VICTORIA
The Way It Was

VICTORIA

A panorama of the Inner Harbour in the late 1920s. The Canadian Pacific's Coastal Steamship Service had its depot on the James Bay (right) side, and the harbour was usually plugged with ships of every description. Laurel Point, on the extreme right, is now the site of a luxury hotel, but used to be the location of the sprawling Bapco (British American Paint Company) plant.

THE WAY IT WAS

MICHAEL KLUCKNER *with paintings by the author*

WHITECAP BOOKS

M. KLUCKNER
1986

Published by Whitecap Books Limited., 1086 West 3rd Street, North Vancouver, B.C. Telephone (604) 980-9852.

Canadian Cataloguing in Publication Data:

Kluckner, Michael
  Victoria The Way It Was

  Includes index.
  ISBN 0-920620-48-5

  1. Victoria (B.C.) - History.
  2. Victoria (B.C.) - Biography.
  I. Title.
  FC3846.4.K57 1986   971.1'34   C86-091359-7
  F1089.5.V6K57 1986

Printed by D.W. Friesen & Sons,
Altona, Manitoba
Printed in Canada

To The Memory Of

Albert Ralph Kluckner (1911-1985)

Contents

Introduction 9

Fort Victoria 13
  James Douglas 18
  J.S. Helmcken 26
  The Songhees 28
  John Work 30

The Old City 31
  The Union Club 42
  The British Colonist 44
  The Streetcar System 47
  Terry's 50
  Spencer's 52
  Chinatown 54
  Joe North 58
  W & J Wilson 61
  Thomas Trounce 61
  City Hall 62
  Charles Rogers 64
  The Whelan murder 66
  The Telephone Company .67
  The Empress Hotel 68
  Churches 70
  Victoria Wilson 72
  The Smallpox War 75

Victoria Harbour 77

Provincial Politics 81
  De Cosmos & Walkem (B.C. *vs.* Canada) 84
  Smithe to Turner (Island *vs.* Mainland) 86
  Semlin to Prior (Government *vs.* Lieutenant-Governor) . . .88
  McBride Prosperity & Party Politics 90
  W.J. Bowser (The P.G.E. & Other Scandals) 92
  Brewster & Oliver (Prohibition to Moderation) 94
  Tolmie & Pattullo (Prosperity to Depression) 96
  The Coalition 98
  The B.C. Provincial Police 99

Residential Areas 101

James Bay 102
  Dr. G.L. Milne 105

Emily Carr 107
W.W. Gibson 108
The Pendrays 109
Beacon Hill Park 110

Rockland 113
  The Pembertons 116
  The Dunsmuirs 118
  Samuel Nesbitt 120
  The Angus Families 121
  Government House 122
  The Barnards 125
  Sir Henry Crease 126

Fairfield 128
  George Winter 131
  Sir Matthew Baillie Begbie 132
  R.P. Rithet 134

Oak Bay 136
  Francis M. Rattenbury 139
  Sir Charles Hibbert Tupper 140
  Sir Clive Phillips-Wolley 141
  Hugo Beaven 142
  John Tod 145
  The Fairgrounds 146

Point Ellice 148
  The Point Ellice Bridge Disaster 150

Esquimalt 151
  The Gorge 152
  The Royal Navy 154
  The Drydock Scandal 156
  Captain Jacobson 157
  The Puget Sound Agricultural Company 158
  F.S. Barnard 161
  The Esquimalt & Nanaimo Railway 162

Saanich & Beyond 165
  Nanaimo & The 1913 Riots 168

Appendix I: Flowers & Plants 170

Appendix II: Bibliography 171

Index 172

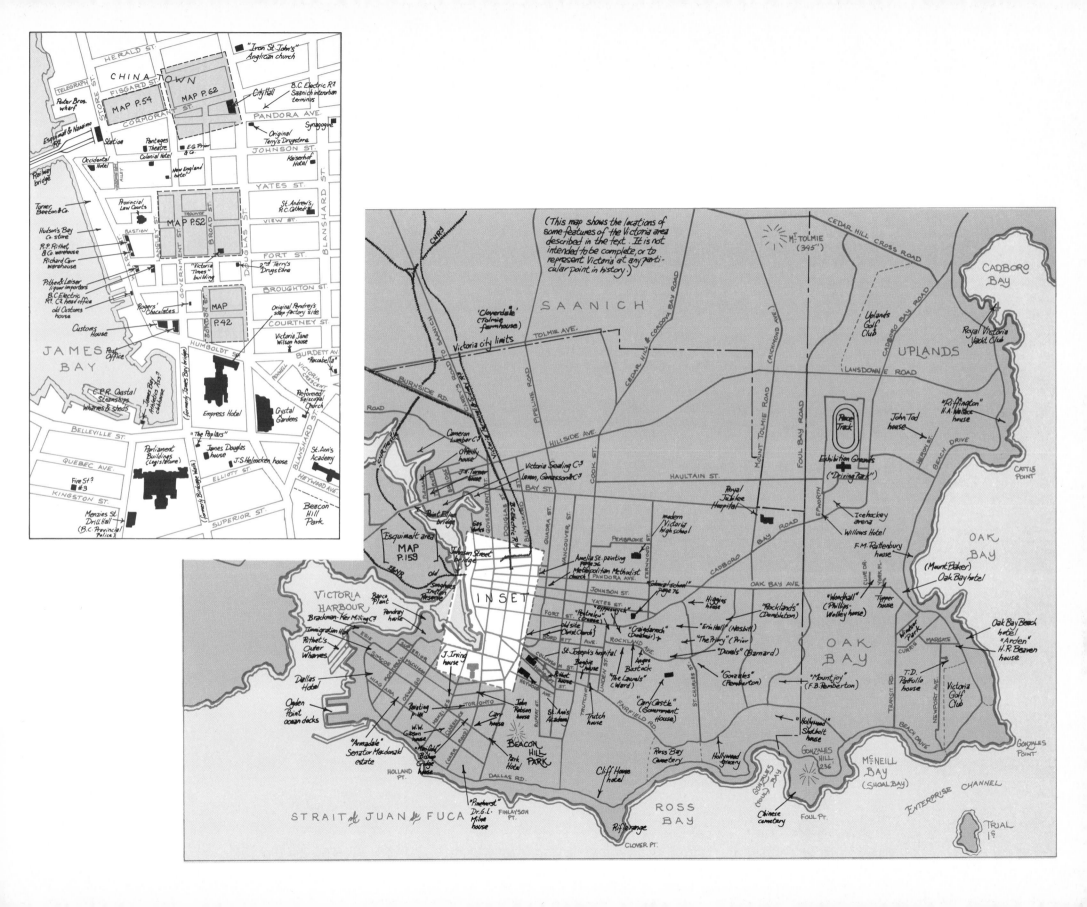

Acknowledgements & Preface

I wanted this book to recreate the atmosphere of old Victoria. The text and paintings follow the "main themes" of the city's early (pre-1950s) years: the search for gold, British colonialism and Imperialism, loyalty to Canada, fear of America, the Oriental question, religion, liquor, rivalry with Vancouver, and the new technologies and fads of the late-nineteenth and twentieth centuries, such as tourism. One of the constant threads running through the book is the youth and adventurousness of many of the early residents of Victoria—men and women, often only in their early twenties, who left comfortable homes in settled countries and travelled to an almost unknown part of the globe. The same story, varying only slightly in its details, could be told of any of the "western" cities on the Pacific Ocean—Vancouver, Seattle, San Francisco, Los Angeles, Sydney, Shanghai.

There are literally hundreds of people who, because of their achievements and beliefs, could have been included in the book; their absence is due only to lack of space. As with this book's "companion"—*Vancouver The Way It Was*—I wanted to give a sense of context to the hodge-podge of little events and curious concerns which have created the physical city of Victoria. The preoccupation with provincial politics, and the parade of governments before our "modern" era began in 1952 with W.A.C. Bennett and the Social Credit Party, is described in a separate section beginning on page 81.

The paintings attempt to recapture the atmosphere of the old city. They were researched from old newspaper photographs, fire-insurance maps, people's written accounts, and—in nearly all cases—the surviving buildings themselves. They do not duplicate any existing photographs. A lot of artistic license went into the composition of people, gardens, and surrounding landscapes. I hope they appear as if they were painted *then*, by someone who was alive at the time and did them on the spot.

A number of people made *Victoria The Way It Was* possible. I am indebted to two authors who devoted a large amount of their long careers to recording and interpreting the events of colonial-era Vancouver Island: Frederick Howay (mainly writing before the First World War) and Margaret Ormsby (writing in the 1950s). As well, I have drawn heavily on the journals of J.S. Helmcken, the writings of Emily Carr, newspaper articles by anonymous journalists who recorded the events of early Victoria while they were happening, and on the newspaper clipping and filing efforts over many decades of employees of the Provincial Archives in Victoria, the Victoria City Archives, and the Vancouver City Archives. I also used as sources many "local colour" articles written by old-time residents of Victoria, including James K. Nesbitt, Cecil Clark, Ainslie Helmcken, Archie Wills, B.A. McKelvie, R.E. Gosnell, Eileen Learoyd and N. deBertrand Lugrin. The following people gave me assistance and information: Joseph Lawrence, Ernest Simpson, Henry Ewert, Mike Steele, Mrs. Mary Wood, Craig Butler, Mr. & Mrs. Ian Angus, Mrs. P. Izard, Mrs. Edward Gudewill, Mrs. Frederick Wood, David Angus, and Darlene Sanders. Michael Burch, the president of Whitecap Books, provided (as always) a lot of support and advice. In addition, I would like to thank Penny Seedhouse and Joanne Wegren of the Victoria City Archives; Geoffrey Castle, Rob Harvey, David Mattison and Barbara McLennan of the Provincial Archives of B.C.; and, Susan Baptie and staff at the Vancouver City Archives for help finding some of the biographical material and portrait photographs. (Photographs not from my own collection are credited as PABC [Provincial Archives of B.C.], VCA [Victoria City Archives], or CVA [City of Vancouver Archives].) Finally, my wife Christine Allen is an excellent editor.

Introduction

The Pacific Coast first attracted the attention of European navigators in 1776 when Captain James Cook undertook his third voyage in the hope of finding a Northwest Passage. Cook made a landfall at Nootka on Vancouver Island in 1778, and then proceeded north, entering the Arctic Ocean through the Bering Strait. After confirming, to his satisfaction, the impracticability of a "Northwest Passage," he turned south and landed at the Hawaiian Islands. There, on February 14, 1779, he was killed by natives.

His journals survived and were published in England in 1784, prompting expeditions by navigators and fur-traders including Captain Barkley, Jean Francois Galaup de la Perouse, James Hanna, Captain John Meares, Lowrie and Guise, Colnett and Duncan, and Martinez and Haro. Meares, though commanding a Portuguese vessel from Macao, was a British subject, and, on February 17, 1789, he was seized, along with his new trading post at Nootka, by the Spaniards, who claimed sovereignty over the entire coast north of their California colony. Negotiations followed between Great Britain and Spain, culminating in the Nootka Treaty of 1790. Two years later, Captain George Vancouver explored the area. In the ensuing decades, England's "official" attention was almost completely occupied by events in Europe, particularly the aftermath of the French Revolution and the rise of Napoleon. The Pacific Coast was forgotten.

Traders, however, visited it regularly, principally from Britain and the New England states of the United States. Russia's claims to Alaska were recognized by the Anglo-British treaty of 1825; American claims to the unorganized Oregon Territory, and to regions north of the 49th parallel (today's international border), were harder to conciliate, particularly following the War of 1812 and subsequent treaties between Britain and the U.S.A.

AUTHOR'S COLLECTION

Provincial Parliament Buildings of British Columbia, Victoria, B.C.

The case for British control of the region now known as British Columbia largely rested on the overland voyage of the North West Company's Alexander Mackenzie, who reached the Pacific Ocean near Bella Coola in July, 1793, eleven years before Americans Lewis & Clark crossed the continent to the mouth of the Columbia River in Oregon. John Jacob Astor followed the latter and founded the trading post of Astoria to establish an American-based rival to the two giant British-owned fur companies—the Hudson's Bay Company and the North West Company.

Ownership of much of Canada (38.8 percent, in fact) had, since 1670, been vested in the "Governor and Company of Adventurers of England Trading Into Hudson's Bay." The Hudson's Bay Company had such a dominance of Canada, and had had it for so long, that its initials were taken to mean "Here Before Christ." The defeat of the French in Quebec in the mid-18th century removed one obstacle to their trading monopoly; an amalgamation with the aggressive North West Company in the early part of the 19th century removed the other.

The HBC was able to coordinate decent trade on the Pacific Coast, supplied from ships sent around the Horn. In 1824, Fort Vancouver was founded on the Columbia River. In 1835, the Company brought "a smoking tree," the steam-powered sidewheeler Beaver, to the Pacific Coast to expedite trade for sea otter with the Indians. The Puget Sound Agricultural Company, with John McLoughlin in charge at Fort Vancouver, was established to feed the Pacific coast and Russian-Alaska forts. Regular commerce began with San Francisco and Hawaii. Coal was discovered, first in the vicinity of Fort Rupert, later in huge quantities at Nanaimo on Vancouver Island.

Oregon, dominated administratively and commercially by the Hudson's Bay Company's Fort Vancouver, but in reality under the joint sov-

Gorge Park, Victoria, B. C.

link of sentiment with the Motherland." The site was known by the Indians as Camosun or Camosack, "the place for gathering Camass," after the starchy bulb with the blue flower which was a major food source for local Indians.

The job of establishing Fort Victoria fell to James Douglas, McLoughlin's chief assistant, who dominated the affairs of the Island colony for decades. The fort, occupying a 100-yard-square enclosure bounded by Government, Wharf, Broughton and Bastion streets, was erected in 1843, and the Hudson's Bay Company quickly moved all its western operations there. The decision was made none too soon, as American enthusiasm for the Oregon Territory, reflected in the successful presidential candidacy of James Knox Polk, was reaching its zenith. Polk received the Democratic nomination in 1844 on two "manifest destiny" issues—the "re-annexation" of Texas, a province of Mexico which had become an ersatz republic; and, the "re-occupation" of Oregon under the slogan "Fifty-Four-Forty or Fight!" (America claimed territory as far north as 54 degrees, 40 minutes latitude, a line somewhat north of Prince Rupert). The boundary dispute was settled peaceably on July 12, 1846, resulting in the acceptance of the 49th parallel as the Canada-U.S. boundary. The "Pig War" on the San Juan Islands during the 1850s and 1860s, which resulted in the San Juans becoming American territory, resolved the division of territory in the Strait of Juan de Fuca.

Vancouver Island, at first a fiefdom of the Hudson's Bay Company, was made a crown colony in 1849, the year when gold fever turned California on its ear. Nine years later, miners began to arrive in sleepy Victoria, lured by reports of wild gold strikes in the practically trackless interior of "New Caledonia." The British government acted promptly, and late in 1858 declared New Caledonia a new colony with the name British Columbia. Victoria, prosperous from supplying the gold rush, incorporated itself as a city in 1862.

The promise of a railway—the ultimate solution to the age-old lack of a Northwest Passage—lured British Columbia into confederation with John A. Macdonald's infant Canada, in 1871. Victoria was named as the western terminus and seemed assured of further prosperity. The collapse of that promise and the creation of Vancouver as the terminus in 1884 increased resentment of Islanders versus Mainlanders, and British Columbians versus Eastern Canadians. Many of the mainlanders who settled at first in New Westminster and the Cariboo gold towns were from Ontario and Nova Scotia. They were Canadian, "small town" and "middle class" in attitude, compared with the sophisticated English colonial spirit which dominated Victoria. Even as early as the 1870s, Victoria was very different from the frontier settlements elsewhere in B.C. and western Canada. It offered a pleasant climate and a refined way of life. Many of the residents brought enough capital from "home" (England) to build large houses with extensive grounds, and establish prosperous commercial operations—mainly in trade with Hawaii, San Francisco, and the outports up the coast. Victoria was also a magnet for retirees from the colonial civil service, the "old China hands," tea planters from Ceylon, and the burra sahibs from the East India Company. Servants were plentiful, Chinese, and cheap (only $20 or $25 a month), freeing their employers for a grace-

ereignty of Great Britain and the United States, was ruled autocratically—a fact that didn't sit well with the roving American trappers who were pushed out of the territory by HBC brigades led by Peter Skene Ogden and John Work. Missionaries moved in, followed by settlers driving the covered wagons along the Oregon Trail of storybook fame. With these came demands for representative, American government. The Hudson's Bay Company, guessing that its claim to Oregon would not likely be backed up militarily by Britain, looked northwards for a strategic fort. In 1842, they chose Victoria.

Victoria's advantages stemmed from its command of the entrance into Juan de Fuca Strait, and—in the political logic of the time—its location on undisputed British territory, "to which British subjects could safely migrate, establishing their children's inalienable heritage and an eternal

ful, formal life and a penchant for politics.

By the turn of the century, Victoria had a population of just over 20,000, and was regarded as a rather English and charming residential city with a high quality of life. "Its atmosphere is laden with invigorating ozone from the sea, and ague and malaria are entirely unknown," noted one report in 1906. Victoria had ceased to dispute Vancouver's commercial domination, and was content with its role as the permanent seat of British Columbia's government, the location of which had been disputed furiously during the early 1890s. Victoria also looked very different from Vancouver: wealthy residents occupied rambling farms and estates in the English tradition, even in "inner-city" neighbourhoods like James Bay; in Vancouver, there was one big landowner—the Canadian Pacific Railway—which developed patches of cleared forest directly into planned subdivisions, and surveyed much of the city into a neat checkerboard.

Victoria did get its share of suburban development, during the frenzied North American land boom of the years before 1913. That burst of activity pushed the city beyond its early boundaries, through the Hillside area, Fairfield, and Oak Bay. Then came the horror and dislocation of the First World War, followed by the rise of the new gods—the motor car, leisured travel, and motion pictures. Few descendants of Victoria's early residents wanted to (or could afford to) maintain the lavish, formal estates. The big properties in James Bay, Rockland and Oak Bay were broken up, and comparatively small houses filled in the spaces between the old wooden mansions. That process accelerated after the Second World War, when thousands of servicemen and their families moved to the west coast. In the old days, the land was more open and parklike. Houses were built in splendid isolation, on rocky outcroppings with views of the sea. Today, although many of the old houses, English-style gardens, and oak trees survive, there are few with grand vistas.

In the late forties, Victoria's downtown slipped into a deep depression. Much of it looked as shabby as the old Angel Hotel, in the painting on page 59. The Rithet warehouses on Wharf Street, which have recently been beautifully restored, were vacant. It was a very quiet little backwater of a city. The restoration and refurbishment since has recaptured some of the unique atmosphere of the last century—an odd combination of San Francisco and English colony.

Victoria continues to be perceived as a "little bit of Olde Englande," in spite of some derision by writers like former *Times* journalist Bruce Hutchinson, who described it in 1950 as "about as quaint as Niagara Falls." For most residents and visitors, though, it retains something of the atmosphere and quality of life from an earlier, very different time.

AUTHOR'S COLLECTION

Victoria & Inner Harbour, Victoria, B.C.

(Next page) Looking west toward Fort Victoria in the late 1840s. The bastion stood where Bastion and Government streets meet today, and the fort's gate was at Fort Street. James Douglas thought that the "large Tract of clear Land" in the vicinity would be ideal for "tillage and pasture," and thus could replace those in the vicinity of Fort Vancouver in Oregon. He noted that more than two-thirds of the land between the Inner Harbour and Gonzales Point was "Prairie Land." The Indian name for the district was "Camosun," meaning "Place for Gathering Camass," and this cleared "prairie" resulted from the centuries of constant digging by Indian women for the bulbs. (This explanation for 'Camosun' was first recorded by artist Paul Kane, who wandered across North America and arrived in Victoria in 1847. Hudson's Bay Company official Roderick Finlayson wrote that 'Camosun,' in the Indian dialect, signified the rush of the waters in the Gorge waterway.) In the springtime, the Indians gathered the bulbs beneath the purple-blue camass flowers; later in the season, they collected the seeds of the woolly sunflower (the yellow, brown-eyed flower in the painting) and the Indian consumption plant (the scattered, tall plant with the small purple flowers, a type of lomatium whose ground-up seeds were used for treating consumptive diseases). The other plant in the painting, with bunches of small, yellow flowers, is a lomatium called spring gold or hog fennel. Camass was by far the most important, as it provided much of the starch in the local Indian diet. The camass bulbs were usually cooked in a hole lined with stones, in which a fire had been built; once the stones were heated, the embers were raked out, the stones covered with green leaves, the bulbs placed upon them and then covered with more green leaves, then the whole heaped over with earth and left to steam for a day and a night. The bulbs were also sometimes boiled in water until the latter evaporated, leaving a highly-valued molasses used for festive occasions. Ethnobotanist Charles Saunders wrote that "white settlers, in the days before their orchards and gardens were established, found in camass a welcome addition to their meagre and monotonous bill of fare, and Camass pie was a not uncommon dish in many an old time Oregon or California household." Indians on southern Vancouver Island got much of their protein from March through August eating halibut, cod and shellfish, and lived through the winter on salmon, caught at the heads of the inlets and dried.

Looking northwest across the Inner Harbour in the late 1930s, towards the Victoria Industrial Reserve—the old Songhees Indian Reservation. Not much has changed on the downtown Victoria skyline, but the James Bay area on the left and in the foreground is now much more built-up with highrise apartment buildings and hotels.

Fort Victoria

With the decision to replace the Hudson's Bay Company's Fort Vancouver with a safer, more northerly, indisputably British fort, 38-year-old Chief Factor James Douglas was dispatched across Juan de Fuca Strait in the sloop *Cadboro*. He made a careful survey of the southern shoreline of Vancouver Island, and finally concentrated his attention on three harbours—Sy-yousung (Sooke), Is-whoy-malth (Esquimalt) and Camosack (Victoria).

Douglas reported in July, 1842, that Esquimalt was "one of the best Harbours on the Coast, being perfectly safe and of easy Access." He noted, however, that the shores were "rugged and precipitous, and I did not see One level Spot clear of Trees of sufficient Extent to build a large Fort upon." There was, in addition, a scarcity of fresh water—"there are several good Runs in Winter, but we found them all dried up, and we could not manage to fill a single Beaker in the Harbour."

Concerning "the Port and Canal of Camosack," however, Douglas noted that the adjoining land, extending southeast to Point Gonzalo (Gonzales) at the southeast corner of the Island, was "Prairie Land, and may be converted either to Purposes of Tillage or Pasture, for which I have seen no part of the Indian Country better adapted." As Douglas was primarily interested in finding a replacement for the fertile breadbasket at Fort Vancouver, it is not surprising he chose a site for Fort Victoria which lent itself to cultivation. His "Prairie Land" became the City of Victoria.

Douglas returned on March 14, 1843 on the steamer *Beaver*, with a party of company men, and set to erecting an enclosure of about 100 yards square on the steep bluff above the Inner Harbour, land now bounded by Government, Broughton, Wharf and Bastion streets. The front gate was at the foot of Fort Street, where the Company built a wharf. One bastion was built on the site of the Army, Navy & Air Force Veterans Club on Wharf Street; a second at the corner of Government and Bastion Street. These octagonal bastions each contained six 6-pounder guns, covering the northeast and southwest angles. The back gate into the fort was on Government Street, near the modern Canadian Imperial Bank of Commerce building at Fort Street. The local Songhees Indians, who lived across the Inner Harbour from the fort site and at Cadboro Bay, were pleased that the fort was to be built, and helped cut the 22-foot cedar pickets for the fort's stockade, ranging far and wide to find suitable trees. Douglas lent them about 20 axes to help them procure the pickets. They were paid one blanket for each forty pickets they brought to the fort site.

The fort was originally (in its planning stages, before Princess Victoria's ascension to the throne in 1837) to have been named Adelaide, after William IV's queen; it was called, briefly and unofficially, Fort Albert, but, shortly after its erection, word arrived from Hudson's Bay Company headquarters at Norway House that it was to be named Fort Victoria.

The HBC's enthusiasm for the site was not shared by British military authorities, who preferred the "very commodious Squirnal Harbour" three miles away. Lieutenants Warre and Vavasour of the Royal Engineers visited Victoria in 1845 at the tail end of a military mission to Oregon. They described the entrance to the harbour as "rather intricate,"

and said that the fort was "badly situated with regard to water and position, which latter has been chosen for its agricultural advantages only." The deep water fronting on the fort site, below a steep wall of rock and the fort, was, however, ideal for the repair of ships; a pair of iron mooring rings was set into the ground a few feet west of Wharf Street, beside the old Customs House, for canting ships over for the removal of the algae below the water line, acquired as ships passed through the tropics on the way to Victoria from England. These mooring rings are now all that is left of Fort Victoria.

The Chief Trader at Fort Victoria and the supervisor of its construction was Charles Ross, a native of Kingcraig, Inverness, Scotland. His second-in-command, Roderick Finlayson, arrived on June 1, 1843, and stayed in Victoria until his death nearly half a century later. Finlayson took over from Ross following the latter's death in the spring of 1844, and quickly expanded the colony. Captain George William Courtenay, who sailed the frigate HMS *Constance* into Esquimalt Harbour on June 24, 1848, described the Hudson's Bay Company's settlement as "300 acres under tillage, and a dairy farm of 80 Cows, together with numerous other cattle & 24 brood Mares, the whole thing under the superintendence of a Civil but hard Scot named Finlaison (*sic*), who has about 30 people of all descriptions under him." Courtenay's arrival was a boon to Finlayson, who had been worried about a possible uprising by Indians living near the fort. Courtenay arranged for the landing of a party of sailors and marines who performed salutes, marched about, brandished sidearms, and fired cannons. This had "a good effect on the natives, as they were evidently afraid to pick any quarrels with us for some time afterwards."

Another early arrival, in March, 1850, distinguished himself as a medical doctor and politician in the young colony, and managed to outlive all the fort's oldtimers. His name was John Sebastian Helmcken. He described the fort's interior as "about a dozen large block storey-and-a-half buildings, say sixty by forty, roofed with long and wide strips of cedar bark. The buildings were for the storage of goods, Indian trading-shop, and a large shop for general trade. The mess room, off from which lived (Chief Factor) Douglas and family, was at the corner of Fort and Government streets. The 'counting house' was near Wharf Street. Mr. Finlayson occupied this post and lived there with his family. A belfry stood in the middle of the yard and its bell tolled for meals, for deaths, for weddings, for church service, for fires, and sometimes for warnings. . . ."

Outside the fort, there was little evidence of civilization, except the occasional log cabin and the cultivated fields, which started just outside the fort's walls and extended up the hill to the site of the high school. The fort's vegetable garden was at Government and Broughton streets. Water was available nearby, from a spring in the Spring Ridge area. There were barns on Fort Street, which ran east from the fort towards Cadboro Bay. The forest commenced north of the Johnson Street ravine; the harbour was lined with "pines" (likely cedars), its bowers overgrown with flowering shrubs.

Helmcken learned quickly that life in the little fort was different from

Six-foot-four-inch John McLoughlin, James Douglas's commander in the Hudson's Bay Company, established Fort Vancouver at the mouth of the Columbia River for the North West Company and was one of the "wintering partners" who led the amalgamation with the Hudson's Bay Company. With the help of brigades led by Peter Skene Ogden and John Work, he ran a prosperous operation in Oregon Territory until the land was ceded to the United States in 1846. The Hudson's Bay Company, and James Douglas, moved to Victoria, but McLoughlin stayed in Oregon and became an American citizen. He died in 1857, convinced that neither the Oregonians nor the Hudson's Bay Company appreciated his role in the settlement of the west.

that in England. Upon his arrival, he was presented to Chief Factor Douglas and Mr. Finlayson, then turned over to the care of the man he was to replace, Dr. Albert Benson, "known by the soubriquet 'Commodore'." Helmcken was to share the "Bachelors' Quarters" within the fort, a portion of a large storey-and-a-half block building, with a common room in the centre and a couple of rooms leading from it on each side. In the common room was a stove, "square, made of sheet iron, bent in all directions by the heat, with a cast-iron door, . . . fed with large billets of wood, of which plenty existed in the Hall. It looked mean and dilapidated, but it was soon found capital for roasting native oysters upon." The stove-top harboured Benson's large, blackened coffee pot. "Every room had sporting weapons in it—muskets and rifles of great variety—swords, a saddle and bridle, tobacco and pipes, lots of dust, and the usual utensils," Helmcken recorded. On his first night at the fort, he slept well, "and was awakened in the morning by the loud ringing of a bell, and a concert proceeding from a host of curs—these curs assembled under the bell at every meal and, looking up to it, howled, the howling being taken up by some dogs in the Indian village opposite" (the Songhees village across the Inner Harbour).

Dr. Benson—the "Commodore"—was perhaps the most eccentric of the fort's residents. He wore a pair of "sea-boots," into which often only one pant-leg was stuffed—"ah," he said to Helmcken, "you laugh, but if you were to remain here a few months you would of necessity become the same!" Helmcken was then still wearing his thin-soled London-made "Cockney" boots and proper trousers. When the pair set off across the muddy fort yard and along a pole sidewalk to the fort's stores, Helmcken slipped every few steps, and "the wretch" Benson laughed. A trip to the Beacon Hill Park area, jumping from hillock to hillock, walking along fallen trees, and wading through swamps, finished Helmcken's boots and trousers, leaving him a "wiser but not sadder man." "I told you so," laughed Benson, "you will soon be like me."

Salmon was a regular feature of the diet—often even at breakfast. They were not, however, like the English salmon, and had to be taken with trolling gear or a net. This disappointed Captain Gordon, the brother of the Earl of Aberdeen, the British Prime Minister. During a visit to Victoria in 1845, while in the midst of negotiating the Oregon Boundary dispute, Gordon lamented that "such a lordly fish had to be caught in such an awful manner." Gordon's sad tale was oft told, and improved with the telling, and it was later said that the British gave up the Oregon Territory because "the salmon did not know enough to rise to the fly."

The Hudson's Bay Company took its security seriously—the trading ship *Beaver*, moored just outside the fort, carried nettings to repel boarders, cannon on deck, and muskets and cutlasses arranged for quick access. The crew was described by Helmcken as "active, robust, weather-beaten, jolly good-tempered men—fat from not being over-worked—some grey, some grizzled, some young," all under the command of Captain Dodd. Officers' cabins were beautifully furnished and commodious; there was a trading place for Indians, who were only allowed on board a few at a time.

The closest the local Indians came to war was over the issue of the killing and eating of some of the Hudson's Bay Company's cattle. After the Indians refused to surrender the perpetrators to justice, Finlayson blew up an empty Indian lodge with grapeshot from one of the six-pounders, completely demoralizing the Indians. They henceforth lived according to the Company's laws.

Dinner at Fort Victoria (announced by the bell and the dogs) was a ceremony about which James Douglas was very particular. All of the bachelors, married officers, and Company officials—generally twenty or more men—were expected to dine together, while wives, children and underlings dined elsewhere. The mess room was about twenty by thirty feet, with a large, cordwood-stacked fireplace at one end and a clock on the wall. The long table in the middle was set with a spotless linen tablecloth and bright decanters, and lined with Windsor chairs brought from England. Dinner, prepared by the Kanaka cook, was several courses, inevitably soup followed by salmon, followed by meats—sometimes venison or duck—washed down with wine during numerous toasts "to the Queen." Afterwards, the Kanaka steward brought tobacco, and following Douglas's lead, the men selected clay "churchwarden" pipes from a pile or drew old, bitten briars from their pockets and smoked calmly and deliberately. Conversation was never allowed to be frivolous in Douglas's presence; Helmcken suggested that Douglas always came to the table primed with some intellectual or scientific subject, or he rehashed military history for the edification of the HBC clerks at the table. The atmosphere of stiff formality was not helped greatly by Douglas's breathtaking conundrums and *non sequiturs*. Once, Douglas asked Benson at dinner, "Why are so many of the Hudson's Bay Company officers bald?" Benson replied, with sparkling wit, *"pro pelle cutem*—they had sent their furs home." Douglas responded gravely, "Perhaps, having given us the poetry of the thing, you will give the prose—the cause."

After considerable conversation, Douglas generally retired to his family in their quarters, leaving a crowd of young men to entertain themselves in the Bachelors' Hall. Further drinking would ensue, and the jollity often became quite intense, as in one case witnessed by Helmcken, when a Captain Grant entertained everyone with swordplay, splitting candles with his cutlass and trying to cut a button off Benson's coat (where there were none too many). "After a while," wrote Helmcken nearly forty years later, "Grant wanted to 'escort Her Majesty to Windsor Castle.' All were to be cavalry. So down everybody went kangaroo fashion. Grant being in command, took the lead, and so we hopped in this style round the room, and made considerable of a racket. In the midst of which, some naughty schoolgirl overhead, probably not being able to sleep, poured some water through a crack in the ceiling right down upon the cavalry." This, he noted, put an end to the diversion, though everyone ended up singing until far into the night.

The arrival of settlers on Vancouver Island eventually solved the evident problem of lack of women. Be it ever so primitive, though, Fort Victoria was still the only speck of civilization on the Hudson's Bay Company's western map. Religious observance—a priority of the pious Douglas, who insisted that all had to go to church every Sunday in the mess hall—was handled by the Rev. Robert Staines, something of an Episcopalian but not a regularly ordained minister. In addition to presiding over religious activities, Staines and his wife ran a school for HBC officials' children out of the upper floor of the building that held the Bachelors' Hall, approximately on the site of the Bank of Commerce at Fort and Government streets. Established in 1849, the little school by the next year had 22 children, including nine-year-old James and eleven-year-old Eliza Anderson, children of Alexander Caulfield Anderson, who had travelled overland from Fort Colville with a fur brigade to reach the school. Staines, "of rather uncertain temper, and disposed at times to be unduly severe in administering corporal punishment, was nevertheless a good student and teacher in Natural History." Douglas considered him "a fomenter of mischief & preacher of sedition" who was a better pig farmer than preacher—Staines, having established farms at Mount Tolmie and Metchosin, was leaving the school increasingly in Mrs. Staines's capable, energetic hands.

Mrs. Staines, "with a row of curls down each side of her angular face, and, when walking, holding up her skirts on each side and ordering the girls to follow her example," dressed the children to a standard of fashion: Eliza Anderson, when she arrived at Fort Victoria, wore a print gown "like a bag with holes for the head and arms and tied round the waist," moccasins, and a poke bonnet "like a coal scuttle"; this was replaced with a dress and a small straw bonnet. Young James's suit of leather shirt and trousers, peaked cloth cap and moccasins was acceptable, but his shirt was changed for a moleskin blouse, belted below the waist and decorated "with enormous white buttons like saucers."

The beds were boards, covered with an Indian mat and a Hudson's Bay blanket, and another blanket as a cover, located in the unlined, bare-log garret of the building. The line where the roof joined the wall was a runway for the hundreds of rats which infested the building, sometimes joining the boys in bed and fighting over their meals, to the point that Staines offered a bounty of a shilling a dozen. Fresh air entered freely through chinks in the walls and cracks in the roof, and in winter, the supply of water upstairs froze solid; the heating system was a box stove in the room at the other end of the building where they had their meals and lessons. A loose board in the floor, when lifted, offered a view of the "mild orgies" of oysters, sherry, port and brandy of the bachelors in the room below. Sunday was a terror—a dreary afternoon learning the Collects, and woe betide anyone who fell asleep during either of the two church services. Both breakfast and afternoon tea were bread and treacle with milkless tea; the children were allowed one tallow dip at night, which they economized by placing salt around the wick to extend its life.

Bright spots in the children's stern existence included the arrival of the HBC steamer *Mary Dare* from the Company's trading post in Honolulu, when Captain McNeil presented them with oranges, sugarcane and fire-crackers. Marbles had to be made of clay and baked in a fire, but still cracked almost immediately. Horse-riding, exploring, fighting Indian boys and stoning the Indians' woolly dogs occupied more time. Captain Grant presented them with a cricket set, which they played near the Burns Memorial in Beacon Hill Park. Shinny and rounders balls were made of hair covered with dressed deer hide.

While the Hudson's Bay Company's priority was trade, that of the British government was colonization. The latter envisioned a Vancouver Island colony with a landed aristocracy, giving security to a village society of servants and tenant farmers. Douglas, on the other hand, wanted sturdy freemen for settlers. A compromise was reached and, on January 13, 1849, a charter was granted to the HBC for the control of Vancouver Island, with the stipulation that within five years a settlement of resident colonists was to be formed; in case of the Company's failure, the Crown retained the right of repurchase. Richard Blanshard was proclaimed the governor of the new colony, and set out from England for Victoria, to be greeted coldly by the snubbed James Douglas.

Blanshard arrived March 9, 1850, aboard the paddlesloop HMS *Driver* (the second naval steamship at the Royal Navy's new Esquimalt station), after an exhausting journey via Panama. His first discovery was that no official accommodation had been provided, so he was forced to ask the *Driver's* Captain Johnson if he could live on board for the indefinite future. Douglas and Blanshard were seldom "brought into actual collision," in Dr. Helmcken's words, except when Blanshard took a rare opportunity to show his authority, as in the signing of ships' registers, a minor function which the Company had always performed. He was certain that Douglas and the Company were plotting against him, and that he had likely been appointed over Douglas by the British government because the latter felt that Douglas would be too autocratic and hold the new settlers at the Company's mercy. Despite his lack of private capital, he was expected to pay his own expenditures while in Victoria. To make matters worse, when he commandeered Captain Wellesley's Esquimalt-based frigate *Daedalus* in October, 1850, for a mission to Fort Rupert to investigate the murder of three white men by the Nahwitti Indians, the Colonial Office notified him that this too was at his own expense. Disillusioned, he left Victoria on September 1, 1851, after only eighteen months as governor; the Colonial Office made him pay his own fare home!

Other groups had expressed an interest in colonizing Vancouver Island, hoping to capitalize on the widely-held feeling—by Gladstone and others—that "The Great Monopoly" had already received enough land. A certain James Edward Fitzgerald promoted a joint stock company to colonize the Island with "gentlemen of birth, intelligence, education and enterprise." Thomas Brown of Liverpool, a Mormon, presented a petition to Queen Victoria, proposing "The Relief by Emigration of a Portion of Her Poor Subjects." Queen Victoria, as much offended by the Mormon's attitude to polygamy as she was afraid of another American invasion—this time by Latter Day Saints to join British Mormons—rejected it outright. The Hudson's Bay Company was thus granted control of Van-

Richard Blanshard, the first governor of the colony of Vancouver Island, did not get on with the Vancouver Island establishment—James Douglas and the Hudson's Bay Company. He was so disappointed with his life in Victoria that he only remained for 18 months. His rather imperious, military manner hid an agreeable, gentlemanly personality. His depression was aggravated, according to J.S. Helmcken, by his poor health—"dic doloreaux of a bad kind," due to the malaria he had contracted in the tropics, the morphine he took against the attacks, and his heavy smoking.

couver Island at an annual rental of seven shillings, though it was common knowledge that the Company's officials realized the incompatibility of colonization and fur-trading. The few new settlers found it difficult to make a living farming on Vancouver Island, as the HBC's Puget Sound Agricultural Company completely dominated the local market, and tariff walls blocked off the U.S. market. As well, for every 100 acres purchased (at £1 per acre), a settler had to bring out from the old country, at his own expense, five single men or three married couples. Not surprisingly, many young men forgot their British allegiance and settled in Washington and Oregon, where land was free or nominally priced.

Soon after Blanshard's precipitate departure, a party of naval officers, bearing the commissions appointing James Douglas governor of Vancouver Island, arrived at Esquimalt harbour. They travelled on foot over the trail from Esquimalt to the fort, through the Indian village—"a very hold-your-nose kind of place"—and were ferried across the harbour in a dugout canoe after making a payment of tobacco. It was late at night, and Douglas received them in a paisley dressing gown and tasseled smoking cap. The formalities completed, the officers passed a few days in the area and entertained some of the local ladies on their ship. One young lady confided to an officer that she was very glad to see him but dashed his romantic hopes by revealing that "the governor kills once a week when a ship is in, instead of once a month." Cattle were in short supply.

The announcement of the agreement to colonize Vancouver Island attracted some interest in England. The Company's annual supply ship from England, the barque *Tory*, arrived at the fort on May 10, 1851, carrying letters, supplies, and the first family of colonists—Captain Edward Edwards Langford, his wife, son and five daughters. Langford, a retired officer of the 73rd Battalion, knew Governor Blanshard, and had been appointed manager of one of their Esquimalt farms by the London headquarters of the Puget Sound Agricultural Company (a subsidiary of the Hudson's Bay Company, formed in London in 1840 to control all of the farms in the Company's western operations, page 158). Being a man of some capital and used to comfort at "Colwood," his Sussex estate, Langford was shocked at the crudeness of his surroundings—the Company had provided, within the fort's walls, two single-room log huts, one for the family of eight, the other for the farm helpers whom Langford had brought with him. This first disappointment led to a life-long, active dislike of James Douglas and the Hudson's Bay Company; it was suggested that Langford built the new "Colwood" as far as possible from Fort Victoria and the Esquimalt naval base, in order better to shield his daughters from unwise liaisons. (On the voyage over, daughter Mary had fallen in love with a very junior officer on the *Tory*. Despite her father's disapproval, the lovers remained true to each other. Twenty years later, the young man, by this time Captain Lewis, followed her to England, married her there, and returned with her to spend many years in Victoria.) Senior officers, however, and eligible bachelors from the fort were welcomed at "Colwood" to share in the carefree social life of the vivacious, accomplished daughters—a bright spot in the isolation of life at Fort Victoria.

Captain Langford wasn't the only settler to hold grievances against the Hudson's Bay Company. Captain W. Colquhoun Grant, a dashing young cavalry officer late of the Scots Greys, complained that all the lands within a reasonable distance of the fort were reserved for HBC officials; he took land in Sooke, far to the west of the main colony. Langford kept a steady flow of abuse and indictments concerning the HBC and Douglas to the Colonial Office in England. Langford managed to get elected to the first legislative assembly of Vancouver Island in 1855, but as he did not own freehold property on Vancouver Island to a value of £300, he was prevented from taking his seat. He claimed that Company officials had delayed the approval of his application to purchase property on Dallas Bank in Esquimalt Harbour. In 1860, he withdrew from another election race following the publication of a broadsheet lampooning his hypocritical attitude to his employers at the HBC and the PSAC (it was rumoured that the broadsheet was written by Judge Begbie). Langford finally quit the Island in January, 1861, and returned to England.

Lieut. Charles Wilson, a 22-year-old Royal Engineer who spent much of the late 1850s working on the International Boundary Commission and later went into law practice with Theodore Davie, described the available diversions in the Colony in 1858: "Last Saturday I made a great expedition to go to a dance. I started in torrents of rain rigged up in long boots and enveloped in a macintosh & rode 8 miles, through the woods, over a most dreadful road, if road it can be called at all, the stumps of the trees in many places still sticking up in the road. I however spent a very pleasant evening for my trouble, but the ride home in the night was dreadful; it rained so hard I could not keep my cigar lighted & had not even that comfort. On Monday we had a ball which went off very well, though the ladies are rather limited, there being barely 20 unmarried ones on the island; we kept it up with great spirit till 3 in the morning, after which I escorted a party of ladies home, a distance of 2 miles, through mud nearly up to the knees; so you may imagine under what difficulties the pursuit of pleasure is followed in a newly settled country."

On another occasion, Wilson and the officers of the *Satellite* and the *Plumper*—sloops-of-war stationed at Esquimalt—got together, determined to give "a grand ball to the ladies of Vancouver Island." For a venue, they were only able to find the Hudson's Bay Company salmon warehouse on Reid's wharf, "a most dismal-looking place, enough to drive all thoughts of dancing out of one's head." To disguise it, "we got all the flags we could from the ships & turned in 30 or 40 sailors, and in a short time a fairy palace of flags was erected, so that not a particle of the building was visible; we then rigged up some large chandeliers & sconces of bayonets and ramrods wreathed in evergreens which when lighted up produced a regular blaze of light & made it quite a fairy scene." They also managed to produce "a first-rate supper," and entertained nearly 200 people "from the governor downwards" until after three in the morning. "Nobody says 'ball' in this part of the world," Wilson noted in his diary. "It is always 'party'." He also thought that the ladies were nicely dressed, "though they would look much better if they would only learn to wear

James Douglas

James Douglas dominated the political and social affairs of Fort Victoria and British Columbia for 35 years. As chief factor of the Western Department of the Hudson's Bay Company, he chose the site and founded Fort Victoria in 1843, then ruled it autocratically until 1864, first as a Hudson's Bay Company official, later as governor of the two colonies of Vancouver Island and British Columbia.

Douglas was born of a Scottish father in 1803 in the Caribbean colony of Demerara, British Guiana. (Many rumours were to circulate in Victoria that his birth had been illegitimate. According to historian M.A. Ormsby, the elder Douglas had entered into "an attachment" with a woman who was likely a creole—rather than a mulatto, as was often whispered. Three children were born to the couple.) Douglas joined the North West Company at age 15 and, after several postings, was sent in 1830 to Fort Vancouver, at the mouth of the Columbia River on the present Washington-Oregon border. He quickly became Chief Factor John McLoughlin's assistant, and was placed in charge of the explorations of Vancouver Island when it became likely that the Hudson's Bay Company would lose its monopoly over the Oregon Territory.

A stiff, rather severe and formal man, he was described by J.S. Helmcken as "a handsome specimen of nature's noblemen—tall, stout, broad-shouldered, muscular, with a grave, bronzed face, but kindly withal." On April 27, 1828, at Fort St. James on Stuart Lake in northern B.C., he had married Amelia Connolly, the sixteen-year-old eldest daughter of Irishman William Connolly, a North West Company clerk, and Susanne, the daughter of a Cree chief. Connolly's marriage, at Rat River House in 1804, had been "according to the custom of the country"; Douglas's marriage two dozen years later was also without the formality of law or clergy. Mrs. Douglas was "as modest as a wood violet," and "an auburn-haired body of considerable activity—orderly and very neat and cleanly."

When Douglas was transferred to Fort Vancouver, his wife, who was expecting her first baby, remained behind, making the journey a year later with her father's fur brigade. Over the ensuing fourteen years at Fort Vancouver, ten more children were born. Women at Fort Vancouver—as later at Fort Victoria—were segregated from the semimilitary social life, and kept house and raised their children in their own quarters. The men ate together in the officers' mess. There were no white women in the Oregon Territory at that time, and it was said that Mrs. Douglas was "the lightest woman." Mrs. McLoughlin was a full-blooded Chippewa.

Douglas demanded that Hudson's Bay Company employees honour their marital commitments; according to biographer Marion Smith, "whatever the original intentions of the parties, marriages between traders and Indian or half-breed women usually turned out to be permanent unions." Sons were often sent to school in Montreal, but daughters generally got by with no education. Fort Vancouver was quite civilized

compared with the northern forts, where trader Ross Cox wrote in 1827 that the mixed-blood wives "are kept in great subjection by their husbands, to whom they are slavishly submissive. They are not allowed to sit at the same table, or indeed at any table, for they still continue the savage fashion of squatting on the ground at their meals, at which their fingers supply the place of forks." Although skilled at European-style tailoring and quite aware of contemporary fashions, "they wear no caps in the house; in travelling, hats are used instead of bonnets."

Douglas did not abandon Amelia in spite of repeated snubs from the likes of Jane Beaver, wife of the chaplain at Fort Vancouver, and Mrs. Staines, the schoolmistress at Fort Victoria, who had "too much uppishness" about her. The Douglases were formally married according to Church of England rites by the Reverend Beaver in Oregon in 1836. As Victoria became more established in the early 1850s, "rude simplicity gave way before the desire to put on airs and graces and make a little splurge," and Douglas began ordering, for his wife and daughters, black lace overjackets, gloves, "caps suitable for wearing in the house," and even a copy of Burke's "Peerage" from England for their education. "What we were in England & Scotland," noted Helmcken, "was burnisht and made the most of."

The Douglases owned a 500-acre estate bounded on the north by the Fort Street hill and comprising part of the Fairfield area east of Beacon Hill Park—its subdivision in the 1880s created much of the Rockland dis-

James Douglas's home, built in the early 1850s on the south side of James Bay, was demolished in 1906. It occupied the "Douglas Gardens," land now covered by the Provincial Museum and Archives. A plaque behind the archives notes the location of the house, and points out the last surviving black cherry tree from his orchard.

Governor James Douglas

Thunderbird Park was opened on May 24, 1941, by Premier Duff Pattullo, as part of a developing heritage area which included J.S. Helmcken's little white house (recently made vacant by the death of his daughter Dolly). A feature of the park when it first opened (on the right of the photo) was the modified dugout canoe "Tillicum," sailed around the world by Captain John Voss in 1904 and now housed in the Maritime Museum in Bastion Square. A new awareness of Indian culture, partly because of the paintings and writings of Emily Carr, and a realization of how fast the old totem poles were deteriorating, prompted the government move. The totem poles could not be modified or replaced without a potlatch—illegal since the 1880 Indian Act. Following the passage of a new Indian Act in 1951, master-carver Chief Mungo Martin and several assistants set to work building a Potlatch House, which opened in December, 1953. The park has been a centre of pole-carving ever since.

trict of the city. They built a rambling, clapboard house on the Provincial Museum site at Belleville and Government. Douglas was a bit ahead of his time in moving to James Bay in the early 1850s—the James Bay bridge (now the causeway in front of the Empress Hotel) was not built until 1859, and the isolation and fear of roaming Indians at night unnerved them. Douglas's friend J.S. Helmcken was induced to move to James Bay for company; evidently, this presented no problem, as Helmcken already had his eye on Douglas's black-eyed 18-year-old eldest daughter, Cecilia. Regardless of his friendship with Douglas, Helmcken had to produce evidence of his character and background before receiving permission to marry her. (Cecilia Helmcken died in 1865, leaving three young children in Mrs. Douglas's care.) Of the thirteen Douglas children, five daughters and one son survived to adulthood.

Douglas's life as governor became increasingly difficult in 1861 and 1862, when Colonial Secretary Sir Edward Bulwer-Lytton and the Lords of the Treasury became impatient about the cost and indebtedness of British Columbia. Douglas's salary, which over the years had risen from £1,800 to £3,800, became an issue. Although the Colonial Office had paid little attention to B.C., and didn't seem to understand the demands of its geography and scattered population, it began to listen to the complaints of disaffected English colonists like Edward Langford, and the "constant tirade" of Canadians like Amor de Cosmos and John Robson for responsible government. The Duke of Newcastle, who had the ultimate responsibility for colonial affairs, became distinctly chilly toward Douglas. At the

Thunderbird Park, Victoria, B.C.

end of 1863 he suggested that Douglas might consider retirement rather than cope with a partially elected legislature on the mainland and the separation of the two colonies' administrations. Douglas readily agreed.

Upon his retirement, Douglas was knighted; he and Amelia then travelled in England and Scotland for two years. They returned to the James Bay estate and a retirement of horseback riding along the seashore, walks in Beacon Hill Park and nursing their fruit trees (Douglas wrote to youngest daughter Martha, when she was at school in England, "I would we could send you some of our delicious pears; they are very fine this year"). Lady Douglas had almost constant dinner and luncheon parties, especially when naval ships were in port; New Year's Day was always open house, and the Douglases fêted scores of callers with wine and cake. She also had seemingly endless amounts of time for friends in difficulty, and helped women like Mrs. Yates through childbirth; one of her grandsons, Colonel Harris, recalled in 1957 that "Granny" always bought venison, fish, ducks and berries from the Songhees Indians who landed their canoes at the bottom of her garden. The food would be distributed to the poor, and the Indians sent away loaded up with fruit and vegetables from her garden.

Lady Douglas, having worked most of her life to establish her legitimacy in the English atmosphere of Victoria, had to suffer through the much-publicized Connolly Case of 1867-1869. Her father, William Connolly, having retired from the fur trade in 1831, had taken his Indian "wife" Susanne to Lower Canada to settle down. A year later, he abandoned her and married his cousin, Julia Woolrich. Upon the cousin's death, one of Susanne's sons sued Connolly's estate for the share which he felt he had been denied. Lady Amelia Douglas had her legitimacy questioned, and her past made a subject of gossip throughout Victoria. Initially, in 1867, Justice Monk had upheld the legality of Connolly's marriage to Susanne, but Woolrich's children appealed and dragged the matter through the courts for two more years. The appeals failed.

Sir James Douglas died in August, 1877. Like many Victoria pioneers, Douglas was a supporter of the renegade Bishop Cridge, so his funeral was conducted at the Reformed Episcopal Church on Blanshard Street. He is buried in the Ross Bay Cemetery. Lady Amelia died in January, 1890. A monument to Douglas was unveiled in the lobby of the legislative buildings on November 19, 1946. "By his firm and wise rule," it states, "he laid the foundations of this province."

their crinolines properly."

Douglas's autocratic manner sprang from knowledge that the Hudson's Bay Company was, in fact, a fur-trading oligarchy masquerading as a legitimate government. "Settlement was the pretence," wrote historian R.E. Gosnell at the turn of the century, "but sovereignty to restrict settlement was the ulterior object." The Company, behind its Britishness and all the implied traditions of representative government, was a law unto itself. This contrasted with the nearby Oregon settlement (organized as a territory in August, 1848), which no one thought ideal, but which still represented the rights and expanded according to the desires of most of its settlers.

Pressured by the newly arrived settlers, Governor Blanshard had appointed a Council of Vancouver Island in August, 1851, consisting of "senior member" James Douglas, John Tod, and James Cooper. Later members, beginning that November when Roderick Finlayson was appointed, included John Work and Justice David Cameron. The council wrestled with the problems of what, if anything, to tax in order to raise money for schools, bridges, roads and a parish church. These prosaic concerns were superseded in July, 1854, when news of the Crimean War reached the colony. It was initially suggested that all white men in the colony be drafted, trained and armed, and that an auxiliary body of natives be conscripted and armed. The latter suggestion was speedily rejected, due to the feelings that the native brigade might prove more formidable to the colony itself than any foreign enemy. After further discussion, the council resolved to leave the colony's defence to Her Majesty's government. Strangely, no attempt was made by the British to take Alaska, nor by the Russians to take Vancouver Island; apparently, both the Hudson's Bay Company and the Russian-American Fur Company put subtle pressure on their respective governments not to extend the war into North America, thus leaving the fur-trading monopolies to trade in peace.

The Vancouver Island council, though quite representative of the few interest groups in the colony, was an illegal attempt to govern British subjects without democratic representation. The Secretary of State for the Colonies, Henry Labouchere, sent a directive to Governor Douglas on February 28, 1856, ordering him to establish a properly elected legislature. Accordingly, the Island was divided into electoral ridings: Victoria Town sent James Yates and J.W. McKay as representatives, while the District sent Dr. Helmcken and surveyor Joseph Despard Pemberton. Helmcken was elected Speaker of the Assembly. For this parliament, the electoral privilege was confined to property owners. (Douglas extended it in 1859 to include tenants, likely because he wanted more taxpayers in order to raise money for road-building. His only meagre source of revenue until then had been the sale of land—his suggestions of taxing liquor and sawn lumber from San Francisco having been wildly unpopular.) Some electoral districts returned members to the Leglislature with as few as four votes—in the Nanaimo election in 1859, A.R. Green was returned with one vote!

The first Vancouver Island Assembly met to advise Douglas on governing an underpopulated, isolated community. During the latter part of 1856, however, rumours began to trickle out from the mainland that gold had been found on some of the interior creeks. In 1857, news of the finds was published abroad and, on April 25, 1858, with the landing of the sidewheeler *Commodore*, Victoria's isolation ceased.

The gold rush was the catalyst which made British Columbia a province, and provided the wealth and population (mainly Californian) to make Victoria a city. The *Commodore* alone brought 450 men, only 60 of whom were British. Instantly, the muddy streets and small shops of the townsite were crowded with men in red flannel shirts, carrying packsacks and bowie knives, who camped in tents around the outskirts of the little town. Victoria's inhabited limits included the fort, a few buildings on Wharf Street, and Government Street from James Bay to the ravine at Johnson Street. That December, Charles Wilson wrote in his diary: "The roads are nearly impassable from the steady rain for days together. In the town of Victoria the mud is so deep that it comes up to the horses' girths & foot passengers can only cross on planks laid across; indeed it is so bad that a story is told of a merchant who wished to carry on a conversation with a person on the other side of the street, hiring an Indian to shoot letters over with his bow & arrow." Pit latrines defiled the air, and instant streams wound between the tents and shacks and through the cow-dung-strewn vacant lots. Drays sank to their axles in the mud, and "No Bottom Obtainable" signs were common on the edge of expanses of water on the roadways. In six weeks, 225 buildings were erected.

Eventually, 25,000 miners had passed through, all seeking supplies and information before starting their trek into the wilderness (the permanent population of Victoria in 1859 was 600). Unlike the 1849 rush to California, where potential gold-diggers had to cross a hostile continent, the rush to B.C. was a simple matter of purchasing a $15 boat ticket in San Francisco. "Never was there so large an immigration in so short a space of time into such a small place," wrote one visitor.

Initially, publicists, speculators and Yankeephiles in San Francisco, "under the spacious cover of American patriotism," had attempted to promote "The Bellingham Bay Trail" and Port Townsend as the only suitable entry points into the Northwest (partly because of Douglas's blockade of the Fraser River with HMS *Satellite* to enforce the Hudson's Bay Company's trading monopoly—a move which earned him a sharp rebuke from Colonial Secretary Bulwer-Lytton. Victoria, even with its "exorbitant prices" at the HBC store, was soon discovered to be the only spot with any reliable information and decent provisioning. The store in the fort was besieged day and night by these "outscourings of the world," all of whom were in such a hurry that a half-day wait for supplies was intolerable. Jailbirds, thieves, desperados, and "the halt, the lame, the blind & the mad," all "let loose by the Government of California for the benefit of mankind," flocked to Victoria. San Francisco merchants moved their stocks completely into new premises in Victoria, and advertised their previous business addresses to jog the memories of former customers.

William Charles (1831-1903) joined the Hudson's Bay Company in 1854, and served at many of the forts and trading posts in western Canada and the United States before his promotion to chief factor at Victoria in 1874. He was an amateur naturalist and bird painter, and did sketches which "illustrate in an originally clever way the many phases of fur trading life of the frontier wilds." He lived at 1038 Fort Street, just west of Cook. One of his daughters married the Hon. David M. Eberts, one-time attorney general of B.C.

James Allan Grahame (1825-1905) was one of the Hudson's Bay Company brigade which ran Fort Vancouver in Oregon. In the decades before his retirement in 1884, he was chief factor in the outposts at "Quesnelle" and Fort St. James, in charge of all the Pacific Coast operations of the Hudson's Bay Company, and finally chief commissioner, following Donald Smith's (Lord Strathcona and Mount Royal of the Canadian Pacific Railway) retirement. His second wife was one of John Work's daughters.

Esquimalt, with its easier access, became the preferred port for the overloaded vessels bringing miners to the colony. The Old Esquimalt Road, built by the bluejackets from HMS *Thetis*, changed almost beyond recognition. Captain Mayne wrote that "a few months before, we used to flounder through the mud without meeting a single soul; now it was covered with pedestrians toiling along, with the step and air of men whose minds are occupied with thoughts of business; crowded with well-laden carts and vans, with Wells Fargo's, or Freeman's 'Expresses,' and with strangers of every tongue and country, in every variety of attire." The town was surprisingly peaceful, though one incident in late July saw some rowdies who had freed an arrested American attempt to hoist the Stars & Stripes above the fort. Douglas called out the heavily armed HMS *Plumper* from Esquimalt to restore order.

Alfred Waddington, an Englishman who had been a "Forty-Niner" and had arrived in Victoria in 1858, decided to make his fortune as a merchant, rather than as a gold-digger. In his curious and colourful book, *The Fraser Mines Vindicated, or the History of Four Months*, published in November, 1858 (the first book produced on Vancouver Island), Waddington wrote that "as to business, there was none, the streets were grown over with grass, & there was not even a cart. Goods there were none, nor in the midst of this Comedy of Errors had a single California merchant thought of sending a single bag of flour to Victoria! We were obliged to replace [bread], first by pilot bread, & afterwards with soda crackers."

The excitement peaked in July, 1858, when, during a ten-day period, four San Francisco steamers landed 5,500 miners in Esquimalt. The price of lots along the Victoria and Esquimalt harbours shot from as little as $5 up to $500, $1,000 and more. Saloons popped up on Government, Yates, and around the Bastion. Most of the miners moved on as quickly as they had come; most were respectable and law-abiding, but some were chagrined to find British laws and authority—personified by James Douglas—firmly in place. On the unorganized mainland, Douglas acted quickly, although at first with no Imperial authority, to forestall the threat of an American take-over (and to protect the trading monopoly of the Hudson's Bay Company). On the 20th of August, 1858, the mainland territory—known vaguely as New Caledonia—was named British Columbia; two weeks later, by order of the Queen-in-council, James Douglas was made governor (as a condition of same, he had to resign as head of the Western Department of the Hudson's Bay Company); on November 19, under the auspices of Governor Douglas and the new chief justice, Matthew Baillie Begbie, officials of the new mainland colony were sworn in at Fort Langley.

Douglas stationed the HMS *Satellite* at the mouth of the Fraser River to collect license fees and levy customs duties on all ships entering the Fraser River. To ensure Victoria's prosperity, he proclaimed it a free port on January 18, 1860—and taxed all goods entering either colony, other than through Victoria. (Only Hong Kong and Labuan shared this status within the British Empire. Free-port status for Victoria and Vancouver

was later to be a campaign issue for the United Farmers of B.C. in 1922.) The mainlanders, particularly the merchants at the mainland capital, New Westminster, were incensed, and were further irritated by Governor Douglas's residency at Victoria.

With the collapse of the gold rush in the early 1860s, a movement began to unite the two colonies of Vancouver Island and British Columbia. Expenses of the two separate governments were very high, and both Douglas and the Imperial government favoured the efficiency of union. Victoria and Vancouver Island, in the beginning, were in favour, as it was felt that Victoria's commercial and political prestige and wealth would be greatly increased. New Westminster and the mainland, however, were jealous of Victoria, and moreover were, by 1865, more prosperous than the Island colony. Britain had little interest in the location of the capital, but had always insisted that its colonies pay their own way. As England slipped into a depression in the early 1860s, it cut public works spending to the bone. Pundits floated rumours that the two colonies would be abandoned, and thus eventually absorbed by the United States (which was preoccupied with its Civil War at the time and was temporarily uninterested). In the spring of 1865, the expected rush to the gold fields failed to materialize; the colonial governments were heavily in debt to the Bank of British Columbia, which refused further credit. Finally, in 1866, a petition in favour of union was signed by 450 people. The British government finally acted, and extended the authority of the Executive Government and Council of British Columbia over Vancouver Island. On the 17th of November, 1866, the union of British Columbia and Vancouver Island was accomplished, and Victoria lost its free-port status.

Two years earlier, in March, 1864, James Douglas had resigned his governorships of Vancouver Island and British Columbia. On March 14, twenty-one years to the day from the arrival of the *Beaver* off Clover Point to commence the construction of Fort Victoria, Douglas and his family boarded the *Enterprise* for a journey to England. "Long before the hour fixed," said the *Colonist*, "the city was decked in all directions with flags and banners, and the shipping in the harbour gaily ornamented with streamers and signals, and as the time of embarkation approached a multitude of people streamed down towards the Hudson's Bay Company wharf and congregated in dense masses." A band played "For He's A Jolly Good Fellow," and, as the little steamer moved off the wharf, struck up "Auld Lang Syne," while a battery on the far shore "sent forth a thundering salute."

When Douglas returned, two years later, the union of the two colonies was almost accomplished. His successors—Arthur Edward Kennedy on Vancouver Island and Frederick Seymour at New Westminster—were, in their separate ways, opposed to union. Seymour thought Victoria only suitable as "a fishing place," and moved from New Westminster (after union, Kennedy was redundant) only under duress.

Douglas had no intention of resuming public life when he again resumed residence at his James Bay home. He had had a change of heart on the matter of union and wrote on November 19, 1866: "alternate rain

and sunshine . . . the Ships of War fired a salute on the occasion. A funeral procession, with minute guns, would have been more appropriate to the sad, melancholy event." Mainlanders apparently rejoiced, though, and the New Westminster *Examiner* editorialized that as "a copious rain immediately followed the reading of the proclamation, British Columbia shed tears in folding to her embrace her long lost sister!"

The union of the two colonies, in 1866, closely paralleled the movement in Eastern Canada towards confederation. A debate began in British Columbia on the advisability of joining in this new consolidation of British North America. Meanwhile, Governor Seymour had temporarily—by refusing to move to Victoria—made New Westminster the capital of the colony. The British Columbia legislature first met in Victoria, following

relentless pressure by Island residents, on December 17, 1867, and a keen debate began on the question of joining Canada. Initially, the popular argument for confederation ("the lucubrations of extreme politicians") rested on the removal of the "despotic" colonial government and the establishment of "responsible institutions"; John A. Macdonald's new Canadian government was willing, and talked about taking over the intervening prairie country from the Hudson's Bay Company (which happened in 1869—the British government bought nineteen-twentieth's of it for £300,000, then allowed Canada to annex it). Lined up against confederation were the strange bed-fellows Seymour, a United States-annexationist group, and those residents (mainly on Vancouver Island) who could foresee transferring no allegiance from England to Canada.

Government Street in the early 1860s, after the wild activity of the gold rush died down, was a collection of wooden shacks and saloons fronting onto board sidewalks and muddy streets. Water came by the horse-drawn barrel-full from Spring Ridge, and was pumped into pails and cisterns at prices as high as 25 cents a bucketful (S.R.W.W.C. on the barrel stands for Spring Ridge Water Works Company).

Roderick Finlayson

One of the builders of Fort Victoria who later was successful buying and selling City of Victoria land was Roderick Finlayson. A "civil but hard Scot" from Loch Alsh, Ross-shire, and the son of a sheep farmer, Finlayson left Scotland for New York shortly after his nineteenth birthday in 1837. He obtained an appointment as an apprentice clerk with the Hudson's Bay Company, and was almost immediately sent west to the Pacific. He spent 1841 and 1842 in the trading posts on the north coast—Forts Simpson, Stikeen, Durham and McLaughlin—and was ordered south to help with the construction of Fort Victoria in June, 1843.

Upon Charles Ross's death, the following year, Finlayson was placed in charge of Fort Victoria. He ruled there until 1849, when James Douglas moved over from Fort Vancouver. Finlayson was then appointed chief accountant for the Hudson's Bay Company, a position he held until 1862. When a "rough-looking" group of miners arrived at Fort Victoria in late 1849, Finlayson wrote in his diary that he took them "to be pirates, and ordered our men to prepare for action—they had leather bags, full of gold nuggets, which they offered in exchange for goods." Finlayson had never seen gold nuggets before: "I took one of the pieces to the blacksmith shop, and finding it flattened out thin as a wafer, I offered to take it at $11 per ounce in exchange for goods." He recorded that no complaints were offered about the low rate, either from the miners or from his delighted superiors, who said the transaction was "entirely satisfactory."

In 1852, Finlayson began to purchase property in the Victoria area, and in the late 1850s built a large house on his estate between Government and Douglas, near Bay Street. Early city directories list his occupation as "capitalist." The house was surrounded by meadows, orchards and formal gardens, and had several barns and stables. He also owned the Spring Ridge springs area at about Fernwood and Vining near Victoria High School—the city's water supply. Water was brought into the city by individual carriers from the springs, at prices which varied from sixpence for three bucketfuls in the early fifties to a high of 25 cents a bucketful in 1858 to twenty buckets for a dollar in the depressed early seventies. (Joseph Despard Pemberton, the surveyor-general, had written to the Hudson's Bay Company in the late fifties, suggesting that a water pipe "to supply not less than 40 persons" be laid from Spring Ridge to the city; the foundation of the modern city waterworks system was laid on October 7, 1873.) Control of the water supply became an issue in April, 1861, when Finlayson's agent J.J. Cochrane tried to shut off the people's supply and charge the water carriers for use of the springs. There was a concurrent rumour that a group of speculators, said to include Attorney General G.H. Cary, were attempting to gain control of the land. It later transpired that Finlayson was out-manoeuvring the speculators—he allowed the es-

tablished water carriers to "dispense Adam's Ale," and later turned the springs over to the city.

In 1849, Finlayson married Sarah Work, a daughter of Hudson's Bay factor and Hillside-area farmer John Work. The couple had seven daughters and four sons. Finlayson gradually dissociated himself from Hudson's Bay Company affairs—his final posting was as superintendent of the company's operations in the interior of Vancouver Island. He was elected Mayor of Victoria in 1878, and got the first phase of the current City Hall built. He, with brother-in-law W.F. Tolmie, owned the Thetis Cove site of the Esquimalt Graving Dock, and sold it to the provincial government for $15,275. Trying his hand at property development, he erected buildings including the warehouses at 1202-1214 Wharf Street in 1882. He died January 20, 1892. Sarah Finlayson survived him by fourteen years, dying January 25, 1906 in the family home on Douglas Street.

Frederick Whymper, a nurse, and Eleanor and Arthur Fellows, in front of the Fellows's little home on Birdcage Walk in the early 1860s. Eleanor was the daughter of penny-postage inventor Sir Rowland Hill. They moved to Victoria in 1859, initially living in Capt. James Cooper's Thetis Cottage on Dyke Point in Esquimalt. (The white-painted house was a navigational landmark which could be seen from outside Race Rocks. It, along with 385 adjoining acres, a barn and outbuildings, were "second to none as a stock farm" in the 1850s.) Fellows and his brother opened a business on Yates Street, offering English hardware "at a modest advance on manufacturing prices." Thieves broke in through a rear window in February, 1860, and took a cash box containing $30 in silver coin, which was concealed under a mattress, but missed $500 in gold in the office. "As it was probably overlooked by accident," said the Colonist, "they are invited to call again for it." In 1880, the Fellowses took E.G. Prior into the partnership, and three years later sold out to him. (Capt. Cooper moved to New Westminster, where he became, like John Robson, a thorn in Gov. Douglas's side. Douglas hated the avid ambition of the businessmen there, writing that "social meetings and country rides are beyond the aim of even the most ambitious pleasure hunters.")

One of the leaders in the fight for confederation was Amor de Cosmos, a Nova Scotian who saw himself as the William Lyon Mackenzie of B.C. He had founded the *British Colonist* newspaper in 1858 to fight James Douglas and the Hudson's Bay Company. His cherished goal was independence and responsible self-government, which translated in the 1860s into a call for confederation with Canada. During the confederation debate in Victoria, in March, 1870, he stated prophetically that "I would not object to a little revolution now and again in British Columbia, after Confederation, if we were treated unfairly, for I am one of those who believe that political hatreds attest the vitality of the State."

J.S. Helmcken suggested that the United States would likely, eventually, absorb both British Columbia and Canada. "The people of this Colony have, generally speaking, no love for Canada; they have but little sentimentality, and care little about the distinctions between the form of government of Canada and the United States," he wrote. "Therefore, no union on account of love need be looked for." As such, he was expressing obliquely the feelings of the old Crown Colony group—prophetic words,

given the catastrophic fate of B.C.-Canada affairs in the 1870s. "The only bond of union outside force," he wrote, "will be the material advantage of the country and the pecuniary benefit of its inhabitants."

Former Colonial Surveyor Joseph Despard Pemberton expressed the pro-English feelings of the old-time colonists in a rhyming letter to the *Colonist* newspaper: "True loyalty's to Motherland / & Not to Canada / The love we bear is second-hand / To any step-mama." Canadians were "North American Chinamen," who saved their money and sent it home to the east. Americans at least were more generous, spending freely what they made.

Henry Pering Pellew Crease, then attorney general of British Columbia, publicly expressed more positive feelings toward Canada, writing in March, 1870, that "our only option is between remaining a petty, isolated community 15,000 miles from home, eking out a miserable existence on the crumbs of prosperity our powerful & active Republican neighbours choose to allow us, or, by . . . becoming the prosperous western outlet on the North Pacific of a young and vigorous people . . . ." Two months later,

Arthur Edward Kennedy, the last Royal Governor of Vancouver Island, was a retired army officer and Anglo-Irish aristocrat who had been governor of Sierra Leone, Gambia, and Western Australia, and had served on the Irish Board of Works during the potato famine. His nickname, "Old Deportment," hinted at his combination of gentlemanly and tropical experience—ideal for running a colony, his admirers felt. Kennedy, however, had never had to govern educated political agitators like Amor de Cosmos and Drs. Tolmie and Helmcken, who provoked his famous remark that there were only two classes on Vancouver Island, "those who are convicts, and those who ought to be."

Governor Seymour, "vacillating, lymphatic and procrastinating" in the words of historian F.W. Howay, was in favour of New Westminster as B.C.'s capital "as strongly as his effeminate nature could be." Seymour described British Columbia (the mainland colony) as "a road with a gold mine at one end and a city in a neighbouring colony at the other." Victorians who thought New Westminster to be a place with "too little soil and too much climate" and didn't forgive Seymour even when he moved his official residence to the Island. His death removed the final obstacle on the path to confederation with Canada.

Anthony Musgrave was appointed governor of the Colony of British Columbia with specific directions to encourage confederation. He was chosen for his popularity with the Canadian element in Victoria—the aristocratic Henry Crease described him as a "creole," meaning he was from the colonies and "not such good form" as pure-British Seymour. No one doubted his intelligence, though his judgement was questioned when he wrote to Seymour, before his appointment was officially announced, to enquire about the quality of the furniture in Government House.

Benjamin W. Pearse, with his partner J.D. Pemberton, surveyed the townsite of Victoria in 1862, and bought a large piece of land in the Spring Ridge area. He was appointed resident engineer of the Public Works Department of Canada. His marriage to Miss Jennie Palmer ("in white tarlatan with satin basque") of Great Yarmouth in June, 1876, was the social event of the season, and the couple took up residence at "Fernwood Manor" at the corner of Vining and Begbie (demolished March, 1969).

Crease was appointed a judge of the Supreme Court, and later revised British Columbia's laws to fit them within Canada's judicial system.

On March 25, 1870, the great confederation debate ended, all having agreed on the terms by which British Columbia would join Canada. These included the assumption of all of B.C.'s debts by the Dominion, an annual subsidy of $35,000, financing for a graving dock at Esquimalt, the care of the Indians, and support of the lieutenant-governor, judges, customs, postal and telegraphy services, the fisheries and the penitentiaries. The Dominion was to ensure a fortnightly steam mail service between Victoria and San Francisco, and a weekly service with Olympia. And, the Dominion was to build a transcontinental railway, starting it within two years of the date of confederation, to a Pacific terminus at Victoria.

The promise of a transcontinental railway, which would end British Columbia's isolation and make it an integral part of a European & Far Eastern link (the solution to the Northwest Passage problem of centuries past), was the most potent argument for confederation. It finally convinced Governor Seymour; regardless, he died of dysentery during an expedition to Bella Coola in January, 1869, and his replacement, Anthony Musgrave, was an avowed advocate of confederation. Musgrave, whose previous posting was as governor of Newfoundland, came with formal instructions from England to bring the confederation debate to a favourable conclusion.

The document containing the terms of union with Canada arrived in Victoria on July 18, 1870. An election was held in British Columbia that November; Helmcken and de Cosmos represented Victoria City and District in the session which began in January, 1871, to ratify the terms of union. On July 20, 1871, in the hyperbolic prose of the *British Colonist*, "British Columbia and Canada joined hands and hearts across the Rocky Mountains, and John Bull the younger stands with one foot on the Atlantic and the other on the Pacific." At midnight the previous night in the city bells were rung, guns fired, Roman candles shot, and "Christmas" crackers snapped. A torchlight parade wound its way through the streets, people shook hands and "cheered and cheered and cheered," for, the newspaper said, "they were celebrating the Birth of Liberty."

The old fort had long since vanished, and the city, with a population of about 8,000, had expanded south into James Bay and east up the Fort Street hill. The fort's site had been subdivided and the lots sold at auction; the highest price, $12,250, was paid by J.J. Southgate for the lot at the southwest corner of Fort and Government Street (the Bank of British Columbia building)—the site of the Bachelor Hall and Staines's little school. The stockade and bastions were demolished in November, 1864.

Prosperity and a glowing future seemed assured for the new Canadian province of British Columbia; it was felt that no one would ever look back.

J.S. Helmcken

The white clapboard house at 638 Elliott Street, in the shadow of the Provincial Museum, was the home for nearly seventy years of John Sebastian Helmcken, who built it in 1852 next to the house of his father-in-law, Governor James Douglas. He was the longest-surviving founding member of both the colony and the province of British Columbia, "a figure of a former generation" often seen walking quietly through Beacon Hill Park.

Born in London on June 5, 1824, Helmcken studied medicine and became "an expert dispenser of pills and potions." (His birth year was the subject of some confusion: the *Colonist* noted his 87th birthday in 1912, and he reportedly celebrated his 90th birthday in 1913. As was the custom of the Victorian period, he was referred to as Mr. Helmcken rather than Dr. Helmcken.) Intrigued by the possibility of life in a new land, he signed on with the Hudson's Bay Company to become the resident surgeon on Vancouver Island. He arrived at Fort Victoria in March, 1850, and quickly became an active force in the little colony's affairs.

Two years later, he was betrothed to Cecilia Douglas. "I have so fallen in love with Cecilia," he wrote, "that I spend much of my time courting." Later, he described the courtship as "a very simple affair—we had hot chocolate and singing—early hours kept." On the day before his wedding, on December 27, 1852, it had snowed heavily, and the only carriage available to the bride and groom was a two-wheeled cart which became impossibly bogged down. Helmcken borrowed a dry-goods crate, which he flipped over, filled with blankets, and hitched to the horse as an impromptu sled.

Helmcken was elected to the first Vancouver Island legislative assembly in 1855, and was appointed Speaker. His actions seem to have been motivated by the practicalities of life in the little colony; in particular, the matter of the colony's "bloated" Civil List in the 1860s strengthened his early distrust of the British colonial system. Helmcken led the group opposing the "specified and unalterable salaries" for Governor Kennedy and his entourage, and, with Amor de Cosmos amongst others, pushed for union with mainland British Columbia in the hope that retrenchment and some financial responsibility would ensue. In July, 1866—about the same time as confederation became a discussion topic in B.C.—the Banks Bill was passed in the U.S. Senate, stressing the desirability of the annexation of British North America. An annexation movement, "confined to Vancouver Island," sprang up, with Helmcken wrongly identified as one of its members (he maintained he was anti-confederation, not pro-annexation). By 1869, a substantial body of opinion within the U.S. Senate considered the annexation of B.C. as part of America's manifest destiny, and pushed

for early construction of the Northern Pacific Railway. Pamphlets were distributed, bearing doggerel such as "You want the mail / You want the rail / You want the cars to hie on / Come join us & we'll thread your land / With passageways of iron." The first annexation petition was circulated in Victoria in the autumn of 1869, and received over 40 signatures. The machinations of eastern Canadian politicians and the Earl of Granville to achieve B.C.'s federation with Canada were seen as insulting, both by the pro-annexationists and the "Family-Company-Compact"—the colonial administrators and Vancouver Island establishment. A further annexation petition ended up being signed by 104 men—about one percent of the white population of B.C.—but the pro-confederation and established interests noted darkly that over half the signatories were either Germans or Jews.

The confederation efforts of Canadians from Canada West (Upper Canada before 1841) including de Cosmos, Walkem, Dr. R.W.W. Carrall, Dr. I.W. Powell, and John Robson, and the Dominion of Canada's hints of a transcontinental wagon road or railway, swayed British Columbia opinion. When new Governor Anthony Musgrave selected a trio of British Columbians to negotiate confederation with Canada, Helmcken was chosen to accompany Joseph Trutch (who had opposed confederation in the years before Musgrave's appointment) and R.W.W. Carrall. Musgrave shrewdly felt that the three represented the varied interests of British Columbia. De Cosmos, the great champion of the cause, was not asked, partly due to his erratic behaviour, but also because of the feeling that he wanted to ensure Victoria's political domination of the province.

Helmcken retired from public life late in 1871, following B.C.'s entry into confederation. He remained active with St. Joseph's Hospital for many years. His wife Cecilia had died very young in 1865; Helmcken lived on in the little house, dying there in September, 1920, aged 96.

Of his children, Harry Dallas Helmcken made the greatest mark. "The People's Harry" joined the Drake & Jackson legal firm, and went from there to become an influential Conservative MLA. His legal career, which included the negotiation of the Songhees Indian Reservation trade, was overshadowed by his flamboyant personal life. In September, 1896, he married a stylish, plump San Francisco widow with an operatic voice. The couple lived for years in a red-plush suite in the Driard Hotel, and moved to a similar suite in the Empress in 1908. Crowds used to gather to watch the couple leave the Driard for an evening's entertainment, with Ogg the chauffeur behind the wheel of their Pierce-Arrow. In 1912, during a visit to London, Helmcken died suddenly, aged only 52. Mrs. Helmcken eventually returned to San Francisco.

Harry Helmcken, with wife and chauffeur, were regular visitors to father John Sebastian Helmcken's little Elliot Street house. The house is now restored as part of the Provincial Museum complex. J.S. Helmcken passed his final years quietly there, puttering in his garden, long after the death of father-in-law James Douglas and the demolition of the latter's much larger house immediately to the west. Harry's nephew, Ainslie, recalled that the enormous Pierce Arrow was "one of the wonders of Victoria. Getting it into Bastion Square, to Uncle Harry's office, was quite something—it had to be backed up about five times to make the turn from Government Street." Harry's political career also occupied the nephew's weekends: "Once, Uncle Harry took me for a drive out to Sooke, and at every farmhouse I had to hop out and deliver newspapers which contained articles about his political and legislative speeches."

John Sebastian Helmcken

The Songhees

The land directly across the Inner Harbour from downtown Victoria, at the western end of the Johnson Street bridge, is the site of the old Songhees Indian Reservation. Today, it sits largely abandoned and unused, bordering the industrial area around the old Esquimalt & Nanaimo Railway yards in Victoria West. Its surrender by the Songhees tribe was—as was the Kitsilano Indian Reservation deal of the same period in Vancouver—a black mark on the record of the McBride government and several prominent lawyers and businessmen in Vancouver and Victoria.

The popularity of Fort Victoria caused the Songhees to move from Cadboro Bay to the Inner Harbour by 1850. Dr. John Sebastian Helmcken visited the Songhees Village shortly after he arrived at the Fort in 1850 and noted that it housed five or six hundred Indians living in "dirt and filth" in a collection of huts along the shoreline, practically on top of the mud. "By far the greater number had a blanket only for clothing," he wrote, "but 'King Freezy' had on a tall hat and a long coat and considered himself somebody, as indeed he was, and friendly to the whites" (Chief Freezy drowned after falling from his canoe in October, 1894; he had once demonstrated his authority by decapitating one of his wives, who had been accused of adultery with a white man, on the beach in front of the village). As for their appearance—"all the Indians had flattened heads, fearful foreheads, retreating backward." Helmcken, with companion Dr. Benson, saw the head-flattening process underway on babies, "a pad and pressure being the instruments; they did not seem to suffer—perhaps it made them good. The cradles were hung on a flexible pole, stuck in the ground at an acute angle, so a slight touch on the pole put it into an up and down motion." Helmcken and Benson also noted the Indians' "woolly dogs," which were regularly sheared for their long hair.

The whites' curiosity about the Songhees rapidly changed to distrust as the city outgrew its trading post status following the gold rush of the late 1850s. Citizens demanded action against the "proximity of this wigwam settlement, with its possibilities of depravity and vice being injurious to the appearance, morals & business of the city, & to the character & best interests of the Indians themselves." Governor Douglas, whose wife was of mixed blood, responded to this hue and cry in the Vancouver Island House of Assembly on February 5, 1859, noting that "the presence of the Indians so near the town is a public inconvenience, but their removal would be neither just nor politic."

Through the 1890s, the "119 acres occupied by 50 Indians" became more of an eyesore. The Indians—especially the *klootchmen* (women)—draped in shawls, blankets and "funny, fancy hats," walked across the railroad bridge from the reserve, up Johnson Street, and squatted down on the sidewalk to sell clams, salmon or potatoes from the sacks they carried. Saunders' grocery, at 571 Johnson Street, offended by their habit of sitting on the store's front window ledge, put a row of spikes along it. Other klootchmen wandered up and down Government, "making terrible sounds, noise—shouting and screaming and all that sort of thing," according to one young woman's reminiscence. Some made fine baskets, or got work selling fish to, or working at, the Todd cannery. Others were objects of crude sport and mild derision. None were accepted as domestic servants. Some hung around across the street from Richard Carr's wholesale store next to the Hudson's Bay Company warehouses on Wharf Street, and were given any provisions, like sultanas, which had gone too maggotty to sell to whites.

The province received the jurisdiction, through section 13 of the Terms of Union with Canada, for resolving the reservation problem. R.E. Gosnell, writing for the Bureau of Provincial Information, described B.C.'s position in the 1911 *Year Book of British Columbia*: "At no time prior to the union did the government of B.C. recognize that the Indians had any legal interest in the reserves set apart for their use. These reserves were increased or diminished as the government thought fit. The Indians were not allowed to transfer any interest in such lands. If, at any time, the Indians abandoned the occupation of such lands, the lands were in the hands of the government, free from what is sometimes called the 'Indian Title,' that is, occupation by the Indians." Thus the Dominion, as trustee of the Indians under the British North America Act, had the right to administer the lands for the Indians' use, but no right to sell or dispose of them, or to grant any mineral or timber leases for anything beyond the Indians' own immediate uses.

Richard McBride's Conservative government made the first attempt to get Victoria, the province of British Columbia, and the Indians together "to settle the matter of the latter's removal": the Songhees Indian Reservation Bill was introduced into the legislature on February 22, 1905, by The Hon. R.F. Green. It passed March 14, and the government sat down to consider its next move. The Dominion, which supposedly held the lands only in trust, threw a spanner into the works by transferring Indian land in Prince Rupert to the Grand Trunk Pacific Railway for its western terminus. Lawyer H.D. Helmcken, K.C., the Indian agent and son of J.S. Helmcken, was appointed by McBride to negotiate a deal with the Indians.

Helmcken reported back to the legislature on October 25, 1910, with an agreement signed by McBride and several chiefs of the tribe, whereby 43 families would leave their reserve for a new site to be chosen jointly by McBride and five members of the band. The Victoria reservation was to revert to the Province of B.C. (its value, in 1905, before the land boom, had been thought to be about $100,000 to $150,000), and each head of a Songhees family was to receive a bonus of $10,000. The group quickly selected a new reservation in Esquimalt, facing into the harbour. The province, it was announced in March, 1911, had set aside $750,000 for the purchase. The Dominion Government, as guardian for the Indians, gave its assent and, on April 4th, Chief Michael Cooper received $421,552 and ratified the agreement with McBride. The Songhees were so delighted that they presented Helmcken with a gold-filled pocket matchbox, in-

An Indian canoe race at a regatta in the Inner Harbour around the turn of the century. The Customs House, slightly to the left of centre in the picture, is still the major building on the water side of that part of Wharf Street. The pitched-roof Hudson's Bay Company warehouse, to the left of the Customs House, was demolished in the 1930s.

pleted by a lawyer named Hamilton Read, who received a fee of $39,525 and shortly thereafter joined the Bowser law firm). Premier McBride, besieged by the effects of the war, economic depression, and the collapse of the Pacific Great Eastern and Canadian Northern Pacific railways, resigned in late 1915. His replacement was Bowser, who had to deal with the Songhees issue through the sessions of 1916.

Legal fees became an issue again when M.A. Macdonald, the president of the B.C. Liberal Association who was running in a Vancouver by-election in February, 1916, said that a $30,000 fee had been paid to Helmcken (by then deceased), on top of the $75,000 paid to Matson. The case was reported in the Legislature, where Liberal leader H.C. Brewster called the Conservative government's position a "whitewash" and said that $30,000 of Matson's fee was a bribe paid directly to some influential Indians.

Coming as they did in 1916, these allegations of bribery against an agent of the government and a press report quoting Bowser as saying that sometimes "it is necessary to grease the palm of an Indian," drew comparisons with the Kaiser's violation of Belgian neutrality—that is, a justification of bribery on the grounds of necessity. Sir Charles Hibbert Tupper, a lifelong Conservative like his father, announced in August that he would support the Liberals against Bowser, whose government was described as "wholesale plunderers of the Province." Tupper's switch to the Liberals was national news, and the *Toronto Globe* editorialized that "the Indian with itching palm is everywhere, in white skin far oftener than red."

scribed "from the members of the Songhees Band, to Harry Dallas Helmcken, for many kindnesses. April 15, 1911. Victoria, B.C."

Everyone felt they had a good deal. The following January, McBride announced that he had secured railway terminals and harbour facilities for the capital, to be located on the Songhees land; following a trip to the East in November, he specified a joint CNR & CPR passenger terminal for it. Nothing materialized—the deal foundered in the depression of 1913 and the bankruptcy of the Canadian Northern Railway system.

Also in 1913, the Liberal press (the *Victoria Times*) struck a sour note by disclosing that J.S.H. "Sam" Matson, the publisher of the province's two biggest Conservative newspapers—the *Victoria Colonist* and *Vancouver News-Advertiser*—had been paid $75,000 for his services in negotiating the Songhees deal. Matson responded on April 20th, stating that the work had taken ten months, and that there were "certain large and necessary expenses which it was not wise to detail" but which had left him with only $15,000 personally.

It was the successful solution to the Songhees question which led the provincial government into negotiating the deal for the Kitsilano Indian Reservation in Vancouver—one which was far less successful ethically (Attorney General Bowser started the negotiations, which were com-

John Work

PABC 14355

John Work's Hillside Farm occupied much of the modern Hillside area of Victoria. Its 600 acres took in most of the northern shoreline of Selkirk Water between Rock Bay and the site of Staines's piggery just west of the CN Railway bridge. To the east, his farm shared a common boundary with part of the Hudson's Bay Company's Uplands Farm (map, page 114).

Victoria's first retiree was John Work, who served with the Hudson's Bay Company until, in 1850, he bought 600 acres to the north of the fort and started the Hillside Farm. He died eleven years later, in December 1861, and all accounts describe him as a simple soul and honest worker, content to leave ambition and the colony's political machinations largely to contemporaries like James Douglas.

Work was born John Wark in 1791 in County Derry, Ireland. He anglicized his name when he joined the Hudson's Bay Company in 1814. He was among the first of the traders across the Rocky Mountains in 1822, and spent the next dozen years ranging from Vancouver Island to San Francisco Bay, trapping beaver and helping to operate the HBC's network of trading posts. From 1835 through 1849, he was in charge of Fort Simpson, then moved to Fort Victoria as one of its resident managers. He retired soon after.

Work's hospitality was extended to Victoria visitors like Captain Mayne, who wrote that even the long hike from Esquimalt in sea boots, with another pair in the pocket for indoor wearing, was well worth it for the few hours of pleasant conversation by Work's warm fire. The farm was one of the first in the area to supply regular produce for the markets, including a 108-pound pumpkin in the 1858 season. He served on the Council of Vancouver Island, appointed in April 1853, to sit with James Cooper and John Tod as advisors to Governor Douglas, and held the position until his death in 1862. He is buried in Pioneer Square, immediately to the east of Christ Church Cathedral on Quadra Street. The location of the old homestead is disputed—James Nesbitt wrote in the 1940s that Work's descendants believed it to be a much-altered old house on Vancouver Street near Kings Road.

AUTHOR'S COLLECTION

John Work

The Old City

Victoria—outpost of British civilization and the only free port on the northwest coast—was destined for greater things than a mere Hudson's Bay Company fort. In 1853, only ten years after the founding of Fort Victoria, the Victoria townsite was laid out by surveyors J.D. Pemberton and B.W. Pearse, and little wooden shops and saloons began to spring up amongst the mud puddles. The inner city's streets—Government, Bastion, Broughton, and Wharf, fitted themselves neatly around the Fort Victoria stockade. Grass grew in the ditches and between the boards of the wooden sidewalks; summer winds turned the town into a dustbowl; merchants and passers-by spent lazy afternoons trading stories (more often than goods) outside the little shops in the shadow of the fort's bastions. As artist Emily Carr recollected: "Victoria was like a lying-down cow, chewing."

The bucolic pace of life continued until the 1858 gold rush. Overnight, saloons, hotels, and cigar factories sprung up, followed not long afterwards by tinsmiths, crockery importers, ironmongers, chemists, and the thousand-and-one trading buildings which make up a city. The legacy of the gold rush was a land boom along Government, Yates, and Johnson streets, prompting James Douglas to establish the government buildings on cheaper land, conveniently accessible to his own home, on the south side of James Bay. In May, 1859, with prices at record heights, the government sold 22 lots along Government Street between Yates and Bastion; finally, in late 1864 the fort was demolished, and the Hudson's Bay Company subdivided the land and sold all the lots at auction. Victoria, in the early 1860s, was a small collection of brick buildings interspersed among rows of shacks, wooden-balconied hotels and saloons, with board sidewalks and muddy streets. Nevertheless, it was a city, and the

residents moved to incorporate it in 1862.

The civic spirit manifested itself, according to the *Colonist*, in a desire to act honestly, advance the public interest "unactuated by ambitious or selfish motives," while keeping an eye on the "powers that be across James Bay" (James Douglas and the colonial administration). All of Victoria's "whole-hearted patriots" were to work under the "half-a-loaf charter by which the city has been incorporated," and turned out on Saturday, August 16, 1862, to vote for the city's first mayor. When it came time to vote, "a perfect forest of hands above the heads of the crowd" showed that butcher Thomas Harris, the former Member for Esquimalt Town District, was the popular favorite over merchant Alfred Waddington.

Harris, just "an 'umble tradesman," he said, had arrived in Victoria about the same time as Waddington and had, like the latter, decided there was more gold to be made as a merchant than as a miner. His Queen's Market at Government and Johnson was a favorite butcher shop, and his square, four-chimneyed brick house at the corner of Bastion and Government, on the site now occupied by the Bank of Montreal, was one of the best in the city. The best-remembered story of Harris's term as mayor concerns a council meeting over which he was presiding in the barracks within the fort, which at that time was serving as city hall and police station. Harris, who weighed 21 stone (300 pounds), leaned back on his chair, and, after a sudden splitting noise, disappeared from view below the edge of the table, landing on "that portion of his breeches which wears out first." The chair was reduced to kindling, reminding the council of "a crushed eggshell." The newspaper reported the next day that the crash was so loud that it set the doors and windows to rattling loudly.

Harris served as mayor until 1865. Although his business fell on hard times during the depression of the 1860s, he spent extravagantly, maintaining race horses and punting at the Beacon Hill Park jockey club. After he was injured in a fall from his cart while driving to his Saanich farm, he became a melancholic drunk, and died at the end of November, 1884. His name survives in Harris Green, the strip of park running east along Pandora from Douglas to Quadra, made possible supposedly by a surveyor's mistake. (The surveying misalignment also caused a kink in Blanshard Street at Pandora, and Cormorant at Blanshard. Blanshard Street between Cormorant and Pandora was only half the normal width. The modern widening of Blanshard Street has created a graceful curve at Pandora, across the site of the original First Presbyterian Church.)

Most of the city's first ordinances were directed at cleaning up the smell and mess caused by the influx of gold miners. Several of the ordinances sought to make it easier for citizens to get around, especially at night when it was so dark that pedestrians constantly fell through holes in the board sidewalks and even occasionally missed the bridge across the Johnson Street ravine on Government. Anyone erecting a building was required to build a fence around it during the construction and to keep lights burning at night—gas street lights were not introduced for another year. Another set of bylaws regulated the movement of pigs, goats, and cattle through the city and set a speed limit of eight miles per hour on the

Government Street from Post Office, Victoria, B.C.

city streets (one violator was Attorney General George Cary, who was fined $20 by Judge Pemberton for riding his horse at "breakneck speed" on the Fort Street sidewalk, and had his expensive rifle seized when he refused to pay). Six separate bylaws regulated rubbish and offensive smells: slaughterhouses, tanneries and distilleries were banned within the city limits; no one was to throw or deposit any "rubbish, filth, ashes or offal of any kind" on public land or into the harbour, or shake or beat any carpet, rug or mat after eight in the morning; no privy could be emptied or night-soil transported through the city streets between six in the morning and eight at night, and no privy could be sunk closer than two feet to a neighbour's premises, or closer than twenty feet to the street.

Victoria rapidly outgrew its frontier-town mentality, and by the 1870s had the substantial look of a proper city—the most important one west of Toronto and north of San Francisco. Most of the shanties and shacks of gold rush days had disappeared by the turn of the century—though, due to the diligence of the volunteer fire brigades, they were not burned out in a conflagration like the one which destroyed youthful Vancouver in 1886.

Before the Empress Hotel was built in 1908, a small tidal inlet of James Bay covered the Empress Hotel site nearly as far east as Blanshard Street. The few residents of and visitors to the James Bay area walked from the corner of Government and Humboldt, by the Australia Hotel, past "Kanaka Row" (the shacks of the Sandwich Islanders who came to Victoria, mainly to work for the Puget Sound Agricultural Company), through the muddy reeds and around to higher ground at Governor Douglas's residence (the Provincial Museum site). With the proceeds of the 1859 land sale, Douglas built a bridge from Government Street across James Bay, and erected the Birdcages, as the first government buildings were called, on the south side of the Inner Harbour. The bridge was not considered very safe—after the 1896 Point Ellice bridge disaster schoolboys were told not to march in lockstep across it for fear of bringing it down. The James Bay mudflats stank terribly in the summer, and everything, from the soap lees from Pendray's first soap-making plant (just south of the current site of the Union Club), to wood chips from the Weiler Bros. furniture factory at the east end of the mud flats, to the occasional dead horse and floating fish, decorated the water and the muddy edge around the bridge. Mrs. Helen Hood, the daughter of Colonel Edward Prior, maintained that Victoria was noted for "a weird smell that used to come up sometimes with the different winds"— possibly clam shells but more likely rubbish and offal at low tide. A man named Bill Nye, who was the local rag & bone man, punted around the shallows under the bridge in a sort of "enlarged tub," scavenging the flotsam.

(Top) Looking north on Government Street, from Broughton, about 1906. The awnings of Weiler Brothers furniture department store, on the right, mark the location of the St. James Club, a banquet hall which was briefly Victoria's city hall. The West End grocery location, diagonally across the street, is now the Pemberton-Holmes building. The sign on the cowcatcher of the streetcar, visible in the original photograph used to make this card, advertised an illustrated lecture on the San Francisco earthquake. (Below) Looking south along Government Street from Fort towards the James Bay bridge, in the mid-1890s. The new legislative buildings are visible under construction in the background. On the right-hand side, farthest down the street, is the old Post Office, and next to it the modest building of the B.C.

Land & Investment Co. Ltd. at Broughton Street. The B.C.L&I was founded following the arrival in 1886 of Cuyler Armstrong Holland, a "supercilious young man" of 22 with a Cambridge law degree and impeccable British contacts. He went into partnership with Thomas Galpin, a member of the company which printed the Illustrated London News; together, they acquired so much land that "every important corner in Victoria was owned by them," plus land in Rockland and Fairfield, the Dallas Hotel, and the Cliff House. They landed boatloads of cattle from Gang Ranch at a wharf on Cadboro Bay, and either slaughtered them there or drove them all the way around Dallas Road to the Outer Wharf. BCL&I was later run by Robert Hugh Shanks (1889-1968), who started as an office boy and retired 57 years later as president.

The downtown butcher shops also contributed to the odour. (There was no refrigeration, so the meat was well aged and succulent, and carcasses of hogs and sheep—sometimes even an entire bullock—hung outside the shops, above the dusty roadway. The butcher shops had no doors, just a wire grating which was pulled across at night.) Goodacre & Dooley, Harris's Queen's Market, the B.C. Market, and future mayor Robert J. Porter's father's provision merchants provided everything on credit, including the Christmas goose. Van Volkenburgh's, at the southeast corner of Yates and Government, landed its cattle near the Royal Victoria Yacht Club site on Cadboro Bay.

Three of the most famous saloons of early Victoria occupied the lower end of Government Street. The Australia Hotel occupied the site of the Empress Hotel's rock garden. Across Humboldt Street, on the site of the Belmont Building, stood the John Bull, and two blocks up the street, on the southeast corner of Government and Fort in the building now occupied by the Irish linen store, was the Brown Jug saloon—renowned for its elegant interior and high-class clientele. There were bars on practically every corner, with drinks at two for a quarter, no chairs, and the open bottle of the patron's favorite brand placed on the bar in front of him. Government Street was often plugged with hacks, their horses waiting patiently while the cabbies killed time in the bars waiting for a fare. Drunks who were kicked out of one bar, and managed to avoid landing face-down in the mud outside, could practically fall into another one. In fine weather, there was Mr. Gowen's lager beer wagon on the street, ready to "refresh the inner man" from its capacious depths. Regular drunks did time doing roadwork on a rather casual chain gang. The free-wheeling bars and relaxed attitude toward drinking and public intoxication ceased quite abruptly in 1917 with the advent of Prohibition.

Victoria was also renowned for its brothels. Two of the most famous were run by Jennie Morris and Alice Seymour, the former on the site of the old Woodward's store at the southwest corner of Douglas and Courtney, the other across the street from the Union Club on Douglas. Rumour always had it that an underground passageway connected the Club to Morris's house; when the old Club building was razed in the early 1950s, a three-foot by two-foot tunnel was discovered, heading in that direction. One of the Club's secretaries passed many an afternoon at Morris's, and his dog waited patiently outside on the street. When the secretary was required back at his duties, so the story goes, the hall porter had no difficulty locating him.

The inner-downtown streets were lined with little stores, "places that sold all sorts of fittings for women," Angus & Gordon Grocers & Wine Merchants at the northwest corner of Fort and Government, the West End Grocery at Government and Broughton, Henry Young's White House, the W & J Wilson Clothiers at Trounce Alley, and Spencer's between Fort Street and Trounce Alley on Government. Families journeyed from the outskirts on the Oak Bay, Esquimalt and Hillside trams for their Saturday shopping at places like Copas & Young at the southeast corner of Fort and Broad. Clerks relayed the customers' money to the cashier by means of little metal boxes like trolleys on an overhead network of wires.

Grocery store interiors were full of the smells of sultanas, ripe fruit, wine and spices. There was no refrigeration and little packaging. Alleys were overrun with sleek, healthy cats, employed in all the shops, warehouses and stables to catch the myriad rats. Emily Carr's father, Richard, brought scraps of meat from home for his warehouse's strays, as he felt that no cat would long be healthy on a diet of pure rat.

The expansion of a few of the businesses, like Spencer's and Weiler Bros. (whose large showroom at Broughton and Government sported the words "Furniture, Carpets, Wallpaper & Complete House Furnishings" painted on the building's sidewall in ten-foot-high letters) dominated the small, specialized shops of old Victoria, prompting the eventual disappearance of many of them. Prohibition knocked out a number of the little grocery stores.

The old Windsor Hotel, at the northeast corner of Courtney and Government (now the Indian Crafts Shop), is reputed to be the first brick building in Victoria. Built in 1859 and originally named the Victoria Hotel, it barely survived an explosion in 1876, when owner George Richardson went looking for a gas leak with a candle. Other hotels in the downtown area, built mainly to serve commercial travellers, included the Occidental at the northeast corner of Johnson and Wharf (now the site of approach roads for the Johnson Street bridge); the Janion Hotel, built in 1891 at 1614 Store and, like the Occidental, adjacent to the E&NR terminus; the Oriental at 552 Yates, the Clarence—a favorite of the bachelor captains from the sealing schooners—at the northeast corner of Yates and Douglas; the Colonial Hotel at 555 Johnson; the Senator Hotel at 548 Johnson Street; and the Strand Hotel next door at 554 Johnson. These Johnson Street hotels were the most convenient for businessmen with dealings in the import warehouses and factories along Wharf and Store streets. The Dominion Hotel, still operating at the corner of Yates and Blanshard after many expansions and modernizations, was started by Steve Jones in 1876. The New England Hotel, at 1312 Government between Yates and Johnson, was built in 1892 for the same clientele, drawn to Victoria by the prosperity of the sealing industry and the newly connected E&NR railway. The hotel was built on the site of the renowned New England restaurant, founded at the beginning of the gold rush in 1858, and operated by German-born Englishman Henry Young, who

Frank Campbell had a cigar and news business at "the Adelphi stand" (the southwest corner of Yates and Government). He wrote bulletins and posted them outside, and his customers gathered to discuss the day's events. "It must be true," people said, "because I saw it on Campbell's board." Campbell broke readily into verse in his British Colonist ads for particularly good shipments (above). Born in Ireland in 1832, he arrived in Victoria with his bride from San Francisco in 1858, and tried looking for mining properties with his friend Sewell Moody. His wife died of Bright's disease in 1888, and Campbell died a few years later. Daughter Martha, the organist at St. Andrew's Cathedral, married the "distinguished French scholar" Henri E. Melnut, who visited Victoria in 1892 to write about B.C. resources.

later founded The White House dry-goods business; the restaurant was forced into bankruptcy by its unpaid waiters in 1936, during the middle of the Depression, and sold at auction for $1,100.

The most prestigious hotel in the downtown area was the Driard, on View Street between Douglas and Broad Street, which opened originally in 1862 as the St. George's. It was sold nine years later to Sosthenes Driard, the asthmatic, corpulent ("a tribute to his cuisine") former proprietor of the Colonial Restaurant, and reopened as the Driard Hotel. The upper portion of the hotel burned in October, 1882, and was rebuilt and reopened within the year. In the late 1880s, the hotel was extended over the Victoria Theatre, which had opened in 1885 at View and Douglas, and a grander hotel entrance was built facing Douglas. In 1892, a new, six-storey Driard was built facing Broad Street. This completed block, partly damaged in the downtown fire, was bought by David Spencer in October, 1910, for an expanded Spencer's (now Eaton's) Department Store.

The Victoria Theatre was perfectly situated so that patrons could slip into the red leather and brass bar at the Driard for a quick drink between acts. The opening of the theatre in October, 1885, was one of the most festive occasions in the city's history, as "hitherto lovers of the drama and opera have had to witness the art in buildings inadequate and lacking in almost every requirement necessary for the proper rendering of a play."

The first theatre in Victoria, in 1858, was, according to a commemorative program distributed at the Victoria Theatre on opening night, the 200-seat upper story of a large wooden building called The Star & Garter Hotel—now the site of the Masonic Lodge—at Government and Fisgard. A year later, ships' officers from Esquimalt converted a Hudson's Bay Company salmon warehouse on Reid's wharf into a ballroom. That same year, the Colonial Theatre, later called the Lyceum, was erected on Government Street. Miss Lulu Sweet, who had flowers thrown at her feet and tolerated a constant parade of stage-door johnnies, was a regular performer there (she was reportedly the namesake of Lulu Island, now Richmond municipality near Vancouver). Subsequently, theatres competed for the public's favour in the Royal Hotel on Wharf Street, at the Omineca on Yates, and in "The New Idea" in the basement of Lawrence Goodacre's butcher shop. The first official theatre, seating 500, was converted from a Hudson's Bay Company storehouse within the fort's palisades, bought by Sir Matthew Baillie Begbie when the fort was dis-

mantled. Called the Theatre Royal, it "echoed the deep, tragic tones of Charles Kean, the gentle voice of Julia Dean Hayne, and the 'smirks and grimaces' of John Wood."

The new Victoria Theatre was organized with a capital of $50,000; its directors included D.W. Higgins, R.P. Rithet and Robert Dunsmuir. On opening night, illuminated by gaslights, "every seat in the parquette and dress circle was filled—the ladies, in their many lovely and contrasting costumes, and pretty faces, in contrast with the sombre attire of the stern sex, formed a bright and charming scene." The drop curtain, with a "life-like picture, with the groves, lake and castle in the background, and Claude Melnotte and his sweetheart standing in the foreground," was received with a spontaneous round of applause, for "there was nothing more gorgeous north of San Francisco." The opening night performance, by a splendidly-rehearsed local amateur company, was very up-to-date: Gilbert & Sullivan's *Pirates of Penzance*. E.G. Prior, a future premier and lieutenant governor, played the pirate king.

When he wasn't indulging his hobby for amateur theatre, Prior was one of the prominent businessmen in Victoria, long before he was lured into the political arena in the 1890s. His huge hardware business, which he had developed originally with Arthur Fellows, had its office and showroom at the northeast corner of Government and Johnson, and a warehouse further up Government at Pembroke. In 1912, the firm had 95 employees, and published an 800-page hardware catalogue and a smaller machinery catalogue. The company amalgamated with McLellan & McFeely in 1920, following Prior's death, and continued operation until 1962, when it discontinued retail sales. The wholesale firm retained the name "Mac & Mac & Prior."

The building next door to E.G. Prior & Co., at 1407 Government Street, showed moving pictures as early as 1903. Alexander Pantages, the Klondike bar-sweep who separated the gold dust from the sawdust on the floor and came home with a fortune, opened a vaudeville theatre on Johnson west of Government (now occupied by Jeune Brothers, who expanded west from their original store). Pantages had a chain of theatres throughout the Pacific Northwest, and his own vaudeville circuit. His next Victoria theatre, north of Pandora on Government, became the shell for the McPherson Theatre. Pantages's empire thrived through the twenties, but he eventually succumbed to the studio-controlled distribution of the "talkies," and ended his career in iniquity and lurid publicity following his arrest on vice charges.

J.H. Turner, another B.C. premier in the mid-nineties, owned Turner, Beeton & Co. Ltd., the manufacturers of the "Big Horn" brand of shirts and overalls in denim and duck. His plant at 1244-52 Wharf Street (called the Yates Block after developer James Yates, now the McQuade's Chandlers Building) had 100 employees and turned out 2,000 dozen garments a month. In addition, Turner imported and wholesaled dry goods, wines, cigars and liquors.

The biggest liquor importer in Victoria was Pither & Leiser Ltd., established in 1858 by A. Casamyou. The company passed into the hands of four gentlemen with the extraordinary names of Camsusa, Raggazzoni,

Coigdarripe, and Boucherrat, before becoming Pither & Leiser in 1893. The company had the exclusive license to import the products of G.H. Mumm & Co. and Gordon & Co., and also distributed tobaccos from all over the world. Their Victoria operation, managed by George Gardiner, was in the six-storey building at the corner of Wharf and Fort; it had a well-appointed display and sampling room, an elevator, and electric lights throughout the upstairs warehousing area. Pither & Leiser competed strenuously with companies like the Tulks' Gold Seal Liquor Company for the lucrative, by-the-case, wine and spirit tastes of Victoria's moneyed families. Following the establishment of the Liquor Control Board in the early twenties, the Tulks quit the business altogether, and the Pither & Leiser building became Victoria's first Liquor Control Board warehouse, and was a liquor store until 1966.

The block to the northwest of Fort Street along Wharf Street contains the Rithet Building, recently restored as provincial government offices. R.P. Rithet & Co. Ltd. were importers and commission agents for groceries and liquor, and were exclusive agents for the Distillers Co. of Edinburgh. The firm was founded in September, 1871, when Rithet was

James Hunter, the Pither & Leiser liquor company manager.

27. His interest in developing the harbour front led to the construction of ''Rithet's Outer Wharves'' at Dallas & Simcoe, which before World War I handled most of Victoria's deep-sea shipping business. The building just south of Rithet's at 1107 Wharf was erected in 1862 by wholesale merchant Richard Carr, the father of artist Emily Carr, and is now a gallery devoted to the latter's paintings.

Another successful Victoria businessman was Samuel Nesbitt, who made enough money in California with the Forty-Niners to move to Victoria and open a bakery at the southwest corner of Broad and Yates in 1858. Several years later, after the fort was dismantled, he moved the bakery to Fort Street between Langley and Wharf. The bakery was something of a novelty in early Victoria, ''equal to anything of the kind we have met with on the Coast,'' said the *Colonist*. Prior to Nesbitt's arrival, bread was either baked at home or else came from Port Townsend. The local Indians also approved, as they supposedly liked to use the biscuit tins for the personal effects of their deceased. Nesbitt became ''Purveyor of Bread & Biscuits to Her Majesty's Navy,'' and built another bakery on a dock at Esquimalt harbour. When the dock collapsed early in 1867, Nes-

bitt rebuilt it, this time with an oven "capable of baking three barrels of flour at once." Following his death in April, 1881, Nesbitt's widow carried on the operation of the Fort Street bakery and expanded the business to the point that, in 1884, seven men were employed and $120 a week was paid in wages. She allowed the men to organize into The Practical Baker's Association—the first labour organization in Victoria (her grandson, Victoria newspaperman James K. Nesbitt, considered *that* a blot on the family's escutcheon).

Victoria's warehousing and importing buildings occupied Wharf and Johnson streets. North of the Johnson Street bridge, past the edge of Chinatown, is the old industrial area centred around Rock Bay and the edge of Point Ellice. One of the biggest operations—"the best equipped machine shop north of San Francisco"—was the Albion Iron Works, founded in 1861 on Discovery Street by Joseph Spratt, an entrepreneur who later owned Spratt's Ark and Spratt's Oilery (for fish oil) on the Vancouver waterfront. The company expanded so that, by 1890, it occupied most of the area between Government and Store streets, on Pembroke, Discovery, Chatham, and Herald streets. It operated as engineers, desig-

ners, brass and iron founders, builders of rail cars for the E&N Railway, prefabricators of decorative architectural ironwork (as installed on the facade at the southern end of the Rithet Building), and manufacturers of an excellent line of woodstoves, which were retailed from a showroom at 515 Pembroke. The last remaining part of the complex is the Stove & Plate Works building at 622 Pembroke.

Albion Iron Works' foundry department was managed for years by John Dougall, whose father had established the Caledonian Iron Works in the city in 1858. The latter firm collapsed in the doldrums of the 1860s. Andrew Gray operated the Marine Iron Works on Pembroke, next to the B.C. Electric Railway car sheds on Store Street. The Victoria Machinery Depot, which now dominates the southern approach to the Point Ellice bridge, had a smaller operation further to the east—the land on the south side of the bridge was the site of the Victoria Sealing Co. sheds and wharf.

The Rock Bay area always had its share of sawmills. One of the biggest was W.P. Sayward's, at the Rock Bay bridge, across the street from the Victoria Gas Works. Other mills crowded into the Rock Bay area, including Moore-Whittington Lumber Co., Jos. Leigh & Son Sash & Door,

Amelia Street south of Cormorant, between Blanshard and Quadra streets. Today, five remain of the seven little workingmen's houses, dating from the late 1880s, which used to line the block. The brick semidetached pair on the left would not be out of place in London, Toronto, Montreal, or Sydney.

Lemon, Gonnason Company Ltd. Sash & Door, and the huge Cameron Lumber Co. Sawmill across Selkirk Water from Point Ellice—now the B.C. Forest Products mill. Sayward's mill, established in 1858, had become by the First World War part of the Canadian Puget Sound Lumber Co., one of the giant forestry firms of the period, with 54,000 acres of "the ubiquitous Douglas fir," sash & door factories and other sawmills on the island, a shingle mill and box plant, and ten miles of private railroad at Jordan River.

The Vancouver Island lumber industry benefited greatly from German investment, coordinated from Vancouver by Alvo von Alvensleben Ltd. and the German-British Columbia syndicate. Von Alvensleben himself had six large logging camps and valuable timber leases on the Island. While in Victoria, he operated from the Kaiserhof Hotel behind the Carnegie Library on Blanshard. The German presence was so strong in B.C. that the German Club held a banquet for 150 on January 26, 1912, in honour of the Kaiser's birthday. Toasts were made by leading B.C. politicians, stressing the Kaiser's love of peace and his blood-relationship to the British royal family (he was Edward VII's nephew). Following the declaration of war, Von Alvensleben was forced to stay out of the country, and his assets were seized after the collapse of the Vancouver-based Dominion Trust Co. in Vancouver in 1914.

The Victoria Gas Works occupied the area between Store and Government streets at Rock Bay. Founded in 1859, it had considerable difficulty actually getting into operation. Amor de Cosmos, then the editor of the *Colonist*, bitterly denounced the company's demand for a monopoly; the gas mains were difficult to lay on Victoria's rocky ground; the steamer from Scotland carrying some of the plant's equipment ran out of water, and the crew mutinied. The company built a brick coal-roasting plant and one gasometer (eventually, there were three on the site), and coal barges from Nanaimo tied up at the company's wharf at the foot of Store Street. The first gaslight was illuminated in front of Caroll's liquor store on September 28, 1862, and several days later other stores and saloons in the downtown area had the steady, bright light of coal gas. It was hoped that street lighting would reduce the size of the chain gang. (Coal gas production also yielded useful by-products, like roof-pitch and creosote, which were sold on the commercial market. After its tar and napthalene were removed by scrubbing and purifying processes, the gas had useful medicinal properties—asthmatics and sufferers from consumption, catarrh and croup got almost instant relief from a whiff of it, before it passed into the sulphur-extracting process. Local chemists purchased the coal tar by-product and mixed potent salves, pills and potions using it as a base.)

The following year, the City of Victoria entered into a contract with the company for street lights—the city bought the lamps and posts, and the company agreed to light them and keep them clean for $40 a month. Freezing temperatures presented problems for gas customers, as the meters needed water in them to operate; the company suggested that in cold weather, ordinary whiskey poured into the meter would ensure a continuous flow of gas. The Victoria Gas Company was finally incorporated into the B.C. Electric Company, which since 1897 had run the city's electricity and street railway systems, in April, 1905.

(Above) Thomas Napier Hibben, born in Charleston, South Carolina in 1827, joined the California gold rush at age 21, established and then sold a bookstore in San Francisco, and arrived in Victoria in 1858. He formed Kurskis Book Store with a Mr. Carswell, then after the latter retired took a Mr. Kammerer and Mr. Bone into partnership with him. Although Hibben died in January, 1890, the business expanded through the efforts of his sons, Thomas and James. The Hibben-Bone Block on Government Street (now the Bastion Inn) was built before the First World War. The postcard of the building was used to notify customers that their special order book or magazine had arrived. At one time, the building had a huge pencil on the roof as an advertisement.

Coal-gas technology—for illumination purposes—was quickly superseded by the new science of electricity. Entrepreneur Robert McMicking, who later installed the province's first telephone system, entered into an agreement with Victoria to provide street lighting. After many changes to the cumbersome and unreliable equipment, Victoria in 1889 had acquired 79 streetlamps scattered throughout the city. (Not all were pleased—Captain John Irving threatened an injunction if a lamp were placed in front of his home at Menzies and Michigan in James Bay.) Very few houses had electricity before the First World War years. The city's power house, on Store Street near Herald, survived until 1912, when the B.C. Electric Railway Co., under the name of Vancouver Island Power Co., brought power from its Jordan River hydroelectric plant to the city.

Transportation through Victoria before the turn of the century was

The Victoria Public Market on Cormorant Street (see map, page 62) served as the railway station for the Victoria Terminal & Sidney Railway. The eastern (right-hand) half served as Number One firehall. Number Two firehall, at Broad and Yates next to Bossi & Giesselmann's grocery store, was the headquarters for the Deluge Company—one of three volunteer fire brigades in early Victoria. The last horse was retired from Number One firehall in 1918.

waiting for horses to be hitched to them."

Vacant lots downtown were often leased as woodyards. One of the biggest was on Herald Street just west of Wilson Bros., where the cordwood was stacked fifteen feet high, and an electric chopping machine occupied the centre of the yard. Some of the inner-city residential streets, like Courtney, Broughton and Burdett east of Douglas, had a mix of occupants which must have made life unattractive for the residents. Lumber yards and a stone-cutting operation took up much of the block between Courtney and Broughton behind Victoria Wilson's house. The elegant houses on Victoria Crescent (now Blanshard south of Burdett) looked down on the stinking James Bay mudflats and the shacks, boathouses and laundry lines of little Penwell Street and "Kanaka Row."

Most families, if they had a field and a horse, also kept a cow. Even the small houses on the outskirts of the business section often backed onto vacant land. Horses were kept tethered nearby, cows were milked, gardens weeded, and the rich often had grooms, hired hands and even coachmen to manage "the back forty." Almost everyone could afford a $25 a month "Chinaman."

Heavy English chaises were slow and difficult for horses to pull, and the iron tires made a loud rumbling on the rutted, stony roads. Houses with a sick person inside had straw spread on the roadway in front to cut down on the rumbling. Gentlemen hurried by in their high, two-wheeled dogcarts. The cracking of whips and whinnying of horses mingled with the shouts of the cabbies and the newsboys on the streets of the little town.

The horse and buggy era, for personal transport and freight, began its decline in February, 1890, when the newly incorporated National Electric Tramway & Lighting Company commenced its electric railway service on two routes—the first from the Work Estate area above Hillside Avenue to Rithet's Outer Wharves in James Bay; the second from the company's Store Street depot across the street from the Albion foundry via Fort Street to the Jubilee Hospital. The tramway company, which barely weathered the 1893 world-wide depression, was brought to its knees in the aftermath of the Point Ellice Bridge disaster in 1896. The B.C. Electric Railway Company was formed to take over the service both on the Island and the Lower Mainland, and ran trams throughout Victoria and Esquimalt until the late forties, when—as in Vancouver—rubber-tired buses were brought in as the "wave of the future."

mainly by horse and buggy. Well-dressed young men in spats rode horses through the downtown streets. Emily Carr wrote that in the city "the smell of horse manure was so much a part of every street that it sat on your nose as comfortably as a pair of spectacles." Baker and butcher boys did their deliveries on horseback, "carrying their loaves and joints in huge wicker baskets rested against their hips." Downtown, there were livery stables everywhere—ten in Victoria in the 1880s. The biggest was Frank Barnard's Victoria Transfer Company, the forerunner of the first electric tramway, which had room for 100 horses in its wooden building at Broughton and Gordon (now a parkade). Passers-by "heard horses chewing and stamping, and saw long rows of tails swishing out of stalls on either side of a plankway while ugly, square vehicles called hacks stood

Yates Street looking west from Douglas in the twenties. The almost illegible billboard in the middle distance, past the White Lunch sign, advertises Swift's Premium meats. The turreted building on the corner, now a Cole's bookshop, housed Edward C. Kellogg's drugstore.

Thomas John Trapp, a commercial salesman, moved to Victoria from the east in 1873, when he was 31, but found most of the business opportunities sewn up. He then hiked back and forth between New Westminster and Hastings Mill, but was able only to get work loading spars at the sawmill. On his return to Victoria, he dug ditches at Spring Ridge and cut dry wood at $1.25 a cord (he received one dollar for each cord of green wood). A.B. Gray gave him brief employment in his dry goods operation, but Trapp soon left for the Rockies, where he spent years as a packer. On his return, he settled in New Westminster, where his activities with T.J. Trapp & Company, and the Great Northern's New Westminster Southern Railroad, made him a rich, prominent citizen.

Noah Shakespeare came to Victoria from Staffordshire in 1863, when he was 24 years old. He became mayor in 1882. That same year, he was elected to the House of Commons, and was appointed postmaster of Victoria in 1887. Shakespeare was a spokesman for the Lord's Day Alliance before the First World War. The first post office was opposite W&J Wilson on Government Street. When the mail steamer arrived, usually signalled by a flag raised atop the Driard Hotel, crowds lined up for delivery, often until as late as ten o'clock at night. An earlier postmaster general, Arthur Bushby, had had to keep a large supply of American stamps on hand. Mail to the outside was sent to San Francisco on a steamer subsidized by the colony, but was then treated as American, and not delivered unless the full American postage was prepaid. Governor Musgrave wrote that he "had never heard of anything as undignified as importing the stamps of another nation for use in a British colony." Mail to the Interior in the 1850s usually went by Ballou's Express, which cost a half-dollar but was a certainty compared with the erratic five-cent postal service.

The 1910 fire which destroyed Spencer's Arcade presented an opportunity for some rebuilding in what had become a seedy, decaying downtown. Victorians profited greatly from the real-estate and economic boom before 1912—fortunes were made developing land, particularly in Fairfield and Oak Bay. Downtown, new bank and trust company buildings were erected, most notably the Royal Bank Building on Government Street, now Munro's Bookstore; the Bank of Montreal at Douglas and Yates, which became the bank's Victoria head office in 1924, superseding the old chateau-style bank at Government and Bastion; the Yorkshire Trust Building at 737 Fort Street; and the Union Bank Building at 1205 Government, now the Royal Trust Building. At the same time, the eight-storey Belmont Building was erected across the street from the old post office at Humboldt and Government; the Fairfield Block, with money from the Fairfield land boom, was built on Douglas; the *Victoria Times*

building at the northeast corner of Fort and Broad demonstrated the prosperity of that Liberal newspaper after fifteen years of the Laurier government.

Victoria changed very little during the period from the outbreak of the First World War in 1914 to the building of the new post office at Government and Yates—the site of the old Adelphi Saloon—in 1949. Aptly enough, the erection of that austere edifice caused the demolition of the old Bank of British North America on Yates, the first stone commercial building in Victoria. In the three-and-a-half decades since, British Columbia—and its government—has grown tremendously; the provincial government has built many new offices in Victoria, but has also converted many residences (like Premier Robson's house on Government, now the Queen's Printer bookstore) and other buildings (like the Menzies Street drill hall, formerly the Provincial Police headquarters) into government offices.

Much of the province's business activity, with its accompanying demolition and replacement of old buildings, has long since moved to increasingly cosmopolitan Vancouver. Victoria's downtown still looks like what it was—a prosperous, well-established, modern, turn-of-the-century city.

The Bank of British North America building on the south side of Yates Street, between Government and Langley, spent its final years as a gospel church. Built in 1858 following the quick decision of the bank's London directors to get in on the financing of the Cariboo gold rush, it was the first building in Victoria to use Haddington Island stone. Prosperity from the Klondike rush in the late 1890s prompted renovations and expansion, most notably a stained glass dome to replace the flat roof. During the First World War, with its employees in uniform overseas, it was staffed by women who became known as Doig's Beauty Chorus, after David Doig (1859-1929), the manager. Doig (who was Dr. Israel Powell's son-in-law) ran the Yukon's first bank, in a tent in Dawson City guarded by Royal North West Mounted Police. The Bank of BNA amalgamated with the Bank of Montreal in 1918, and the Yates Street branch was closed in 1924, following the opening of the Douglas Street head office. Francis H.A. Norton's Northwestern Creamery, "The Home of Velvet Ice Cream" at 1311 Broad, had horse-drawn wagons which were a familiar sight until the late forties. Norton, born on Salt Spring Island, founded it in 1912. The dairy was bought by Silverwood in 1966.

The Union Club

Most men of social prominence in Victorian and Edwardian times were clubmen; most prominent Victoria men were members of the Union and Pacific clubs, sometimes the Vancouver Club, and frequently also the Royal Victoria Yacht Club and a golf club. Before the Second World War, the quintessential clubman was "a bachelor of the most confirmed kind" (whether married or not), whose life centred around the same chair, at the same hour, with the same newspapers, brought by the same servant, in his club.

The concept of the Union Club developed over some casual billiard games and discussion in a hall over Morrison's Drug Store at the northeast corner of Fort and Government. Frank Barnard canvassed the city for members, and, in April, 1879, a group chaired by Sir Matthew Baillie Begbie met above Van Volkenburg's butcher shop at Yates and Government (the Poodle Dog Cafe location). The first clubhouse, at the same premises, had two billiard tables, an American carom table, a reading room, a card room, and a larger room with a bar in one corner.

The Union Club achieved some notoriety in late 1881, when bartender John Creden and the club's executive were charged with conducting a club without a municipal business license, and with selling liquor without a license. Heavy legal talent—A.E.B. Davie and C.E. Pooley—represented the club, and another future premier, Theodore Davie, represented the City of Victoria. The provincial government supported the city, and even amended Victoria's charter to help it with the prosecution of the club, but the Supreme Court ruled in favour of the latter. The government, and its champion *The Standard*, harboured suspicions that the club had been formed in order to create a political party to oppose the Walkem administration. When the governor general, the Marquis of Lorne, innocently accepted an invitation to dine at the club during his Victoria sojourn in the fall of 1882, *The Standard* blasted him for being "misled by the unwise counsel" and "spurious gentility" of the members. Future distinguished guests—including Lord Lansdowne, Lord Stanley and the Earl of Minto—avoided any whiff of controversy, as the Union Club had by then managed to justify its contention that the club was merely an extension of the members' private homes, and thus nobody's business.

By 1884, membership had reached 149, and a new clubhouse was built at the northwest corner of Courtney and Douglas, fronting on the latter. The design, "a sort of composite, in which the French style largely predominates," was executed in red brick, with towering chimneys outside and little black iron fireplaces inside. Big-game heads adorned the walls, including, it was claimed, the two biggest moose heads ever taken. At the turn of the century, the club's dominant concern was the dogs kept tied up there by many young English remittance men. Some members had even installed private kennels in the basement, but the wailing and yelping was too much for many. The dogs, plus an invasion of rats and cockroaches, the lack of heat in winter, and the drunkenness and discourtesy of some of the members, prompted a blizzard of complaints in the club's suggestion book, to wit: "that a certain gentleman of the late Committee be *ordered*

to discontinue using the soup dishes and other plates for the purpose of feeding his dog"; "that the door from the Billiard Room to the Racquet Room be glazed and 'Wait for the Stroke' be conspicuously posted"; "that the present cooks be got rid of as soon as possible as the cooking is abominable"; "that the windows of the lavatory be screened *at once*, as there is a plague of flies there" (answer was: "Attended to—flies cannot now use the lavatory"); "that whoever the gentleman is that has not $1.50 to buy an umbrella, kindly apply to me and I will make good—provided he leave mine alone"; "that the Club discontinue to supply toilet paper for a gentleman who insists in using sixteen sheets everytime he participates in his hobby"; "that the club flag is a disgrace—ditto the secretary's tie"; "that the Secretary be instructed to supply gum boots and umbrellas to members using the lavatory"; "that the cockroaches should be removed from the stewed apples before being offered to the members for breakfast" (answer: "steps will be taken to remove such"); and, in October, 1914, "that gentlemen of German or Austrian birth and parentage be requested for their own comfort and that of the members, to abstain from using the Club." (When plans for the club's new quarters on Humboldt Street were discussed in December, 1910, it was unanimously agreed that "Ladies' dining, sitting, and retiring rooms" be included.)

Before 1914, about one-third of the club's members were under thirty years of age. Many of these "young bloods" participated in ice hockey games against the rival Pacific club, and were wild participants in the famous Saturday night rat hunts and relay races which predated the club's move to its new premises at Humboldt and Gordon. Twenty-three of these young club members didn't return from France. The depression years of the thirties forced out most of the remaining ones. The extravagance of the new clubhouse, built in a booming, prosperous time with free advice on interiors and fittings from the rich, oft-travelled F.M. Rattenbury, brought the club to the brink of ruin. In 1934, the heating plant broke down and there were no funds to repair it; only the offer of $3,000 from one Colonel Villiers saved the day. In September of the following year the club defaulted on its city taxes.

The old Union Club on Douglas became first a returned serviceman's club for veterans of France during World War I, and then served throughout the twenties and thirties as a veterans' beer parlour. During the Second World War, it was called Prince Robert house—the home away from home for bell-bottomed, white-capped sailors from Esquimalt. The new Union Club site had been home to Senator W.J. Macdonald before he built "Armadale" in James Bay in 1877. The house and grounds—"an acre in extent, with rustic walks, oaks, a small orchard, & flower beds with a fountain"—were then turned into a residential hotel, later called the Badminton Club, with splendid views of the harbour and the Olympic range from many of the windows. Macdonald sold the property to the club in December, 1909, for $50,000.

(Club life was one of the attractions which Victoria held for Englishmen. Due to the unrest in India in the twenties, there was a concerted ef-

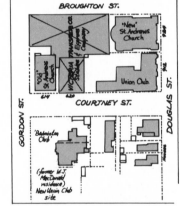

Harry Pooley, MLA and rat-hunter.

The old Union Club, at the northwest corner of Douglas and Courtney, was vacated in 1913 in favour of the new clubhouse at Humboldt and Gordon. Most of the problems at the old location stemmed from the Victoria Transfer Company stables next door. Hay was often piled on the dusty sidewalks, and flies invaded the club through every open window. The biggest problem, however, was rats, which gave rise to the regular Saturday night rat hunts. The most famous of these was held on the eve of the move to the new clubhouse, with future attorney general Harry Pooley and architect F.M. Rattenbury as head huntsmen. The rats, which had chewed large holes above the kitchen sink, were forced out of their den there by banging on a specially constructed biscuit tin. The hunters, armed with walking sticks, then charged into the room and, "for an hour, the chase about the big kitchen would be on." It was a poor night when less than a dozen were killed. Pooley once won $25 from a visitor to the club, betting he could walk from the new clubhouse to the old, kill two rats, and be back within fifteen minutes (he got three). The civic rat-catcher once caught 120 rats there in a single night. The other club amusement was relay races, in opposite directions around the clubhouse and Transfer Company stables. These generally started in any room where the participants were gathered, and often involved leaping out of the nearest window to get a head start. One drunken participant mistakenly leapt out of a second-storey window, and was later found with his shinbone protruding, still trying to complete the course.

PABC 65092

fort by B.C.'s agent general in London, Frederick Wade, to induce Indian Army officers to retire to Victoria. Wade's efforts were almost stymied by a letter which appeared in the *Morning Post* in April, 1922, signed by Vice Admiral Sir E.R. Pears and seven other officers who had settled in B.C., warning potential emigrants that "their particular needs and social requirements and educational ideals would not be met in this new country." Wade's response made reference to men "who preferred polo to work.")

The British Colonist

A feature of life in North America during the nineteenth century was the impassioned, yellow journalism of newspapers and the colourful partisanship of editors and readers. Victoria was no exception, largely due to the bellicosity of Amor de Cosmos, the founder of the *British Colonist* newspaper and a premier of British Columbia.

De Cosmos was born William Alexander Smith in Windsor, Nova Scotia in 1825. He joined the Forty-Niners in the California rush of 1849, and found in San Francisco—where there were many Bill Smiths—that his mail was constantly getting misdirected. Accordingly, he headed for the state capital, Sacramento, and changed his name to Amor de Cosmos—"love of the universe." Few people could have been less aptly named.

De Cosmos moved to Victoria in the summer of 1858, with the rush of miners heading north to the Cariboo strike. He decided, however, to settle down, and on December 11 founded the *British Colonist* as a soapbox for his anti-James Douglas, anti-Hudson's Bay Company, pro-responsible government ideals. During the 1860s, de Cosmos was the first to advocate the union of the Island and mainland colonies and, in the middle of that decade, the confederation of British Columbia with the rest of British North America. He doggedly pushed for the appointment of the colony's governor from "among our own people," supported compulsory voting, and took every opportunity to oppose monopoly—whether by the little Victoria Gas Company or the huge Hudson's Bay Company.

James Douglas, the governor until 1864, who bore the brunt of the newspaper's attacks, did not respond publicly, although he was privately appalled and once allegedly threatened to throw de Cosmos off the James Bay bridge. On February 2, 1860, when drawing comparisons between the colonial social life at New Westminster graced by Colonel Moody's wife, and similar occasions at Victoria from which the mixed-blood Mrs. Douglas was often absent, de Cosmos wrote that Douglas was unsuited to be governor; however, "were a good Indian agent required, it would not be too difficult to discover a suitable incumbent, qualified by long experience and intimate associations."

Anyone powerful was a target. One day, when Robert Dunsmuir and Roderick Finlayson were conversing on the street, they were approached by de Cosmos, "who applied opprobrious epithets to Mr. Dunsmuir. Mr. Dunsmuir requested his insulter, who seemed to be labouring under some strong excitant, to pass on, whereupon Mr. de Cosmos struck him on the side of the head with his fist. Mr. Dunsmuir retaliated by wearing out an umbrella on his assailant's head and shoulders. The combatants were then separated."

The "strong excitant" was likely liquor, as de Cosmos had a reputation as an extraordinary drinker, even in a drunken town like 1860s Victoria. His electioneering was highlighted by band music and free drinks, but, acknowledged J.S. Helmcken, he was also the best orator in the colony: "he knew all the captivating sentences for the multitude . . . a free-thinker in religion, a radical, a demagogue, a sort of socialist, he was vainglorious

and egotistical to the utmost degree," and on the platform "he boasted of travelling through California with a revolver in each boot," striking theatrical attitudes to help him make his points. Once, in the legislature, de Cosmos spoke for seven hours nonstop, by the end of which, as his former employee David Higgins's *Victoria Chronicle* noted, his voice, "never the most musical, had sunk into a mere squeak, like that emitted by a half-drowned rat, and he appeared at times scarcely able to stand." Energy was provided by "a tumblerful of eggnog, from which he occasionally imbibed." (De Cosmos's speaking record doesn't even approach that of Leonard McClure, in the old Colonial Legislature on April 23, 1866, speaking against Governor Kennedy's purchase of Cary Castle. McClure spoke from three that afternoon continuously until nine the next morning, "on his pins with a resolution in one hand and a glass of port in the other." The exertion, it was said, brought McClure to an untimely grave.)

De Cosmos sold his interest in the *Colonist* to pursue a career in the sphere of politics, although he later owned the *Victoria Standard*, which defended his excesses during the time he was B.C.'s premier. His passion was confederation, and he introduced the first resolution into the British Columbia legislature, on March 10, 1867, for the admission of the colony into Canada. He was elected federally in the first election after confederation, and also gained a seat in B.C's first provincial legislature in February, 1872. He was the clot around which coalesced the dissatisfaction with Premier McCreight, and was appointed premier after the latter's defeat. As premier of B.C., he introduced a resolution into the B.C. legislature objecting to the early introduction of the Canadian Tariff, then abandoned Victoria for Ottawa nearly six weeks before the opening of the April, 1873 session. Both Ottawa and Victoria promptly passed statutes banning dual representation, so De Cosmos resigned the B.C. premiership on February 9, 1874. He spent the balance of the seventies as an MP, and was the most active B.C. member, advocating the construction of the Pacific Railway and the banning of Chinese labour. He became insane, and died in an asylum in 1897.

(De Cosmos's time as B.C. premier was marked by the "Texada scandal." Sewell Prescott Moody, the owner of the Moodyville sawmill in North Vancouver, took de Cosmos, Walkem, Beaven and the other members of the provincial government on a secret visit to Texada Island in August, 1873, to examine an ore body there. On their return, they all put in applications to purchase the land, and when De Cosmos travelled to Ottawa and England on government business, he spent a good deal of his time trying to interest capitalists in the project. Just before the 1874 federal election, the *Colonist* spilled the beans. A Royal Commission was appointed on March 13, 1874, composed of Supreme Court judges Begbie, Crease and Gray, with MLA John Robson acting as "prosecution." The Commission's report, released that October, said that "the circumstances were apparently suspicious, but nothing unlawful or prejudicial to the public's interests had occurred." Walkem, by that time premier, survived

AUTHOR'S COLLECTION

Amor de Cosmos, the founder of the British Colonist.

Crowds gathered outside the Times *building at Fort and Broad, on December 10, 1936, to follow the bulletins from London reporting King Edward VIII's impending abdication. Radios were set up in Spencer's Department store (in the background, now Eaton's), so shoppers missed none of the news. The King's resolve to marry the twice-divorced American, Wallis Warfield Simpson, caused a constitutional crisis when the British government refused to sanction it. The unfolding drama "caused usual reserves to break down, and stranger talked to stranger freely." That day's civic election faded almost into insignificance. "Except for the death of King George V," said the* Times, *"no subject since the Great War has created greater discussion in Victoria." The King's radio broadcast, in which he stated that he could not reign without "the woman I love," was so avidly followed around the world that a temporary cease-fire was declared in the Spanish civil war. The* Times *headline the next day said: "Tears Shed as News of Abdication Read."*

the uproar; so did Amor de Cosmos, the MP.)

The *Colonist*, after surviving its first century as an independent newspaper, entered into a joint operating agreement with the rival *Times*, until the two newspapers were amalgamated by the Thompson newspaper group in 1980.

The *Province* newspaper, long the Vancouver morning daily, was established in Victoria as a weekly on March 3, 1894, by Hewitt Bostock and Walter C. Nichol. At first located in the former Presbyterian Church at the corner of Gordon and Courtney, the paper appeared every Saturday on glossy paper, about eight inches by twelve, containing about twenty pages. Bostock claimed he created the name from Shakespeare's ''a province I will give thee'' in *Anthony & Cleopatra*. When Bostock gave up his interest to pursue politics, Nichol expanded the paper's size, improved its journalistic quality, and moved it to Vancouver at the turn of the century. The Victoria *Province* heaped withering criticism on the Turner government, especially over its subsidies to railways and stock promotion schemes in the Klondike. Premier Turner and Speaker C.E. Pooley had allowed their names to be placed on the boards of directors of two companies—Dawson City & Dominion Trading Corporation and the Klondike & Columbian Gold Fields Ltd.—by a glib promoter named J. Maurice Catton. After a few months, the companies collapsed, and many small investors in England lost everything. Nichol, in a *Province* editorial, accused Turner of gulling the British folk into wild speculation. Turner sued, and used his influence to get Nichol charged with criminal rather than civil libel. Nichol's solicitor, the famed Vancouver KC, E.P. Davis, tore every witness to shreds, including the hapless newspaper boy who had bought ''the evidence''—the copies of the *Province* at the newsstands—and was ordered on the stand to prove that he had bought it, and to remember his activities on the Saturday mornings before and since. The jury couldn't agree on a verdict. A second trial was ordered, and when the second jury likewise couldn't agree, the Crown finally dropped the case. By that time, Turner's government had long since been dismissed. Nichol went on to sell the *Province* to Southam in the early twenties.

The appointment of Thomas McInnes to the lieutenant-governorship in 1897 created a Senate vacancy which was filled by William Templeman, a prominent Liberal who had founded the *Victoria Times*. The *Times* was almost permanently the opposition paper in Tory Victoria. Only after the four disastrous federal Conservative governments of the early 1890s, did Victorians briefly follow the national love affair with Wilfrid Laurier, and elect Liberals.

Templeman was appointed to the post of Minister of Inland Revenue in 1906. George Riley, who had defeated E.G. Prior in a run-off called to settle the dispute over the latter's narrow victory in the 1901 election, resigned his federal seat in 1906 to allow Templeman to run. Templeman won, and Riley was appointed to his Senate seat. The 1908 election was hotly contested, with popular local Conservative Harry Barnard finally beating Templeman by 2179 votes to 2166. Barnard was hoisted on the shoulders of his supporters and carried through the Victoria streets at the head of a torchlight parade.

In the 1911 campaign, Templeman had even more of an uphill fight, attempting to sell Laurier's trade reciprocity policy to a hostile west coast. He had to bear the blame for every one of Laurier's unpopular policies, which had been consistently attacked by Premier McBride. Templeman was taken to task for alleged relaxation of immigration regulations which allowed Chinese into the west coast, and failure to provide construction contracts for war vessels in Victoria yards. Although he promised to improve Victoria's port, and released correspondence showing that the Laurier government would spend $3 million on new breakwaters and deepening the inner and outer harbours, he got nowhere at his public meetings. On reciprocity, Templeman refuted Conservative claims that food prices would rise and told a women's meeting on September 17 that ''every good housewife should be able to buy everything for the family table which she did before, and still have a considerable sum left for pin money.'' Premier McBride retaliated that the Laurier government would view even British Imperial questions ''through American spectacles.'' The day before the election, the *Victoria Times* summed up the Liberal position: ''the fight for trade liberty is to be turned into a fight for personal, civil and political liberty.'' The Conservative view was expressed as: ''A vote for Borden is a vote for King and Flag and Canada.'' In the election, Conservative Harry Barnard was returned to the seat, and the Tories swept the province and much of the country, ushering in a dozen years of national Conservative governments.

During the twenties and thirties, under the editorship of Benny C. Nicholas, the Victoria *Times* consistently supported what were said to be Liberal, progressive candidates, particularly Duff Pattullo provincially and MacKenzie King federally in 1935. Like the independent *Colonist*, it became the victim of modern newspaper economics, and was submerged under the *Times-Colonist* banner in 1980. The *Times* building, at the northeast corner of Fort and Broad, was superseded by the Victoria Press building on Douglas Street, which now houses the combined operations of the two Victoria dailies.

William J. Templeman, the Liberal workhorse in Tory Victoria, founded the Victoria Times.

Thomas W. Paterson, the B.C. lieutenant-governor after James Dunsmuir, hid his Laurier-Liberal sympathies for policies like trade reciprocity with the U.S., and managed to get along well with staunch Imperialist, Premier Richard McBride. Before assuming the viceregal position, Paterson directed the Victoria Terminal & Sidney Railway.

The Streetcar System

*A National Electric Tramway &
Lighting Company streetcar in
the mid-1890s. The bowler-hatted
man "driving" at the front is E.A.
Morris, who had festooned the
tram with signs for his tobacco
shop on Government Street.*

Victoria's last streetcar, draped in black crepe in mock mourning, ran on July 5, 1948 from the Outer Wharves, past the Empress Hotel, and along Government Street, ending at the car barns at Pembroke and Store. Old number 383 was the successor to four cherrywood and polished brass, sixteen-foot-long streetcars which, 58 years earlier, had dragged Victoria out of the horse and buggy era. Like their B.C. Electric Railway counterparts in Vancouver, Victoria's streetcars became dilapidated through lack of maintenance and capital investment in the thirties and forties, and were replaced by rubber-tired buses.

The first streetcars arrived in 1889 and created a sensation with their electric lights, bells, and hand-painted route signs and advertisments. They were a daring investment in almost untried technology—the first electric railway in the world had run successfully only six years before. The owner was the National Electric Tramway and Lighting Company, headed by Captain J.D. Warren, with a board of directors including former *Colonist* owner David Higgins, Premier Robson's son-in-law Joseph Hunter, physician Dr. G.L. Milne, dentist Dr. T.J. Jones, druggist Thomas Shotbolt, and foundry owner Andrew Gray.

The NET&L system started with two lines: the first being from Hillside down Douglas to Yates, Government, across the James Bay bridge, along Birdcage Walk, Superior, St. Lawrence, Erie to the Outer Wharf; the second from the car barns at Pembroke, along Store, Johnson, Government, and Fort to the Royal Jubilee Hospital. It expanded in 1890 with a line to Esquimalt; then added extensions to Oak Bay and the new fairgrounds at the Willows.

Victoria and the NET&L became indispensable to each other, despite continual griping in the newspapers about poor service, bark peeling untidily from the street-side power poles, and discourteous men crowding together on the rear platform to smoke their pipes and cigars, obliging women to elbow their way through in order to enter the car to take a seat. Boys caused the conductors considerable grief by leaping on and off, stealing rides and placing stones on the tracks, which on several occasions derailed the small, light trams. During the snowfall of February, 1893, the NET&L's tracks in the downtown area were covered with snow, in some places as much as six feet deep, as a result of residents and businesses along the line shovelling snow from sidewalks and rooftops. The line was out of service for nearly a week before a thaw finally cleared it. In early 1894, the NET&L started using standardized car-stopping places, eliminating the old, much-abused practice of stopping the tram wherever a passenger wished to alight.

Victoria's depressed financial state in the early nineties (reflecting the state of the world economy, but aggravated locally by the decision of the Bering Sea Arbitration Tribunal), caused David Higgins and co-investor Major Dupont to look to London for financing, a move which induced financiers Robert M. Horne-Payne and Sperling & Co. to invest in the NET&L. One of their first moves was to change the tramway's name to the Victoria Electric Railway & Lighting Co.

Nothing much improved, and on May 23, 1895, Dunsmuir's Union Colliery served a writ on the VER&L for payment of its coal account. The tramway was pushed into bankruptcy. Frank Barnard, who had been engaged by Sperling & Co. to manage its Lower Mainland-area street railways, also took over the Victoria system on May 1, 1896. Renamed the Consolidated Railway & Lighting Company, it had just over three weeks of trouble-free operation before Car Number 16, grossly overloaded with picnickers heading for the Victoria Day celebrations at Macauley Point, broke through the rotting Point Ellice bridge. Fifty-five people were killed (page 150). On October 13, the Yorkshire Guarantee Corporation of Vancouver, which held the mortgage, foreclosed and took possession of the railway's property. The following April, in London, the B.C. Electric Railway Co. was formed by Horne-Payne, Sperling & Co., and other English investors; its consolidation of the Vancouver street railways with the Victoria system, and its development of hydroelectric generators, were the basis of its dominance of British Columbia's utilities for the next 60 years. The first manager was Frank S. Barnard. (The B.C. Electric, headed by G.P. Norton and Horne-Payne, was part of the same corporation which funded the Canadian Northern Railway system, bought

David William Higgins was a Haligonian who came to Victoria at age 24, in 1858, after a brief career in journalism in San Francisco. He worked for and later purchased the Colonist, turning it into the opposition paper against Amor de Cosmos, Walkem and their supporter, The Standard. The antagonism became so intense in September, 1878, that Higgins assaulted Standard editor Robert Holloway with a cane in front of the Supreme Court room. Higgins claimed provocation due to an article critical of his family, and was fined only five shillings by a sympathetic Justice Crease. Higgins built the recently restored "Regent's Park" at Fort and St. Charles streets, and had six children—Frank was a leading Victoria lawyer, Will married Dolly Helmcken, and Elizabeth married Vancouver lumberman James Raymur. Higgins was the Esquimalt MLA in 1886, and became Speaker of the legislature. He was the first manager of the Victoria streetcar system. Following his retirement, he wrote local history stories, and attracted quite a following with books like "The Mystic Spring" (page 99).

Dunsmuir's Vancouver Island coal mines, and owned sawmills throughout the province. Its political influence on Sir Richard McBride's government resulted in the extensive railway guarantees granted to the CNPR, now the Canadian National, in B.C. The B.C. Electric was taken over by the provincial government in 1961 and reconstituted with the B.C. Power Commission to form B.C. Hydro.)

Under the direction of R.H. Sperling after 1904, the BCER introduced a standard five cent fare (eight for 25 cents during rush-hours) and put the streetcar system in order. New lines were extended to the Gorge, Foul Bay along Fairfield Road, Burnside and Uplands. Luxurious new cars with separate smoking compartments were introduced on the Fort Street & Oak Bay line. As in Vancouver, an open-topped observation car gave tourists the best three-hour sightseeing ride in the city, visiting Esquimalt, the Gorge and Oak Bay, for 50 cents.

The Number 2 Outer Wharf-Cloverdale line was often crowded with Sikhs, Chinese and tweedy Englishmen on the run into town from Rithet's. Going south, it was full of civil servants, and the conductor jokingly called out "Resthaven" at the stop outside the legislature. The Number 3 James Bay line ended at Niagara Street and Douglas at the entrance to Beacon Hill Park. It was also called the "Resthaven Special" when it passed the legislature; regular passengers included throngs of picnickers, Tom Plimley the bicycle man, and Emily Carr with her white rat. The eleven o'clock Number 4 Esquimalt car on Saturday night was always full of drinkers heading back to Victoria from the Esquimalt pubs (Victoria had no taverns until 1953), and the corner of Yates and Douglas was called "Pusser's Corner" after all the sailors there in their "pussers" (bibs and tuckers).

Sperling was succeeded as general manager in 1914 by George Kidd (1874-1962), an English accountant who had gone directly to Horne-Payne's London home to apply for a job as B.C. Electric secretary.

Jitneys (unlicensed private cars operating as mini-buses on the same routes as the streetcars) began to appear on Victoria streets in November, 1914. By the next May there were about 50 of them operating, and the BCER protested to City Hall. In late 1918, the provincial government finally passed legislation to ban the jitneys from Victoria and Vancouver. They nevertheless persisted until December, 1920, when a Victoria by-law forcing compliance with safety regulations finally eliminated them.

(Preceding page) Looking southwest towards the city, from near the corner of Fort and St. Charles, about 1900. The house in the left foreground is "Regent's Park," owned by David Higgins, the original manager of the Victoria streetcar system. In the centre distance is the Nesbitt's "Erin Hall," and on the right through the mist loom the towers of Joan Dunsmuir's "Craigdarroch." There were only a few large estates on that part of Fort Street; some years later, however, the land between Higgins's and Nesbitt's was subdivided, the driveway into "Erin Hall" becoming Carberry Gardens. The Fort Street mud was notorious: on November 22, 1863, Augustus Pemberton's house on Fort near Moss Street caught on fire, and a runner was dispatched to the Deluge Company at Number Two firehall. The fire wagon became so bogged down that another runner was eventually dispatched to tell the firemen to turn back, as the house had already burned down. After 1915, this point on Fort Street, where the road narrows and curves, became known as "the Dardanelles," after the strait leading into the Gallipoli battlefield near Istanbul.

Kidd promptly increased streetcar fares to six cents. In 1921, following the disbanding of the Public Utilities Commission (which had approved the six-cent fare), the fare reverted to five cents. Kidd threatened a wage cut, then applied to the Dominion Railways Commission to remove the Vancouver and Victoria street railway systems from the jurisdiction of their local municipalities. The Commission was asked to extend the Dominion charter of the BCER's Vancouver, Fraser Valley & Southern Railway so that the latter could purchase both the Victoria and Vancouver tram systems. Both Victoria and Vancouver protested; BCER finally withdrew its application when the municipalities caved in and agreed to the six-cent fare. On January 1, 1922, the rule of the road changed from the left to the right, and the BCER received $400,000 compensation from the provincial government to pay for changing over the tram doors from left to right and altering its track-switching mechanisms.

The BCER built its Victoria head office building at 1016 Langley. It retained its old car sheds at Pembroke and Store streets, and established a depot at 1505 Douglas Street for its Saanich interurban line. This latter line, much like the Chilliwack one on the mainland, was intended to serve farmers on a meandering milk run through the rural land on the Saanich peninsula to a terminus at Deep Cove. It was in competition with the Victoria Terminal & Sidney Railroad, which operated a rather irregular service from its terminus at Douglas and Cormorant. Both systems had folded due to lack of business by the mid-1920s.

The BCER began bus service in December, 1929, on Haultain Street, with three 23-passenger buses. A second line was established in February, 1940, to serve the Esquimalt naval barracks. Although the BCER's streetcar franchise in Victoria expired in 1938, the service continued into the war years, with an eye to the impending petroleum rationing (invoked April 26, 1940). By the end of the war, the system needed renewal but voters rejected a bylaw in December, 1946 which would have eliminated the streetcars. A better-organized campaign the next June urged a complete rejection of the old streetcars in favour of a modern system using buses to serve Victoria, Esquimalt, Oak Bay and Saanich. It passed, and tracks were removed commencing in October. Many of the old streetcars were sold, at prices from $100 to $150, for use as bunkhouses, chicken coops, and cottages. One ended up as a private movie theatre in the garden of the McGill residence on Tattersall Drive in Saanich.

Terry's

One of the most popular meeting places in Victoria was Terry's, at the southwest corner of Fort and Douglas. Terry's was a drugstore, originally Terry's Cash Chemist at the southeast corner of Pandora and Douglas. By the twenties, everyone went there, especially after the theatre on Saturday night, to dine and dance to the fine orchestras in the separate dining room. "Meet You At Terry's" was the popular slogan, and many evenings there were line-ups out the door for seats, and waitresses with loaded trays dodged the dancing couples in the aisles who overflowed from the dance floor during "Dancing Cheek to Cheek" and "Begin the Beguine." According to one story, a woman whose society husband had been having an affair sought out her rival one evening at Terry's, armed with a horse-whip. The "other woman" barely had a chance to stand, before being whipped down into her chair. In the mid-1940s, Terry's was advertised on streetcar sideboards as "The Talk of the Town."

Terry's was founded by Wallace Samuel Terry. Born in 1869 in Ontario, Terry came to Victoria in 1890 and opened the drugstore seven years later. He was a long-time director of the Victoria Tennis Club and a grand master of the Masonic Lodge. He volunteered as the vice-consul for Belgium shortly before the outbreak of the First World War, and organized the Belgian relief drive following the German invasion in August, 1914—Victorians contributed thousands of packages of food, including tinned salmon, and clothing. He died in November, 1932, aged 61.

The Terry's site is now occupied by the Bentall Building. When the building was demolished, the soda counter was saved, and installed in Fanny's restaurant, at the southeast corner of Blanshard and Fort.

(Left above) The original Terry's Drugstore at the southeast corner of Pandora and Douglas in 1917. The young man in the white jacket is the 24-year-old pharmacist, Bert Emery. (Left below) The interior of the original Terry's in 1917, with the famous soda fountain on the right. The archway in the middle of the photograph led into a small dining area, designed and decorated by architect Samuel Maclure. (Above) The interior of the second Terry's, at the southwest corner of Fort and Douglas, during the thirties, when it was advertised as "The Talk of the Town."

Other popular meeting spots in Victoria included Clays' Metropolitan Bakery and Tea Room on Fort Street, the Poodle Dog on Yates Street, and, for those with a bit more "mazuma," the Empress—with dancing to Billy Tickle's orchestra. The Crystal Gardens was very fashionable for Saturday night dances in the twenties.

Spencer's

The Eaton's department store which occupies the area between Douglas and Government south of View Street used to be Spencer's, the largest department store in early Victoria. Spencer's was one of two large store chains (the other being Woodward's) which got their start in B.C. By 1948, when the Spencer family sold out to Eaton's, the firm had stores in Victoria, Vancouver, New Westminster, Nanaimo, Courtenay, Duncan, Chilliwack and Mission.

David Spencer arrived in Victoria in 1864, too late to strike out for the goldfields. He was 27, and had left South Wales with his friend Joseph Wilson, in response to the encouraging letters of the latter's brother William (with whom Joseph formed W & J Wilson Clothiers at Government Street and Trounce Alley). Spencer opened a stationery and fancy-goods business which shrewdly featured a bookshop and lending library. His first advertisement in the *British Colonist* on January 29, 1864, was pitched directly at the homesick and entertainment-starved residents of the little town. It said: "Cheap reading! Three thousand popular novels, also standard works on history, biography and travels. One bit per vol., or one dollar per month. All the English and American periodicals and magazines received by every steamer! Valentines! Sensational and Comic, New and Beautiful!" (Valentines and Christmas cards were offspring of the newly devised penny-postage service.)

After six years, Spencer sold his shop to Hibben & Carswell; he then entered a partnership with William Denny to buy "Victoria House," which opened on January 14, 1873. The firm prospered, and led the way in advertising and stocking the latest goods from England. In his frock coat, top hat and striped trousers, Spencer was the epitome of a respectable merchant. In his spare time, he was active in the Methodist church and sang in the choir at the Pandora Street church with his wife Emma. Their family grew, eventually to thirteen children, and Spencer built a large house called "The Poplars" at Belleville Street and Birdcage Walk on the southern end of the James Bay bridge. (Mrs. Spencer used to delegate one child to watch for Father's approach from town at lunchtime. When he started at the north end of the bridge, the child hurried to notify her. The table was set and lunch placed on it as soon as he walked through the door.)

In March, 1879, Spencer dissolved his partnership with Denny and went into business under his own name. Three years later, he bought an L-shaped block with 33 feet of frontage on Government and 56 feet on Broad Street, and built the Arcade Block to fill in the remaining store space between Fort Street and Trounce Alley. At first, he used only the main floor for retailing and leased the second floor for a YMCA centre and offices. Both floors were completely lighted with skylights. David Spencer Ltd. expanded with each passing month—he branched out from the drygoods business into Oriental carpets, dressmaking and millinery, and the manufacture of ladies' bath gowns and tea gowns. He sent his eldest son Chris every year to France, Germany and England on buying trips,

and by 1890 had an inventory valued at $120,000. One evening in October, 1910, a fire broke out in Spencer's and spread quickly, demolishing everything in the block bounded by Fort, Government, Broad, and Trounce Alley. Also damaged was the Driard Hotel, which had fallen on hard times in the couple of years since the Empress Hotel opened. Spencer bought the Driard, and the attached Victoria Theatre, and spent three feverish weeks converting it into a department store. Spencer's Arcade was rebuilt several years later to serve as an annex to the main store.

David Spencer died in 1920. The Vancouver operation—by then the biggest—was managed by "Mr. Chris," while the Victoria store was run by "Mr. Will." The latter started a 25-year-club for long-serving employees, and earned a considerable loyalty from Victorians with old-fashioned service, familiar faces, English imports, and a superb tobacco counter. To celebrate both its golden and diamond jubilees (in 1923 and 1933 respectively), Spencer's "purchased" the Victoria streetcar system

The central downtown area, before the disastrous 1910 fire.

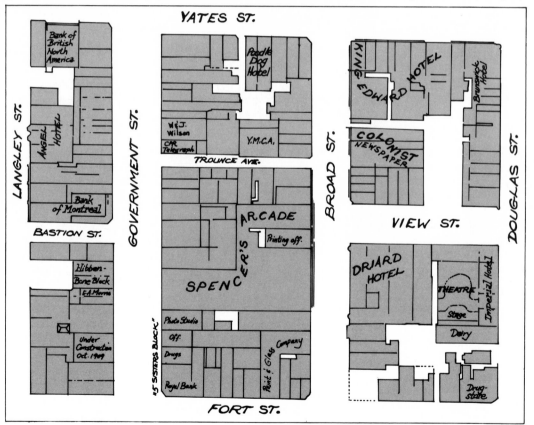

52

Looking east from Government Street, across the blackened ruins of the Spencer Arcade to View Street, shortly after the 1910 fire. David Spencer purchased the damaged Driard Hotel, in the background, and worked feverishly to reopen his department store there. The old Arcade building site stayed vacant through the early part of the First World War, and returned soldiers created a replica of the trenches on the Western Front out of its mud and rubble. Victorians were invited to tour the earthworks, at a 25-cent fee for charity. A building permit was issued for the new Arcade building in August, 1915; it seemed to be as jinxed as the previous one, and was gutted by a $300,000 fire on May 10, 1922. Six shops and ten offices were destroyed—Wilkerson's Jewellery and Plimley & Ritchie Bicycles each suffered $40,000 losses.

David Spencer

for the day: schoolchildren flocked to joy-ride to Deep Bay and back on the interurban, and plugged the streets at the end of the line in Esquimalt. The newspaper said: "All Victoria To Ride Free." After the changeover in 1948, Victorians took their time transferring their loyalty to Eaton's, which reflected founder Timothy Eaton's puritanical streak (much sterner even than David Spencer's devout Methodism): the tobacco counter was removed, and drapes were drawn across the window displays on Sundays.

After Will Spencer died in 1946, the Victoria store was taken over by his sister, Sara Ellen. She was a woman of strong principles and active in many causes: she was one of seven commissioned Canadian women (an Honorary Lieutenant) overseas during World War I with Captain Mollie Plummer and the Canadian Field Comforts; in the thirties, she was one of the few people to picket ships carrying scrap metal to Japan. While she lived at the Moss Street home (page 115), before giving it to Victoria as an Art Gallery in 1951, she hosted the meetings of the many societies she patronized, including the Victoria Symphony Society, the Alpine Club, and the Society for Preservation of Alpine Plants. She lived to a great age, dying in January, 1983 at age 97.

Chinatown

Chinatown is not nearly as exotic now as it was in the first half-century of Victoria's existence. The Chinese residents are different—familiar with white customs and assimilated into white society. The white population is different—more open-minded, better travelled, less prudish and credulous, and less racist. The old Chinatown, on the few blocks on either side of Government Street on Cormorant (now Pandora), Fisgard, and Herald, was a place which few whites probably ventured into, but many talked of. Stories, through endless repetition and variation, told of an alley barred by a gate with a round, head-sized hole and "an unremovable stain"; Chinese girls, it was said, went straight into opium, prostitution and slavery; killings and suicides were common and "never found by the authorities," as undertakers whisked the still-warm bodies away.

In truth, in the late 1850s, Chinese in B.C. were "either washing gold or washing laundry." In 1864, reliable estimates said there were 2,000 Chinese in the province, mainly patient golddiggers who had wandered north from California. Victoria's Chinatown developed quickly on undesirable land north of Johnson Street; more Chinese moved to the coast, especially after the CPR construction contracts ended in 1885 and the imported railroad coolies found they hadn't earned enough money to pay their passage back to China. There was plenty of domestic work, at $20 or $25 a month, for the white households. Chinese laundries had "a raised platform at the back, shamelessly displaying all sorts and conditions of white men's undergarments." Benevolent societies were formed and joss houses and schools erected. By the turn of the century, people said, "half of Victoria was Chinese."

Chinatown was marked by "the aromas of unnameable viands, burning joss sticks and damp bamboo," the shops always in a gloomy half-light, with quiet figures watching from the deep shadows. Shop windows were filled with strange herbs, little human-shaped ginseng roots, dried fungi, and other objects "suggesting all sorts of skinned small animals." Bottles and jars had bizarre medicinal contents, like tonics made from the fetus of barking-deer. Doorways and windows were decorated with bright red parallelograms, covered in "hieroglyphics." Chrysanthemums in pots stood on balconies and the landings of the endless flights of stairs between the fire-trap tenements. Chinese women were the more exotic for being rarely seen—there weren't many of them, most of the men having immigrated as single coolies. Those who had come over as wives of prosperous businessmen walked little and painfully on their compressed "Trilby feet." As well, their lips and cheeks were painted, at a time when no respectable white woman would paint hers. When the bride of Lee Chong of the Moon Song & Co. arrived at Rithet's wharf in February, 1898 aboard the *Empress of China*, the newspaper noted that "her feet are the smallest, her nails the longest, her lips the reddest, and her hair the blackest." She was not meant for work.

White Victorians followed the accounts of the slave-girl traffic in the 1880s with tremendous interest. A battle for control of the trade caused a series of vicious killings by rival Tong factions, some based in San Francisco. One of the earliest murders was that of Tue Guay, the wife of Fisgard Street merchant Wong Chuen. She was abducted, and an attempt was made to extract a ransom, followed by an attempt to sell her in Seattle. She was eventually found murdered on the beach at Narrows Island, her body tied to a rock and sunk in the shallows. The murderer, Wong Fat, was hung at the Hillside Jail.

An Englishman who had lived in San Francisco and China, John Gardiner-Vrooman, set up a home for wayward Chinese girls on Frederick Street, where he gave them an elementary education and sewing lessons. In 1888, in his role as Immigration Service inspector, he intervened in a slave-girl transaction and gained custody of a 17-year-old girl. The girl successfully petitioned to Judge Begbie to have her custody revoked; concurrently, Gardiner-Vrooman had his life threatened. The police investigated, and initially took into custody the "magnetic healer Professor Menzies," who claimed that Gardiner-Vrooman had lured the girls away from their homes and was mistreating them. Menzies did eight months on the Topaz Street rockpile for his "false pretences." The police eventually caught Lim Sam and Lum Hip, and charged them with conspiracy to commit murder for writing the death note. A letter from the former, the head of the Chee Kung Tong, to the latter, setting out his terms of employment as a "salaried soldier" of the Chee Kung Tong, was published and caused a sensation. Lum Hip was supposedly insured for $10 a month medical expenses, $100 a year to his family if he landed in jail, and a $250 pension and return to China if he was disabled in the course of his duty. He and his fellow "soldiers" were said to be fighting a steady battle with the "flying squad of hatchetmen" from San Francisco's Hip Sing Tong. Both men were acquitted by a jury.

A few months later, a 19-year-old woman named Yow Kum, who had come to Victoria from California and couldn't return due to the newly enacted Chinese Exclusion Act, was sold to a man named Yip Tang. She became "an inmate" of the brothel at 71 Fisgard—the site of the modern police station—and sat every night at the open window, talking with the men passing by. She fell in love with Chan Ah Hang, a bed-maker at

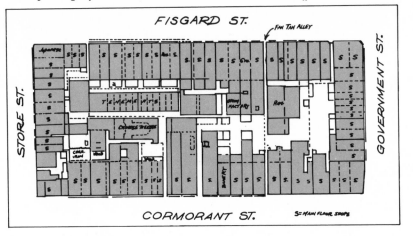

White people rarely saw beyond the solid wall of shops ringing the block of Chinatown bordered by Cormorant (now Pandora), Fisgard, Store and Government. The entrances into the labyrinth of tenements, gambling houses, opium factories, and alleged girl-slave brothels which made up the interior of the block were through the closely watched Fan Tan Alley (next page) or by Theatre Alley, at the opposite end. Part of the lure of Chinatown was fantasy—the credulous minds of unsophisticated whites speculating about exotic, Oriental mystery in the midst of prudish Victoria. Another, for the police, was the desire to shut down the gambling joints, especially in the anti-vice 1910s and 1920s. The result was incredibly elaborate security precautions—men with hats pulled over their eyes in doorways and at the entrances to the alleyways, secret door-locks, and a rabbit-warren of staircases, alleyways and rooftops—all to keep the games of Fan Tan, Pi Gow, Don Gow and Chuck Luck going. The only numbered landmark on Fan Tan Alley was number five—Sam Fun's Man Hop Cafe (translated as "foodstore suitable for ten thousand occasions"), which closed in December, 1953. Sam the cook regularly demonstrated his kick-boxing style to patrons there.

55

Burns House in Bastion Square—at least he thought so, and suggested poisoning Yip Tang. However, Chan was soon warned that Yip Tang had learned of the poison plot, and realized that his lover had betrayed him. At 10:30 on the Sunday night of May 12, 1889, Chan walked up Fisgard to the window, smiling at Yow Kum. Suddenly, he grabbed her head, pulled it across the window-sill and nearly severed it with a cleaver. Chan ran west, then south, and hid in the coal bin beneath Burns House. When he finally emerged two days later—looking for food—he was captured, and taken to the Hillside Jail, where he hung himself in his cell.

In other reported instances of the slave trade, a young woman named Chan Sui was sold for $1,330 by an English-speaking woman named Ah Die to a labourer named Chung Man; he kept her locked in a cabin at 27 (now approximately 1617) Store Street. And, on the 23rd of September, the *Empress of China* docked, carrying six young women. They were met by two Chinese merchants, who sent the two youngest to Wah Chong and his wife above 13 Cormorant Street (now 517 Pandora); the others were sent to the flat above the See Wah tinsmith shop at 50 Fisgard (now 570). Bonds were posted by the merchants with immigration inspector Dr. G.L. Milne "to ensure their morality," but a *Colonist* reporter found them soon thereafter, at 50 Fisgard, dressed in costly silks and jewellery, with several men all smoking opium and "listening to a native band." At the same time, a man named Ah Kim, who was an actor with the local Lee Pong Opera Company, returned from China with several young girls, whom he passed off as members of his troupe. He was allegedly paid a total of $2,500 (equivalent to about ten years' wages) to land the girls in Victoria.

A better level of education, and a rise in Chinese nationalism directed against the Manchu dynasty, resulted in a decline of the evil Tongs and an end to the slave traffic. The Tongs became more fraternal and social. None of this affected the opium business, which was a traditional relaxation for Chinese men, and entirely legal in Canada. Temperance-minded ladies, like Mrs. Carne of the Angel Hotel (page 59), employed Chinese cooks. When Mrs. Carne's cook was late for work, she sent her son Fred to fetch him from the opium dens. Several opium factories operated full-time in Victoria, including one in the centre of the block just west of Fan Tan Alley, and another—the Tai Yune Company—on the "triangle" at Pandora and Government (map, page 62).

A sense of Chinese culture was instilled in young people by the Lock Quon, the first Chinese school, which opened on the north side of Fisgard, at Government, on July 1, 1889. It moved in 1909 to the current grand Chinese school, a block east on Fisgard opposite the police station. With knowledge came a better awareness of the local oppression of Chinese. (All Chinese, alive or dead, were said to want to return to China. The little Chinese cemetery on Gonzales Bay, at the end of Penzance Road, was notorious amongst whites for its "bone house" and the "associative haunting" of the nearby Smith house at 2120 Penzance. The "bone house" contained the remains of thousands of Chinese, who were to be returned to China for reburial. Problems with various occupying and revolutionary governments in China for thirty years before 1961 kept the

bones in Victoria. Brazen white children stole the Players and Millbanks cigarettes left by Chinese families who were "feeding the dead" with ricecakes, earthenware cups of tea, and cigarettes. The bones were returned to China for reburial in 1961, and the old "bone house" razed soon after. The belief that all Chinese wanted to return home and send their money home caused Canadians from Upper Canada who sent their money home in colonial days to be dubbed "North American Chinamen.")

The Manchu dynasty brutally oppressed the Chinese people. The commonly-worn pigtails came from the Manchu saying that "a horse has a tail and a rider, and you will wear pigtails to prove we are in the saddle." Many Victoria, Vancouver and San Francisco Tongs threw support behind Sun Yat-Sen's Nationalists, although the community was divided on its loyalties. On November 15, 1908, the newspapers carried news of the death of Emperor Kwang Su. Reports quickly followed that the Dowager Empress, Tse Hai An—"a complete non-entity," according to the British ambassador—had died soon after, "exciting suspicions of foul play." Lord Lee, the Chinese ambassador in London, sent an order throughout the British dominions for all Chinese to mourn for three days. Nearly every door promptly had a white cloth hanging from its knocker—white being the mourning colour—and the rooms of the Chinese Reform Association were draped with white cloth inside and out. During a mass meeting outside the Chinese Benevolent Association, a young man created a sensation when he made a speech dissenting from the command and opposing any mourning. Simmering disputes sparked many fights, including "a first class old-time Tong War" in the meeting rooms of the Fisgard Street schoolhouse on October 8, 1916. In September, 1918, when Chinese government minister Tang Hua Lung was visiting Victoria, he was assassinated on the street by Chang Wong, who blew his own brains out when cornered by the police. During the twenties, a man named Chan Dun operated a flying school at Lansdowne Airport to send trained pilots to China to aid the revolution. The Chinese community only became more united in opposition to the Japanese invasion of Manchuria in 1932.

Rumours of constant payoffs to the police and city officials crystallized in 1915 into a concerted effort to shut down the gambling dens (the concurrent public sentiment for prohibition was but one aspect of a general move to rid the community of all vice). A secret raid—to avoid tipoffs by corrupt police—was planned for the night of December 15, with Sergeant John Fry as the battering ram. The target was "the Oriental Club" on Fan Tan Alley. The sentry in the alley caught sight of the charging police through his peephole, and managed to seal the lock, but Fry charged right through the door and captured 147 Chinese. Most couldn't make the $25 bail or the $10 fine, so were sent to the Wilkinson Road Jail. The same night, another raid, on the Empire Club on Fisgard, netted 80 more. Victorians angrily protested at the cost of feeding and transporting the manacled prisoners from Wilkinson Road to the Cormorant Street terminus of the interurban, then marching them to Government House for gardening duty. The next month, Sergeant Fry led a raid on the Fan Tan Alley premises "above #1 and #2, west side." Police broke down three doors, and arrived in the smoke-filled main room with its green-shaded

Chinese merchants who sold opium were usually supplied by a local factory like the Tai Yuan Company on the "triangle" at Pandora and Government. A visit to Tai Yuan was a highlight of Governor General the Earl of Aberdeen's tour of Victoria in 1895. Accompanied by Chinese ladies in traditional costume, the Earl watched the cooking and preparing of opium, then visited the local joss-house for tea. About 60 tons a year of opium was imported from Hong Kong and processed in a half-dozen plants in Victoria, mainly for shipment to San Francisco, where it retailed at $7-$8 a pound. The opium business also thrived in Vancouver's Chinatown until the race riots of September, 1907—Dominion labour expert (and future Prime Minister) William L. MacKenzie-King was sent to Vancouver to arbitrate the Chinese merchants' claims for compensation, and was appalled at the size of the loss-of-business claims by opium factories. He was also lobbied strenuously by the Wesleyan Methodists, led by future Conservative cabinet minister H.H. Stevens, and told how more and more white men were falling victim to opium and Chinese gambling. Canada's first Narcotics Control Act, banning the processing and sale of opium, was passed the next year.

One of the few whites who argued in the thirties for political rights for Orientals was Victoria-born Henry Forbes Angus (b. 1891), a graduate of Victoria High School, McGill, the Lycee Descartes in Tours, and Balliol College, Oxford, where he received a doctorate of laws in 1914. Following a military career in Mesopotamia and India with the Wiltshire Territorials in World War I, Angus joined the UBC Economics faculty in 1919, becoming department head in 1930. He served as a member of the Rowell-Sirois Commission on inter-governmental relations in the late thirties. His statements in late 1940 that suspicion against Japanese-Canadians was "unwarranted" led him to be branded in the legislature and the House of Commons as "notoriously pro-Jap" and "disloyal to the Province." He also predicted at that time that the use of French outside Quebec would be the crucial problem facing Canadian unity. His best friend in Victoria was actor Freddie Wood, later prominent at UBC; his wife, Anna, was a niece of Hudson's Bay Company explorer and writer Alexander Caulfield Anderson. Henry Angus was a nephew of James Angus of Rockland Avenue.

drop-lights only to find the "inmates" disappearing through trapdoors, out windows and across rooftops. Police seized loads of paraphernalia, including opium pipes, pads of marked tickets, stamps, and the buttons, brass cups and black cotton sleeves used by the dealers. Quai Kwan, who was in the process of escaping down a trapdoor when he ran into the ascending Inspector Heatley, was arrested with $62.50 in dimes. He was found guilty in police court of being the keeper of the premises, although he claimed to be just a tailor, who had gone there for coffee at the end of his twelve-hour working day.

The allegations of corruption prompted the mercurial Joe North to campaign against Mayor Porter (page 58). After that affair, and the swing of the pendulum away from prohibition and "blue Sundays," Chinatown ceased to occupy so much of the public's attention. John Fry, named Police Chief in 1921, survived Joe North's antics and stayed in the job 10 years, before retiring to his house at 219 Superior, where he died at age 75 in 1946. Chinatown was in danger of a general "urban renewal" and bulldozing until the late Sixties, when its unique character was formally recognized by the city. The Gate of Harmonious Interest, erected in the early 1980s by a group of citizens led by University of Victoria professor Chuen-yan David Lai, spans the "entrance" to Chinatown at Fisgard and Government.

White resistance to Oriental immigration was the single unifying theme of B.C. provincial politics before the 1930s. The idea of a head tax on all Chinese entering B.C. was first proposed by John Robson in 1872. Premier Walkem, whose opponent T.B. Humphreys had received a lot of votes from Chinese in the Cariboo, passed an act in 1875 declaring that neither Chinese nor Indians could vote—this, said historian F.W. Howay, "was the first definite statement against Chinese voting." The head tax of $50, similar to one in place in Queensland, Australia, was established in 1885. It was increased to $100 in 1900, and $500 in 1903. Almost all Chinese immigration was prohibited from 1923 to 1947. Orientals finally received voting rights in 1949.

Whites felt that at least the Chinese were useful as domestic servants and in industries like fish-packing (the automatic fish-cleaning machine, which revolutionized the industry when it was introduced in 1903, was universally called "The Iron Chink"). The Japanese, though, were considered a real economic and political (later military) threat.

In 1905 Richard McBride's government—under strong pressure from the two Socialist members on whose support the government depended—passed an act imposing an arbitrary language test on any immigrating Asiatics. It was vetoed on January 20 by the governor-general, as "it is opposed to the Federal and Imperial policy of friendly relations with Japan."

Two years later, Lieutenant-Governor Dunsmuir came under fire for refusing, on April 25, 1907, to assent to a similar act (popularly called the Natal Act, after a law in that colony, and also the Bowser Bill, after the attorney-general, it had a clause which said that no one could immigrate who couldn't read and write "any test submitted to him" in English or a European language).

Dunsmuir, a Conservative, was exposed by Liberal Labour Minister MacKenzie King for contracting for 500 Japanese miners (Attorney-General Bowser's law firm was accused of acting for Gotoh, the labour contractor). The debate over Dunsmuir's alleged conflict of interest raged on into January, 1908. Dunsmuir was bitterly denounced by Nanaimo member J.H. Hawthornthwaite, who moved

a motion of censure and impeachment. By February 11, when the B.C. legislature unanimously passed the bill, Dunsmuir had about-faced and assented to it. However, the federal government indicated they would disallow it, and on February 20, Chief Justice Hunter, in a test case involving Japanese, disallowed the B.C. Bill as contrary to the Imperial treaty with Japan. An appeal court upheld Hunter's decision, and Justice Clement went so far as to say that B.C. was being disloyal. A similar case against 18 "Hindoos" in March was thrown out by Mr. Justice Morrison. Attorney-General Bowser appealed unsuccessfully; then suspended the Immigration Act.

Meanwhile, the Hon. Rodolphe Lemieux had gone to Japan, at the behest of the Dominion Government, and returned with a "voluntary" agreement by the Mikado to limit Japanese immigration to Canada to 150 a year. By 1914, the immigration problem was mainly a "Hindoo" one, as East Indians attempted to exercise their British Empire citizenship—climaxing in the ugly *Komagata Maru* siege in Vancouver that spring.

The Anglo-Japanese treaty was signed on June 13, 1911. It was the outgrowth of understandings, dating back to 1902, whereby Chinese and Korean independence were assured, and the co-signatories agreed to keep expansion by third parties like Russia, Germany and the United States out of Asia—especially India, in Britain's case.

The Japanese issue resurfaced following World War One—the Japanese had been staunch allies of Canada and Britain, and her navy had protected the west coast of North America, leaving Britain's free to concentrate on the Atlantic. In June, 1920, though, the province was at it again, attempting to exclude Japanese subjects from public works contracts. Final judgement—that B.C.'s actions violated the 1911 Anglo-Japanese treaty—was given November 18. The next year the 1911 treaty came up for renegotiation.

American attitudes played a large role in Canadian feelings. Japan had been too competitive with American commercial interests in China; there was suspicion of Japanese navy collusion with Britain; Californians, especially, were antagonistic to Japanese economic expansion. The Hearst newspapers led the fight in the U.S. against the new treaty. Both China and Canadian Prime Minister Meighen were opposed to it. In B.C., the "peaceful penetration" of the province was the issue; fruit growers complained bitterly about Oriental competition; the B.C. government lobbied Ottawa for revisions to the British North America Act, so it could control its own immigration. The Asiatic Exclusion League, formed in July 1921 with Trades & Labour Council president F.W. Walsh in the chair, led the agitation. The Victoria Chamber of Commerce passed a resolution on November 28 to ban all Oriental immigration, and to segregate Victoria public schools (this suggestion, picked up by the Victoria School Board, caused a boycott by the Chinese, led by Lim Bang, who with Lee Mong Gow filed suit against the Board, lost, then raised funds for Chinese public schools; the segregation attempt was abandoned soon after).

Further sporadic attempts during the twenties to eliminate Japanese immigration met with failure, although the legislature retained its unanimity for the cause. In the 1930s, following Japan's military ascendance, the cries became more insistent. After the Japanese declaration of war in late 1941, the federal government invoked the War Measures Act, and moved all Japanese away from the B.C. Coast.* Common sense, and political rights for all Canadians of Oriental ancestry, had to wait until the late forties.

---

*The relations between whites and Japanese in the decade leading up to the 1942 evacuation are covered in considerable detail in *Vancouver The Way It Was*, pages 29-33. The effects of Japan's militarism on the Chinese community during the thirties is described in the same book, pages 36-40.

Joe North

Joe North's antics during the decades before 1950 added a lot of humour and controversy to Victoria's sometimes staid civic affairs. His outrages overshadowed his good works—he collected over $50,000 for charity (his favorite cause being orphan children), published the *Christmas Herald* newspaper once a year until 1960, and was named Victoria's best citizen in 1937.

Born on January 13, 1878 in Wellington, New Zealand, Christopher Rowland North came to Victoria at the turn of the century and got a job as hoseman for the fire department. He was elected to the Police Commission in 1921 and, with his crony Dr. Ernest Hall, proceeded to clean up the city's allegedly graft-ridden police department.

The pair visited the speakeasies and blind pigs operating in Victoria in the summer of 1921 in defiance of the government's tough new Liquor Act (public sentiment was still strongly prohibitionist). At Harris & McAvoy's Lodge Cabaret, at 586 Johnson, they witnessed a table with a half-dozen gentlemen "under the influence of liquor" accompanied by a young lady of decent family, "dancing and kicking up her heels." At Hazen Hepburn's Borden Cabaret, at 825 Fort, there were "over 100 people, old women of sixty, young girls of sixteen, all sorts of people—not more than ten were sober."

North then claimed he talked to a "Chinaman" in Chungrane's Fish Store, who suggested North take money to protect the Chinese gambling joints. He was then approached by Charlie Bo, a tailor, who told him to "fix the police," in return for which the white men would be kept out. North named "protected" Chinese gambling houses, operated by Charlie Quong, Pong Lee and Kew Lee, at 1415 Store, and 507, 511, 519, 537, 550, 552 and 556 Cormorant Street. Police Chief Fry was not amused, and had Police Commissioner North arrested in August, charging that he had caused the police chief to neglect his duties by permitting the operation of lottery and gambling resorts in Chinatown. After sensational testimony, North was acquitted on September 13.

A month later, North was arrested on Blanshard Street in front of the YWCA for intoxication. He claimed, to much laughter from the 200 people who packed the courtroom for the trial, that he had bought the whiskey from the government vendor, and had consumed only two drinks with dinner. He was fined $100.

The mayoral campaign, leading up to the December, 1921 election, was dominated by North and Hall's pro-temperance stance and their charges against Mayor Porter. North and Hall rented the Royal Victoria Theatre on December 8, and told a foot-stamping, cheering, overflow crowd of 1,600 of their year's work against "the alcoholized forces of iniquity." North claimed collusion among the gambling elements, Mayor Porter, the police and the city detectives, warning the crowd not to vote for "the graft, corruption, bribery, and civic rottenness that are camouflaged under his candidature." He alleged that Mayor Porter was directly involved in rum-running to the United States, and told the henceforth-famous horse story: "A horse had been seen to load an automobile with whiskey, take it to Sooke, and load it on a schooner which had then sailed across the Sound. There are two kinds of horse. There's the mare, and there's the horse. I leave it to you who drove that automobile."

North then launched into a tirade against the city detectives. He claimed that his drunkenness charge was a frame-up, that Det. Sam Sicialano had tried to pick a fight with him on the CPR wharf, that they kept a couple of girls in a motel on Burnside Road, and that, because of their corruption, "human lives were traded for Chinese gold." Not surprisingly, Porter and the detectives launched lawsuits the next day. The mayor dropped his suit on December 13, but the suits of the detectives versus Hall and North opened in January to jammed courtroom galleries. A fundraising campaign, sponsored by city temperance elements led by Methodist minister Dr. Sipprell, raised money at banquets for the "Hall-North Defence Testimonial Fund." On March 23, 1922, Hall and North were defeated in all the actions; the city detectives collected over $6,000 in fines.

North, unbowed, made plans to go on a temperance crusade to California with William Davison, alias Billy Caine, a former vaudeville star and self-confessed bootlegger, accompanied by a 30-piece band and a 500-voice choir. Nothing came of it.

The most famous Joe North story concerned his 1948 lawsuit against the Victoria Baseball Athletic Co. Ltd., which had denied him admission to baseball games even though he held season's tickets. North had been ejected for his alleged "drunk & objectionable" behaviour, and his habit of giving Bronx cheers to any coach or player who didn't meet with his approval. In court, wearing his Victoria Good Citizen medal from 1937, he demonstrated his Bronx cheer and argued that the baseball club had breached its contract with him. He lost, and was ordered to pay $96.80 to the club's solicitors for legal costs.

North died on January 17, 1963, aged 85. His crony Dr. Hall (1852-1932) kept out of politics after his costly grandstanding with North. "A brilliant and unorthodox surgeon" and one of the few Conservatives who hated the liquor traffic, he ran unsuccessfully against John Hart in the 1916 provincial election.

Joe North, "a leathery man in a bowler," campaigned enthusiastically against anything he considered vice. One of his victims was Mayor Robert John Porter, who was defeated in the 1921 civic election following North's accusations of corruption. The demoralized Porter died the following April 24 from pneumonia—"an untimely end to a useful career," according to his obituary. Born in Victoria in 1867, Porter was the son of a Burnside district farmer who owned Porter & Sons meat market at the northwest corner of Johnson and Douglas. The son was president of the B.C. Agricultural Association following S.F. Tolmie's retirement, entered politics in 1912 as Ward V alderman, and topped the poll in the first civic at-large election in 1913. His accomplishments included the planning for the Johnson Street bridge, and his work with the "wooden ship delegation" to Ottawa in 1920, which attempted to get ship-building contracts for Victoria to ease the readjustment problems following World War I. Porter was defeated by prohibitionist William Marchant (page 70).

(Next page) The Angel Hotel, on Langley Street opposite Chancery Lane beside the Law Courts (today's Maritime Museum), was a run-down building in a run-down area before its demolition in the late forties for the new post office. However, at the turn of the century, it was the leading "temperance hotel" in Victoria—it didn't have a bar (the original owner had removed it following a tax dispute with the city). The hotel, run by the "very motherly" Mrs. Frederick Carne (whose husband was away gold prospecting for most of every year), was a popular spot with the "shabby genteel" people from up-island who came to town and then changed into their English finery. Mrs. Carne charged $6 a week for board and lodging, and darned the socks of the respectable young men who lived there. She was an active Methodist, and travelled to Europe with Mr. and Mrs. W.J. Pendray after her husband's death.

M.KLUCKNER 1986

B. Williams's little store at 97 Johnson Street (in the old street-numbering system) was next door to the Atlantic Hotel between Broad and Douglas Street. Gentlemen bought few shirtwaists (displayed in the left-hand window), but maintained a good collection of collars and cuffs, which were fastened to the shirtwaists with studs. During the Klondike gold rush in the late 1890s, Williams changed his inventory to outfit cheechakos for the long hike over the Chilkoot Pass.

Herbert Goulding Wilson, one of five sons of Government Street clothing merchant William Wilson, was president of the Board of Trade. The other sons were Joseph, who took over W & J Wilson from his father in 1900, and later passed it on to his only son, Harold; William, who was a California businessman; Charles, who was a Victoria solicitor; and Biggerstaff, who started the ice and cold storage business on Herald Street.

**THOS. TROUNCE,
ARCHITECT, ETC.**

OFFICE ON KANE STREET, ABOVE DOUGLASS.

PLANS AND SPECIFICATIONS CAREFULL
prepared for Public Buildings or Private Resi
dences, and the usual business of an Architect prompt
ly executed   3m

A group of prominent Victoria Methodists on the stairs of the Trounce residence in James Bay: (top row) Thomas Trounce and Mrs. Trounce; (middle) merchant David Spencer, unknown woman, and John Teague; (front) Mrs. Chris Spencer, Mrs. McCrossan, and Mrs. David Spencer. John Teague settled in Victoria and became a full-time architect in 1874, after nearly two decades following gold rushes in California and B.C. He survived many hardships, including a hike from Murderer's Bar to Langley on the ice of the Fraser River in the winter of 1859, and a nine-and-a-half day forced march from the Interior to the coast with only six pannikins of flour to eat. He designed the Royal Jubilee Hospital, St. Joseph's Hospital, St. Ann's Convent, the Victoria Public School, the Reformed Episcopal Church, the Driard Hotel, and City Hall.

Trounce Alley, the narrow street connecting Broad with Government just north of View Street, was the result of a real-estate fight between architect-developer Thomas Trounce and the colonial administration. Trounce owned property facing onto Government and Broad sStreets. Although the city had not yet been officially surveyed (that was done in 1862, by J.D. Pemberton and B.W. Pearse), Trounce believed that View Street would be opened through to connect Broad with Government. However, in 1858, the View Street right-of-way was sold and a fence built across it; the surrounding owners were outraged, and said that View might as well be used as a potato patch. Capt. Edward Stamp—later the founder of the famed Hastings Mill on Burrard Inlet—erected a wooden barrack-like building on the former right-of-way in 1862. It was later replaced with a block of stores with stone piers and cast-iron columns, the home of T.N. Hibben's Stationery, Henry Young & Son drygoods, and—adjoining it at the southern end—Spencer's Arcade.

Trounce opened the alley through his property in 1859 to provide access to his Broad Street stores. To prove it was privately owned, he closed it one day a year—a tradition that continued until the turn of the century. The alley became somewhat redundant after the 1910 fire, which destroyed everything in the block bounded by Fort, Trounce, Government and Broad. View Street was extended through to Government, and the Royal Trust building was erected on Trounce Alley before the outbreak of the First World War in 1914. The hole where Spencer's Arcade had stood remained unfilled with anything except water—during the War, returned soldiers dug replica trenches there and charged 25 cents admission to people curious about life on the Western Front. The new Arcade Building was erected in 1917, and today houses Eaton's Annex.

Thomas Trounce took his architectural training in England; then followed gold rushes to Australia, California, and finally to Victoria in 1858. He lived with his wife in a tent on Douglas Street during the 1858 miners' rush, before building the first stone house in Victoria, on property bordered by Michigan and Superior streets west of Menzies. The house, built of fieldstone rubble, was demolished in 1967; originally it faced Superior, but the property was subdivided and Trounce's address became 436 Michigan, across the street from John Irving's house (Irving Park). The Trounces were renowned gardeners: their orchard produced apples which won a bronze medal at the Colonial & Indian Exhibition in London in 1885; the garden produced splendid geraniums, fuschias, roses and heliotropes. They were very prominent in the Methodist church. Trounce died on June 30, 1900, aged 87.

The oldest-established business on Government Street, at the corner of Trounce Alley, is W & J Wilson Clothiers. William Wilson was an accountant with a London silk manufacturing firm; when the business collapsed due to the sudden imposition of a French tariff on silk, he moved to Victoria, arriving in September, 1862, a month after his 24th birthday. Like so many others, he made an unsuccessful trip to the Cariboo, all the good gold-creeks being staked. Upon his return, he purchased the stock of a bankrupt clothing firm, which had been located in a log building at the northeast corner of Government Street and Trounce Alley. His brother Joseph joined him two years later, and the firm became W & J Wilson. They pulled down the log building, replacing it with the one in which the firm still does business a century and a quarter later. William Wilson had a brief flirtation with politics, and was elected to the legislature as one of four Victoria members during the second Walkem administration from 1878-82. His support of Walkem sealed his fate, and he returned to business thereafter. He died in October, 1922.

City Hall

Victoria's City Hall was built on the initiative of Roderick Finlayson, who became mayor by acclamation in January, 1878. Construction proceeded quickly once he overcame opposition to the huge $10,000 budget—the eventual cost was $9,860. It was an ugly, squat little building at the corner of Douglas and Pandora, extending only as far north as today's main entrance, and west to the old boiler room. The original entrance was on Pandora. The additions to the front facade, which gave it its current appearance, started in 1889.

The most colourful incident in the City Hall's past, the story of which has served ever since as a benchmark of civic parsimony, began with Mayor J.W. Carey's 1884 grudge against the law firm of Drake and Jackson. Council had authorized, but Carey refused to sign, a cheque for $707.10 for legal services. On December 12, following a judgement obtained by the lawyers, Sheriff MacMillan seized the city's books, assessment and all the loose cash held by City Treasurer Thomas Russell. The waterworks were told to consider themselves seized. An ex-policeman named Redgrave was sworn in as bailiff, and took charge of City Hall. Mayor Carey tried to enter, but was rebuffed, so sent a policeman named Sheppard to guard the bailiff. The two spent the night stretched out on easy chairs.

Carey served Sheriff MacMillan with a writ, claiming illegal seizure of property. Chief Justice Begbie considered the matter the next day, and ordered the removal and sale of the city's assets. A large crowd gathered at Byrnes' auctioneers on Wharf Street on the morning of the 19th. Some were in a party mood, calling out: "Let's put His Worship up and see what he brings," and "I'll bid ten cents!"; others, however, felt some shame over the proceedings. Edgar Crow Baker, the city's MP, tried to stop the auction and offered, with other ratepayers including Messrs. Higgins, Loewin, F.S. Barnard, Robert Dunsmuir, and Joseph Spratt, to pay all the costs of the judgement and indemnify the sheriff against all claims. When the auctioneer, on legal advice, continued with the sale, Baker and his supporters bought most of the items. Mayor Carey made an appearance, and tried to make a speech, but was ordered away.

The citizens who put up the money to buy the city's goods and chattels were eventually repaid. Carey was thrashed in the next election by R.P.

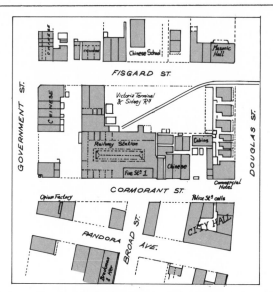

Mayor Joseph W. Carey, photographed with a granddaughter.

(Next page) Looking south down Douglas Street, in the late 1930s, from the corner of Cormorant past City Hall and the B.C. Electric's former interurban station. This part of Douglas Street changed drastically in the early 1960s, with the closing of Cormorant Street, the rerouting of Pandora at Government Street, and the creation of Centennial Square. City Hall got its first paint job in preparation for the 1939 visit of King George VI and Queen Elizabeth. Biggerstaff Wilson's ice wagons had been common on the streets since his cold storage business opened next to the E&N Railway station on Store Street in 1901. Boys lined up in the morning outside the plant at 536 Herald to get their family's daily ice block; homes to which ice was delivered used window cards to indicate how much they wanted. Wilson's main competitor was the Victoria Ice Company, started in the 1890s by James Baker, who cut blocks of ice from Swan Lake in the winter and packed it into sawdust-filled ice houses along the shore. In 1910, he sold out to his nephew, Stan Baker, who ran the business from his house at 2626 Rose. With his sons, Gordon and Jimmy Baker and his stepson, George Harris, the firm survived until 1967. They delivered five wagon loads of ice every morning before seven to the Northwestern Creamery on Broad Street for the manufacturing of "Velvet" ice cream. The Douglas Hotel was built by Victoria-born banker and merchant Lim Bang (1881-1974), who owned a number of greenhouses and a brick plant in Sidney.

Rithet. City Hall survived a demolition threat in the early sixties, and was restored under the leadership of Mayor Richard Biggerstaff Wilson to become the centrepiece of the Centennial Square project.

Charles Edward Redfern came from London to Victoria in 1862, when he was 24—one of the few men on the brideship Tynemouth—and prospered in the jewellery business. Elected as an alderman, first from the James Bay ward in 1878, he was mayor in 1883 and again from 1897-99. He ordered the City Hall clock from colleagues in London, and made silver-handled scissors for the ribbon-cutting ceremony which opened the additions in 1891. At his shop on Government Street, Redfern provided the city with standard time: he had "a large dial in position above his store, operating it by machinery placed at the rear of his building."

John Grant, mayor of Victoria when the city hall was expanded to its present dimensions, was from Alford, Scotland. He mined for gold in the Cassiar region, and was the MLA there from 1882 until his election as mayor in 1890.

AUTHOR'S COLLECTION

Charles Rogers

Rogers Chocolates, at 913 Government, still makes its custard creams and plum puddings "as big as tea biscuits," though the price has climbed considerably above the original five cents. The building, like the E.A. Morris Tobacconist up the street, has been meticulously preserved. Charles W. Rogers, the founder, had a fruit business in the original building at 913 Government, but moved to larger premises across the street in the 1890s. He married Miss Leah Morrison of James Bay in 1888, and soon thereafter, while continuing to run the fruit business, started experimenting with candy recipes. The chocolates' reputation was carried all over the world by tourists and Royal Navy men. The Rogerses became a fashionable and prominent family; they moved the business back across the street to the newer, opulent building in 1916.

Their son, Frederick Morrison Rogers, had "a mania for explosives," and had lost three fingers playing with them. He carried sticks of dynamite around with him as he rode on the streetcars. In January, 1905, at age 15, he took a room in the New England Hotel and shot himself to death. The parents were grief-stricken, and buried themselves in their work. Their eccentricities became notorious. They lived at 421 Kingston Street and, although wealthy, never installed lights, telephone or inside plumbing. They paid no attention to their dress, and often didn't bother going home, sleeping instead in rocking chairs by the wood stove in the back of the store. They developed a paranoia about holdups, but never dealt with a bank—when they walked home, she carried the money in a black bag and walked a block ahead of her husband to avoid recognition. People said they had hundreds of thousands of dollars tucked away in their house.

A card in the window of the shop stated: "My candies are made in the morning and sold in the afternoon." Charles Rogers worked in the back at a marble-topped table, with only a short-handled spade as a tool. Sometimes he locked the door in the face of customers or refused to sell them more than one box of candy. He died in 1927, aged 73, leaving a $295,985 estate. His wife gave most of the money away, and lived on in a nursing home on a modest pension until 1952, when she died at age 88.

A man with the same surname, identified as "an heir to a chocolate fortune, the importunate Ralph Rogers," figured in two versions of one of the many Rebel Mowat (page 167) yarns. This Rogers lived in the Empress Hotel, and his arrogance was said to be matched only by his wealth and laziness. Apparently, Rogers went bear hunting in Sooke, and had his picture taken with a dead bear hanging from a tree. He showed the picture around and bragged about his bravery. Mowat, who loved to deflate any pompous person, had *his* picture taken with a bear lying on top of him, and had it printed in the *Times* that afternoon. In the second, later version of the story, the bear was delivered through the Empress lobby, carried by three porters. That evening, while Ralph Rogers was describing his great bravery, a boy—bribed by Mowat—interrupted Billy

Charles and Leah Rogers

Tickle's orchestra on a pre-arranged signal and said, loudly, "Mr. Rogers, my Dad says that the bank okayed the cheque for $100 that you gave him when you shot our pet bear, but he wants you to return the bear's collar and chain."

(Next page) Jim Bryant's bicycle shop at the southwest corner of Johnson and Broad streets in the early 1920s. Bryant (1895-1977) came from Cornwall in 1913, learned the bicycle business from Tom Plimley, and, after a brief stint working for Biggerstaff Wilson's ice company, founded his own shop. Plimley survived and prospered by switching to selling automobiles; Bryant quit and went to work in the Esquimalt dockyard from 1931 until his retirement in 1960. He lived at 883 Head in Esquimalt, near Captain Jacobson, and was married by the Rev. Clem Davies. Tom Plimley started in the bicycle business in Victoria in 1893, on Yates Street between Broad and Government. Shortly after the turn of the century, he started importing English cars, like the Swift, Coventry and Humber. In 1910, he moved to expanded premises on Johnson Street, and sold the Overland Friction Drive Metz, Hupmobiles, and Detroit Electrics. He died in 1929, but the family automobile business has continued and prospered. Bryant's concession to the automobile age was a sidewalk gas pump, fairly common in Victoria in the twenties.

The Whelan Murder

View Street at Blanshard, beside the St. Andrew's (Catholic) Cathedral, was the site of one of the most bizarre, dastardly murders in Victoria's history. On Christmas Eve, 1890, David Fee, a young shop-owner who had been attending the midnight service at the old church at 740 View (where the Bishop's Palace now stands), was gunned down by a drunken Irish night watchman, who either took Fee to be an anti-Fenian, or—as defence attorney Charles Wilson claimed during the murder trial—a white-coated, high-hatted ghost.

The night watchman was Lawrence Whelan, a pro-Fenian Irishman who had been cautioned by Irish community leader Tom Deasy not to show the green-spangled Fenian flag around Victoria. (The Fenians were an Irish-American organization, founded in 1861 to forcibly separate England from Ireland. In 1865, a Fenian convention in New York decided to establish an independent government in the United States, and the following year there were several armed raids across the Canadian frontier into Ontario. San Francisco was a hotbed of Fenian sympathizers, and a number of the brickworkers engaged in the building of the St. Andrew's Cathedral were Irish-Americans from there.) Despite Deasy's warning, the Fenian flag had been raised above the derrick on the construction site. It was removed by the cathedral's contractor, Aeneas McDonald, but the workers figured that Deasy had taken it down. He was "marked" in Victoria, and a letter was sent by Whelan's friend Joe Silk to a Fenian organization in San Francisco, saying that if Deasy ever visited there, "you will know how to treat him." Deasy, who was a member of a volunteer fire brigade, often quietly patrolled the business section at night, like an apparition in his long, white, rubber fire coat.

A notice appeared on a post near the construction site, saying that the cathedral would be burned to the ground before its completion. The contractor employed a watchman, who was so nervous and regularly drunk that he attacked the foreman one night when the latter dropped by for a visit. Whelan was hired as the replacement a few days before Christmas; he was reportedly teased by young sports on the street, who told him that "ghosts would come and steal him away" and to beware his enemies, who would drop things on him from the scaffolding above.

On Christmas Eve, Whelan, who had been drinking copiously at local bars, borrowed a shotgun from Joe Silk before starting his vigil at the construction site. Silk also provided him with a bag containing several cartridges, all said by Silk to be blank.

Meanwhile, David Fee and a friend, Frank Partridge, both fashionably dressed in long white coats with silk top hats, had been attending a Christmas Eve dance at the Philharmonic Hall. They left the dance shortly before midnight, as Fee wanted to see in Christmas day at the church at 740 View. After a brief period at the church, they left to return to the dance and were walking quietly across View Street when they came upon Whelan, who had left the construction site and was standing in the street, holding an umbrella and the shotgun. As the two young men passed him, Whelan raised the gun and shot Fee in the heart. Whelan fled, but surrendered to the police later that night.

The trial created a sensation, with Attorney-General Theodore Davie acting as crown prosecutor, and the aged Chief Justice, Sir Matthew Baillie Begbie, on the bench. Davie maintained that Fee had been shot by mistake—the intended victim was Deasy, in revenge for his lowering of the Fenian flag. Silk's letter to San Francisco had been returned by the dead letter office, and was entered as evidence. The jury, after lengthy deliberation, returned to the courtroom late on Saturday night. Their verdict was that Whelan had intended to do bodily harm, but had acted without premeditation. Begbie, enraged, shouted at the jury: "How can it be without premeditation, and still be with intent to do grievous bodily harm?" He ordered the jury to retire and reconsider their verdict. They returned at ten minutes to midnight with a verdict of "murder, but unpremeditated." Begbie again yelled at them that he couldn't take that verdict, and threatened that if they didn't produce a verdict either of murder, manslaughter or acquittal before midnight, he would lock them up until Monday. The jurors hastily conferred, and reached a verdict of manslaughter.

Whelan, who had just twice heard himself declared guilty of murder, stood convicted of manslaughter. Begbie, who was convinced that Whelan had wilfully committed murder, said "I will protect you from the dogs—you shall not be torn to pieces by your indignant fellow citizens, but shall go from here to be made miserable, to be a slave for the rest of your life."

Whelan, as he was taken away, managed to speak to a *Colonist* reporter, saying that he had been so frightened he hadn't been able to account for what happened. "I didn't hear anything till I went to turn to go back across the street," he said, "and then I sees right in front of me two men in white with plug hats on." Begbie's words to Whelan—"never again will you be allowed to go on your drunken brawls"—were evidently not shared by the federal authorities, who, ten years later in 1901, pardoned him.

The Telephone Company

A typical B.C. Telephone Company exchange during the First World War years.

A little building on Trounce Alley was the location of B.C.'s first telephone exchange switchboard. Although first seen only as a novelty, or as a method of spreading gossip, the telephone quickly gained respectability in North America (much faster than in England), and "is a great public convenience, which, once adopted by a business house, will not be dispensed."

The telephone system was operated by Robert Burns McMicking—one of British Columbia's electrical pioneers. Born in Ontario, he came west with the Overlanders in the spring of 1862. McMicking was one of a small group which spurned the lure of the Cariboo gold diggings, and descended the Fraser River in canoes. Several were lost by drowning; the survivors included lumberman R.H. Alexander of Vancouver, Victoria Member of Parliament J.A. Mara, and Provincial Museum founder and curator "Jack" Fannin.

During the late 1860s and early 1870s, McMicking acted as superintendent of the Western Union telegraph line from New Westminster to Quesnel—the surviving piece of the Collins Overland Telegraph, which was to have connected London with New York via Siberia, but was abandoned following the successful laying of the transatlantic cable. A telegraph cable was laid to connect Victoria with the Portland-New Westminster line at Bellingham Bay and, in 1879, Victoria was linked with Nanaimo.

In January, 1878, following years of frustration with the underfinanced telegraph service (by then operated by the federal government), McMicking became the agent of the Bell Telephone Co. in B.C. With his small consignment of telephones, he hooked up the Pendray soapworks at Douglas and Humboldt with Jeffrey's store at Government and Yates, then connected the Victoria telegraph office with the *Colonist*. The effect was sensational—particularly on McMicking, who was fired from the government telegraph service at the end of March, 1880, due to his conflicting telephone interests.

Businessman Edgar Crow Baker, who had just formed the Victoria & Esquimalt Telephone Co. with five friends (A.A. Green, R.P. Rithet, E.A. McQuade, Capt. J.D. Warren, and James Innes) each contributing $500, offered McMicking a job. On May 5, the line to Esquimalt was completed, and poles were erected along the city's principal streets. The *Colonist* hyperbolized that a Rip Van Winkle, upon seeing all the posts with projecting arms, would describe Victoria as "a glorious place for Jack Ketch, where so many gallows-trees are needed." By the end of July, the *Colonist* suggested that "parties having news, or other information to communicate, will confer a favor by transmitting it to this office through the instrument of the nearest subscriber." Other prominent early customers were Theodore Davie and the police station. The Trounce Alley switchboard was installed to tie the system together.

McMicking, though manager of the V&E Telephone Co., had only about 50 subscribers to look after, so maintained his business activities as an electrical dealer and as the City of Victoria's electrician in charge of the generating and street lighting systems. By the 1890s, though, general acceptance of the telephone brought the need for large amounts of capital for expansion. As in the case of the B.C. Electric Railway Co., English investors from Yorkshire, under the banner of G.P. Norton's Yorkshire Guarantee & Securities Corp., provided the money. By 1898, Edgar Baker was able to sell his $500 one-sixth share for over $70,000! Nevertheless, the Yorkshire group lacked faith in the future of the telephone, and allowed their associate, William Farrell, and a group of minority Canadian shareholders to buy the system. The B.C. Telephone Company was thus formed in 1904, in an amalgamation of four regional telephone systems, after strenuous lobbying of the anti-monopolistic provincial legislature. Vancouver Island was connected with the mainland the following year.

A company called the International Telephone & Telegraph Company was organized in Washington, and laid a cable from Bellingham through the San Juan Islands to Telegraph Cove on Cadboro Bay. The first cable was a two-pair one. Business increased slowly at first, but was so substantial by 1911 that the company laid another one of seven pairs. There were 3,904 telephones in Victoria that year, just under one-fifth of the provincial total.

An automatic exchange was introduced into Victoria in 1930. At that time, there were five city telephone prefixes—Albion, Belmont, Colquitz, Empire and Garden. For years, the Victoria telephone company's main office was in the Temple Building at 521 Fort Street.

The Empress Hotel

The magnificent, stately Empress Hotel did for Victoria what the Chateau Frontenac did for Quebec City. With its completion in 1908, Victoria became an acceptable port of call for the Canadian Pacific's world-class cruises and first-class tourists. The *Colonist* described the Empress as a hotel which would "make the Western gateway of the great transcontinental system a fitting companion to the historic pile on the heights of Quebec." A more prosaic problem was also addressed—the fate of the stinking James Bay mudflats, which were filled to provide land for the hotel.

The Canadian Pacific had begun making moves into the Pacific Coast tourist market at the turn of the century; the company bought the Canadian Pacific Navigation Co. in 1901, thereby gaining control of much of the coastal shipping business, and had not denied a rumour that it might purchase the Driard Hotel. The two Victoria promoters of tourism Canadian Pacific-style were Capt. Troup of the CPN, and lawyer-politician Harry Barnard—both of whom were well ahead of their time in seeing the possibilities of closer, tourist-oriented connections between Vancouver, Seattle and Victoria. The possibility of being a CPR town like Quebec intrigued Victorians; nevertheless, the city needed revenue, so Troup and Barnard set out to prepare the citizens for a short-term economic sacrifice. Presentations were made to the Board of Trade, which agreed that the Douglas Gardens—part of the former governor's residence grounds on the south side of the mudflats—would be an ideal location. Concurrently, the newspaper was filled with James Bay horror stories about floating dead horses and soap lees from Pendray's soap factory, and the city Health Department warned children away due to the possibility of typhoid. A by-law was approved by the city voters, authorizing the construction of a causeway and the filling of the flats, but no plans were confirmed for the use of the new land.

Then, in June, 1902, Sir Thomas Shaughnessy, the CPR president, arrived in Victoria on his annual inspection tour. Presentations were made to him touting the advantages of a large CPR hotel, but he remained publicly non-committal. The next May, during a visit to the Driard, he said that the CPR didn't want any more hotels, and was having enough problems with its mountain hotels in Banff National Park, but that the company might reconsider if there were concessions on land, water and tax. Architect F.M. Rattenbury published in the newspaper the next day a detailed sketch of the Inner Harbour, showing the post office, a new Carnegie Library on the site of the Belmont building, a large CPR hotel, a college on the Douglas Gardens site, and his own legislative buildings on the far right.

This grand vision produced the desired effect. On August 24, alderman and butcher Lawrence Goodacre, seconded by Ross Bay Cemetery stonecutter and alderman Alex Stewart, called for a plebiscite to strike "an agreement with the CPR Co. for the erection of a tourist hotel at James Bay & to grant certain lands & exemptions in consideration thereof." The motion passed, and the next June, in order to clean up Kanaka Row and

Looking north towards the Empress conservatory, which, in this postcard, has been tinted green for visibility. Most of the beautiful gardens beside and behind the hotel have since been paved over to provide bus and automobile parking spaces. The hotel's first gardener was Arthur Robillard, who had been overseer and gardener for an estate in Normandy. He emigrated to Victoria shortly after the turn of the century, and tended grounds for the Pembertons, McBrides, Todds, Arbuthnots and Rithets. His work for Dr. Henry Esson Young, the Minister of Education, led him to Point Grey in the early twenties to lay out the UBC campus gardens, and from 1919-22 he put in the Alpine Garden at Butchart's. The garden at the Empress was perhaps most famous during the fifties, when Welshman A.F. Sanders and an eleven-man crew supervised it. There were 120 varieties of roses in the one-acre garden, including tea and moss roses, American pillars and "the newcomer, Ruth Alexander." Sanders planted 125 varieties of dahlias, all grown from cuttings, around the nine-hole putting green on the east side of the hotel.

Humboldt Street, the city bought out all the landowners there. On July 7, 1904, the city ratepayers voted 1205-46 to extend the tax-free status to that land.

The enthusiasm for Harry Barnard's role in the scheme helped get him elected mayor that year. Rattenbury was hired as architect, and had his plans for the hotel, reminiscent of the Chateau Frontenac and "beautiful in its magnificent stateliness," ready soon after. A forest of Australian gum pilings were driven 125 feet into the James Bay fill to support the structure.

Construction proceeded without delay, and the Empress opened on January 20, 1908, with Mrs. Stewart Gordon, the wife of the manager, signing the register first. It originally had 160 rooms, and was quickly ex-

The Crystal Gardens, on Douglas Street behind the Empress, was one of the few edifices built in Victoria in the twenties. Like the CPR coastal steamship terminal on Belleville (now the Undersea Gardens), the Crystal Gardens was built by the CPR to aid its tourist business. The idea was launched in 1921 by the Chamber of Commerce, and F.M. Rattenbury did sketches for an amusement centre with heated swimming pools, a ballroom, shops, galleries, and a greenhouse roof over a lush, tropical garden. The design and the effect inside, once it opened in 1924, were unmistakably modern and American. Its habituées, sporting cloche hats, silk stockings, feather boas, and cigarettes, arrived in automobiles to dance in what became Victoria's most fashionable nightspot.

panded with the addition of north and south wings in 1910 and 1913 respectively. Eventually, there were 570 guest rooms, including seven special suites and the royal suite, which had eight rooms, eight baths, and a serving pantry for the dining room. The hotel was decorated by Kate Reed, the wife of the hotel chain's manager-in-chief Hayter Reed.

Life at the Empress during the thirties continued the traditions of the just-passed "jazz age" and Victoria's versions of flappers. Parties, as described by writer Peter Stursberg, often became wild on dollar-a-mickey rye until broken up by "Four Eyes, the house dick." Couples BYO'd to the Empress without fear of police raids, unlike at other less protected clubs in the city. The Empress dinner dances, which cost two dollars a couple before the price went up by 50 cents in 1936, featured a three-course dinner of consommé, chicken à la king, and ice-cream parfait, followed by coffee. And, always, there was Billy Tickle and his orchestra, The Toe-Tappers, which expanded from three to eight pieces for the ballroom dances. Americans who wanted him to play the "Star Spangled Banner" and "God Bless America," were always refused. When misinformed Imperialists accused him of disrespect for only playing the first six bars of "God Save The King," Tickle produced a newspaper clipping

which said that it was incorrect to play the entire piece unless the sovereign was present in person (which he was, once, in 1939). Tickle played "Tell Me Tonight" for newlyweds, and "It's Later Than You Think" for wedding anniversaries, and did requests, like the one for a regular from Montreal who liked "I've Got a Lovely Bunch of Coconuts."

The other side of life at the Empress during the Depression was not so gay. The north wing was closed, and top floor rooms were offered for one dollar a day, which "brought in a lot of widows" who took breakfast in their rooms, skipped dinner but had the 35-cent afternoon tea, and entertained their friends in the lounges. One lady regularly ordered a pot of hot water and brought her own tea bag, and was tolerated by the management. Bridge teachers reserved parts of the lobby and music teachers used the pianos for lessons. One couple had a ritual of dinner at 6:15, followed by silent sitting on a chesterfield, at opposite ends, until the orchestra played "The King," then to bed.

One memorable person was John Rowlands, an English rugby player and coach of Victoria teams who composed the "British Columbia March"—and presented an autographed score to all his good friends. He occupied, for over 25 years, the same long-backed, tapestry-covered chair next to the grandfather clock in the lobby. He was "unusually posted on provincial affairs," and maintained his vigil in the seat all day when the legislature was in session.

To promote Victoria as a mid-winter tourist paradise, the CPR sponsored a February golf tournament at the Colwood course, with accommodation at the Empress. One winter there was a heavy snowfall, so the Georgian Room was converted into a nine-hole course, heavy rugs being set up with undulations for fairways and traps. The course was played with putters and the event was a great success. The snow fell a second year, and the course was set up again, but thereafter the CPR changed the golf tournament to April.

The Empress suffered along with Victoria in the tourist doldrums of the fifties. The CPR, which cut back its steamship service on the coast, publicly considered the abandonment of the hotel and, in the early sixties, floated a plan for its demolition and replacement with a motor-hotel. The boom in auto-tourism, spurred by the opening of the Swartz Bay-Tsawwassen ferry route in 1960, brought new visitors to the city, but forced the CPR to modernize the Empress. Before 1966, the hotel had its own direct-current power supply, installed when the hotel was built. (The steam-heat and generating plant, behind the hotel, had a 167-foot-high chimney, twelve feet across at the base with five-foot-thick walls, which was demolished in January, 1968.) There was only one alternating-current line down one wall of the hotel, giving television reception to the bar, executive suites and lounge. Every night, manager Les Parkinson distributed 160 radios and 25 sanitized electric shavers among the guests, for use in the strange d.c. plugs in the walls. The modernization program began in 1966.

The famous Boston ivy, which has covered the front façade of the hotel since the thirties, was all killed by the sudden Armistice Day frost in 1955, but has grown back since.

Churches

Victoria's skyline is still dominated by its church steeples. Christ Church on Cathedral Hill at Burdett and Quadra and its predecessor on the site of the Law Courts just to the west have commanded that hillside for over a century. The other massive churches of downtown Victoria—Metropolitan United at Quadra and Pandora, St. Andrew's Presbyterian at Douglas and Broughton, and St. Andrew's Roman Catholic at View and Blanshard, date from the 1890s, an era when prosperous Victorians put wealth and effort into their religion. Businesslike Vancouver, which was little more than wooden shacks at that time, has few churches of comparable size and splendour.

The Anglicans' activities in Victoria became mired in a series of controversies after the death by drowning of Rev. Robert Staines, Fort Victoria's "man of frills." Staines's replacement was Edward Cridge, a cello-playing, pugnacious, evangelical missionary who disliked the formal liturgy of his Cambridge and London colleagues. Cridge's views met with the favour of James Douglas, who built the Victoria District Church, also known as Christ Church, in 1856, to serve the local populace. Cridge's appointment and the appropriation of public funds to pay his salary prompted a denominational foofaraw which lasted a year. Although the Roman Catholics under Rev. Modeste Demers stayed uninvolved, a Protestant missionary complained about the favouritism. The attack was taken up in 1858 by de Cosmos and others, who felt that a state church—the Church of England—had no place in Victoria. Eventually, even the glebe on Church Hill was reduced by the Island Assembly to less than 30 acres. (Governor Douglas didn't make the same mistake on the mainland, where he made land grants to four denominations.)

Four years after Christ Church opened, the Rev. George Hills—not too fondly nicknamed "Beau Brummell" for his elegant, aristocratic manners—arrived in Victoria. Hills's influence on Miss Angela Burdett-Coutts, who had launched the Anglican Diocese of British Columbia with a donation of £15,000, resulted in the erection of the "Iron St. John's" at Douglas and Fisgard—the current site of the Hudson's Bay Company store.

Iron St. John's was paid for by Burdett-Coutts, prefabricated of corrugated iron in England and sent around the Horn to Victoria. Hills thought there wouldn't be enough trees for a proper cathedral, and erected the Gothic edifice—"the height of Victorian fashion," according to architectural historian Barry Downs—in five months in 1860. Acoustically, it was a disaster: to those inside, rain sounded like "machine gun fire" and wind caused a "moaning and shrieking" with which only the organ could compete; in later years, even the passage of a tram made the church service inaudible. The interior decoration, as one parishioner recalled, had been done by the Rev. Jenns, "in stencils in the queerest shapes and brilliant yellows and blues." Following the iron church's demolition in 1913, a new St. John's was built just up the street.

Meanwhile, the first Christ Church burned down in 1869, and three years later was replaced by a fine, tall, wooden church designed by surveyor, engineer and lieutenant-governor Joseph Trutch. At the consecration, under the direction of Bishop Hills, the Archdeacon of Vancouver (Oregon Territory) spoke of how parishioners' lives would be enriched at the new cathedral by an increased devotion to formal ceremony and ritual. Rev. Cridge jumped to his feet, and addressing his "dearly beloved friends," said that "this is the first time ritualism has been preached here, and I pray God Almighty it may be the last." Obviously, the congregation was with him, as witnessed by "the clapping of hands and stamping of feet." Cridge was expelled from the Anglican Church by Hills, and established the Reformed Episcopal "Church of Our Lord" at Humboldt and Blanshard, which today backs onto the Canadian Pacific Lawn Bowling Club and the Crystal Gardens.

Cridge's new congregation and supporters were practically a who's who of nineteenth century Victoria. James Douglas's funeral was there in 1877; Judge Begbie, a prominent member of the St. John's congregation, gave Cridge small gifts of money and attempted to help him pay his legal costs following the Church of England's successful action against him and his renegade congregation; Judge A.F. Pemberton, the warden of the first Christ Church, became an active member of the Reformed Episcopal; J.S. Helmcken counted Cridge as one of his best friends; merchant James Angus developed "a frightful distaste for bishops who pretended to be Church of England," and crossed horns with them constantly; many of Victoria's businessmen, like stationer T.N. Hibben, contributed funds towards the building of the new church. Steadfast Anglicans included the Works, Pearses, Trutches, O'Reillys, Hetts, Mackenzies (of Craigflower), Tyrwhitt-Drakes, Grays (John Hamilton), Creases, Tolmies, Walkems, J.D. Pembertons, Finlaysons, Richards, Todds, and Priors.

Cathedral Hill is the site today of a third Christ Church, begun in 1926. The parklike block to the north is Pioneer Square, where many of the early Hudson's Bay Co. explorers, like John Work, are buried.

The Presbyterians also had their difficulties, in particular a dispute between Rev. Hall and Rev. Somerville over property, which resulted in the establishment of a new St. Andrew's Presbyterian and the splitting of the congregation. The St. Andrew's church on Douglas, erected in 1890, is the product of their happy reunion. The most prominent Presbyterian families in Victoria were the James Dunsmuirs, the Barnards, the Robsons, and the Nesbitts.

The Catholic church in Victoria started with the 1858 arrival of the Rev. Modeste Demers, the Bishop of Vancouver (Oregon), and four sisters from the Institute of St. Ann. The little St. Ann's school, which has since been moved behind Dr. Helmcken's house in the Provincial Museum gardens on Elliott Street, offered a course of studies to the white settlers in the colony, with subjects ranging from grammar, rhetoric and history to bookkeeping and needlework. Demers also built St. Joseph's hospital and St. Ann's Academy at Humboldt and Blanshard, just east of

Rev. Ephraim Evans, with his colleagues—the Revs. White, Robson, and Browning—established Methodism in Victoria at the Pandora Avenue church (at Broad Street), where James Douglas laid the cornerstone on August 15, 1859. The Methodists led the struggle to maintain temperance (page 94) and the Lord's Day, especially during the First World War years and the twenties when many of the traditional institutions of society were threatened. Their political ally was William Marchant (1853-1934), an early prohibitionist who became mayor following the Joe North-Mayor Porter circus before the 1921 election. Marchant's political Waterloo was his antagonism to the anti-Blue-Sunday petition of May, 1922; he was defeated by Reginald Hayward at the next election. He operated Marchant & Futcher oriental importers on Fort Street. His Liberal connections (he ran against Edward Prior in 1891) got him a customs inspector job from 1897-1921. He was one of the few in Victoria to speak out against the Boer War, lobbied for the Carnegie Library grant, and also managed to be Victoria's chess champion for many years.

Bishop Edward Cridge of the Reformed Episcopalian Church, photographed here at his lily-decorated Easter-time pulpit, had a voice, wrote Emily Carr, "as gentle as if it came from the moon." Born in Devonshire in 1817, he was ordained in the Church of England and noticed the newspaper advertisement seeking a replacement at Fort Victoria for the drowned Rev. Staines. After his split with Bishop Hills, he went to Ottawa and was consecrated Bishop of the Reformed Episcopalian Church.

Dr. W.J. Sipprell's pastorate at Metropolitan Methodist was the longest in the church's history. He campaigned relentlessly during Prohibition to prevent a return to the abuses of the liquor years.

Few Victoria churches have suffered so ignominious a fate as the old St. Andrews' Presbyterian at the northeast corner of Courtney and Gordon streets. After the new, larger church was completed at the corner of Douglas and Broughton streets (visible in the background), old St. Andrews had a variety of tenants, including the Province newspaper and this auto garage.

Cridge's Church of Our Lord.

The Methodist presence dates from the arrival, on February 10, 1859, of Rev. Ephraim Evans, Rev. Ebenezer Robson and Rev. Edward White from eastern Canada. They held their first service three days later in the Police Court room. "It was a great failure, but I did the best I could," wrote White. "The room, 22x32, was crowded to excess." Robson, the brother of future Premier John Robson, started missionary work among the Chinese in a vacant saloon at the corner of Government and Herald. The congregation, including the Spencers, Pendrays, and Carrs was able to move from its first church at the southwest corner of Pandora and Broad to its present church in 1890. Victoria's Methodists, led by Dr. W.J. Sipprell, were leaders in the People's Prohibition Association during the Great War years, and contributed to the anti-vice "Hall-North Defence Testimonial Fund" in the early twenties.

There was little observance of the Lord's Day in Victoria before the 1870s. All the Sabbath laws were enacted on the mainland and, even after union, Victoria continued to ignore them. Then, in 1873, 142 Victoria residents led by George Jay and A.J. Langley successfully petitioned the government for the enforcement of all the "blue laws." Premier Walkem's counsel advised that all the English Blue Laws, dating back to Charles I, were in force.

The city's observance of the Lord's Day grew lax again after the turn of the century. A campaign led by the Women's Christian Temperance Union and the Lord's Day Alliance, with Noah Shakespeare as spokesman, resulted in a plebiscite in January, 1909. It was argued that, during the tourist season, thousands of people would get a bad impression of the city by seeing so many business places open on Sundays. The referendum passed 1,198 to 1,090, and the city was shut tight on Sundays through 1913. The following March, cigar and fruit stands began to agitate for equal rights with the indoor hotel stands which had been operating on Sundays. The former were allowed to open, "if not too ostentatious a parade of their actions is made."

The Police Board started active prosecutions under the Lord's Day Act in the early 1920s. The Anti-Blue-Sunday League, led by Herbert Kent, managed to get a Sunday-closing question on a civic plebiscite on May 13, 1922, which was seeking an additional $110,000 to complete the Johnson Street bridge (the provincial government had initiated it, but had not allocated enough funds). Prohibitionist Mayor William Marchant, backed by most of the city's ministers, urged citizens to stay home to kill the effectiveness of the plebiscite, and predicted that fewer than 2,500 would vote. To his chagrin, by an overwhelming margin of 3,853 to 509, the citizens voted against enforced Sunday closings. Marchant's credibility never recovered, and he was defeated by Reginald Hayward in the civic elections at the end of the year.

The Rev. Clem Davies gave "prophetic scriptural lectures" from the City Temple in Victoria after his arrival in 1922, and started CFCT radio (later called CJVI), the first standard broadcasting service in Western Canada, to spread his gospel six nights a week and three times on Sunday. Born in England in 1890, he studied at an American bible college before moving west. Like Detroit's Father Coughlin, he became identified with "crypto-fascist" political trends in the thirties. He argued against the Canadian radio commission, claiming that all thought in Canada would be controlled from Catholic Montreal. He moved his ministry to Vancouver in 1937, and, dressed in white tie and tails, held "outdoor church" evangelical meetings for crowds of 10,000 on the old Arena site. He made international headlines in 1938 when he claimed that the Duke of Windsor had abdicated because he was drugged and "hypnotized by an international gang of Jesuits seeking to undermine the British throne." Like many of his colleagues, he gravitated to Los Angeles, opening a ministry there in 1940 to give the "Kingdom Message," including guidance to "blow Japan off the face of the earth." After the war, he hired a train and toured North America with Arak the Great, a mystic healer from Iran. He died of malaria in Los Angeles in 1951.

Victoria Wilson

On the hill behind the Empress Hotel, on the site of the Chateau Victoria, there used to stand a rambling, white-painted house with a three-storey tower—a landmark on the edge of downtown until the early 1970s. In the Chateau Victoria, a lounge called "Victoria Jane's" commemorates the house's eccentric owner—Victoria Jane Wilson. The penthouse restaurant, called "The Parrot House," recalls Miss Wilson's pets and the bizarre legacy she left them upon her death in 1949.

Victoria Jane Wilson was a granddaughter of Alexander Munro of the Hudson's Bay Company—thus, Mrs. Elizabeth Rithet was her aunt. Her father, James Keith Wilson, made a lot of money in real estate, and built his mansion on Churchway Avenue on the hill just above Douglas. ("Churchway" was changed to Burdett Avenue, to honour the generosity of the Baroness Angela Burdett-Coutts, the patroness of the Anglican diocese which built Christ Church at the top of the hill.) The grand house was gradually encroached upon by smaller houses, and overlooked the odorous shamble of Kanaka Row and the James Bay mudflats. Miss Wilson enclosed the house more and more as the city expanded around her. There were fine Oriental gardens and lily pools behind the stone wall and high hedges, but she never entertained and wouldn't let anyone onto the grounds.

Like her aunt, she purchased an electric brougham—in her case, a $7,000 Hupp-Yeatts from Plimley's in 1909—but drove it only 45 miles. It had less than one charge on its battery. She developed a strong dislike for the sight of the man who came occasionally to fill the house's fuel oil tank, so had a tunnel-like alley built for him, to connect the street with the house; the tunnel made it impossible to get the car out of the garage. She collected closets full of exotic clothing, but never went out in it.

When she was five years old, in 1882, she was given a parrot named Louis, which was already supposedly 18 years old. The parrot, and another 60 exotic birds she collected, outlived her, and her 1949 will left a large sum of money for their care. Yue Wah Wong (also called Ah Wong)—the gardener while she was alive—was hired by the executor at $200 a month to care for Louis, which he did from 1949 until his death in 1966. The parrot thrived on brandy, walnuts, almonds and hard-boiled eggs, and was reputedly moved to a secret new home in 1967 to discourage kidnapping and ransom attempts.

The provisions for Louis were a bizarre sideline to Miss Wilson's will, which generously endowed a number of Victoria charities, and left $250,000 to Royal Jubilee Hospital. The Burdett Street home became a rooming house, and was modified and renovated repeatedly, so that final pictures of it look little like its simple profile at the turn of the century. Around 1970, the Pacific Club expressed an interest in purchasing and renovating it, but the plans never materialized, and it was demolished two years later.

Looking east from near the corner of Humboldt and Burdett, around the turn of the century. The hillside was dominated by the white-painted, three-storey tower of Victoria Jane Wilson's house, now the site of the Chateau Victoria. At the top of the hill, on the site of today's Law Courts, stood Christ Church Cathedral. In the early days, Wilson's few neighbours were people like the Wilson-Browns, who ran the high-society "Church Bank House" girls school at the northwest corner of Rae (Courtney) and Blanshard. By the turn of the century, though, more modest interests had intruded—the house on the near corner backed onto a greenhouse operation, and both sides of Rae (Courtney) behind Wilson's were home to stone-cutting and lumber-chopping operations. "The Corner Grocery" (on the corner in the middle of the picture) was located on the site of today's Executive House). W.J. Pendray's soap works and paint plant on Humboldt Street had water access at their back doors onto slimy James Bay—Pendray was bought out, and moved to Laurel Point, following the Empress Hotel plebiscite. No photograph of Victoria Jane Wilson appears to have survived.

Pharmacist Bert Emery, like many other Victorians, couldn't resist photographing the city paralyzed under the "big snow" of February, 1916. The photograph above was taken looking south on Douglas Street from Pandora, where Emery was employed at Terry's Drug Store. Victoria got about four feet of snow in the first three days of February, and a strong wind kept piling it higher and higher until the drifts in some places reached ten feet. Streetcars were stuck and stranded, and B.C. Electric used a snowplow-equipped locomotive pulling a flat car (visible ahead of the streetcar in the picture) to deliver supplies to isolated parts of Esquimalt and Oak Bay. Fortunately, Victoria was full of soldiers preparing to go to the Western Front, so there was enough manpower to dig out the streets and sidewalks. Life returned more or less to normal on February 11. B.C. Electric was so pleased with the help the soldiers had given that all men in uniform rode free for a month.

The Smallpox War

The most heated Victoria vs. Vancouver battle occurred in the summer of 1892, when Vancouver "quarantined" Victoria following a smallpox outbreak on the Island. Premier Theodore Davie, who was having the fight of his life making Victoria the permanent capital, found it even more difficult to gather pro-Victoria political support on the mainland.

The first smallpox outbreak in Victoria was noted in March, 1862. It mainly affected the "depraved and dissolute" Indians living on the outskirts of the city. Thirty of seventy Indians in a camp on Ogden Point died, as did the white policeman who was helping bury the bodies. It eventually ran its course, "for want of material to work upon." A decade later, the mail ship *Prince Alfred* hove to off Ogden Point, flying the yellow flag. A young girl named Bertha Whitney was afflicted. She was sent with her family to George Nias's vacant farmhouse at Holland Point, on the Beckley Farm property, where she died; a small memorial at the Holland Point park on Dallas Road commemorates her. The other passengers—hissing and throwing old potatoes at the health officials—passed a nine-day quarantine at Macauley Point.

Another smallpox scare, in 1889, involved a passenger on the Canadian Pacific Navigation Co.'s steamer *Premier*, but passed with little incident. In late April, 1892, however, a Chinese man on the *Empress of Japan* came down with smallpox. All the Chinese aboard were quarantined, and the liner continued on to Vancouver. In early July, a man named Hilton, who lived on the Cadboro Bay Road and had been in the Orient and on the ship, came down with the disease. Two days later, a prostitute named Ella, who lived in the red-light district on Dupont Street on the edge of Vancouver's Chinatown, became very ill. She told health officials she had got the disease in Victoria.

By eleven o'clock on the morning of July 12, following panicked meetings of the Vancouver Board of Trade and city officials, the Board of Health and port authorities declared a quarantine against Victoria. Seattle, New Westminster, and Nanaimo cooperated with Vancouver to shut off all the traffic. The first ship to attempt to land from Victoria was the CPN's *Yosemite*—it was met by a barrage of water from firehoses directed onto its gangplank to prevent anyone from disembarking. The CPN promptly applied to Mr. Justice Crease in Victoria for an injunction against the Vancouver quarantine order, arguing that anyone who had been vaccinated, and had complied with the health regulations in Victoria, should be able to go ashore. Crease granted the injunction, but the Vancouver authorities completely ignored it.

Any steamer that attempted to land cargo had to submit to a complete fumigation; moreover, any passengers who had faith in Crease's injunction and attempted to go ashore through the fumes of burning sulphur, were tossed into the quarantine building at the City Hospital. On the 19th, Victoria *Daily News* reporter Freddy Laing journeyed to Vancouver on the *Yosemite* and, with seven others, marched down the gangplank "into the arms of the waiting policemen." The *Daily News* ran a quick dispatch, entitled "They Gobbled Our Fred—And He's In Quarantine." The next day, a dispatch from Laing was spirited out of Vancouver and appeared in Victoria under the headline "They Are Half Starved." Laing wrote that the accommodation consisted of half a dozen up-ended nail kegs, later supplemented with two hard chairs, and that the food, "a large bucket of porridge, a bucket of coffee, several loaves of bread and other things in keeping were deposited upon the floor at the entrance." No towels or soap were provided.

The *Vancouver World* responded, and increased Victoria's indignation, by lampooning Laing's articles as "The Wail of a Vag," claiming that he had answered an ad for "200 tramps and vags (vagrants) who would like free room & board at Vancouver's expense for 14 days." Libel threats, and half-hearted apologies, followed. One man—a Bengal army doctor returning to England on furlough—attempted an escape, and flattened a guard before being tackled by some of Vancouver's Finest.

Meanwhile, on July 26, the sheriff at Vancouver, responding to a contempt of court order from Justice Crease, arrested Mayor Cope, city solicitor A. St.George Hamersley, and the city health officer and detained them at the Hotel Vancouver pending transportation to Victoria. The trio were released on July 28 and required only to pay court costs, as Crease felt they were acting in the spirit of their civic duty. They were heroes in Vancouver. Laing and the other "prisoners" were also released, though the English doctor was detained until he paid a fine for assault.

In Victoria, meanwhile, yellow flags flew from many windows that summer. Families moved to the seashore at Gonzales, Oak Bay and Esquimalt and, after they got used to camping (many had no equipment, and their Chinese servants didn't like sleeping in tents), had a wonderful summer. Doctors advised everyone in the city to clear out, and hotels in Seattle and Banff were full of refugees. The epidemic passed with the summer.

(An earlier incident, unrelated to smallpox, involved Vancouver Mayor (1886-1887) Malcolm MacLean, who stood on a pile of boxes on the Evans, Coleman & Evans wharf in Vancouver, "like Liberty on her pedestal," and warned *Princess Louise* passengers of the danger of night travel to Victoria. The mayor then offered to find all passengers hotel accommodation in Vancouver. He made a second attempt the following day to boost Vancouver's tourist revenue, this time actually on board the *Princess Louise*, but was ordered off by the mate, who was carrying a large stick.)

Victoria Harbour

(Preceding page) Looking southwest from Yates Street, toward Ormond Street, in the early 1880s. The little wooden building is the colonial schoolhouse, built in 1853, and from 1876 to 1882 the province's first high school. Built practically in the woods on "Minnie's Meadow," amid wildflowers, willow swamps and oak trees, the school was replaced in 1876 by the brick public school in the background; in 1882, the high school was relocated in a brick addition attached to the east wall of the public school, and the old schoolhouse was demolished three years later (no photograph has survived of the little schoolhouse; a rough sketch was made in 1917 by a former pupil). A new high school, later known as Girls' Central, was built in 1902 at the east end of the school reserve, facing Fernwood Street; the 1876 public school became known as Boys' Central. These buildings were demolished in the 1950s for the construction of Central Junior High School. Victoria High School moved in 1914 to its current site at Spring Ridge, a few blocks to the north. From 1902 to 1915, when the University of B.C. opened in Vancouver, Victoria High School was affiliated with McGill University in Montreal; called Victoria College, it provided the first year of university arts education (Second Year Arts was offered beginning in 1907). Victoria College was later revived at "Craigdarroch."

Victoria's Inner Harbour has been, since the earliest days, crowded with ships of all descriptions. Only the big liners—especially the white *Empress*es of the Canadian Pacific Railway—took on their passengers outside the harbour entrance until R.P. Rithet's Outer Wharf was completed in 1891 at the western end of Ontario Street. The Number Two streetcar line terminated at Rithet's, and brought the disembarking passengers from their ships into the centre of the city. A tremendous number of businesses quickly located nearby, some with their own wharves and railway spurs. Pendray's Bapco paint plant and soap factory moved from James Bay in the early years of the century to Laurel Point; adjoining it were the Bullman-Allison lumber company, Bannerman & Horne Hay & Feed, the Victoria Chemical Company, and Brackman-Ker Milling. (In the twenties, airmail seaplanes used the Chemical company's wharf for loading. The first airmail letter from Victoria was from Mayor Porter to the mayor of Seattle, on May 10, 1919. Pilot Bob Rideout, a twice-shot-down veteran of World War I, had to land his Curtiss "Jenny" in a pea-field on Whidbey Island when he ran out of fuel. The local army detachment discouraged souvenir hunters while Rideout found more fuel, and the letter was delivered on the second day.)

The Inner Harbour was plugged with sidewheelers, sternwheelers and screw-steamers, dominated by the fleet of the Canadian Pacific Navigation Co. The shoreline was continuous wharfage for companies like the the Hudson's Bay Company and Turner & Beeton. Wharf Street had filled up with wholesale houses by the 1870s. In the twenties, enterprising Victorians used the warehouses and docks for importing, storing and loading liquor for illegal shipment to the "dry" United States*. Port of Victoria statistics in 1922 showed a sudden increase in deep-sea clearances (400 more than the previous year), attributed to the "mosquito fleet" with manifests stamped for Ensenada. The *Jessie*, owned by the famous navigator Capt. Voss, was a regular transporter, as were many converted motor-torpedo boats, yachts, and rusty steam-packets.

After 1901, when the CPN was purchased by the Canadian Pacific Railway Co., the shoreline in front of the legislative buildings and west to Laurel Point was occupied by the wharves and sheds of the CPR coastal service, connecting Victoria with the railway mainline at Vancouver. Other ships linked with the Northern Pacific at Seattle, and the Union Pacific at Portland. Regular connections were made with San Francisco, and with the myriad of little ports to the north. By the 1950s, changing travel habits—the modern desire to move in relatively straight lines with few delays, the popularity of automobiles, and the sheer numbers of people on the move—outdated most of them.

*Rumrunning was legal—or at least not illegal—and the customs officials turned a blind eye to it. See pages 58, 94 and 95 in this book, and pages 220 and 221 of *Vancouver The Way It Was*. On June 24, 1922, Senators G.H. Barnard and R.F. Green in the Canadian Senate blocked a B.C. attempt to ban private importation of liquor. This helped not only the rumrunners, but the local bootleggers, making B.C. "the moral sink-hole of the Dominion," in the words of *The Prohibition Bulletin*.

The triangle run between Victoria, Vancouver, and Seattle—with luxurious, leisurely steamships allowing pleasant stopovers—was one of the first to go. (The triangle run has since been revived a few times, most recently in 1985 with jetfoils providing a service not much slower than the harbour-to-harbour floatplanes. The "new" *Princess Marguerite*, brought to the coast in 1949 ostensibly to revive the triangle run, was saved from the wrecker in the early seventies by the provincial government, and plies the Victoria-Seattle run as an excursion ship during the summer.)

Captain John Irving's Canadian Pacific Navigation Co. was founded in 1883 with capital from the Dunsmuirs, Rithets, Wards, and other prominent Vancouver Island families. It had a fourteen-vessel fleet which included the famed sidewheeler *Princess Louise* and the old East Coast Mail Line steamers *Maud* and *Wilson G. Hunt*. The *Yosemite*, a former Sacramento River sidewheeler with a walking beam "that was the delight of small boys," was first put on the Burrard Inlet run on July 4, 1886, when 700 Victoria excursionists went to Port Moody to watch the first train arrive. The service prospered, and the famous *Islander*, with its red plush and stained-glass-decorated staterooms, was launched on the Clyde

The Dallas Hotel, on Dallas Road opposite today's Ogden Point docks, was a popular spot for farewell parties. Its observation tower provided a clear view past Race Rocks; in the early days before Rithet's Outer Wharves opened, the night porter awakened travellers at the sight of a ship's light and rowed them out. The hotel operated from 1891 to 1915. Torn down in 1928, it was doomed by the new mobility of the motorcar and the ease of steamship navigation into Rithet's and, later, Ogden Point.

LITHOGRAPH FROM VICTORIA THE QUEEN CITY

in 1888 (it sank in 1901, after hitting an iceberg near Skagway). It was soon joined by the *Charmer*, originally launched in San Francisco as the *Premier*, which was rammed by a collier and beached at Point No Point in 1892. Relatives of the dead and injured had her held for damages, but Captain Irving supposedly refloated her at night and got away "from under the eyes of the U.S. marshall." The *Islander* and *Charmer* alternated on the Vancouver-Victoria run, and made some trips directly to Seattle; their success caused Seattle ship-owners to fight for a share of the traffic.

A number of luxurious steamers were built by the CPR during the following decades, including the *Princess Beatrice*, the *Princess Victoria*, the *Princess Charlotte*, the night-boats *Princess Alice* and *Princess Adelaide*, the *Princess Joan* and *Princess Elizabeth* (both sold to Greek interests in the 1960s), the *Princess Kathleen* (which hit a reef and sunk in Alaska), the *Princess Sophia* (which ran aground in Lynn Canal in 1918 during a hurricane and sunk two days later, drowning 343 people), and the first *Princess Marguerite* (torpedoed and sunk in the Mediterranean on April 17, 1942).

The CPR commenced its triangle service in early 1908, first with the *Princess Victoria*, which offered a $1.25 round-trip to Seattle, leaving at 10 p.m. daily; in June, it added the *Princess Royal*, with a morning departure, to the run. Seattle interests, under the banner of the Puget Sound Navigation Co., a subsidiary of the coastal and Alaskan Black Ball line, ran the S.S. *Iroquois* and *Chippewa* from the Evans, Coleman & Evans wharves in Victoria and Vancouver; on June 15, they cut their triangle round-trip rate to one dollar. The next day, the CPR matched it. On July 11, the CPR cut its rate to 50 cents, which was matched by the Black Ball line. On the 28th, the CPR's rate dropped to two-bits for the *Princess Royal*, which was also matched. The two companies continued nose-to-nose with the 25-cent rate until October 24, when the CPR suddenly raised fares to $2. The *Chippewa* kept its 25-cent fare until the following May 19, when the two companies agreed to end their rate war, and fares promptly went to $3 one-way or $5 round-trip.

Business was booming everywhere, and competition quickly arrived in the form of the Grand Trunk Pacific Coast Steamship Co. Ltd., founded in 1909 as a subsidiary of the transcontinental railway which was building cross-country toward its Prince Rupert terminus. Its first ship, the S.S. *Prince Rupert*, arrived in Victoria from England in June, 1910, and commenced a weekly schedule, calling at Seattle, Victoria, Vancouver, Prince Rupert and Stewart. Later, the S.S. *Prince George* arrived at the coast, and a twice-weekly service was offered. Following the collapse of the Grand Trunk Pacific Railway, and its absorption into the Canadian National system, the steamship service was reorganized; the Victoria and Seattle stops were discontinued, and the ships began a coastal and Alaskan cruise service under the CNR's flag. The CNR made an attempt, in 1930 on the eve of the Depression, to uproot the CPR from its entrenched domination of the triangle run, and brought the twin-screw, 22-knot luxury liners *Prince Henry*, *Prince David* and *Prince Robert*—with air conditioning and foam mattresses—to the coast. The service only lasted a year. The

Prince Robert served as royal yacht during the visit of King George VI and Queen Elizabeth in 1939, before all three liners were commandeered by the Admiralty for war service. The *Prince George* burned at Ketchikan at 1945, and a new *Prince George*, which cruised Alaska waters until the early eighties, was launched in 1948 at Yarrows in Esquimalt.

The years before World War II were the heyday for the CPR midnight boats. One night boat arrived in Victoria at 7 a.m., and passengers disembarked for breakfast in the Empress. "Everyone sleeps in our beds," said the advertising slogan. The Prince of Wales, Gary Cooper and Katharine Hepburn were amongst those who did. A trip on the midnight boat could also be an escape from the tight confines of home: the Victoria High School rugby team, for a great portion of one night in December, 1909, were guilty of language and rowdyism which would be "a disgrace to a bawdy house," according to a complaint from a passenger in the next cabin. During the war years, painted grey and equipped with guns and armour, the midnight boats ran without lights for fear of prowling Japanese submarines. Soldiers stationed in Victoria complained that they were not allowed to take the Sunday night boat back from Vancouver following their 48-hour furloughs; as it was "not essential travel," their tickets were stamped "Not For The Midnight Boat," so they had to catch earlier sailings and sacrifice valuable hours of their leave.

Tourists on the triangle run caught the *Princess Victoria* in Seattle in the morning, often with over a thousand fellow passengers, and had a couple of hours to stop over in Victoria—long enough to wander through the shops and take the tally-ho through Beacon Hill Park. The ship then departed for Vancouver, arriving at seven in the evening, and making connections with trains for the CPR's Rocky Mountain resorts and points east.

In 1948, Puget Sound Navigation Co. bought out the Black Ball Ferries line, and, four years later, bought the old *City of Sacramento* ferry to compete with the CPR's *Princess Pat* on the Vancouver-Nanaimo run. Renamed the *Kahloka*, she went into service in June, 1953, and was the first west-coast ferry to accommodate all highway vehicles. The CPR at that time offered five daily trips to Victoria—three of which had a coach connection from Nanaimo. Pacific Stage Lines began its through bus to Victoria, via Nanaimo in December, 1953, with two round trips daily and a one-way fare of $5.45. Black Ball, which also ran smaller steamers on the B.C. coast, bought out the old Gulf Island Ferry Co. from Gavin Mouat in 1954, moved its Victoria-Port Angeles ferry M.S. *Chinook* to the Vancouver-Nanaimo run in 1955, and took over the Bowen Island run from Union Steamships the following year.

Victoria was clearly being superseded as the Island's transportation centre by Nanaimo. "It is a dead-end port," said one CPR source. The Victoria city council put pressure on the CPR early in 1958 to recommence its Sidney-Steveston car ferry, to save motorists the long drive up to Nanaimo. That May, the Seafarers' International Union and Canadian Merchant Service Guild went on strike, and by early June the Island was completely cut off from the mainland, with no Black Ball or CPR ferries

Captain John Irving's Canadian Pacific Navigation Company dominated the coastal steamship business before the turn of the century. Irving (1854-1936) was born in Portland, and moved to New Westminster in 1858 with his father William, a renowned steamboat captain. At sixteen, he began working for his father, then took over the business two years later when the latter died. In 1883, he founded the Canadian Pacific Navigation Co. with $500,000 capital from Victoria families, including the Dunsmuirs and the Rithets, and built a number of coastal steamers, amongst them the R.P. Rithet, Princess Louise, Maude, Yosemite, and Premier. He sold the CPN to the Canadian Pacific Railway in 1901. He was married to Alexander Munro's daughter Jane—thus, R.P. Rithet was his brother-in-law. They lived in James Bay, at the southwest corner of Michigan and Menzies streets (now Irving Park).

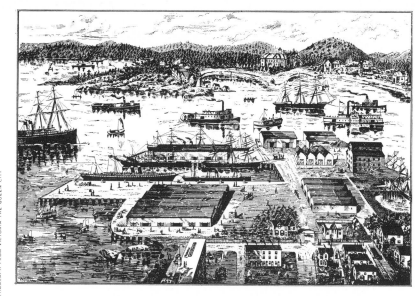

Rithet's Outer Wharf, at the western end of Ontario Street in James Bay, provided the first dock for ocean-going vessels. The view across the harbour entrance in this 1891 etching shows the beginnings of the army barracks on Work Point.

The Brackman & Ker Milling Co. warehouses were built a stone's throw to the north of Rithet's Outer Wharves. David R. Ker was born in Victoria in 1862, "where he was educated in the public schools," and learned the flour milling business in San Francisco and at the Saanich Mills, where he entered into partnership with the German-born Mr. Brackman. Their five-storey plant, with boiler and engine house attached, had five runs of stones on the main floor to grind the different cereals, and a series of bins and elevators on the floors above run solely by "automatic contrivances." Brackman & Ker's main competition was the Victoria Rice and Flour Mills Company at 1900 Store Street (now Capital Iron), the owner of the Thermopylae, a sailing barque which brought rice from Bangkok, Saigon and Hong Kong for grinding, then returned it as flour for sale to ports in the Far East.

Alexander Roland Milne was collector of customs for the Port of Victoria. He was a brother of Dr. G.L. Milne, the physician and businessman (page 105). He was appointed Collector of Customs and Controller of Chinese for the Port of Victoria in 1890; later, his brother (who was a Liberal) received the latter position. Alexander Milne married Annie Frye, the widow of one of his predecessors in the customs department.

that May.

Ironically, the major loser from the government's decision to get into the ferry business was not the CPR. It was TCA—Trans Canada Airlines—whose short-hop DC-3 service to the Pat Bay airport lost half its passenger traffic.

One of the most important industries in Victoria in the 1880s and early 1890s was pelagic (open water) sealing. Victoria interests had $780,000 invested in boats and equipment—a fleet of about 50 schooners, with more than 500 Indian hunters and 200 canoes—a common sight at anchor in the Inner Harbour and along Selkirk Water.

Originally, fur traders on the west coast were after sea otters, worth $20-$30 each, but hunted the seals—worth less than a dollar, as they were so easy to catch. The unlimited hunting brought the sea otter close to extinction, and in 1821 Russia attempted to ban all foreign vessels from approaching within 100 miles of the coast north of 51 degrees. The dispute which followed was settled by treaties with the United States and Great Britain in 1824 and 1825, respectively (the southern boundary of Russian America was then fixed at 54 degrees, 40 minutes, leading to the famous Fifty-four-forty disputes of the 1840s, page 11).

In 1867, the U.S. purchased Russian America (Alaska), and granted a sealing monopoly to a U.S. company which closed the Pribilof Islands to outsiders. Only the pelagic sealing was left. The previous year, Hugh MacKay had made the first attempt to seal on the open water in the schooner *Ino* from Victoria. The seals were either swimming or sleeping on the surface of the water, sometimes more than 30 miles from shore. Initially they were killed with spears by the native crew in canoes, then with rifles, finally with shotguns. Obviously, thousands sank and were lost, but the typical schooner took home about 2,000 skins in a season. By 1883, the schooners were pursuing the diminishing seal herd as far as the Bering Sea, led by the American *City of San Diego* (notorious 40 years later as a rumrunner) and Captain Jacobson's *Mary Ellen* out of West Bay in Victoria (page 157). Although the Alaska Commercial Company held the U.S. land monopoly, it saw its profits diminishing because the herd was intercepted before it got to the Pribilofs.

In 1886, the U.S. decided to take action to protect the monopoly's interests. The U.S. revenue cutter *Corwin* was sent to seize all vessels, flying U.S. and British flags, sealing in the Bering Sea, even though it was part of the high seas. Three Canadian schooners were seized and towed to Oonalaska for trial—they were beached and stripped of their supplies, riggings, and skins; the captains and mates were fined $500 and $300, respectively, and given a month in jail. The other Victoria sealers hurried away, but returned the following year. More were seized—20 in total in the four years to 1889. The U.S. was treating the Bering as its own sea (*mare nostrum*), although it had accused the Russians of the same thing in 1821. The Americans began negotiations in 1887 with Great Britain, Russia, France and Japan, proposing a closed pelagic season between April 15 and November 1 to conserve the resource. Great Britain would have signed, but Canada protested strongly that the only result would be to enhance the value of the land operation.

On December 18, 1891, each government appointed two commissioners to the Bering Sea Tribunal (one of the British representatives was

operating. On June 24, using its extraordinary powers under the Civil Defence Act, W.A.C. Bennett's provincial government took over Black Ball ferries and made moves to "shanghai" the striking men back to work. News of any ferry leaving the Island, even for Anacortes or Port Angeles, caused a near stampede, and car line-ups extended for blocks. An airlift was actually commenced, on July 19, to supply the Island with food. Premier Bennett, claiming that he was forced to use almost dictatorial powers (earning him the nickname "King Cecil") by the failure of John Diefenbaker's federal Conservative government to intervene to settle the strike, announced late in July that the government was going into the ferry business, "to ensure a fast, reliable service" with the mainland. Swartz Bay and Tsawwassen were chosen as the terminals for the Victoria-Vancouver run, and the M.V. *Sidney*, the first of the government's fleet, was built at Victoria Machinery Depot. The service started on June 15, 1960—cars cost $5 one way, passengers $2. Victoria business interests were ecstatic.

The government bought out Black Ball in 1961, almost coincidentally with the takeover of B.C. Electric. With the launching later that year of the *City of Vancouver*, the free-enterprise B.C. government was tied with Washington State for the title of world's biggest sea-going ferry system. The slogan "Follow The Birds to Victoria," coined in 1921 by George Warren of the Victoria Publicity Bureau, was adopted by the government

a Canadian, Professor Dawson). Sealing was halted, although the commercial interests complained bitterly. Great Britain wanted a three-mile limit, while the U.S. claimed that the seals were domestic animals, only temporarily out of its possession while in the ocean. Finally, in February, 1892, the matter was submitted to an international panel of jurists, which sat in Paris from March to August. The decision technically went against the United States, but the jurists framed regulations which effectively stopped all pelagic sealing, leaving the land operations untouched—they "gave Canada the shell and handed the kernel over to the U.S.," said the newspapers. Theodore Roosevelt, then the New York Police Commissioner, thought it was a sign of weakness even to allow the arbitration—a belligerent attitude which, when he was U.S. President, made the Alaska Boundary dispute of 1900-03 a particularly bitter one (that arbitration handed the "Alaska panhandle" to the United States).

Although the U.S. had "won" the sealing arbitration, they were forced to pay damages to the Victoria sealers—$473,151.26 was finally agreed to in 1896. British sealers continued to work the western part of the Bering Sea, and Russian and Japanese sealers continued to hunt around the Pribilofs. Although the U.S. government prosecuted any Americans in the area, the Canadian government refused to control Canadians who continued pelagic sealing. Finally, in 1911, Great Britain and the U.S. agreed to ban all pelagic sealing north of 35 degrees, and to give fifteen percent of the land catch to the Canadians. In July, 1912, the agreement was extended to Russia and Japan.

The sealing arbitration helped depress Victoria's economy in the nineties, but represented a real landmark in the history of the conservation movement. As well, it was one of the few times in history when a complex issue was arbitrated by an international panel, rather than as the aftermath of a war.

C.P.R. Landing Place, Victoria, B.C., Canada

The Harbor, showing C. P. R. & G. T. P. Steamers
Victoria, B. C.

(Above) Looking north from the legislative buildings to the classically-styled Canadian Pacific Coastal Steamship Terminal on Belleville Street in the late twenties. In the left distance, on the site of the former Songhees Indian Reservation, is a rag-tag collection of industrial buildings—not the major industrial and railway terminus envisaged by the McBride government before the First World War (which was to be connected with the Ogden Point docks by a railway bridge across the Inner Harbour entrance). In the right distance is the bascule-span Johnson Street bridge, finished in 1924, and one of the few provincial government-sponsored civic improvements in Victoria during the twenties, although it took a civic referendum to raise the money required to finish it. The CPR Steamship terminal is now the "Madame Tussaud's" waxworks museum. The CPR's expanded activity helped displace the James Bay Athletic Association clubhouse from the site of today's Undersea Gardens. The clubhouse, with billiard room and showers, opened in 1891 and provided a home for the "James Bays" baseball team. The J.B.A.A. later moved, with its four- and eight-oared shells, to the Gorge. (Below) Looking west, from the front windows of the Empress Hotel, about 1920. The Inner Harbour, the headquarters of the coastal trade since Fort Victoria days, was unsuitable for ocean liners, so Rithet's Outer Wharf, "around the corner" to the left, provided moorage for the trans-Pacific CPR Empresses and the Royal Mail boats from Australia before the turn of the century. The construction of the Ogden Point docks, which at last provided Victoria with docking facilities "second to none on the coast," were a Liberal election plank in 1911. Completed before the end of World War I, they are practically abandoned today, due to the decline of Victoria as a shipping port. The CPR's coastal wharves are on the left of the picture, on Belleville Street; Pendray's Bapco paint factory is in the distance on Laurel Point; the Grand Trunk Pacific, with moorage on Wharf Street, connected Victoria with its Prince Rupert terminus before abandoning the steamship service in 1923. Small vessels, including much of the rum fleet in Prohibition

years, used the Evans, Coleman & Evans wharf. Founded in Vancouver in 1888, EC&E specialized in stone, coal, cement supplies and coastal shipping. After 1910, the business was dominated by the Barnard brothers and R.P. Butchart. "Boss" Johnson, later premier of B.C., was president in 1946. The corporate successor to EC&E became Ocean Construction Supplies, following a merger in 1957.

Provincial Politics

Victoria's role as provincial capital has turned a lot of politicians into Victoria residents, and helped foster in the city an obsession with the day-to-day cut and thrust of provincial politics. In the last century, partisans often held torchlight parades through the Victoria streets for their champions. For the rest of the province, "Victoria" is a synonym for "provincial affairs." Politics today, though conducted with unbending partisanship within the confines of the legislature and the press conference, has none of the volatility of political life in Victoria a hundred years ago. Government today rests in the hands of the Cabinet; the backbenchers bide their time serving on committees, and are expected to limit their grumbling to closed-door caucus sessions, while the Opposition is resigned to its role until the expiry of the government's term of office after three to five years.

Before the 1903 election, there was no such loyalty, as there were no formal political parties in the legislature. Individual men were elected as individuals, though federally they had Liberal or Conservative memberships and leanings. Governments rose and fell with astonishing regularity, and premiers with their small cabinets were constantly bullying and cajoling their supporters in the legislature in order to retain their toehold on power. In the 32 years between the province's entry into confederation and 1903, fourteen men held the office of premier—one (G.A. Walkem) on two separate occasions. In the eighty-odd years since, only thirteen men have been premier, the record being held by W.A.C. Bennett, who was the head of a Social Credit government for the 20 years after August, 1952. (In the earlier period, while some of the instability of political life was due to the lack of political parties, an equal part was due to the mortality rate of the premiers. During the extraordinary Smithe-to-Turner ministry, commencing in January 1883 and continuing until August, 1898, three premiers died in office: William Smithe, A.E.B. Davie, and John Robson.) Lieutenant-governors exercised a lot of discretion, too, when one government fell and another alignment of members around a different leader appeared, thus eliminating the need for frequent and often indecisive elections.

The political issues which dominated British Columbia—both in colonial days and in the years before the turn of the century—concerned the Island's economy and traditions: first, was there to be a railway, which would make Victoria, as the logical terminus, a great and prosperous city; second, was it worthwhile joining Canada, and severing the direct Imperial link with England; third, would the railway terminus be Victoria, or the Burrard Inlet area; and, fourth, once the railway terminus was settled, and Vancouver had begun to dominate the province's economic affairs, which city was to be the provincial capital.

Running through these issues in the nineteenth century, and continuing as major public concerns until the Second World War, were a thread of anti-Orientalism—which reflected itself in everything from civic development to school policy—and an obsession with liquor.

The provincial government buildings command the south shore of the Inner Harbour. Their location dates from 1859, when Governor James Douglas, intent on selling downtown lots to the highest bidders during the Cariboo gold rush boom, decided to locate the government buildings on cheaper land to the south. His own house and that of his son-in-law J.S. Helmcken were among the few south of James Bay at that time. Douglas allocated funds for the construction of the James Bay bridge across the tidal mudflats which are now the Empress Hotel site, and commissioned Hermann Otto Tiedemann to design a set of buildings for the Colonial Administration. Five buildings were erected by contractor Gideon Hallcrow, a Scots crofter and handyman who had built J.S. Helmcken's little house eight years before. Four were removed when the current legislative buildings were erected in the 1890s, and the final one, closest to Belleville Street, burned down in 1957.

Hallcrow's contract for the buildings ended up exceeding $100,000, and this, plus their location, design, and erection without the approval of the colonial assembly, caused a storm of objection. Douglas "proceeded with them regardless of his censors." Victoria's pundits criticized the isolation and detachment of the various government departments in separate buildings—there was a legislative hall, a central administrative department, a court house, an office of the chief commissioner of lands and works, and a printing bureau. Many people objected to the design—a picturesque, quaint style of architecture "somewhat suggestive of Chinese pagodas"—which, combined with the individual departments' isolation in the five buildings, earned them the nickname "the Birdcages." (Another Tiedemann building, the old Court House on Bastion Square, now the Maritime Museum, built 30 years later, is equally odd-looking and was "supposedly based on a building in his native Munich," according to the Victoria Heritage Advisory Committee.) The continuation of Government Street south of the James Bay bridge past the Birdcages was called Birdcage Walk; at the turn of the century, the most common story was that the name originated from Birdcage Walk in London, England, though J.S. Helmcken, for one, logically claimed it came from the street's proximity to the Birdcages. Birdcage Walk, before the James Bay causeway was built about 1905, extended only as far south as Michigan Street, two blocks into the James Bay residential area.

By the 1890s, Victorians had grown quite fond of their curious Birdcages, which "caused a feeling of regret on account of their demolition, but the business of the public office having long ago outgrown their capacity, their fate was inevitable." There was no such fondness on the mainland for the decision, following elaborate manoeuvring by Theodore Davie's government in 1892, to anchor the capital permanently in Victoria. When the legislature opened on February 10, 1898, Victoria gained a magnificent edifice.

An international design competition was held in 1892; the two judges, non-competing architects from eastern Canada who were holed up in the Roccabella guest house on Victoria Crescent, reviewed 67 sets of plans, including a picturesque Inner Harbour sketch signed by a "B.C. Ar-

A gathering —perhaps the opening of the legislature —on the lawn in front of the "Birdcages" at the present site of the province's legislative buildings on James Bay.

The legislative buildings, lit up at night during the 1930s. They were first outlined with lights in October, 1901, for the visit of the Duke and Duchess of Cornwall and York, later King George V and Queen Mary.

chitect." The B.C. architect was, in fact, from Leeds, England, with an ego in inverse proportion to his amount of experience. Nevertheless, Francis Mawson Rattenbury got the commission, and moved to the Driard Hotel from Vancouver to complete the plans; Victorians watched over the next four years as his brilliant conceptual sketch was translated into stone and glass.

Rattenbury designed a magnificent façade, but paid little attention to interior details, reflected in terrible acoustics within the legislative hall (which was corrected by stringing salmon netting from the ceiling), no writing facilities in the press gallery, and no washroom in the lieutenant-governor's suite—a host of little problems that pushed the price up by more than fifty percent to the enormous figure of $950,000, and the completion date all the way to 1907.

Nevertheless, all approved of the end result. Contemporary accounts waxed eloquent over the "huge masses of grey stonework, in stately outline with the expanse of green sward and the blue waters of James Bay in the foreground and the glorious Olympic Mountains behind, producing a most beautiful, and, in its way, unequalled, effect." The design's antecedents were hazarded as "Renaissance in style, though treated in so original a manner as to make any particular description somewhat misleading." Rattenbury's career was launched, the government had a new home and Victoria had an unforgettable landmark.

Additions were made to the legislative buildings from 1911 to 1916. The government precinct was expanded in April, 1929, when the Tolmie government purchased all the lots facing Government Street from Elliott to Superior, and those on Superior between the Government Printing Office at Government Street west to Menzies. One feature of Premier Tolmie's expanding government—a harbinger of the massive governments of

recent years—was the appointment, on June 25, 1929, of newspaperman B.A. McKelvie as director-general of the brand-new Bureau of Public Relations. Since then, government offices have expanded into many James Bay houses, including Premier Robson's house at Michigan and Government, now the Queen's Printer bookstore. As well, provincial government departments occupy many buildings downtown.

The civil service first began to grow like Topsy during the early 1890s, when Theodore Davie was premier. The cost of civil government salaries went from $61,763 in 1886-7 to $145,000 five years later. By 1908, the civil service had grown in such a haphazard fashion that Dr. Henry Essen Young introduced the first bill for classification and grading of employees. Young and the McBride government wanted promotion by merit with standard examinations, and proposed a superannuation system to "improve the tone and capacity of men." The superannuation clause, which was strongly supported by the legislature's two Socialist members, caused such controversy within the Conservative caucus that it was dropped. The maximum salary for a chief clerk was set at $1,800; deputy ministers received $2,700 per year.

Civil servants were expected to be strictly non-partisan, and were felt to have no political rights. Their political activities became an issue in early 1918, when clerk R.G. Duggan was dismissed from the civil service after accepting the appointment of president of the Victoria branch of the Great War Veterans' Association, which was active in provincial politics; Duggan had already incurred the disfavour of the Liberals by campaigning for the Unionists in the 1917 federal election. T.D. Pattullo, then Minister of Lands, dismissed Duggan on January 8th.

De Cosmos & Walkem (B.C. *vs.* Canada)

The first eleven years of British Columbia's history as a province, following its confederation with Canada in July, 1871, were an amazing charade of petulance, gerrymandering, and secession, dominated by Amor de Cosmos, George Walkem, and the promise of a Pacific Railway. British Columbia politicians behaved, in the opinion of central Canadians, like "spoiled and thankless children" over the promised Esquimalt terminus of the railway, and spent the province deeply into debt during the depression which lasted for the entire decade. In Victoria, the issue was simple—without the railway, the city would never be more than a minor colonial outpost.

The province's first elections were held from October to December, 1871, in the various parts of the province, with oral nominations and open voting by show of hands—many bands were hired and drinks bought to woo the undecided. In Victoria City, John Foster McCreight, Simeon Duck, Robert Beaven, and Dr. Tolmie were elected; Amor de Cosmos was elected for Victoria District. McCreight, who had been acting attorney-general during Governor Musgrave's tenure, was asked by the new lieutenant-governor, Joseph Trutch, to form a ministry. McCreight was no particular friend of the "Crown Colony clique," which was seen by Trutch as an advantage for unifying the province.

The first legislature met on February 15, 1872. Confederation had blotted out most of the issues from colonial days—the old "party" issues of British loyalty vs. American annexation vs. Canadian federation had been submerged, but the "island vs. mainland" dispute still had plenty of force. In the distribution of seats, the mainland elected thirteen members versus the Island's twelve, but McCreight allocated two salaried portfolios to Island members and only one to a mainland member—Walkem. McCreight made no secret of his feeling that the province was not yet ready for complete autonomy, and infuriated the mainland members by refusing to increase the sessional allowance. The opposition members, dominated by de Cosmos and mainlanders John Robson and T.B. Humphreys, could have defeated him in the legislature in the first session, but were united only in their dislike of him. By the time the second session opened in December, 1872, McCreight was fuming publicly about "local politicians with narrow views." On the third day of the sitting, Humphreys moved no-confidence in McCreight's administration; four days later, the latter resigned.

Trutch was chagrined at the sudden, capricious demise of McCreight's ministry, and asked Amor de Cosmos to form a government. There was little need for another election as de Cosmos liked most of the old government's policies (including secret ballot voting), and accepted its Speech from the Throne with only a few minor, verbal alterations. De Cosmos was a shrewd politician—although he had used Humphreys and Robson to help him unhorse McCreight, he refused to offer either of them seats in the Cabinet. He objected to McCreight's introduction of the Canadian tariff, which, according to the Terms of Union with Canada, only had to be introduced after the Pacific Railway was completed. De Cosmos's decision to fight the tariff—from his seat in the House of Commons in Ottawa—and abandon Victoria while doing it, resulted in an Act disallowing anyone from holding seats both provincially and federally.

De Cosmos had quietly requested, from the federal government, changes in the Terms of Union in order to raise funds to build his pet project—the Esquimalt drydock. The word leaked out and, on February 7, 1874, a crowd of 800, including prominent politicians like Senator Macdonald and J.S. Helmcken, stormed across the James Bay bridge and invaded the legislature. The Speaker, Dr. Trimble, was forced from his chair, and de Cosmos wisely hid in the Speaker's office. De Cosmos took the opportunity to resign, and beat a hasty retreat to his Ottawa House of Commons seat. George Anthony Walkem—who thought that de Cosmos had "all the eccentricities of a comet without any of its brilliance"—was the beneficiary, and was offered the premiership on February 9, 1874.

Interest in the transcontinental railway was "intense and personal"—everyone stood to benefit personally from the prosperity it would bring, *if* they held property and business interests along the line or at the terminus. New Westminster, obviously, held out for a Burrard Inlet terminus and a route down the Fraser Canyon, while Victoria wanted the line to run down Bute Inlet, across Seymour Narrows, and down the island to a terminus at Esquimalt. By an order-in-council in June, 1873, the federal government had named Esquimalt as the terminus, without having any idea how it would bridge Seymour Narrows. The decision was "a flagrant bribe to the voters of Victoria." Walkem, the member from Cariboo, was able to gain support in Victoria, as both areas would benefit only if the Bute Inlet route was chosen.

Walkem moved quickly, in the spring of 1874, to force the federal government to commit to the Bute Inlet line. The federal government sent its emissary, Mr. Edgar, to negotiate a modification of the Terms of Union in an attempt to mollify volatile Victoria. Walkem refused to deal with him, then prepared a memorandum to the Crown on June 15, 1874, crying foul and threatening secession if England didn't push Canada to honour the original terms. Into the stalemate came Lord Carnarvon, the Secretary of State for the Colonies when the British North America Act was introduced, who offered to arbitrate. Walkem went to London, and after lengthy discussions with Carnarvon, accepted new terms.

These Carnarvon Terms, framed to keep B.C. within confederation, offered an immediate start on a railway line connecting Esquimalt with Nanaimo, the active pursuit of railroad surveys on the mainland, and the expenditure of at least $2 million a year on railway work within the province. In return, B.C. accepted that the completion date on the transcontinental railway could be delayed until the end of 1890 (not the ten years after confederation, which was promised in 1871).

Walkem returned to Victoria from London, and was serenaded at his house by a crowd of torch-bearing citizens. According to his arch-enemy, the *Colonist*, the premier then "poured out a tale of the intense suffering he had undergone in consuming green turtle soup, fat capon, and Widow

George Anthony Walkem (1837-1908) enjoyed his physical resemblance to Rudyard Kipling, though Henry Crease thought him best described as a fence-sitter or weathercock. Judge Begbie, who had permitted American lawyers to defend Americans during the 1858 gold rush, refused to grant Canadian lawyers like Walkem admission to the bar. Walkem petitioned Governor Douglas and finally received permission to practice in February, 1863. Begbie and Walkem feuded thereafter for years—once, when Walkem was premier, Begbie threatened to jail him for contempt. Walkem countered that he would only be held for 24 hours, as the Justice Minister would order his release. Walkem was despised by the English in Victoria for his low political morality and "the intellectual frailties engendered by his professional antecedents," as Lord Dufferin put it.

Andrew Charles Elliott (1829-1889), B.C.'s fourth premier, had none of Walkem's political skills. His "retiring and studious nature" was better suited to his modest Victoria legal business.

John Foster McCreight, B.C.'s first premier, was a lawyer, not a politician. Following his defeat, he was appointed to the Supreme Court. Of all the judges in the early days of B.C. (including Begbie), he was said to be the most learned in the law, and "woe to the counsel who had not made an exhaustive examination of all the relevant authorities" before appearing before him. McCreight later returned to England, where he died on November 18, 1913.

Robert Beaven, Walkem's minister of finance, took over the government after Walkem was appointed to the bench. With Walkem gone, there wasn't a lawyer left in the Legislature, so Beaven invited his cousin, J. Roland Hett, into the Cabinet as attorney general. In the provincial election in July, 1882, Hett was declared elected in Esquimalt, by 74-73 over C.E. Pooley, but as one of Hett's voters was illiterate, and another an alien, Pooley was declared elected by one vote. During the visit of the Marquis of Lorne and Princess Louise, Beaven asked rather wistfully whether Vancouver Island could become a separate kingdom, with Princess Louise as Queen.

Cliquot champagne, and of his interviews with Lord Carnarvon." Then, "with a wild whoop" and with Mayor Drummond leading the way, "the crowd adjourned to the nearest saloon to take 'a wee drap' at the Premier's expense."

Although the Carnarvon Terms were drawn up on November 17, 1874, Walkem claimed in the legislature at the beginning of the following March that he had not received any official documents on them (he had received them, but not through "channels," so he claimed it was private communication). He had not disclosed that he had agreed to an alteration of the Terms of Union, and wanted to hold off so doing until after he had been re-elected. However, on March 19, Prime Minister MacKenzie introduced the Esquimalt and Nanaimo Railway Bill at Ottawa, with the proviso that he would build it only if he didn't have to raise taxes. It passed the House, but the "treacherous" Canadian Senate, feeling that the little railway was an absurdity, refused it. Thus, the Bute Inlet route was killed, and the Burrard Inlet route—with the subsequent domination by the city of Vancouver—became inevitable. Victoria became even more outspokenly hostile. "Secession," said John Robson, "is the next card to be played." The province's economic depression deepened.

By the time of the fall provincial elections in 1875, word had leaked out about the Carnarvon Terms, and Walkem was attacked for changing the Terms of Union without consulting with the people. Also, it was apparent he had given the Island everything, and the New Westminster mainlanders nothing. He was nevertheless returned with a majority of two. On January 10, 1876, when the legislature opened, he announced that he had decided again to petition the Queen. Robert (Peg-Leg) Smith moved a resolution to secede, and become an independent country under the protection of England (and demand $30 million compensation from Canada). However, although Walkem was lambasting Ottawa for defaulting on its railway obligations, he had approached them for a $450,000 loan to meet the government's operating expenses. A motion of non-confidence in Walkem passed on January 25, 1876, and he went down to defeat.

Andrew Charles Elliott, a Dublin lawyer and member from Victoria City who was only fair at law and inept at politics, was asked to form a government. The Island's politics were dominated by the Carnarvon Club, made up of people like Robert Beaven, T.B. Humphreys, W.F. Tolmie, J.S. Drummond, and Elliott—who was an Island member but had managed to gather considerable support in New Westminster for his government. As such, "he was trying to ride two horses at once," and wasn't up to the battle with a man like Walkem. Although business and morale improved following Lord and Lady Dufferin's visit in August, 1876, there was no resolution to the matter of the Island railway. Elliott was defeated in the house on March 29, 1878, but refused to resign. The legislature continued to meet, attracting larger and more hostile crowds. Finally, on April 12, he resigned, and in the subsequent election was completely routed, losing even his own seat.

Walkem was returned, with the recognition that he would fight Ot-

tawa. Elliott had been "conciliating and dignified" on Dominion affairs, but Walkem stoked the fire again by reintroducing his secession motion on August 9 (indicating, also, how much he owed to the people of Victoria for his re-election). By the time the resolution reached Ottawa, John A. Macdonald was back in power, having defeated MacKenzie in the federal election.

In making the decision on the railway's transcontinental route, Macdonald, in 1879, had new strategic worries. The Russian war scare of the previous year had underscored how difficult the Bute Inlet route would be to defend; as well, the Northern Pacific Railway was advancing rapidly across the United States to its Puget Sound terminus, threatening economic penetration and domination of southern B.C. His formal decision, on October 4, chose the Fraser Canyon-Burrard Inlet route.

Islanders, however, still wanted their railway, and an "Island Railway or Secession" movement started. Walkem, angered by Macdonald's refusal to consider the Esquimalt to Nanaimo line as anything more than a local public work, tried his secession resolution for a third time. The vote was 20-4, and both London and Ottawa were worried about the strategic implications of the threat to their "all-red route to the Orient." Walkem, however, got into local trouble of his own over the Esquimalt dry dock (page 156). Fortuitously, Judge Alexander Rocke Robertson, aged 40, who had badly injured his knee while bathing at Kamloops, died of the resulting infection at Victoria in December, 1881. Macdonald, assured that Walkem had separated himself from his "rabid" Carnarvon Clubbers, appointed him to the bench to fill the vacancy on May 23, 1882.

Robert Beaven, Walkem's Minister of Finance, took over. A provincial election was held in July, in which Beaven was completely routed. Beaven refused to resign, and during the three-month visit of the governor-general, the Marquis of Lorne and his wife, Princess Louise, "the ship was allowed to drift." Lieutenant-Governor Cornwall, who had said that "the party-ties" of the newly elected members weren't sufficient to ask for Beaven's dismissal, finally ordered the Legislature to convene on January 25, 1883, after receiving a rather angry petition from three-fifths of the elected members. Beaven's government "went calmly on against all hostility," but was voted down on a no-confidence motion by William Smithe.

Walkem, after his 1879 marriage to Sophie Edith, the fifth daughter of prominent merchant Henry Rhodes, lived at "Maplehurst," the Rhodes family home at Princess between Blanshard and Quadra. In the mid-1880s, he was a judge at Yale, and although he was often carried away from the dinner table dead-drunk, he never hesitated to convict the railway workers brought before him for public drunkenness. He spent much of his spare time drawing animals, especially lions, and had enough talent to be nicknamed "a modern Landseer." In his final years on the bench, he would often and without warning introduce anecdotes of his early days at Williams Creek in the Cariboo in the 1860s, to the bewilderment of all present. He died in 1908, aged 71.

Smithe to Turner (Island *vs.* Mainland)

The defeat of Robert Beaven in the legislature on January 30, 1883, ushered in an administration which, with five different premiers, governed B.C. until August, 1898. As Beaven had been drifting along since the previous July with no mandate to govern, the lieutenant-governor felt justified in asking William Smithe, the acknowledged leader of the opposition group, to form a government.

William Smithe had come to British Columbia from England to farm in the Cowichan area in the 1860s. He married Martha Keir, the daughter of a well-established farmer there, in 1873, two years after he had first been elected to the legislature. Once he became premier, he embarked on a program of land "giveaways" to aid capitalists to construct railways. His rationale—highlighted by the inaction of the Walkem years—was that the province had few assets other than land and no ability to raise the capital itself to construct large-scale public works. The major beneficiary of this policy was the Esquimalt & Nanaimo Railway, which had been stalled in political controversy since its suggestion as part of the Carnarvon Terms of 1875. A syndicate of Robert Dunsmuir, John Bryden, and three of the "Big Four robber-barons" of California's Southern Pacific Railway—Collis Huntington, Leland Stanford and Charles Crocker (Mark Hopkins was already dead)—were granted 1,900,000 acres of prime Vancouver Island land, plus other concessions, in return for building and operating the E&NR. Other railway lines in the Kootenays and the interior received land grants, and the Canadian Pacific Railway received 6,000 acres of prime Vancouver land—enough to ensure its domination of Vancouver's development ever since—for extending its main line fourteen miles west of Burrard Inlet tidewater at Port Moody. The public was pleased with the value obtained from these land grants, as they stimulated considerable economic activity.

By 1886, Smithe had decided to build a fine James Bay house: "ten rooms; the best Minton tiles and facings adorn all the fireplaces; the whole cost is between $8,000 and $9,000." Before the house was ready, on March 29, 1877, Smithe suddenly died.

His attorney-general and the member from Lillooet, Alexander E.B. Davie, was selected premier by his colleagues. He was one of five sons of Victoria physician John Chapman Davie, who in 1885 built one of the first houses in the Rockland area ("Fairholme" at 638 Rockland Place). Alex came to Victoria from England with his father in 1862, returned to England for his legal education, and articled in Victoria with Robert E. Jackson, the partner of Justice Tyrwhitt-Drake. He decided to practice in Victoria, but travelled on the Cariboo circuit with Chief Justice Begbie until his 1875 election to the Legislature from the Cariboo riding. His legal workload so increased that he entered a partnership with Charles E. Pooley of Esquimalt, but he continued in politics, and was re-elected in 1882 at Lillooet. When he became premier after Smithe's death he continued as attorney-general. "Close application to his duties and to his law practice so undermined his health in the fall of 1887 that he never recovered, and a gradual decline brought him to the end of life's journey on the 1st of August, 1889."

John Robson, the fiery former New Westminster editor of the *British Columbian*, took over the premiership on August 3rd. Born in Perth County, Ontario in March, 1824, Robson came to B.C. in 1859, attracted by the gold fever. He soon abandoned his gold digging, and moved to New Westminster, where he cleared roads for a year before becoming editor of the *British Columbian*, "preaching union with Canada in and out of season" until 1869. He moved to Victoria to become editor-in-chief of the *Colonist*, and built a fine house at the southern end of Birdcage Walk, at Michigan Street—the house now occupied by the Queen's Printer Bookshop (page 103). Robson, who had in his early days been identified as a Liberal, became a Conservative—the only choice for anyone in 1890s Victoria who didn't wish to court social exclusion.

The old mainland vs. Vancouver Island issue was more or less dead, as too many people who didn't know of the past had emigrated to the province since the 1870s. In the campaigning for the June 13, 1890 election, though, the distribution of legislative seats became an issue. Sixteen Island members were elected by 7,111 voters, while only six (on the lower mainland) were elected by 6,556 voters. Robson found himself under fire for favouring the Island, and for granting public lands to speculators.

By 1892, Robson was in a battle with the press, especially the *Columbian* in New Westminster, and its editor, Mr. Kennedy. Kennedy had accused the Robson government of some shady dealings in the granting of land for the New Westminster & Vancouver Tramway. In order to deal with Kennedy, a law was passed to enable a libel prosecution, where none before had been possible (the only previous case had seen Amor de Cosmos brought before the bar of the legislature for libelling Speaker J.S. Helmcken in 1861; de Cosmos apologized and was set free).

Robson was in London on government business on June 29, 1892, and while entering a carriage jammed his finger in the door. Blood poisoning developed and he quickly died. His funeral in Victoria on July 28 was conducted by his brother, Rev. Ebenezer Robson, with no music or any ostentatious display. The procession of mourners from St. Andrew's Presbyterian to the Ross Bay Cemetery was nearly a mile long.

Alexander Davie's younger brother, Theodore, the member from Cariboo who had been Robson's attorney-general, assumed the premiership on July 2. He had a much rougher time as premier than any of his three predecessors in that administration, as the issue of fair representation turned into a fully-fledged Island vs. mainland dispute in 1893 (the "smallpox war" of the previous summer didn't help, page 75). The issue which raised tempers to the boil was Davie's decision to build extravagant new legislative buildings in Victoria, thus permanently anchoring the capital on the Island. The government Act to authorize a $600,000 loan was bitterly opposed on the mainland.

Francis Carter-Cotton, a Vancouver MLA and publisher of the Conservative *News-Advertiser*, headed the mainland fight against Davie's Conservatively-inclined government. In early 1894, shortly before the

Alexander Edmund Batson Davie was premier of British Columbia from 1887 to 1889, when he died, likely from overwork. He was a staunch Roman Catholic and federal Conservative. His marriage to Constance Langford in 1874 produced seven children, two of whom died in infancy. Sophie became the wife of the Hon. Albert E. McPhillips, President of the Council in Richard McBride's government and a prominent Victoria K.C. Cyril Francis Davie (1882-1950) also became a K.C., and was Conservative MLA for Cowichan-Newcastle from 1924-33, serving the final three years as Speaker. He was an early Tory advocate of state health insurance and split with the Tolmie government in May, 1933, charging it with "a wanton disregard for the rights and privileges of the poorer people." Winifred Mary married Frederick J. Fulton in 1909. Fulton was MLA from 1901-09 and later served as MP for the Cariboo. Their son, Edmund Davie Fulton, born in 1916, was elected Progressive Conservative party president in B.C. in 1952, following the demise of the Coalition government, the rise of W.A.C. Bennett's Socreds, and the ouster of Herbert Anscomb's "old guard." E. Davie Fulton

became Justice Minister in John Diefenbaker's federal Conservative government in 1957, and fought viciously with W.A.C. Bennett over the international treaties on the Columbia river, which cleared the way for the three B.C. Hydro dams in the Kootenays. Following the return of the Federal Liberals to power in the early sixties, he returned to B.C., assumed the leadership of the provincial Conservative party, and attempted to unseat Bennett. He was unsuccessful, and spent the rest of his career as a judge.

Theodore Davie, the younger brother of Premier Alexander Davie, assumed the premiership on the sudden death of John Robson. His early attempts at land development created the Adelphi Block at Yates and Government Street—usually known as "Campbell's Corner." His successful political juggling of mainland vs. Island interests resulted in the permanent anchoring of the provincial capital in Victoria in 1893, and the construction of the legislative buildings on the Inner Harbour.

elections which were planned for that July, a redistribution bill was passed, giving the mainland nineteen members and the Island only fourteen. That February, the government had let the first contracts for Rattenbury's legislative buildings, with a cost estimate then of $686,000. Davie's masterful political skills had gathered enough support on the mainland for the legislative buildings, but, as an opposition election pamphlet of June 19 claimed, it was only achieved by "a wild carnival of gormandizing and boodling by the Davie Compact." The pamphlet claimed that Interior MLA's had received massive amounts of road-building money for their ridings as a "sop" for their support of the buildings, and that James McQueen, a bitter opponent of the government and supporter of the Mainland Movement, was brought into line by Davie with a directorate in the Nicola Valley Railway Co., whose president was Vancouver-based CPR physician Dr. Matthew Lefevre. The government's supporters were "principally real estate and mine boomers, land or railway grabbers" who had either had, or were after, "a pull at the government teat." The pamphlet also drew attention to the Conservative *Colonist's* government advertising revenue, which had shot from $858 in 1891-2 to $1,960 in 1892-3. It pointed out to the mainlanders that Ontario's legislative buildings had cost 65 cents a head, while B.C.'s would cost $10, and that it cost $2 a head to govern every white man, woman and child in Ontario, but $22 a head in B.C. The money to build that "tremendous act of folly & extravagance" (the legislative buildings) could have built 2,000 miles of good roads, they claimed, or dyked most of the Fraser (which had flooded disastrously the previous winter).

Government had become expensive: civil government salaries had gone from $61,763 in 1886-87 to $145,000 in 1893-94. The public debt, which had stood at $770,812 early in Smithe's term in 1884, stood at $3,187,456 in 1893, and more than doubled to $7,425,262 before Premier Turner's ministry was dismissed in 1898.

Nevertheless, Davie was returned for another term, but his health had begun to fail due to a weak heart and he took the appointment, following the death of Chief Justice Begbie, of the province's chief justiceship on February 23, 1895. His health became so fragile that an elaborate cage-elevator was installed in the Law Courts on Bastion Square (now the Maritime Museum), so that he wouldn't have to climb the stairs. He died on March 7, 1898.

Davie was succeeded as premier by John Herbert Turner, a Victoria City member who had been the government's Minister of Finance since August, 1887. Turner, who lived on Pleasant Street in Point Ellice and was one of the city's prominent businessmen (Turner & Beeton Co. on Wharf Street), came to power shortly before the rush to the Klondike goldfields turned Victoria upside down. His administration came under fire for its railway policy, especially in 1898 when it chartered railways like the Cassiar Central which, with little capital, had few hopes of reaching the goldfields in the interior and the North.

Turner allowed his name to be on the directorate of the Dawson City &

Dominion Trading Corp., and the Klondike & Columbian Gold Fields Ltd. When the companies collapsed after a few months, a number of Englishmen who had entrusted their savings to the security promised by the premier's (and Attorney-General Pooley's) name, lost everything. Walter Nichol's *Province* newspaper carried a denunciatory editorial, and Turner sued for criminal libel (page 46).

Meanwhile, defections and resignations were withering Turner's majority in the legislature. Elections were held on July 9, 1898. One of the few candidates who publicly supported the government was future premier Richard McBride, who ran as "a straight Turner man," described in one newspaper as a rarity "like the Great Auk." The elections were inconclusive: only sixteen members were returned with decisive majorities. Twenty-nine petitions were filed, attacking the elections of all but six members. The only petition which succeeded was in Esquimalt, declaring Mr. Bullen (a descendant of James Douglas) defeated, and electing David Higgins in his place.

With matters still uncertain, Lieutenant-Governor Thomas McInnes (whose appointment had created a Senate vacancy filled by Liberal Victoria *Times* publisher William Templeman) decided on August 8th that Turner was "no longer endorsed by the electorate" and dismissed his government. He then, curiously, called on former Premier Robert Beaven to form a government. What made it doubly curious was that Beaven didn't even have a seat in the legislature.

Semlin to Prior (Government *vs.* Lieutenant-Governor)

The results of the July, 1898 elections were so indecisive that Lieutenant-Governor Thomas McInnes felt justified in acting somewhat arbitrarily to stabilize British Columbia's shattered political life. He apparently felt that former premier J.H. Turner didn't command an adequate following in the house; as well, he was new to the province, and could see no alignment with one leader who might form a successful government. His choice of former premier Robert Beaven, who had been seriously discredited in his previous attempt at governing the province in 1882 and didn't even have a seat in the legislature, perhaps indicates how confused he was by the local situation. Turner was dismissed by McInnes on August 8th. After four days, Beaven admitted that he couldn't get enough support to form a government, so McInnes was forced to choose among the three acknowledged leaders of the opposition factions in the legislature.

McInnes's quandary came at a time when many people in B.C. were beginning to feel that provincial politics should run along party lines, as federal politics did. The *Colonist* had editorialized in 1885 that "election interests are conducted more upon personal than upon party lines... electors look more toward personal peculiarities than to the principles he professes." This, combined with the free drinks and bands which accompanied most electioneering, meant that "politics are conducted in a happy-go-lucky, go-as-you-please sort of way—the man who can talk the loudest, or the longest, or who can tickle people in their mental ribs 'til they roar with glee, is often elected at critical periods in the history of the country." However, by the time Sir Charles Tupper visited Victoria in the late 1890s, and suggested that B.C. elections should be fought along party lines, the *Colonist* was quick to say he should leave provincial matters alone (during the late 1890s in Victoria, the Tories were discredited by association with the four federal Conservative administrations, including Tupper's, which had tottered along before Wilfrid Laurier's Liberals were elected in 1896). Then came McInnes.

The three opposition factions in the legislature which had opposed Turner and survived the 1898 election were led by Cariboo rancher Charles Augustus Semlin, Conservative Vancouver newspaperman Francis Carter-Cotton, and Liberal Vancouver lawyer Joseph Martin. McInnes felt that Semlin was the only one who could bring the factions together, so he asked him to form a government on August 12. This, following the dismissal of Turner and the courting of Beaven, all at the lieutenant-governor's whim, caused Secretary of State R.W. Scott to reprimand him for "so dashing a method of changing your advisers."

Semlin's government included Martin as attorney-general and minister of education and Carter-Cotton as minister of finance. The latter two began to fight viciously almost from the moment they were appointed. The fighting continued outside the legislature, and included Martin's sudden, highly-partisan dismissal of Victoria Police Magistrate Farquhar MacRae on November 21st. At a banquet in Rossland during a government tour on June 20, 1899, Martin got into such a row with Carter-Cotton that

Semlin demanded his resignation. Meanwhile, Semlin had not called the elected members to a sitting, so McInnes demanded that he convene the legislature by the end of October, or else call an election.

Semlin, outraged at the constant interference by the lieutenant-governor, appealed directly to the Secretary of State. A compromise was reached, whereby Semlin agreed to open a legislative session on January 4, 1900. A bitter six weeks followed, highlighted by Martin and former premier Turner fighting Semlin, and Martin fighting Carter-Cotton. Semlin was defeated by nineteen votes to eighteen on a redistribution bill in the middle of February, but refused to resign, arguing that tradition demanded his government's resignation only on a money bill. McInnes felt differently, and gave Semlin until February 27 either to resign or ask for an election. Semlin did neither, and arranged a coalition, not including Martin, to control the legislature. Nevertheless, he was dismissed by the lieutenant-governor at noon on the aforesaid date.

The next day, while the legislature and public speculated about what would happen next, Martin allowed that he had been asked to form a government. The legislature promptly voted twenty-eight to one that it had no confidence in "the third member from Vancouver." The vote had barely been concluded when the lieutenant-governor arrived to prorogue the session. In an example of defiance unprecedented in the British Empire, every member except Martin walked out of the legislature, hissing and catcalling as they went. Only Martin stayed in his seat, and listened to McInnes read his speech. As the lieutenant-governor was leaving, the members stormed back into the chamber in "a football rush," led by Okanagan member Price Ellison, who shouted "We are The People" and threw his hat repeatedly in the air.

Martin managed to form a small ministry, with the support of his four-man cabinet of Smith Curtis, J. Stuart Yates, George Beebe and J.C. Brown. He didn't attempt to pass any bills, and dissolved the legislature on April 10th. His campaign for re-election was called "the greatest political fight ever waged by any man in Canada," but he was trounced on June 9th by Dunsmuir. The nickname "Fighting Joe" stuck with him through the rest of his career.

Lieutenant-Governor McInnes was again chastised by the Dominion secretary of state, but the MLAs were out for blood. Immediately following the election, a majority petitioned Prime Minister Wilfrid Laurier for McInnes's dismissal. Laurier asked the lieutenant-governor for his resignation, which the latter refused, claiming his action in dismissing a government with a working majority (Semlin's) had been constitutional. Laurier fired him on June 21, 1900.

The recognized leader of the anti-Martin forces was coal mine owner James Dunsmuir, who indicated that his only interest in the premiership was a desire to serve the public by bringing a "non-partisan" stability to provincial politics. The glue which bound the government together was opposition to Martin, so on September 3, 1901, when Dunsmuir took Martin's old minister of finance, J.C. Brown, into his cabinet as provincial

Charles Augustus Semlin, the Cariboo rancher and premier who was fired by the lieutenant-governor on February 27, 1900.

Thomas McInnes, whose erratic behaviour as lieutenant-governor sealed the fate of the non-party system of government and resulted in his dismissal by Prime Minister Wilfrid Laurier after James Dunsmuir came to power in the 1900 elections.

"Fighting Joe" Martin was premier from March 1 to June 14, 1900. Born in Ontario, he came to B.C. in 1897, following a career which included a term as an MP, and one as attorney general of Manitoba. Following his provincial defeat, he made a fortune in Vancouver real estate, moved to England, and was elected MP for East St. Pancras in London. He made two later attempts to re-enter B.C. politics, and died in Vancouver in 1923, aged 72.

secretary, the rest of the cabinet was infuriated. Richard McBride, only 30 years old but the progressive rising star of the government, resigned his portfolio of minister of mines. Brown went back to his New Westminster riding to be re-elected (all Cabinet appointees, in all the governments until the forties, had to face the voters in their ridings in a by-election, to test the public's confidence in their appointment); McBride, the New Westminster native son who represented Dewdney riding, campaigned viciously against Brown. The latter was defeated, and McBride emerged as the undisputed leader of the opposition. (Through the latter half of the Dunsmuir administration, Joe Martin had belligerently occupied the seat of the leader of the opposition—and threatened physical combat with McBride and any other member who attempted to move him out——although he consistently voted with Dunsmuir.)

By late 1901, Dunsmuir's Conservative support was bolstered by Martin and his handful of Liberal followers. On the same day that McBride and any other member who attempted to move him out premier) J.H. Turner resigned to become B.C.'s agent-general in London.

Francis L. Carter-Cotton was the Minister of Finance in Semlin's abortive government in 1898-9. A political Conservative and publisher of the Vancouver News-Advertiser, he fought continually with Liberal Attorney General Joseph Martin, and backed "the CPR line" in provincial and Vancouver civic matters.

Robert Garnet Tatlow made a fortune as a fish packer with Henry Bell-Irving, and entered politics in opposition to James Dunsmuir in the 1900 elections. His resignation as Minister of Finance in 1909 was a blow to the credibility of Richard McBride's government. He was killed on April 11, 1910, when the horse pulling his carriage through downtown Victoria was spooked and ran away—Tatlow was thrown from the careening vehicle and died instantly.

After an almost seven-month delay, Dunsmuir finally called a by-election. The winner of the by-election was Col. Edward G. Prior, who became Dunsmuir's minister of mines, and quickly assumed the mantle of heir-apparent, as the Premier tired of the problems of shared decision-making. Prior took over the premiership the same day that Dunsmuir resigned, on November 21, 1902.

Prior had only the tattered remnants of Dunsmuir's support, and by the end of 1902 was operating with a majority of only two, sometimes three. Debate in the legislature centred on land grants, "not in the public interest," which had been made to the Columbia & Western Railway. There were further revelations that correspondence had been concealed, and that the government had deceived the legislature. Prior's support dwindled further, with resignations and dismissals, so that by May, 1903, he was hanging on grimly with only the consistent support of his minister of finance. On May 28, the legislature was scandalized to learn that Premier Prior, while he had been holding the portfolio of chief commissioner of lands & works in December, 1902, had secretly seen tendering documents for a bridge cable contract in the Interior, and had awarded the contract to E.G. Prior & Co. Ltd. The new lieutenant-governor, Sir Henri Joly de Lotbinière, dismissed him the next day.

Richard McBride was asked to form a government on June 1st. The next day, Robert G. Tatlow, the new president of the executive council, read a letter from McBride to the legislature stating that the government to be formed would be a Conservative government. McBride also wrote that the next election would be fought along party lines. He went to the people in October, and was returned with a workable government. Party politics had arrived in B.C.

McBride Prosperity & Party Politics

The most successful politician before W.A.C. Bennett came on the scene in the 1950s was barrister Richard McBride, the Conservative premier of British Columbia from June 1, 1903 until December 15, 1915. Only 32 years old when he became premier, McBride was tall and well built, with a fleshy handsomeness and easy charm, a great shock of prematurely grey hair (he was completely grey at 30), and the unerring ability to mix with and influence people from every class—not only in "a colony" like B.C., but even in snobbish London. He ascended to the premiership with a reputation for honesty and high principles, following his timely dissociation from Dunsmuir's tainted government, at a period in the province's history when the economy was beginning to boom. He rode that prosperity with his reputation intact until the 1913 crash, and made the good times and optimism synonymous with his leadership—"McBride Prosperity." Born in New Westminster on December 15, 1870, he was the first son of the warden of the B.C. Penitentiary, Arthur McBride (1836-1909), who had come to B.C. as a miner and had served as Victoria city jailer and as sergeant in the Provincial Police.

Premier McBride's nicknames—"Handsome Dick," "Glad-Hand Dick," even "The People's Dick"—indicated how he had most British Columbians at his feet with his Irish charm. He led singsongs around the piano and "danced the night away at political rallies." He was "a glamorous and glittering ambassador who symbolized B.C.," a unique character whose "faith and loyalty were unbounded." McBride was the first B.C. politician with a positive national reputation: in 1910, a movement started in the Conservative party in the Maritimes to draft him as the national leader to replace the faltering Robert Borden, but McBride liked the B.C. stage and his role as a "British British Columbian." Winston Churchill was so impressed with him that in June, 1911, following one of McBride's innumerable visits to London, he described him as "a man upon whose striking visage high destiny has set its seal." (McBride invited Churchill to visit B.C. to shoot grizzlies. Churchill replied that, given his current popularity, "a more popular proposition would be that the grizzlies come to London on the contrary errand.")

The early years of his first administration saw McBride's personal prestige dominating the legislature. Most workers were mollified by the general prosperity, and McBride's compromises and charm gained the support of the legislature's two Socialist members—Parker Williams and James Hawthornthwaite from the Nanaimo coal-mining area—who were needed to keep his minority working. He introduced legislation for an eight-hour day in the coal mines—"pernicious and disturbance-breeding legislation" which proved that McBride, in the words of the Liberal Victoria *Times*, was "under the dominating influence of Socialism." James Dunsmuir threatened to close his Nanaimo mines if the eight-hour day were enacted.

Larger issues, with opportunities for greater public support, soon dominated the province. In 1905, under the direct influence of the Socialist members, McBride introduced the first in a long series of bills to ban Oriental immigration into B.C. Although the legislation was immediately disallowed by the federal government as being "opposed to the Federal and Imperial policy of friendly relations with Japan," the issue became a springboard for a "Fight Ottawa" campaign (see also pages 56 and 119).

McBride began to deal with the Grand Trunk Pacific Railway in 1905, and arranged some ethically questionable land grants in return for an early construction start from the western terminus at Prince Rupert. The shady land transfers for the GTP terminal at Kaien Island alienated the Conservative Party's "old guard" in Vancouver, and made an enemy of Sir Charles Hibbert Tupper, a prominent Victoria lawyer and Conservative who had served in his father's short-lived federal government in 1896; the furore led to the resignation of McBride's lands & works commissioner, R.F. "Bob" Green, in December, 1906.

By then, McBride was fighting Ottawa for "Better Terms," and had made himself immensely popular with the Orangemen's groups in the province by decrying Laurier's separate (Catholic) schools legislation in Manitoba. His "Better Terms" campaign argued that B.C., with three percent of the total population of Canada, paid eight percent of the price of confederation, and got in return one percent of its trade benefits. He called an election for February, 1907, and was returned with a majority government of 26 members, facing 13 Liberals and two Socialists.

The 1908 legislative session was dominated by racial issues—the bitter denunciations of Lieutenant-Governor Dunsmuir by the Socialist members for his refusal to allow a Restrictive Immigration Act; the federal compromise by Rodolphe Lemieux to limit Japanese immigration; and the manoeuvring over the Songhees Reservation transfer (page 29). McBride began negotiating with the promoters of the Canadian Northern Railway (now the CNR main line), Donald Mann and Alexander MacKenzie, who were looking for land grants and government subsidies. On October 18, 1909, following ten months of negotiation, rumour and innuendo, McBride called an election. The next day, he signed a contract and subsidy agreement with the two promoters. Two days later, two of McBride's most reputable cabinet ministers, Finance Minister Tatlow and Minister of Lands F.J. Fulton, resigned. Tatlow, particularly, had maintained firmly that MacKenzie and Mann would build their railway without a subsidy. William J. Bowser, an old friend of McBride's from Dalhousie law school, took over the finance ministry. Regardless of those incidents, the election was another triumph for McBride and "McBride Prosperity"—an overwhelming majority of 34 Conservatives, facing only two Liberals and two Socialists in the legislature.

Every week saw a new announcement of railway lines and industrial activities. In January, 1910, the Canadian Northern Railway Bill was passed, specifically to build a line from Victoria 100 miles to Barkley Sound, and to include "a first class modern passenger, mail, express and car-ferry service between English Bluffs (Tsawwassen) and Victoria." Real estate prices all over the province were soaring; farmland in areas

Richard McBride became premier at age 32, and had prospered enough by age 40 to move to the Gorge Road area. He initially lived in a rambling, red-painted wooden house (demolished 1954) at 502 Rupert Street (now the northwest corner of Quadra and Academy Close), on the edge of Beacon Hill Park, next door to St. Ann's Academy; every morning, he dropped his daughter, later Mrs. McGregor McIntosh, at the back door of the convent, and continued walking west to the legislature. The house was built in 1890 for D.M. Ebert's partner, lawyer W. John Taylor, and had two stables, a closed-in paddock at the back, wide bay windows, a den with a potbellied stove, and Shakespearean picture tiles (each tile a scene from a different play) on the fireplace. A 25-foot-long pantry separated the kitchen from the dining room, as Taylor "didn't like to smell his food before it was put in front of him." One morning in 1926, when Senator Robert F. Green lived there, the house was hit by the Seattle mail plane, which "shattered itself against the house and piled up in the garden, a total wreck, with pilot Smith unconscious amid the wreckage."

The Oriental Way.
—Vancouver *Daily Province*

McBride's attitude to women's suffrage, as to prohibition, helped bring down his government. The suffrage campaign, led by future judge Helen Gregory MacGill, and Mesdames Spofford, Farris, Carter-Cotton, Angus, and Norton, and Misses Gutteridge and Sutherland, to name a few, was finally successful in the plebiscite of September 4, 1916. An anonymous poem received by Mrs. Farris read: "Hush my little one, hush my pretty one / Daddy will rock you to rest, / Sleep my little one, sleep my pretty one, / Here on your daddy's vest. / Mother will come to you soon, my dear, / Only a few hours yet, / She will come home when her speech is done, / For mother's a suffragette." The suffrage bill was enacted on March 2, 1917. Soldiers voted against suffrage, and the Liberals had to put up with a "petticoat government" charge. The first general election with women voting was to have been in the autumn, but women were "all so busy with fruits and preserves, pink teas, outings, etc." that Premier Oliver fixed the date for December 1, 1920.

like Fairfield in Victoria was quickly subdivided; wild booms accompanied rumours of new railway lines and terminuses, especially at places like Port Mann and Fort George.

The year 1911 was the most prosperous in B.C.'s history. McBride turned his activities to fighting the Laurier Liberals' trade-reciprocity plans with the United States, and helped swing B.C. completely for the Borden Conservatives in Ottawa. The debates in the legislature "were not very exciting," as the opposition was completely demoralized—especially the Liberals on January 30 when Esquimalt member John Jardine crossed the floor and joined the Conservatives, as he couldn't agree with his only colleague, Victoria Liberal MLA H.C. Brewster, on which of them was to be the leader of the opposition (page 160). Brewster, said McBride, was "a minority of one, with no following in the country and none in the House."

A massive increase in the number of cars on the roads caused W.J. Bowser to bring in a Motor Vehicle Act, requiring registration and licensing of cars and drivers. A move toward control of liquor consumption resulted in Bowser drafting amendments to the Municipal Act. Increasingly, the day-to-day matters of government and party organization were left in Bowser's hands, while McBride concerned himself with national and British Empire issues.

By 1912, Canada was embroiled in a naval debate: should Canadian money be used to buy Canadian ships (the Laurier Liberal position), or should it be given to the Royal Navy for expansion of its fleet (Borden's & McBride's position, backed strongly by First Sea Lord Winston Churchill). The triumph of Laurier's supporters crystallized British resentment about the disunity of Canada, and investment began to be pulled out of the West. Germany, Austria, and Italy were spending tremendous sums on battleships. German investors, especially in the United States, started to unload large numbers of securities onto the U.S. stock markets, to seek ready cash against the Continental war scare. Many Canadians, especially in the West, who had invested heavily in Mexican railway and power development schemes, had their savings threatened by the civil war and the U.S. refusal to intervene militarily (James Mason, the president of the Home Bank of Canada, visited Victoria on September 14 to reassure investors that an expected resolution of the crisis would cause the west to "resume its bounding stride"). Thousands of people in the west had been hoarding gold and silver, and "making easy money by selling things bought not for use, but for speculative profit."

McBride was above all the common concerns. He had attended the magnificent coronation of King George V in London in late 1911. Rumours circulated that he was to be knighted.

Government guarantees and subsidies to a group of promoters seeking to build a railroad connecting North Vancouver with Prince George, via Squamish, became the major campaign plank when McBride went to the people again in March, 1912. Against them, the Liberals, comprised mainly of H.C. Brewster, John Oliver, and Vancouver lawyer F.C. Wade, campaigned for total prohibition, a white B.C., suffrage for women, and a Canadian navy. The election, held on March 28, was a rout for McBride—40 Conservatives were returned, with no Liberals; only the

standard two Socialists remained as the official Opposition.

A couple of weeks later the *Titanic* sunk. The economy faltered, and suddenly the real-estate boom which had captivated western Canada collapsed. Construction in Victoria dropped from over eight million dollars to four million in one year. Unemployed workers became a regular sight on the streets, and free food distribution started from some churches.

McBride received his knighthood on June 14, 1912, and a further insignia during the Duke of Connaught's visit to Victoria that October. By then, however, his reputation as a charming conciliator was obsolete—Liberal newspapers said he and Bowser were running a machine-type political organization, with payoffs from the many contractors and patronage appointments; Sir Richard himself was in financial straits due to the collapse of some of his many investments; in February, 1913, he had peremptorily dismissed a 10,000-signature petition requesting female emancipation. Now it was his arrogance, not his popularity, which knew no bounds.

Off he went on his regular trip to London in August, 1913, leaving unresolved the workers' rebellion in Nanaimo (page 168). The depression deepened. Only the declaration of war in August, 1914, gave McBride an opportunity to revive his popularity. He spent much of his time in London, working feverishly to attract war orders for the beleaguered west coast—which was too far from the war zone to benefit economically. Meanwhile, his railway guarantees added up to $80 million, atop a $10 million provincial debt. Finally, he dissolved the government on March 7, 1915. A month later, the Rev. A.E. Cooke's sensational pamphlet, *The Crisis in B.C.*, which detailed wild allegations of corruption and boodling in the government, was published.

That December, McBride resigned as premier, in favour of Bowser. He assumed the post of agent-general, forcing his old friend J.H. Turner out. By late 1916, it was clear that something was seriously wrong with his health. On May 1, 1917, McBride's friends announced that they were expecting his return to Canada, possibly to enter federal politics. He died of Bright's disease, aged 46, later that year.

Sir Richard and Lady McBride (the former Margaret McGillivray, whom he married in 1896) had six daughters. One married Lieut. Col. McGregor McIntosh, a Glaswegian who had lost his right arm at the Somme in 1916, and was a Conservative MLA and party organizer on Salt Spring Island during the thirties. McIntosh was a life-insurance agent in Victoria following the war, and was killed in a small-plane crash in 1955. Another of McBride's daughters married the son of Col. the Hon. Francis Hood, son of the 4th Viscount Hood and Helen Prior, eldest daughter of the former premier. The Hoods spent their last years in Victoria, after a lengthy military career in England.

Pensions were magnanimously awarded to Lady McBride ($1,500 a year) and Mary Ellen Smith, widow of Liberal minister of finance Ralph Smith ($1,000) in April, 1931. Following disputes in the legislature and a re-opening of old wounds by the Liberal opposition, however, the Tolmie government on June 23 decided it wouldn't grant the pensions. The Conservative party then paid a pension to Lady McBride, and the Liberals paid one to Mrs. Smith.

W.J. Bowser (The P.G.E. & Other Scandals)

Sir Richard McBride's resignation in mid-December, 1915, left the province in complete disarray. The population of British Columbia had decreased by about 100,000, as men left for the war in Europe, and families moved east and south to find work. In the midst of this depression, with rumours of scandal hanging over the government and with over twelve years of power behind them, the Conservative party hoped that acting leader William John Bowser would call for a leadership convention. Instead, he formed a government.

Bowser, who was first elected to represent Vancouver district in 1903, became McBride's attorney general in 1907 and assumed the finance portfolio following Tatlow's resignation in 1909. Born in Rexton, New Brunswick on December 3, 1867, he graduated from Dalhousie with a law degree and moved west to Vancouver a year later, in 1891. During the years from 1908, he served as attorney general, and introduced progressive legislation to regulate motor vehicles, moderate the abuse of liquor licenses (by saloons, for example), ensure compassionate treatment "in accord with Christian ethics" for "fallen women," and conserve the salmon fishery through a cannery licensing act. He was known, said a contemporary, as "a good fighter," and devoted a tremendous amount of his time to Conservative party organization. He was a machine politician with a passion for political science, and scorned those less organized with an arrogance which led him to be dubbed "The Little Napoleon." One of the nicest things said in his defence was that "You will always find the most missiles under the finest apple tree in the orchard." Part of his trouble stemmed from his lack of "the natural and buoyant personal magnetism of his predecessor." McBride was a hard act to follow, especially during a depression.

Bowser misjudged the force of the two dominant political issues of the time—Prohibition and women's suffrage. The Liberals, led by abstainer H.C. Brewster, judged the mood correctly, and had, in fact, campaigned for both issues as early as 1912. The first test of the Bowser government came in February, 1916, when by-elections were called to gain public approval for two of Bowser's cabinet appointments—C.E. Tisdall in Vancouver and A.C. Flumerfelt in Victoria. The latter ran against Liberal party leader Brewster, with "a minimum of personalities in the contest" and a promise between the two men for "clean politics." Although Brewster managed to avoid slanging Flumerfelt, who promised Victorians a ship-building program while playing down his connections with the British-American Trust Co., he went after Bowser for his "carelessness" in allowing the collapse of the Vancouver-based Dominion Trust Co. in October, 1914. Bowser's law firm, he said, were the attorneys for Dominion Trust, and on February 24th he claimed that "I can show you many old men today digging in ditches, who a few years ago were worth $50,000, because of the Dominion Trust failure." Bowser's law firm was also alleged to be doing business for the discredited MacKenzie & Mann of the Canadian Northern Railway, helping to buy up rights-of-way in the province. Bowser's salary and allowances were also questioned—at $10,600 a year, they were $1,600 above the Ontario premier's.

Hardly an aspect of the Conservative government's record escaped criticism: the alleged $105,000 "patronage" commission on the Songhees Reservation deal; the subletting of the excavation contract for an extension to the legislative buildings allegedly to "a Conservative druggist at a price thousands in excess of the lowest tenderer"; Bowser's liquor law amendments which favored the Conservative "old guard" and protected the liquor importers and hotel owners.

The vote, on February 26th, saw Liberal Malcolm Macdonald defeat Conservative Tisdall by a two-to-one margin. Brewster's defeat of Flumerfelt by a similar margin occurred on March 4. Rumours soon surfaced, however, that the Vancouver by-election had not been fought cleanly. A select committee of the legislature met on April 28 to consider the sensational charges in the public press. It had been a Liberal named Patrick Donnelly, curiously enough, who laid an information in Vancouver on April 19 charging a man named Peter Annance with "trying to induce certain Liberals to act as impersonators"—to vote many times for the Liberal candidate, Macdonald. The Conservative press quickly dug up more names, including a Liberal organizer named John T. Scott who had hired "gangs of pluggers" in Seattle at $10 each, plus transportation and accommodation in Vancouver, to "commit wholesale personation." Seattle witnesses were brought forward, corroborating details such as using names of the dead or fraudulent names to vote for the Liberal candidate. Proprietors of two Vancouver rooming houses testified of the behaviour of the rowdy "squads and crews" from Seattle. A janitor in the legislative buildings, Robert Gosden, who was better known as a leader of the Industrial Workers of the World (the "Wobblies" radical movement) was paid $400 by Scott, and an alleged further $50 by Macdonald, to provide a list of voters who were dead, absent at war, had moved, and so on. Then it transpired that members of the Conservative Association executive in Vancouver had advance information that the "pluggers" were coming from Seattle, and had let them fix the election without notifying the police or press, thus better to frame Macdonald. Gosden was eventually discredited as a witness, but the other charges stuck, even though two witnesses named Clancy and White were dragged up from Seattle to testify that they were employed to "plug" for Mr. Tisdall. Peter Annance went to jail for nine months; Scott fled the country. By that time, the province had gone to the polls in a general election.

The September 4, 1916 election was a landslide for the Liberals, who won 37 seats, while only nine remained Conservative and one Socialist. Bowser only hung onto his seat once the overseas (soldiers') results came in on October 13. Voting day also included the two plebiscites, for women's suffrage and Prohibition, which both passed although the Prohibition vote was clouded in controversy. Victoria returned four Liberals—the new premier H.C. Brewster, future premier John Hart, George Bell and H.C. Hall. Compared with the by-elections, the general election was fought quite cleanly (only J.C. Pendray, the Victoria paint

William John Bowser's nickname was "The Little Napoleon"—due to his party-machine discipline—though he and Premier McBride were also known as the "gold-brick twins" following the patronage and hints of corruption in the 1912 election. Charles Tupper described him as "the embodiment of Prussian 'kultur'" and "the Kaiser of B.C. politics"—strong words from a fellow Conservative, especially following the world-wide outrage at the German invasion of Belgium in late 1914. Bowser lived on Terrace Avenue, off Rockland, with his wife and niece, in a quiet home with a trout pool in the garden and a "soft-voiced Chinese major domo" at the front door.

Thomas "Good Roads" Taylor was McBride's Minister of Public Works and Railways, although McBride and Bowser shared the "supervision" of the PGE contractors. Taylor initiated work on the Trans-Provincial Road—an important project to his constituents in Revelstoke.

A.C. Flumerfelt ran as a Conservative—on McBride's and Bowser's government's record—in the 1916 by-election in Victoria, and was demolished by Liberal party leader H.C. Brewster. An honest man who wanted to keep personalities out of politics, he was nevertheless tarred by his identification with the "big interests." He had owned a shoe company in Winnipeg, and came to Victoria in 1886 on a business trip.

manufacturer, was caught padding a School Board soap tender by $25 and donating that amount to the Conservative association).

The new Liberal, Prohibitionist "petticoat" government was led by Harlan Carey Brewster, the 47-year-old former ships' purser and cannery owner. He chose as his attorney general Malcolm Macdonald, the successful candidate in the 1916 Vancouver by-election. Macdonald entered office still under a cloud from the allegations, and claimed that "by hook or by crook, chiefly by crook and with the perjured evidence of crooks, I must in some manner be linked up with the operation of the gang who were brought from Seattle to vote for the 'wet' candidate." A second set of charges, brought by "the 6th member from Vancouver," a Liberal, clarified the evidence against Macdonald. A representative of the Canadian Northern Railway had placed $25,000 in a Hotel Vancouver safe, which was removed the next day by "the Liberal candidate in that by-election." Macdonald resigned on May 14, 1917. John Wallace deBeque Farris was chosen as his successor.

Prohibition and women's suffrage were positive planks in the Liberals' 1916 election campaign, while the alleged scandals surrounding the Pacific Great Eastern Railway dominated their mudslinging. The PGE route, from Vancouver north via Squamish and the Chilcotin, was originally chartered by the Grand Trunk Pacific, and was intended to connect its main line to Vancouver and Dawson City. Later, in 1912, McBride's government chartered the Pacific Great Eastern to a syndicate including Foley, Stewart & Welch, one of the giant railway contracting firms of the Edwardian years (they built, for example, the double-spiral Connaught Tunnel in the Selkirk Mountains in 1906). McBride's Conservatives had won their massive forty-to-two legislative majority in the 1912 election on the strength of that railway's economic potential, and had guaranteed securities for $35,000 (later $42,000) per mile. The depression of 1913, and World War I, made the project financially hopeless, and construction was abandoned before the Liberal Brewster government came to power in late 1916. Liberal MLA (and future premier) John Oliver said on March 9, 1917 that in order to save Foley, Stewart & Welch from bankruptcy, Bowser had almost bankrupted the province. He established a select committee that day to examine the relationships among the PGE, its contractors, and the former Conservative government—especially McBride and Bowser. The inquiry opened amidst sensational publicity, including reports that certain PGE officials had made a "precipitate departure" to the United States; that Rockland resident D'Arcy Tate, K.C., the vice-president of the railway, had received stock valued at over $6,250,000 as his commission for securing the charter and provincial guarantees, and had undertaken to provide "incidental expenses, including such campaign funds for the Conservative party as might be necessary"; and that a warrant had been sworn out for the arrest of the missing D'Arcy Tate.

The select committee detailed examples of gross price-fixing, excessive costs, lack of proper supervision by the government, and payments to Conservative MLAs (including $9,000 paid to "sub-contractor" A.H.B.

MacGowan, who did no railway work). Disillusionment with the government—with any government—followed, especially among unionized labourers. Both McBride's and Bowser's reputations were badly tarnished. At the end of the inquiry, the PGE, through its lawyer E.P. Davis, agreed to turn over all their assets to the government, but said the line could only be finished at government expense with government supervision. The line consisted only of separated sections of track between North Vancouver and Whytecliffe, and 348 miles from Squamish to Quesnel, indeed "going from nowhere to nowhere." Nicknames were quickly coined for the PGE: "Province's Greatest Expense," "Prince George Eventually," "Please Go Easy."

The PGE curse now fell on the Liberals, even though the inquiry had tarred the Conservatives. Before the 1921 election Premier John Oliver was trying to unload his "white elephant." The original agreement in the charter indicated that the GTP would route its Vancouver traffic over the PGE line; after the war, when the federal government took over the GTP, it was thought they would take over the PGE too. Instead, the Dominion was obliged to nationalize the bankrupt Canadian Northern, thus creating today's Canadian National system. The PGE became redundant. There was a strong possibility, in 1921, that the new Liberal Prime Minister, MacKenzie King, would buy the PGE, but John Oliver had been publicly negative about King's pet project—free trade with the United States. The PGE stayed an issue which dominated politics through the twenties. In 1940, the province had $78 million invested in it. The line finally was completed to Prince George, and from Squamish to Vancouver, in the fifties, but under its new name of "B.C. Rail" it has haunted the province's balance sheets ever since.

The PGE was the motivating factor behind the political protest movements of the twenties. While union men found a political outlet through the various Socialist and I.W.W.-style factions after the First World War, returned soldiers and farmers rallied around the United Farmers of B.C., a party similar to the agricultural-based ones which dominated politics in Alberta and Ontario at that time. When Bowser was re-affirmed as Conservative party leader in late 1922, a group of Young Conservatives in Vancouver formed an alliance with the farmers from the UFBC, remnants of the Great War Veterans' Association, and some established businessmen and lawyers including Sir Charles Hibbert Tupper, George Walkem (nephew of the premier), and super-industrialist A.D. MacRae. They formed the Provincial party, and fought the 1924 election unsuccessfully on charges that both Bowser and Oliver had accepted PGE "slush funds." Massive boodles were alleged, but an audit ordered by Oliver after the election proved nothing. Oliver's final words on the PGE, shortly before his death in 1927, were: "I don't know what to do with the dashed thing."

Brewster & Oliver (Prohibition to Moderation)

Premier Brewster had more to deal with than the "local" agitations for Prohibition and women's suffrage—the war in Europe was dragging on with enormous casualties, and, by early 1917, the conscription issue was threatening to tear the country apart. Conservative Prime Minister Robert L. Borden was attempting to put together a Unionist coalition in Ottawa with conscription as its major plank, but had a tremendous political fight against Liberal Sir Wilfrid Laurier, whose Quebec-based support was strongly against compulsory military service. In B.C., Brewster was a strong conscriptionist, and was approached by Borden in October, 1917, and offered a seat in the federal cabinet if he could successfully convert his pro-Laurier Liberal colleagues, including Attorney General J.W. Farris, M.A. Macdonald, F.C. Wade, former premier Joe Martin, future Vancouver mayor Gerry McGeer, and Victoria's Stuart Henderson. British Columbians who were pro-Unionist included Bowser, Tupper, and Dr. S.F. Tolmie and Joshua Kingham of Victoria. The federal election resulted in a moderate Unionist majority.

Labour strife on the west coast increased during the Unionist campaign. Conscripts were "the most degraded of slaves," said one leader. Radical labour, led by E.T. Kingsley and R.P. Pettipiece in Vancouver, was espousing "Bolshevism," and promoting the Industrial Workers of the World ("Wobblies") and One Big Union. In Victoria, former Socialist MLA James Hawthornthwaite preferred the name "Bolsheviki" to I.W.W., and commented late in 1918: "As to war, in the future if Kings wish to fight, let us give them clubs and tell them to go somewhere and fight all they want; then send the Generals and Colonels with clubs, and every moustached, bandy-legged little officer who is left, even in Victoria!" Through 1919, both the Vancouver and Victoria labour councils were dominated by OBU sympathies, and both joined in sympathy strikes with the Winnipeg General Strike in June (the Victoria one lasted a few days starting June 23). By the end of the year, following a "swarm" of American Federation of Labour organizers into the west, most of the Victoria and Vancouver unions had returned to their moderate, A.F.L. affiliation.

Meanwhile, Premier Brewster had left Victoria on February 9, 1918 for an inter-provincial conference in Ottawa; he caught a chill on his way back, and had to stop in Calgary, where he entered hospital and died March 1. John Oliver, the acting premier, was appointed to succeed him on the sixth. (The Victoria by-election to replace Brewster was the first test of soldiers' sentiments: Private Frank Giolma of the Great War Veterans' Association campaigned for a policy of industrial absorption of returned men, conscription of alien labour, better veterans' pensions and care for widows. He swept the riding against strong Liberal and Conservative candidates.)

Oliver's main problem was Prohibition. The Prohibition referendum had originally been promised by a befuddled Richard McBride on August 23, 1915—he could not see how people could vote for such an extreme policy. On February 29, 1916, Bowser promised a referendum and tightened the Liquor Act. Two weeks later, a deputation of license holders led by the Gold Seal Liquor Co.'s Albert E. Tulk, and Sir Charles Hibbert Tupper, met with Bowser to demand compensation: only a few years before, they had had heavy expenses converting their saloons into hotels to comply with the Liquor Act amendments. Four days later, on March 19, a congregation of eleven Victoria churches endorsed the tightened Liquor Act. Two weeks later, the "Committee of 100," an affiliate of the Peoples' Prohibition Association led by Vancouver businessman Jonathan Rogers, held a massive Prohibition meeting in Victoria, opposing any compensation for the liquor dealers. Bowser attempted to compromise, on May 25, introducing a liquor bill based on the Macdonald Act in Manitoba, which would not interfere with importation for private or sacramental purposes. Though the bill was approved by the legislature, Bowser was still pressured into calling a Prohibition referendum for September 14.

A clear majority of civilians voted for Prohibition, but the soldiers, both at home and overseas, voted strongly against it. The Rev. Ben H. Spence, a Prohibition leader, had published articles describing Canadian soldiers "debauched by British booze"—his book *The Fiddlers* was banned by the Canadian government as inflammatory and disloyal. Allegations of crookedness on the part of practically everyone—especially McBride, who as agent general in London was supervising the overseas vote—resulted in an investigation by the legislature. Eventually, it was determined that about half the ballots were questionable, and that more people had voted against Prohibition than had voted Liberal in the last election. But by that time Brewster's government had chosen Prohibition.

The new act said that any liquor with greater than two-and-one-half percent spirit could only be obtained from the government vendor with a physician's prescription, or be imported from outside (this loophole was partially filled by the federal government's order-in-council of December 24, 1917, and by a Prohibition of the inter-provincial transport of liquor the following April); other restrictions said that liquor could only be kept by occupants of private dwelling houses and served to guests inside (not even on the lawn), and that it was illegal to carry liquor in a car, boat, or pocket. Druggists could keep five gallons, dentists one pint, and doctors two quarts, all for medicinal purposes. The issue, for most people, then became one of finding a sympathetic doctor to write a prescription.

On December 13, 1918, the new Prohibition commissioner, Walter Findlay, was arraigned in Vancouver on a charge of importing and selling whiskey. He pleaded guilty on December 16 to importing 700 cases, and was sentenced to a fine of $1,000 or six months. A hue and cry began, led by Jonathan Rogers, over "the gross fraud and breach of trust." The crown appealed, and the following June 10 Findlay got two years. Between March and October, 1919, B.C. doctors wrote 188,120 liquor prescriptions, one doctor being responsible for 4,000 in a month. Victoria doctors wrote 54,732 prescriptions that year, and the new Prohibition commissioner, J. Sclater, reported that sales of 8,767 cases of rye, 8,323 cases of Scotch and 818 cases of brandy had netted the government $1,579,475.

Harlan Carey Brewster fought for the Liberal cause, and promoted prohibition and women's suffrage, for years before finally gaining power in the 1916 election. His strong stand for conscription, before his sudden death in early 1918, aggravated the radical labour strife on the west coast.

Albert Edward Tulk, a Conservative and a cavalry lieutenant in the First World War, represented the liquor interests in the fight for compensation following Prohibition. His Gold Seal Liquor Company abandoned the B.C. market in the early twenties, following the Moderation referendum and the creation of the Liquor Control Board.

"Honest John" Oliver described himself as a "dirt-farmer," loved to have his picture taken holding a shovel, and always ate at the White Lunch on Yates Street, as "I like to see and pick what I'm going to eat." He had little sympathy with the radical labour movement during the late 1910s, and said that unemployment was caused by a "misplaced" labour force, too many merchants with heavy overheads, and extravagance "in our buildings and our ideas." His defence of himself was: "I started working before I was ten years of age, driving a donkey in the mines of Derbyshire, and I have been working ever since, and never harder than as Premier of B.C."

It was difficult, he said, to keep an adequate supply on hand.

The federal import ban was lifted in January, 1920, and the provincial laws were tightened to limit physicians to 100 prescriptions of eight ounces each a month. Although the prescription business declined, a tremendous amount of liquor started to enter B.C. extra-provincially. One seizure was the $237,000 stock of the Canadian Pacific Wine Co. in Vancouver on August 17: the company appealed successfully all the way to the Privy Council in London, arguing that the provincial government was attempting to restrict inter-provincial trade.

Attorney General Farris rapidly came to the conclusion that Prohibition was unworkable, and, on March 29, announced a referendum. The campaign leading up to the October 20 vote was "vigorous and picturesque," with Mrs. Farris one of the leading "dry" exponents. The Moderation movement—sale from government vendors in sealed packages, and no by-the-glass sales—was supported by Tupper and the *Colonist*. The women's vote was especially large—their temperance, rather than strict Prohibition sentiment, carried the day, and a majority of 27,000 voted for government control. The issue needed a political verdict, and Oliver went to the polls in a general election on December 1, 1920, arguing: "I have no conscientious scruples about making all I can out of the business." Bowser also supported the Moderation bill. "A bewildering medley of two chief parties, plus Farmers, Soldiers, Labour and Socialists, with a large number of hyphenated candidates and opinions"—153 candidates in total—contested the election. Oliver, campaigning for moderation and a new provincial road-building program, carried the election with a 13-seat majority.

Farris introduced a new Liquor Act on February 23, 1921, which allowed for permanent resident liquor permits at $5 per year, set a quart bottle limit on single purchases, banned display signs and provided for a 50-50 sharing of profits with municipalities. A penalty of six months imprisonment at hard labour was set for the first offence of illegal sale of liquor. A strong plea was made by hotels and clubs to sell liquor, beer, and wine by the glass. The government rejected it, so on June 23 the Veterans' Clubs announced they would sell beer to bona fide members. Four days later, police began raiding clubs. Tupper appeared for the Army and Navy Veterans in Victoria on July 29, charging that the Liquor Board was a monopoly in restraint of trade and thus in violation of the British North America Act. When this argument was dismissed, Victoria lawyer H. Despard Twigg, on August 6, sought to prove that the practice of beer-selling by the Veterans' Clubs constituted distribution of property among members, not beer-selling. This also was rejected, but Twigg appealed and won on September 6.

The "Drys" immediately took up the fight. Dr. Sipprell, the Victoria Methodist Minister, spoke out fervently against the public "being engaged in the buying and selling of liquor." Bowser attacked Farris in the legislature, charging that a "liquor ring" made up of Liberal stalwarts surrounded the attorney general. Farris's reply indicated his discouragement: "What is there in political life in this Province good enough to have to stand for this sort of thing?" He resigned at the end of the year, and returned to his private law practice.

Meanwhile, the Moderation League, by now led by Henry Bell-Irving (the Tulks were about to pull out of the liquor business), lobbied the government strenuously for by-the-glass beer sales in hotels and clubs. Violations and police raids continued, especially in Vancouver where, by the middle of December, 18 hotel bars were reported to be open and selling beer, charging their "club members" a ten-cent fee. The Great War Veterans' Association adopted a system of tokens, and although the Province called it "distributing" and prosecuted vigorously, they were unable to obtain any convictions. A local option law was finally passed on December 20, 1923; Victoria for years decided against beer-parlour sales, forcing city drinkers to go to Esquimalt, which permitted them.

Much of the Prohibition sentiment in B.C. stemmed from the powerful influence of American radio in the early Twenties, especially the sermons of Billy Sunday and the agitation of "Pussyfoot Johnson." Maine had been "dry" as early as 1851, and a Prohibition amendment was ratified by 46 out of the 48 states in December, 1917. Full Prohibition ("the Volstead Act") became effective in the U.S. on January 16, 1920, and continued until Roosevelt repealed it in 1934. B.C.'s "anti-Volsteadians" did a thriving business rumrunning down the coast, and hopping across the border on the mainland, during the twenties (page 79).

John Oliver's government struggled through the scandals of Prohibition and the PGE, and went to the people on June 20, 1924, following the sensational accusations of the Provincial party over the PGE. All three major leaders—Oliver, Bowser, and the Provincial's MacRae—were defeated, though Oliver was later returned in a by-election. Bowser retired. The economic boom in the late twenties mainly benefited Vancouver, while Victoria languished far behind. "Honest John" Oliver, who had just passed his 70th birthday, took a holiday in the summer of 1927 in the United States. After a week, a rumour began to circulate that he was at the Mayo Clinic; then, that he had terminal cancer. He returned to Victoria on July 3, "a broken old man," and died on the eve of the visit of the Prince of Wales and Prince George. He was buried in Victoria on August 20.

His successor, picked by the caucus, was the 53-year-old minister of finance and education, Dr. John D. MacLean. A native of Prince Edward Island, MacLean had moved west at age 19 and taught school in B.C. and Alberta. He then went to McGill University, and returned to Rossland in 1905 as a medical doctor. He gravitated to politics, and was elected from Greenwood in the 1916 Liberal sweep. Before he had served a year as premier, his government's mandate was four years old, and he called an election for July 18, 1928.

Tolmie & Pattullo (Prosperity to Depression)

Dr. MacLean, the new Liberal premier, was in much the same position politically vis-a-vis his predecessor, Oliver, as Bowser had been with *his* predecessor, McBride—he had to run his government on his predecessor's record. MacLean was a little smug, not at all modest about his intelligence and organizational ability, and not very daring—his nickname "Velvet Vest" fitted him perfectly. He was obviously out of touch with the electorate—especially with the crucial votes in booming, go-ahead Vancouver—and, like "dirt farmer" John Oliver, neglected to give Vancouver any cabinet representation. The Vancouver *Province* newspaper, which had always been Conservative, and was by far the most influential newspaper in the province, campaigned relentlessly to remove the Liberals from power.

The PGE railway still dominated the news and drained the province's finances, and the Liberals, after more than a decade in power, could scarcely continue to blame it on the McBride and Bowser Conservatives. MacLean announced early in his premiership (on December 1, 1927) that as no offer to purchase the PGE had come from either national railway, the province should complete it from Vancouver through to Prince George. However, during the campaign leading up to the election in July, he waffled, saying his government would complete it if necessary, but would not necessarily complete it. His final position was that he would be better able to sell it to the federally-owned CNR, as, being a Liberal, he was on better terms with Prime Minister MacKenzie King. MacLean was thus "turning what should have been a business proposition into a political deal," said the Conservative press.

Other local issues marked MacLean's ten months in power: Joshua Hinchcliffe and Major Allan Lyons, both Conservative members in Victoria, charged that the Provincial Police was subject to political influence; a Liquor Board inquiry investigated allegations that payoffs and favours to the Liquor Board staff from H.F. Reifel's brewery interests had surfaced during the 1926 customs scandals (which brought down King's federal Liberal government); none was proved.

The Conservatives, in 1926, had chosen Dr. Simon Fraser Tolmie as their provincial leader. The son of the celebrated Dr. W.F. Tolmie of Cloverdale farm in Saanich, he was born in Victoria on January 25, 1867, and graduated in 1891 from the Ontario Veterinary College in Toronto, before returning to Saanich to run the family farm. In 1898, he was named Provincial Veterinary Inspector and six years later was chosen as chief inspector of the Animal Health branch for the Department of Agriculture. He was elected to the House of Commons in 1917, and from 1919 to 1921 served as minister of agriculture in Arthur Meighen's government. When Meighen was re-elected in 1926, Tolmie again became minister of agriculture, but at the first whiff of the B.C. provincial election he resigned his Ottawa seat and hurried home.

By comparison with the colourless and abstract Dr. MacLean, Dr. Tolmie was the epitome of the country vet—warm, simple, genial and plain-spoken. MacLean didn't stump the province, but Tolmie travelled 4,000 miles through the interior in three weeks, speaking to country meetings and city rallies. In the election, on July 18, the Liberals were routed, and even Premier MacLean lost his Victoria seat. The Liberals were reduced from 23 to 12 seats, while Tolmie's Conservative forces ended up with 35 seats in the legislature. The MacLean government resigned on August 20; MacLean himself got the job of federal Farms Loan Commissioner the following January 7th, and a fortnight later Thomas Dufferin Pattullo, the MLA from Prince Rupert, was chosen as the new Liberal leader.

Tolmie's government was notably dull and unimaginative—most of the news it made concerned the wave of patronage appointments of Conservatives hungry after a decade out of power. Its 1929 performance was called the Milk and Water Session, as the two major pieces of legislation dealt with milk (the pooling of surplus milk profits among cooperatives in the Fraser Valley) and water (establishing a Water Board as part of the Public Utilities Commission). As the economy faltered and crashed at the beginning of 1930, Tolmie's government seemed unable to cope.

Vancouver suffered much more directly from the effects of the Depression than Victoria, partly because Vancouver's economy was trade and industry-based, while Victoria's quietly subsided with the diminishing government revenues. Unemployed single men easily reached Vancouver by riding free on freight trains, while the trip to the Island took cash and a boat ride (although there were many stories of unemployed men getting stranded on the Island after "good samaritans" gave them one-way tickets and promises of jobs). Regardless, it was a hopeless period for many people, and the provincial government had few ideas and even less money.

Tolmie was a great imperialist and believer in Great Britain. He decided to move in the same, conservative direction as the British government, which had followed the recommendations of the May Commission, a "non-partisan" group of businessmen who claimed to be able to fix the economy with modern business planning. The B.C. equivalent was the Kidd Report, chaired by chartered accountant George Kidd, a retired B.C. Electric president, and endorsed by some of the big industrialists in Vancouver.

Kidd's group met to demand a balancing of the budget on March 18, 1932, at a luncheon attended by 600 confreres in the ballroom of the Hotel Vancouver. Kidd led the attack against the budget of Finance Minister "One Percent Jimmy" Jones (named for his famous one percent surtax on high incomes), which Kidd claimed would not balance, thereby adding to the province's already massive $114 million debt. Speaking in front of a large canvas covered in figures marked in black and red, Kidd said his desire was only "to point out the seriousness of the situation." Other accusations and recommendations followed: industry could not compete against the high interest rates of government bonds; wages were too high compared with Europe; the legislature should be reduced to 28 members and the Cabinet to six; the University of B.C.'s budget should be slashed from $25 million to $6 million; most of the province's problems were due

Dr. J.D. MacLean (1873-1948) was "the forgotten premier." He took over the premiership following John Oliver's death in the summer of 1927. The Liberals' popularity, after a decade in power, was definitely waning when "Velvet Vest" MacLean took over. He lacked the bright ideas and force of personality to reverse the trend, and lost even his own seat the following summer.

Thomas Dufferin Pattullo was so neat and natty that "he parted his hair with a spirit level." His sartorial splendour was the butt of numerous cartoons, especially as the Depression deepened. Pattullo lived on the edge of the Victoria Golf Links in Oak Bay, and—for his only recreation—started at the hole nearest his house. Otherwise, he had no hobbies except politics, and only one true friend—his Finance Minister, John Hart.

An anti-Pattullo advertisement from 1934, urging financial restraint and responsibility à la Kidd Report.

to the duplication of government employees, rules and regulations. Beneath it all ran an indictment of representational, partisan government; Kidd evoked the panacea of a government run by "non-partisan" economic planners and businessmen. (The same theories dominated the economies of countries like Germany, Italy and Japan during the thirties; a faith in economic planning and business principles inspired Franklin D. Roosevelt's "New Deal" in the United States after 1933; a sincere belief in the power of economics had led to coalition government in Great Britain.)

Much of the opposition was led by Victoria-born economist Henry Angus, who argued that the report was "in the interests of a limited class in the community, rather than the considered advice of business and professional men." That September, Tolmie called for a Union government. Opposition leader Pattullo considered Tolmie's acquiescence to the Kidd Report a sign of weakness, and when the latter approached him about a coalition, he rejected it. Tolmie drifted along and let his government run five years to the day—the absolute end of its legal mandate—before calling an election for November 2, 1933. His campaign plea to the voters was: "Why change? We are the only group with Depression experience."

Duff Pattullo had a more positive slogan: "Work and Wages." He believed in priming the pump—deficit financing to create a public works employment program—and was prepared to wage "an incalculable battle against the Ottawa government" to get a better deal for B.C., specifically to get some special relief to help look after the one-third of Canada's unemployed who had come into the province. Once again, a B.C. politician was seeking election with the promise to "fight Ottawa."

The election campaign featured 219 candidates vying for 48 seats, including 13 Unionists led by Tolmie, following the B.C. Conservative Association's decision to leave its members to choose as they wished; 47 Liberals under Pattullo; 38 Independent non-partisans, including W.J. Bowser, who came out of retirement; and 46 CCFers. Many of the independents wanted coalition government.

The Co-operative Commonwealth Federation (CCF) first appeared in British Columbia in the spring of 1933, following its formation in Regina. Its "visionary socialism" offered the only true alternative to Pattullo, and the messianical radio broadcasts of CCFer Dr. Lyle Telford, like those of Father Coughlin, the Rev. Clem Davies, and Alberta Premier "Bible Bill" Aberhart, had a great power of persuasion with his audience.

A week before the election, Bowser died of a heart attack, so the voting in the six ridings (four in Victoria and two in Vancouver) which he "led" was postponed until November 27. On the 2nd, in the general election, the Tolmie government was almost annihilated—only Attorney General Harry Pooley was returned in Esquimalt. Thirty Liberals and seven CCFers, including father and son Ernie and Harold Winch, formed most of the legislature. Pattullo promptly introduced the Special Powers Act, a piece of emergency powers legislation to move B.C.'s 100,000 unemployed out of the cities and onto the land, which he felt he would need if

he got nowhere fighting Prime Minister R.B. Bennett. The SPA overrode all other legislation on the statute books, and gave the Cabinet sweeping powers over natural resources, borrowing money, public works, property, and civil rights in the province. The Conservative press immediately branded Pattullo a "fascist" and a "dictator," and the label stuck with him throughout his career. Pattullo and his finance minister, John Hart, received initially rather short shrift from Bennett, who thought they were wildly reckless. Eventually, the two governments compromised, and Pattullo's Work and Wages program was able to proceed, with some national financial help and without invoking the SPA.

Conditions had improved enough in British Columbia to guarantee Pattullo a sweeping election victory on June 1, 1937. The CCF retained their seven seats, but although they had gained a lot of public sympathy for their support of the work-camp strikers in 1935, and their championing of the cause of the downtrodden, voters began to return to the orthodox parties as the economy brightened. Eight Conservatives were elected, and the two parties together faced 31 Liberals. The cause of Union government had once again become popular—this time with business groups, which saw a coalition of the two old-line parties as the best way to guarantee inexpensive government and keep out the CCF.

Pattullo's attention turned to the interior and the north, in the hope that a new resource boom would come from oil and gold. Rumours that the Americans were interested in building an Alaskan highway followed President Roosevelt's visit to Victoria in the pouring rain on September 30, 1937 (he disembarked from a U.S. destroyer at the Ogden Point docks, and drove through crowds estimated at 30,000 to a Government House luncheon).

Pattullo, a Prince Rupert "Grit" with something of a built-in fear of the business community's demands, moved in the autumn of 1937 to control the oil industry by establishing a Fuel Control Board. He suspected that the "oil interests," and the Vancouver-based financial interests which identified with his finance minister, John "The Juggler" Hart, were in favour of coalition. Simultaneously, the progressive faction of his Liberal support began to slide away, after he cut relief grants to municipalities, arguing that conditions were much better now and the single men ought to be able to support themselves by dispersing throughout the province, in the hinterland where he was sure the work was. Instead of dispersing, they marched on Vancouver in the spring of 1938 and occupied the Hotel Georgia (briefly), the Vancouver Art Gallery, and the Post Office. Their eviction by the police on June 20 resulted in the worst riot ever seen in Vancouver. Pattullo, who had been busy pursuing a quarrel with Prime Minister MacKenzie King in Ottawa, paid no attention to the sit-down strikers. His callousness damaged his reputation, and many voters felt his narrow partisanship was out of touch with the times. The declaration of war, in September 1939, and the resurgence of the CCF as a constructive alternative, made a coalition inevitable. Pattullo, the old Grit warhorse, obviously had to be moved out in favour of the businesslike, grey-flannel conciliation of a John Hart.

The Coalition

Duff Pattullo's partisan Liberal and provincial attitudes were out of step with B.C. public opinion once the Second World War started in 1939. Finance Minister John Hart and Attorney General Gordon Wismer were more willing to compromise their "Grit" attitudes in order to unify Canada for the war effort.

The conciliatory attitude of the time was apparent in the Rowell-Sirois Commission—the Royal Commission on Dominion and Provincial Relations—which sat from 1937-40. Demands for revisions to the British North America Act had become like "hardy annuals," and the commission's recommendations revamped financing arrangements between the federal and provincial governments. One of the more timely results was that the federal government assumed the entire cost of unemployment relief. War financing was also simplified. The Commission's progressive ideas were epitomized by Victoria-born commission member Henry Forbes Angus, a nephew of merchant James Angus, who was head of the Department of Economics at UBC.

At a federal-provincial conference following the completion of the Rowell-Sirois Report, Pattullo aligned himself with the two maverick Canadian provincial premiers—Alberta Socred William Aberhart, and Ontario Liberal Mitchell Hepburn. Aberhart, especially, had resisted Angus's appointment to the commission, feeling his orthodox economic beliefs were contradictory to Social Credit monetary theories, and thus opposed to progress and "useless in this age." The conference was wrecked by the three premiers' narrow partisanship, and business interests in British Columbia were infuriated. By mid-1941, the people surrounding Finance Minister Hart were openly talking of a coalition government and a new premier.

Pattullo still felt that his "fight Ottawa" stance was giving him votes, and called an election for October 21, 1941. He was so confident of victory that he invited a large number of friends and reporters to his home on the edge of the golf course in Oak Bay to listen to the returns on the radio. They were anything but encouraging: the Liberals dropped ten seats to 21, the Conservatives elected twelve, and the CCF, who topped the polls with one-third of all the votes, elected 14.

Pattullo made overtures in the direction of the CCF, reasoning blindly that he was still seen as progressive compared with the "oil interests" and businessmen around Hart and the Conservative party (the latter were openly antagonistic to Pattullo over his Fuel Control Board; the conflict had peaked in 1940 over the board's power to establish a retail price of gasoline). The CCF, remembering Pattullo's Special Powers Act (and his brief endorsement of Mussolini's economic planning methods in the early thirties), still thought of him as a fascist. Pattullo, certain that Hart and his big-money supporters had ganged up on him, split completely with him in November. On December 3, 1941, Pattullo lost the party leadership at the provincial Liberal convention. He resigned, and recommended that the first member from Victoria, John Hart, be asked to form a government. That Sunday, Japanese planes bombed Pearl Harbour, and the Pacific war began. Hart immediately formed a non-party, Unionist government.

Life in British Columbia during World War II was extremely prosperous, although with rationing and travel restrictions there wasn't very much to spend the money on. Over 30,000 people were at work in the Victoria and Vancouver shipyards. More workers moved to the coast from the prairies and the B.C. interior, creating housing shortages in both cities. Little stucco bungalows were quickly thrown together, filling in the old estates and vacant lots in older parts of Victoria. Streetcars carried record numbers of people. Vancouver Island Coach Lines suspended all its services to the beaches and resorts to save gas. Rockland Avenue resident Kathleen Agnew, who was unable to get new tires for her car, bought a new Packard in order to have something to drive.

The Coalition continued after the war, in the new partnership from 1948-52 of Liberal "Boss" Johnson and Conservative Herbert Anscomb, the former reeve of Oak Bay. There was no further justification of a Union government on the grounds of a national emergency—the Coalition partners were united only in their dislike of the CCF, which in the 1945 election had won ten seats. The Coalition brought in a system of alternative voting, where each ballot was marked with first and second choices and the winner was determined by a complicated formula, ostensibly to make it almost impossible for the CCF to form a government. The old-line parties—the Liberals and Conservatives—were still split into factions and fighting over issues from the twenties and thirties. The rise of a fourth party, with new blood and a constructive program for the forward-thinking 1950s, was inevitable.

In the 1952 election, with the alternative ballot, there was no definite majority, and the weeks dragged on as the results were slowly tabulated. Eventually, it transpired that Johnson and two of his Liberal Cabinet ministers had been defeated. The Social Credit party, led by renegade former Conservative W.A.C. Bennett (who had crossed the floor just before the Coalition collapsed, and formed a new party during the election campaign), led with 19 seats. The CCF had 18, the Liberals six, the Conservatives four, and Independent Labour one. Johnson resigned, and Bennett was asked to form a government.

No one really knew what Bennett represented—was he another protest party offshoot, like the Provincial party from the twenties? Did he believe in Social Credit monetary theories? Was he a renegade Tory, like Bowser in the 1933 election? It turned out that he was a conservative politician and that the name "Socred" was inappropriate. The voters didn't care, and returned the party again and again over the following decades, initially in 1953 with 27 seats out of 48, then in 1956 with 39 out of 52. The old-line parties almost completely disappeared. And Bennett fought Ottawa throughout his career, always looking for a better deal for B.C., just like all the successful B.C. premiers dating back to de Cosmos and Walkem in the 1870s.

John ("call me Jack") Hart was Pattullo's heir-apparent. He was supposed to be "full of Irish blarney," but got his nicknames "the Juggler" and "Trader Hart" for his financial legerdemain, especially the mysterious contingent liabilities in the PGE books when he was finance minister (before his temporary withdrawal from politics in 1924) during John Oliver's government. He dressed like an Ottawa treasury department mandarin, in a double-breasted black coat and grey pants. He retired in October, 1947, and died ten years later, aged 78.

The B.C. Provincial Police

Augustus Pemberton, commissioned by Governor Douglas to establish on Vancouver Island the forerunner of the Provincial Police. He married Chartres Brew's sister, Miss Jane Augusta, who had come to Victoria in 1861 with the intention of keeping house for her brother. The Pembertons lived at the 15-acre "Glenville Estate" above Five Points in Fairfield, at the end of Masters Road. He died on October 18, 1891, two years after his wife. One son, Chartres Cecil, stayed in Victoria and, though trained as a lawyer, worked in the real estate business for years, specializing in Gonzales Hill property.

The most famous police force of early Canada—the Royal North West Mounted—was created fifteen years *after* the B.C. Provincial Police. The Mounties' exploits in preserving law and order in the west were no more glorious than those of the B.C. Police; the latter grumbled that "the prairie brethren" achieved greater glory because they were in uniform (the B.C. Provincial Police didn't get their distinctive khaki uniforms with the olive green pant-stripe and epaulets until the mid-twenties).

The colony of Vancouver Island, and the wild mainland which became British Columbia, had a placid existence until the 1858 gold rush. The arrival of "the worst of the population of San Francisco—the very dregs, in fact, of society," as Governor Douglas described the miners, alarmed him. In London, the Colonial Office's Sir Edward Bulwer-Lytton agreed to dispatch a party of Royal Engineers, under Colonel Richard Clement Moody, to establish roads and a defendable town (New Westminster), and maintain order in the goldfields. The cost of the Royal Engineers was more than the Colonial Office could easily bear, and Lytton wrote to Douglas that "your real strength lies in the conviction of emigrants that their interests are identical with those of the government; a police force must be derived from the people on the spot, who will understand that for their own preservation from internal disturbances, they must rely solely on themselves."

To establish the force, a man named Chartres Brew was commissioned by London and sent to Vancouver Island. Born in Corsfin, County Clare in 1815, he joined the Royal Ulster Constabulary in 1840, and had recently finished service in the Crimea. Brew left England on a ship called the *Austria*, which burned in the mid-Atlantic. He was picked up by a passing ship, which carried him to South America. He made his way north to Victoria, arriving somewhat late, to discover that Governor Douglas had presumed him lost and commissioned Augustus Frederick Pemberton instead. (Brew was given the job of establishing the force in British Columbia, once the mainland colony was created in late 1858. His brother Tomkins became town constable at Granville, now Vancouver.)

Pemberton was a member of the "Dublin Castle Gentry," like his nephew Joseph Despard Pemberton, Peter O'Reilly, and other Irishmen in colonial Victoria. He was born in Clontarf, near Dublin (where his father was Lord Mayor), in 1808, and was educated for the bar, but decided to come to the New World "to follow agricultural pursuits." He arrived in Victoria in December, 1855, following an arduous journey through Panama, during which half of his travelling party were massacred by Indians. Pemberton's appointment in Victoria also carried with it responsibilities as police magistrate and prefect of the city. He made himself extremely unpopular with the southern American element in the city when he appointed a number of blacks as policemen (in the same way, Bishop Cridge drew criticism for permitting Victoria's black community to worship in his church, and Governor Kennedy alienated many citizens by enthusiastically receiving a salute from the former Californians).

The combination of Pemberton, Brew, and Judge Begbie kept lawlessness to a minimum. Brew was able to overawe American gang leaders like the supposed desperado of Boston Bar, Ned MacGowan, and Pemberton's fluency in various Indian languages forestalled uprisings. They were fortunate that one common practice of the California gold rush years—duelling—never got established in B.C. A few duels were documented in the Interior, but only one was recorded in Victoria, in September, 1858. Two Americans, John B. Collins and William "Tipperary Bill" Morris had a dispute, which developed into a scuffle. They agreed to duel, and met past the outskirts of the city, on Vancouver Street east of Kanaka Row. At the third volley, Collins was mortally wounded, and Morris fled by boat for the United States, hotly pursued by Pemberton's constables. Morris was hanged, for another incident, in California the following spring. (A highly coloured, fictionalized account of the duel was published by Victoria politician and businessman David W. Higgins, as one of the chapters in a book called *The Mystic Spring*, in Toronto in 1904).

The B.C. Police had its headquarters in the former Menzies Street drill hall behind the legislative buildings. By the late thirties, it consisted of eleven officers and more than 300 NCOs and constables. Enlistment was limited to British subjects "of good character," between 21 and 35 years of age, five foot ten or taller, and weighing at least 165 pounds. The force modernized itself considerably, following the 1924 appointment of Col. John Hugh McMullin as commissioner by Attorney General Alex Manson. Uniforms were purchased, training was improved, and legislation was passed to allow municipalities to contract with the B.C. Police. They were the first Canadian force to use wireless "to span the great distances," in 1928. Fourteen police boats were maintained, including the P.M.L. 14, berthed in Victoria, with a courtroom on the aft deck and accommodation for five crew members and five prisoners. The B.C. Police also established a Highway Patrol, with a dozen Harley-Davidson motorcycles patrolling the border roads for rumrunners, and 13 white-painted Ford vans as patrol cars. The latter converted quickly into ambulances, and in addition carried brake meters and light testers for roadside vehicle inspections. During the Second World War, they carried spray cans of khaki paint, so that in case of a sudden invasion they could be camouflaged "in twenty minutes."

Col. McMullin was typical of the men who signed up for the B.C. Police in the years around the First World War. Many had been career officers in the territorial regiments, or members in colonial police forces (particularly the Shanghai constabulary, which ceased to exist following the Japanese bombing and invasion in 1938), who wished to work for and retire into a British milieu. McMullin was born in Madras, India, in 1868 and, following an English education, was commissioned to the East Surrey Regiment. He transferred to the Third Hussars, but resigned in 1893 to try farming in the Okanagan after the wide publicity given to the Earl of Aberdeen's ranch near Vernon. He re-enlisted at the outbreak of the Boer War and received the Queen's South Africa medal. In October, 1901, he joined the B.C. Police, and stayed with them until his retirement in 1939 (he died in Victoria on May 10, 1943). Another typical officer was Inspector William Lewis Fernie, described in the Police's "official magazine," *The Shoulder Strap* (subtitled "Colourful Stories of Romance and Adventure of the Provincial Police in B.C."), as a "damned white fellow."

Police officer Bob Owens was a familiar figure between the wars. Born in Bangor, Ireland in 1885, he came to Victoria as a child, was captain of the Victoria lacrosse team in 1909, and a star on the old Cloverdale basketball team. He joined the B.C. Police in January, 1912, enlisted in the Canadian Expeditionary Force in 1914, and returned to the police after the war. Owens helped solve the two major crimes of the Twenties: the *Beryl G* hijacking in September, 1924, and the Royal Bank robbery in Nanaimo on December 12 of that year. The former involved the dastardly murder of a father and son for their illegal liquor cargo on a little rumrunning boat called the *Beryl G* in a cove on Vancouver Island; "Cannonball" Baker and Harry Myers, alias "Cy" Sowash, were eventually caught and hanged. The Royal Bank robbery was a piece of pure gangsterism by "hardened criminals or American gunmen." A U-drive was hired the previous day in Victoria by the gunmen, who drove north and took over the bank on payroll day. The employees were herded into a corner and told "keep still or we'll fill you full of lead"; $42,000 was spirited away across the border. The Seattle police unearthed some clues which eventually led Owens to William Bagley, "hard guy" Harry Stone, and "Big" Johnson. Bagley, "spineless and cowardly at the end," was hanged at San Quentin.

McMullin's retirement coincided with John Hart's rise in power from finance minister to premier. Hart ordered an investigation, in April, 1942, into shortages and supply costs in the force. In what became known as "the shoe-box incident," it was discovered that a Victoria merchant had maintained an open account ostensibly for the purchase of shoes. When he received a cheque from the police, he cashed it and put the money in a "shoebox till," which eventually contained several hundred dollars used for incidental expenses, including paying a contractor to install a heating plant in a building which the force had commandeered for "certain" stores. On August 6, charges of conspiracy to defraud were brought against former police quartermaster Leonard J. Simmons, John G. Simpson of James Maynard Ltd., and drygoods merchant George H. Hall. The charges were dropped, but Hart and his attorney general Gordon Wismer maintained a suspicion of the force thereafter.

In March, 1950, Wismer decided to disband the B.C. Police, and replace

Inspector Robert Owens, guarding child-star Shirley Temple during a visit to Victoria in 1937.

Col. John H. McMullin, born in India and educated in England, was commissioner of the Provincial Police from 1924 to 1939. His colonial and military background was typical of the B.C. Police between the wars.

A police motorcyclist in the thirties, from The Shoulder Strap *magazine. The Provincial Police bought Harley Davidson and Indian motorcycles for its highway patrol. The former were purchased from Fred Deeley in Vancouver. The "Indian agent" in Victoria was Richard "Pop" Shanks (1876-1963), at the Brooklands Motorcycle Works at 937 Fort Street. Born in England, Shanks started with a bicycle shop at Weybridge near the Brooklands racetrack, then moved to Victoria in 1911 and opened a garage "with the chief job of pulling cars out of the mud." He was a charter member of the Victoria Motorcycle Club in 1912, and continued to ride a motorcycle to work till his mid-70s. One son, Reg, carried on the business, while the other, Bob, who was a daredevil motorcycle rider in his youth, raised horses and opened Shanks' Saddlery at Douglas and Market streets.*

it with the RCMP, in order to "save a considerable sum of money." Most of the police were absorbed into the RCMP, but, of the 520, about 30 chose to quit or take early retirement rather than take the cut in pay, $15 to $20 a month, to RCMP rates (B.C. Police pay rates had been $7 a day for sergeants, and $5.55 for first class constables). The Mounties had other rules which caused some bitterness, including one which said that a man must have five years of service and $1,200 in the bank before he could get married. The RCMP took over B.C. policing duties in August, 1950.

Residential Areas

James Bay

The Victoria land map of 1858 shows most of the James Bay area owned by the Fur Trade Division of the Hudson's Bay Company. Called the Beckley Farm, it was sold off piece by piece over the ensuing decades, so that by the turn of the century James Bay was almost completely settled.

At first, the purchasers were men like wholesale merchant Richard Carr and future senator W.J. Macdonald. They bought large acreages, which were developed and cultivated into paddocks, fields, orchards, and formal gardens with long driveways and screens of trees. The roads were lined with bird-filled hedgerows and wildflowers grew profusely in the springtime. Properties were separated by rubble walls with old-style postern gates, and fields with snake fences and stiles; every property had a big house and a number of outbuildings for chickens, the cow, and horses. Servants were cheap and almost invariably Chinese—most English servants responded to the freedom of the new world, married, and became boss of their own properties. The flat James Bay area was lush and easily tamed, like England, helping to ease the homesickness for British colonists 150 sailing days from home. The high land, at Beacon Hill Park and above Dallas Road, commanded a splendid view of the straits and the Olympic Mountains. Wild roses covered the cliff-tops along the Dallas Road drive, and grasses and blue camass and daisies filled the fields.

There was little settlement until the completion of the James Bay bridge and the "Birdcages" in 1859. Then, it became the only fashionable neighbourhood before Rockland was subdivided in the 1880s—close to town, but separated from the hurly-burly of the waterfront and the saloons of downtown and the stink of James Bay itself. Birdcage Walk, the continuation of Government Street south of the James Bay bridge, stopped at Michigan Street, where Mrs. McConnell's cow-yard occupied the land between Michigan and Toronto Street. The "continuation" of Birdcage Walk south of Mrs. McConnell's was a narrow lane called Carr Road (extended between Toronto and Michigan and renamed Government Street following the completion of the causeway in the early 1900s). On the east side of Carr Road in the long block between Simcoe and Toronto was only one house, Carr's; on the west side, set far back from the road in a little copse behind an orchard, with a driveway lined with laurel and yellow roses, was Bishop Cridge's "Marifield." And so it was throughout most of James Bay—a sylvan, gentle setting with the perfume of flowers in sunny fields, breezes from the strait, and lots of space between the houses.

Life was a round of "quite gay" entertainments. Wednesday was the "at home" day for ladies; Sundays, after church, there were lengthy lun-

ches for large parties, and afternoon teas celebrated the arrival of friends from England. As the years passed, and the original estate-owners died, suffered business reverses, or moved to estates in Rockland and Gonzales, the properties were subdivided. By 1900, tight little subdivisions like the one on Avalon and Phoenix (now Huntington) streets had changed the character of the area to an almost "working class" one. "Widow's cottages," like the ones on Paddon Avenue on part of the old Pinehurst estate, were built to provide a modest income for the aging women attempting to hang on to their larger houses.

More little houses filled in the spaces so that, by the end of the 1940s, there was little land left. Two of the former estates—Senator Macdonald's 28-acre "Armadale" and Capt. Irving's at Menzies and Michigan—have become parks. Another estate—"Pinehurst" at 617 Battery Street—once occupied all the land north of Dallas Road and west of Beacon Hill Park to Government Street; its driveway wound through formal gardens from an entrance on Dallas Road. Now, it is very difficult even to see the old house, which is crowded in amongst townhouses, apartments, and little houses on the new streets surrounding it. A lot of the very old houses—like Thomas Trounce's—were demolished in the sixties and seventies for apartment buildings.

Bishop Cridge, the controversial minister of the Reformed Episcopal Church, came to Victoria in 1855 as the Hudson's Bay Company chaplain. Just before leaving London, he asked his sweetheart Mary Winnelle to accompany him. The couple had a number of children rather quickly, but lost four of them to scarlet fever in two months in the winter of 1864-5 (their longest-lived child was Ellen, who married Thomas Laundry of the Bank of B.C.). A decade later, they moved to "Marifield" off Carr Road—their driveway is now little Marifield Avenue. Cridge, like his great friend Dr. Helmcken, outlived his wife and lived to a remarkable age, dying at 96 in 1913 at "Marifield."

Another James Bay resident was Peter John Leech, whose discovery of gold in Sooke touched off the short-lived Leechtown rush in the early 1860s. Leech was a Crimea veteran, a surveyor and explorer, and later Victoria's city engineer. He built "Avalon Villa" across the street from Beacon Hill Park at Avalon Road. His wife, the former Mary Macdonald of the bride-ship *Tynemouth*, "in a red velvet bonnet with strings under the chin," played the organ every day at the Reformed Episcopal. Leech was almost always away.

One of the more notorious residents was Alexander Davidson Macdonald, the founder of Macdonald's Bank, who lived at "Springfield" at 633 Michigan Street, next door to the Alexander Munro home at Douglas Street (now the playground for South Park school). Macdonald had relatives in New Orleans in the banking business, and a pretty bride who was a highlight of the social season. He opened his bank and general store at Yates and Wharf Street in 1859, and issued the first paper money in British Columbia. Originally, the only currency on Vancouver Island was Hudson's Bay Company tokens, supplemented by barter and bank drafts paid in sterling on London accounts. The circulating medium was Amer-

William John Macdonald (above) arrived in the early 1850s, worked for the Hudson's Bay Company, and was Victoria's third mayor, in 1867. Along with R.W.W. Carrall and Clement F. Cornwall, he was appointed to the Canadian Senate on December 10, 1871. He moved in 1876 from "Glendale," his property on the site of the current Union Club, to James Bay, and built "Armadale" near Ogden Point, somewhat on the external plan of the Armadale Castle at Skye. It had 28 acres of grounds, including a proper croquet pitch. The house ended its life as a rather shabby nightspot. A "panther" (cougar) was shot on its grounds in 1905. Macdonald's granddaughter, Flora Hamilton Burns, was a well-known writer and good friend of Emily Carr.

ican dollars. In April, 1861, the steamer *Tartar* arrived carrying £6,900 in sterling, which was put into circulation, but the sovereign was taken for five dollars, the florin a half dollar, the shilling a quarter, the six-penny ("a bit") supposedly 12½ cents, but used as a dime. Governor Douglas issued government notes in dollars to pay Cariboo Road contractors. On November 14, he decided to coin all the gold in the colony's possession into $10 and $20 pieces, to try to stop the flow of gold dust to San Francisco. Only a few were manufactured. Macdonald's bank had a tough time competing with Wells Fargo and the Banks of B.C. and British North America. Then, the Vancouver Island legislature passed a law forbidding the issuance of any paper money after March 1, 1865. On the night of September 23, 1864, Macdonald's bank was burgled for $30,000 under extremely suspicious circumstances; Macdonald arrived back in Victoria from the Cariboo two months later, and attempted to stay the run on his unsecured money. His bank closed late in November. Just before

bankruptcy proceedings could begin, Macdonald was rowed out to a ship standing off Holland Point, and disappeared. (The uncertain money situation in the colonies continued until January 1, 1866, when an ordinance was passed stating that all public accounts were to be kept in dollars, and setting the pound sterling at $4.85. Even as late as 1877, most of the money in circulation in Victoria was American.)

Dr. Israel Powell, the namesake of Powell Street in James Bay, and a prominent real-estate investor and promoter in the late 1880s in Vancouver, married Mrs. Macdonald's sister at "Springfield." Powell gained some dubious fame as a Canadian-trained doctor when Governor Musgrave, who wanted to show his faith in matters Canadian (as opposed to matters British), asked Powell to set his broken leg. Musgrave was left practically a cripple. "Springfield" was later the home of A.A. Green's partner Francis Garesche, who drowned in the S.S. *Pacific* disaster in 1875.

Dr. G.L. Milne

Looking south towards "Pinehurst," the Milne estate above Dallas Road just west of Beacon Hill Park, from a pergola-like "breakfast balcony" on Battery Street. A contemporary account described "Pinehurst" as "set in the midst of over two acres of land, beautified with artistic gardens . . . it overlooks the sea and the Olympic Mountains in the distance." Its address was then 618 Dallas Road; now, with the subdivision of the property, its address is 617 Battery Street.

Dr. George Lawson Milne

George Lawson Milne had an exceptionally active and prosperous life as a physician, developer and politician. He lived for most of his time in Victoria at "Pinehurst," the huge, turreted Queen Ann-style house off Battery Street in James Bay.

Born in Scotland in April, 1850, he graduated from the Toronto School of Medicine, and arrived in Victoria in 1880 after a year in Kansas City. He had left the latter as he felt the town was malarial and had no future. It was one of the few business misjudgements he ever made. He made a fortune with Powell, Dupont, Oppenheimer, Rand, and other partners in the Vancouver Improvement Co. —the only capitalists able to compete with the CPR in Vancouver before the turn of the century—and was active with Victoria tramway and real estate operations. He had a thriving Victoria medical practice, including a term from 1884-90 as city Medical Health Officer, and later, following his presidency of the B.C. Liberal As-

sociation and an unsuccessful run in the 1896 federal election, as Immigration Agent, Medical Inspector and Controller of Chinese for Victoria. Milne thought that the "Oriental menace" was greatly overstated, but cautioned that a relaxation of British standards "would only lead to chaos." He said that "of all classes of Orientals, I think the Chinese are the best and most adaptable."

He was an active Presbyterian, but adapted to the Unionist movement in the early twenties. He and his wife passed their summers at "Speyside," their Beecher Bay resort with adjoining 143-acre grounds. His prescription for a long life was "to get married and, if you are widowed, to marry again"—a nice contrast to his colleague J.S. Helmcken, who was a widower for nearly 60 years, and lived to age 96. Milne died in March, 1933, aged 82.

Emily Carr

(Above) Emily Carr, about 1940. (Preceding page) The Carr family's "great red and white, loose-knit Cow" which walked "with her great bag swinging slowly from side to side."*On her tours of the property with her father, when she was a little girl, Emily Carr would pass through the lily field, where the cow was "knee deep and chewing." She wrote that "nothing, not even fairyland, could have been so lovely as our lily field. The wild lilies blossomed in April or May but they seemed to be always in the field, because, the very first time you saw them, they did something to the back of your eyes which kept themselves there, and something to your nose, so that you smelled them whenever you thought of them. The field was roofed by tall, thin, pine trees . . . at the end of the field, we climbed a stile over our snake fence. On the other side of the fence was a mass of rock, rich and soft with moss, and all round it were mock orange and spirea and oak trees." Father, she wrote, sat on a rock and thought "how splendidly English he had made it look."

*The Book of Small, Toronto, 1942, page 11.

Emily Carr was the first artist to interpret the powerful, oppressive gloom and deep colours of the rainforests and Indian villages on the west coast. Much as Victoria was isolated from the rest of Canada and the world, she was isolated from the "modern" movements which swept the old artistic traditions away in the rest of the world. She developed her style and her ideas, not only in this isolation, but in the teeth of scorn and antagonism from almost everyone in Victoria. Her teachers told her to paint the light and the sunshine, but she wanted to investigate the shadows.

Emily Carr, born December 13, 1871, was the youngest of nine children, and grew up, harassed by her elder sisters, in a deeply religious, Presbyterian home at 207 Government Street at Simcoe. The house was surrounded by ten acres of "English" fields and hedges, hawthorns, primroses and shrubberies, described lovingly and vividly, nearly seven decades after her childhood, in The Book of Small. Her mother died in 1888 and her father in 1890, leaving her in the care of her older sisters and a kindly but conservative executor. She was sent to San Francisco for art studies, and then went to Europe. On her return, she attempted to teach and paint in Vancouver, but health problems and a lack of art opportunities brought her back to Victoria to live.

Her share of the old family property was a block of land on Simcoe Street near St. Andrews. She resolved to erect a boarding house, with a studio, to provide enough income to maintain her independence and freedom to paint. Her writings are filled with the conflicts between the "old-world" sensibilities of her sisters and other Victorians, and her own "new-world" ones. The architect recommended to her was English and too haughty to care for Victoria's building codes, so her house ended up costing far more than it should have. It was finally completed in 1913, at a time of collapsing prices and declining population. Her tenants through the First World War years were an astonishing collection of troublemakers and rent-skippers—she tried pottery, sheepdog raising, and a variety of other little businesses to make money. Finally, in the twenties, she became so frustrated that she quit painting.

Her behaviour became increasingly eccentric, and her part of the house and garden housed a fluctuating menagerie of birds, sheepdogs, a monkey named Wu, and her white rat. She was a common sight walking downtown on Government Street, smoking a cigarette and pushing a baby carriage containing the monkey. Cab drivers disliked "her foul mouth and filthy monkey."

By the late twenties, her work had come to the attention of the Group of Seven painters, and the anthropologists and curators connected with the National Gallery of Canada. However, Victorians still considered her terribly offbeat and profane. The major art organization in Victoria was the Island Arts and Crafts Society, founded in 1909 and dominated by traditional watercolourists like Josephine Crease (daughter of Sir Henry), Maude Lettice, architect Samuel Maclure and his wife Margaret, and Sophie Pemberton (daughter of Joseph Despard). Their social attitudes and artistic ideas were too "pretty" and "stuffy" for Emily Carr.

Victoria took small notice of her at the Island Arts and Crafts Society's annual show in the Belmont Building in 1932. The vast majority of the paintings offered for sale were small, accomplished landscapes in watercolour. For the first time that year, though, a nod was made towards modern art: a separate space, beguilingly called "The Modern Room," featured the comparatively overpowering works of Emily Carr, Edythe Hembroff, Jack Shadbolt and others. This artwork provoked some bemused comment, a little discussion, but no scandal or offers to purchase.

As the years passed, and she approached her seventieth birthday, her health began to fail, and she took to writing. Her first book, Klee Wyck, was a sensation across Canada. It won her the governor general's award and, finally, some recognition and respect in Victoria. That respect was further enhanced by The Book of Small, published in 1942. Appreciation of her art gradually followed, but her health continued to decline, and she died in 1945, aged 73.

Her extraordinary contribution is preserved in the Emily Carr Gallery on Wharf Street—in the same premises where her father operated his wholesale food and liquor business over a century ago. The old family house on Government Street, now surrounded by dozens of little houses from more recent generations, is a National Historic Site.

MORTGAGEE'S SALE
— OF —
FINE SUBURBAN PROPERTY,
—SUITABLE FOR—
HOTEL OR PRIVATE RESIDENCE.

J. P. DAVIES & CO.

Have received instructions from the Mortgagee to sell at Public Auction, at sales-room, Wharf street,

Monday, February 24, 1879,

AT 12 O'CLOCK, NOON,

All that certain Piece or Parcel of Land near the City of Victoria, Vancouver Island, being a portion of the BECKLEY FARM and more particularly known as the

PARK HOTEL, BEACON HILL,

Containing one acre or thereabouts, with all the improvements thereon.
CONSISTING OF

A large two-story Frame Building, lathed and plastered, containing Seventeen Rooms.
—ALSO—

Stables, Outhouses and a fine young Orchard.
BY ORDER MORTGAGEE.

Lots 5 and 6, Block I, Harbor Estate, Esquimalt Road, between the bridges
—ALSO—

Sections XXX, XXXI and XLVIII, Sooke District, containing about 562 Acres.

TERMS AT SALE
J. P. DAVIES & CO.,
Auctioneers.

A constant thorn in Richard Carr's side was the Park Hotel, later called the Colonist, at the corner of Douglas and Simcoe. Carr had sold an acre of his land to the aptly-named Mrs. Lush, on the condition she never build a public house on the land. She promptly broke her word, and hacks filled with "tipsy sailors and noisy ladies" drove past Carr's house day and night. He left the corner of his land adjoining the pub "thick and tangled," with "a deep ditch with stinging nettles about it, and a rank, muddy smell"—avoiding it on his weekly walk-abouts. The pub's closure in 1879 due to William Lush's suicide, was a brief respite, as it reopened in 1882 as the Colonist.

W.W. Gibson

The first all-Canadian airplane was built by William Gibson in the coach house behind 146 Clarence Street in 1910. He disassembled it, loaded it onto a wagon, and pulled it by horse-power to a grassy meadow on the Dean Farm near Mount Tolmie, later part of the Lansdowne airport, for its maiden flight.

The first successful all-Canadian airplane was built in Victoria, in the coach house behind 146 Clarence Street in James Bay. The spruce wings and airframe were designed by 35-year-old William Wallace Gibson, who had arrived in Victoria in 1907 to work in real estate, but tinkered with airplanes in his spare time. Fred Jeune on Johnson Street provided the silk for the wings, Tom Plimley built the undercarriage with four bicycle wheels, and the Hutchinson brothers designed and built the engine at their Bay Street shop near the Victoria Machinery Depot. A western stock saddle strapped to the airframe in front of the engine was the pilot's seat.

Gibson worked on the plane through the summer of 1910, then hauled it to a flat, grassy field north of Richmond Street, between Shelbourne and Lansdowne. On September 8, 1910, he managed a takeoff and flew the plane 200 feet. It was the first flight in British Columbia. The engine—distinctive for the two counter-rotating propellers at opposite ends of the crankshaft—is now on display at the National Aeronautical Museum in Ottawa. The engine's configuration gave Gibson's contraption the nickname "The Twin Plane." Gibson went to the United States to pursue his aviation interests, and after a long career died in Oakland, California in November, 1965, aged 91.

The Pendrays

Grounds of the W. J. Pendray Residence, Victoria, B. C.

The Pendray house on Belleville Street, called "Loretto Hall," was known at the turn of the century for Pendray's hobby of topiary. There was a billiard room in the tower lookout and an attic playroom for the four boys—Ernest, Carl, Herbert and Ray. Mrs. Pendray outlived her husband by 24 years, and died there in 1937, aged 87. The house has been restored as The Captain's Palace, a restaurant with a single room to let.

Laurel Point, the "headland" at the entrance to the Inner Harbour, is now the site of a luxury hotel, but for years it hosted the industrial clutter of the British American Paint Works (Bapco) and the British Columbia Soap Works. The companies' founder, W.J. Pendray, lived just to the east

(Above) Mrs. W.J. Pendray, for over half a century the mainstay of the Metropolitan Methodist (United) Church. (Right) "Satin-Glo Sam," Bapco's trademark, and some of the paints produced at the Laurel Point factory in the thirties.

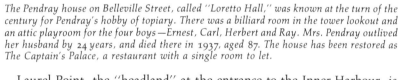

SATIN·GLO
A BAPCO PRODUCT

Enamel, Varnish, Satin Finish . . . with these three Satin-Glo finishes you can do all your interior decorating. Made in British Columbia. Quality guaranteed.

British America Paint Co. Ltd.
Victoria Vancouver Calgary Edmonton Regina

of the plant on Belleville Street at Pendray Street, in "Loretto Hall," the turreted house with topiary in the gardens.

W.J. Pendray's wanderlust took him first to California in the 1850s, where he made about $3 a day panning gold in the Grass Valley area. He wandered north to the Mosquito Creek area of the Cariboo, struck it rich, and retired to England, where he invested his fortune in South African gold mines and lost the lot. He then moved to Virginia City, Nevada, made a small stake, and came north to Victoria in 1875. He and a friend, clothier William Jeffree, noticed that thousands of dollars were spent importing soaps, and that huge quantities of kitchen fats and tallow were wasted every day in Victoria. The pair started a soap factory on Humboldt Street (page 73). Jeffree soon returned to the clothing business, but Pendray prospered, using the slogan: "if people are ever to become contented, happy and prosperous, they first must be made clean." He imported his sweetheart, Amelia Carthew, from England in 1877, and married her at Jeffree's house the day after she arrived, on May 26. They moved into a cottage on Douglas Street near Courtney. Pendray bought the Belleville Street property in 1890, and built "Loretto Hall" about five years later.

Pendray's British Columbia Soap Works manufactured two grades of whale oil soap ("one for killing insects and one for household purposes"), four grades of household soap (white, brown, blue or mottled), and three kinds of toilet soap (carbolic, shaving, and glycerine). He had a power printing press for the labels, a tin shop for the cans, and a box factory for the cartons. In the nineties, "Electric Soap" was the big seller—practically anything that was good and modern at that time was described as "electric," implying it had great health-giving abilities.

Pendray bought a small paint plant on the north side of the E&N Railway bridge on Shore Street, and moved it next door to the soap works on Humboldt Street. In 1906, he moved both plants to Laurel Point, to make way for the Empress Hotel.

Pendray was killed in 1913, when the paint plant's fire-sprinkler feed pipe broke, and fell 40 feet onto his head. Of his sons, Ernest was killed in 1909, thrown from his wagon on Belleville Street practically in front of the family house. Carl had become general manager of the Bapco plant in 1905, and sold the soap factory to Lever Brothers in 1913, following his father's death. He was mayor of Victoria from 1925-28. He turned over the paint company to his son, W.A. Pendray, in August, 1949, and died at La Jolla, California, aged 81, in February, 1961. Herbert accidentally shot himself in the chest on December 5, 1893, with a .22 belonging to his companion, jeweller's son Harry Redfern; he survived to be vice-president of the paint company until his death in 1952.

Beacon Hill Park

Beacon Hill Park occupies the high ground between "Marvin's Hill" and the cliff on both sides of Finlayson Point south of Victoria's downtown. Its lookout on the highest point marks the approximate location of the two beacons which gave the park its name—the westerly one was a triangle, the other a square, and when a ship's navigator saw the square through the triangle, he was on course to avoid the dangerous Brotchie's Ledge.

Governor James Douglas put the land—Lot LXXXVI on the Victoria-area survey—aside for a public park in the late 1850s. It was used for horse-racing, the track circling Beacon Hill, in the early 1860s. Mayor Thomas Harris was the first president of the Jockey Club and the track's major punter. The provincial government gave the park to the City of Victoria on February 21, 1882; seven years later, an expenditure of $25,000 was authorized by the ratepayers, and a plan providing for a lake with a stone bridge, formal gardens, and pathways winding amongst the garry oaks, was drawn up by John Blair.

A visit to Victoria was not (and is not) complete without a ride on a tally-ho through the park. Bicycle clubs met regularly there for picnics, and many James Bay and Fairfield residents—like Mrs. Elizabeth Rithet—rode their horses daily in the park once the vacant land near their homes became built-up.

Beacon Hill Park Victoria B. C.

Spring-time in Deacon Hill Park, B.C.

(Next page) Goodacre Lake, named for butcher and alderman Lawrence Goodacre, who was the driving force (and provider of meat) for Beacon Hill Park's old zoo, established near Cook Street and Dallas Road in 1907 but abandoned after the Second World War. The stone bridge, which was once used by automobiles and carriages, was part of John Blair's park layout of the 1880s. A tremendous number of postcards have featured the park, including the misspelled "Deacon Hill Park" card from the P.E. Company in Toronto in the late thirties. Postcards were published locally by T.N Hibben & Co. (page 38) and by J. Howard A. Chapman (above), a native of Wiltshire who came to B.C. in 1890 to work as a manufacturer's agent. He compiled many cinematographic views of the province used by the Emigration Department before the First World War. Another photographic firm was Spencer & Hastings (later operated by the fashionable John Savannah). Partner Oregon Columbus Hastings was born in Illinois, but spent his second year in a prairie schooner on the way to Portland. After moving to Victoria, he built a house near the water tower in the Rockland area, and had Victoria's first astronomical telescope in his observatory. One of Victoria's first photographers was Hannah Maynard, who arrived in 1858 and took many of the surviving pictures of the fort. Her studio, above the ground-floor shoe-store her husband Richard operated, was located at 723 Pandora—the large windows, necessary for portraiture, are still visible there.

A kitchen of the 1890s, featuring a "Nugget" woodstove from the Albion Iron Works and a coalgas-fired copper water heater. The wooden shelf-and-counter piece, with a flour bin and slots for eggs, beaters and graters, was a "Hoosier Special," and cost $40 at Weiler Brothers. It "saves miles of steps for tired feet," according to the company's catalogue. ("Hoosier Specials" were manufactured all over North America, and often called "the bride's best friend." They were a traditional wedding gift from the mother-in-law. A hoosier is a resident of Indiana.) Weiler Bros. were probably the biggest furniture manufactory in Victoria. Started in 1862 by John Weiler (1824-1899), the company had a large factory on Humboldt adjacent to Pendray's soap factory, and showrooms on Government Street. John Weiler's house, at the southwest corner of Blanshard and Broughton, was demolished only in the late forties. His main competitor in the furniture business was Jacob Sehl, operating as Sehl-Hastie-Erskine after 1891.

John Dougall (above) was in charge of the foundry department at Albion Iron Works, before starting his own company, Atlas Iron Works, at Government and Pembroke. He sold his foundry to a syndicate and moved to Vancouver in 1886, where he profitably operated a hotel for several years before retiring to his Victoria home at 816 Cook Street. He was one of the first volunteers for the Deluge Company fire brigade.

Rockland

A number of the big houses in the Rockland area were turned into private schools after the dislocations of the First World War. "The Laurels" was built in 1885—the same year as Pemberton's "Gonzales," which also became a girls' school—for Robert Ward (below), who worked in insurance and with Welch & Rithet in the shipping business.

"Rocklands," Henry Dumbleton's house at 1750 Belcher (Rockland) Avenue, the name of which likely spurred the street's name-change. Dumbleton was a much-travelled, wealthy English hunter and adventurer—"a sporting Englishman with a large collection of horns"—who settled in Victoria before the turn of the century. His best friends in Victoria included F.B. Pemberton, Major Ridgeway Wilson, Major Dupont, and the Bank of Montreal's A.J.C. Galletly, who lived nearby at "Hochelaga," 1715 Rockland Avenue. Dumbleton's son, also named Henry, lived at 634 Michigan Street. His wife started taking P.G.'s (paying guests) after Henry became a semi-invalid, and her "Dumbleton Boarding House" became a great success.

Following James Douglas's death in 1877, his property south and east of downtown, called the Fairfield Estate, was subdivided. The property fitted around the eastern side of Beacon Hill Park, north to the Cadboro Bay Road, and east to near Pemberton Road. The ocean was the southern boundary. Most of the land to the east had been purchased beginning in 1855 by Joseph Despard Pemberton (map, page 114). Pemberton said he fell in love with the rocky hillside with its spectacular view east to Mount Baker, south to the Olympics, and west across the city to the Sooke Hills, when he was riding one day through the open woods and saw, far in the distance and below him, an Indian stalking a deer near a small lake. Another story, recounted by J. Robert Anderson, said that W.J. Macdonald had been urged by James Douglas to purchase the land. Macdonald consulted Pemberton, who was an acknowledged expert on the island as well as the crown's surveyor, then walked out himself to have a look at it. When he returned to the land office to make the claim, Pemberton, "rubbing his nose in the usual manner, replied: 'I have taken it myself'."

Thus, the lieutenant-governor's "Bleak House," "Duval's Cottage" on Rockland, and Pemberton's first log dwelling were the first residences up there, high above the smoke and smell of Victoria, facing the sea. (One 33-acre piece of the old Douglas estate became the Government House grounds. It had been bought by the B.C. Land & Investment Co., who leased it to the provincial government for a half-yearly rental of $24.25. The government finally purchased it in 1921.) There were two estates built in the early years which had their driveways off Fort Street and the Cadboro Bay Road: "Erin Hall" for the Nesbitt family in 1874, and "Pentrelew" for the Crease family on Fort Street just east of Cook in 1875. Soon they had neighbours: A.A. Green at "Gyppeswyck" (now the Art Gallery); the Dunsmuir's massive "Craigdarroch" on an estate stretching from Fort to Rockland Avenue; David Higgins at Fort and St. Charles (page 48).

Architect Charles Vereydhen was engaged to divide the remaining Douglas-owned land around Belcher (Rockland) Avenue into five- to seven-acre estates. The narrow roads he laid out wound among the rocky outcroppings; fine, English-style homes and gardens were created, where the owners lived like country squires.

Until the turn of the century, the Rockland area was still dominated by these few estates, most with lookout towers and views to Oak Bay, the Olympics and the Inner Harbour. By 1900, further sales and subdivisions heralded a new generation of houses as grand as the original ones (especially as architects like Samuel Maclure and F.M. Rattenbury came into their own), but without the "country-estate" grounds. The wild prosperity of the decade before the First World War saw the remaining lots soon purchased.

It is difficult to imagine the area as it was at the turn of the century—a rolling park carpeted with grass and wildflowers, dotted here and there with Garry oaks and large, wooden houses. As the old estates were broken up for tax sales, or became impractical due to the unavailability and high cost of servants, modest infill housing filled up all the spaces between the old houses, which now crowd their little lots. "The Priory," at 729 Pemberton Road, was once surrounded by acres of woods and had a good view of the sea above the native trees. Now it seems almost lost amongst the large, Edwardian houses on the narrow, winding lanes. Even "Craigdarroch," which used to loom above the town like the castle of a medieval baron, can hardly be seen through the screen of trees and houses.

Hewitt Bostock, together with future lieutenant-governor Walter C. Nichol, founded the Province *newspaper as a Victoria weekly. Bostock was elected to the House of Commons for the Yale-Cariboo riding in the Liberal sweep in 1896, defeated in 1901, then appointed to the Senate on June 6, 1904. He built "Schuhuum," meaning "a windy place," in 1894 on the bank above Rockland Avenue at number 1322. His major interest other than politics was cattle-raising on his ranch at Ducks near Kamloops.*

Looking northwest to Alexander Alfred Green's house, "Gyppeswyck"—a medieval spelling of his birthplace, Ipswich—in late 1889, the year the house was completed but before the major additions were made to Henry Crease's "Pentrelew," visible in the distance. The land all around the few large houses on the Cadboro Bay Road (upper Fort Street) was open gardens and parkland; the properties were often separated by ivy-covered rubble walls with little gates. Alexander Green studied medicine in his youth, but gave it up for travel, and arrived in Victoria from Nevada in 1873 as the Wells Fargo representative. He was later associated with Frank Garesche, in the Garesche-Green banking company. He died at age 56, likely of cancer, in September, 1891, leaving a wife and six children. The house, after a brief stint as the lieutenant-governor's residence, was purchased in 1903 by department store owner David Spencer, who renamed it "Lan Dderwen." In 1951, it was donated by Sara Spencer to the city of Victoria for use as an art gallery.

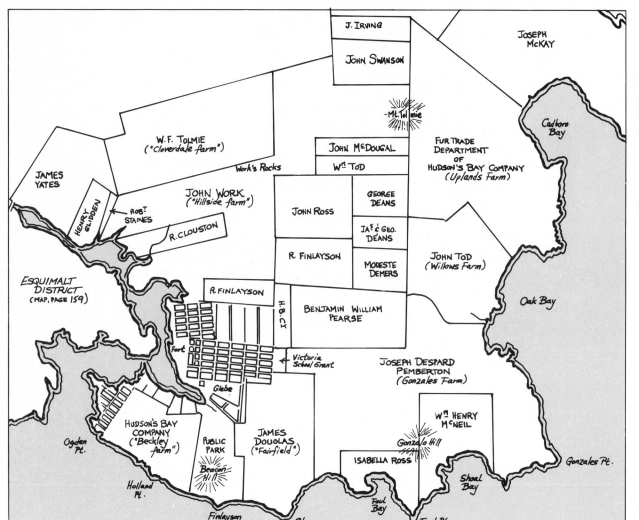

The major landowners in Victoria in 1858.

The Pembertons

The biggest landowner in early Victoria was Joseph Despard Pemberton, whose Gonzales Farm extended from Rockland Avenue and St. Charles streets south and east all the way to the Oak Bay waterfront and Gonzales Point. Pemberton laid out and constructed Oak Bay Avenue through the 1,200-acre farm and presented it to the government. Pemberton lived more like a country squire than anyone else—he loved horses, sponsored regular paper chases (the Victoria version of fox hunts) on the open land of his estate, and built his home, "Gonzales," at Rockland and St. Charles, like an English manor house.

Pemberton was a member of the "Dublin castle gentry," and one of the three colonial public servants whose employment dated back to 1851—James Douglas and Benjamin Pearse being the other two. Contemporary historian F.W. Howay noted his "sunshiny nature" and described him as "polished, gallant and courteous under all circumstances—a fine type of the Irish gentleman of the old school." Born in Dublin in 1821, he was the grandson of the city's Lord Mayor. Before joining the Hudson's Bay Company and moving to Vancouver Island to become colonial surveyor and engineer, he was professor of engineering and mathematics at an English college, engineer for two English railways, and an architectural designer—he entered the famous Crystal Palace design competition, receiving a bronze medal (the winning entry was Joseph Paxton's landmark design, a model for innumerable railway stations and pavilions ever since).

As the colonial surveyor, Pemberton mapped much of southern Vancouver Island. His trigonometrical survey from Sooke to Nanaimo took two years to complete—transit angles often were taken from treetops—but his work was so accurate that there was a discrepancy of only 50 feet in 100 miles (compared with the Admiralty coastline survey done several years later). His survey of the Nanaimo coalfields in 1852 started the chain of events that created the city of Nanaimo, Robert Dunsmuir's great wealth, and much of the prosperity of Victoria and the southern part of Vancouver Island. Pemberton designed and erected the Race Rocks and Fisgard lighthouses, and worked with Pearse to lay out the streets and services for the City of Victoria. He built the first Victoria schoolhouse in 1853, and the Victoria District Church (the forerunner of Christ Church) in 1856. He resigned from the Hudson's Bay Company in 1858, and took the position of surveyor-general of British Columbia when that colony was formed late that year.

In the late 1850s, he paid £40 to some Hudson's Bay Company men to build a 30- x 20-foot log house, a barn and some small outbuildings on the farm. In addition, there was "a log park, wherein to lassoo cattle" and about five acres of cultivated land. Pemberton's sister Susan came to Victoria in 1856 (and ended up staying until 1868, most of the time as principal of Angela College) and hosted dinner parties by candlelight with Joseph in the log house, with modified potatoes as sconces, "and in every available corner would be a shakedown for those coming from a distance." Pemberton returned to England in early 1864 to marry Theresa Jane Despard Grautoff. The couple came back to Victoria in March on the same ship as the new governor, Arthur Kennedy, and his family. Pemberton's subsequent resignation from public service was due either to his disagreements with Kennedy, or to his desire to live as a country gentleman on his farm with his new wife.

The Pembertons were able to erect a "fine type of old English country home" near the corner of Rockland and St. Charles in 1885. The house was massive—over 10,000 square feet with 20 rooms, including a 45- by 18-foot drawing room and a 30- by 18-foot dining room, five bathrooms, a conservatory in the tower with a splendid view of the Pacific Ocean, a billiard room, a writing room and a library. The huge, high-ceilinged rooms were dank and difficult to heat during the winter—guests recalled how elegantly dressed women shivered at the dinner table.

Pemberton continued to be very active through his sixties, in spite of a weak heart. One of his favorite pastimes was the hunt club paper chase, regularly held on the Oak Bay part of his farm—now the golf course. ("The great dearth of winter amusement in this colony" and the ideal that "everywhere the old flag waves, the cheer of the huntsman is heard" caused G.H. Wilson Brown to attempt to establish fox hunting in Victoria; he imported five pairs of English hounds on the *Prince of Wales* in January, 1867, but only seven survived. Having no indigenous beast to hunt, Victorians had to make do with the paper chase. Even the Australian colonials could chase kangaroos. Wilson Brown was said to be too English even for Victoria, and bitterly resented the introduction of baseball, shortly before his death in 1904.) Following the paper chase on November 11, 1893, at about five in the evening, Pemberton and his wife were riding home along Oak Bay Avenue. Near the Cadboro Bay road, his wife noted that he had fallen behind. She turned to urge him to catch up, but saw him lying on the road. An aneurism had killed him, probably even before he fell. He was 72.

Theresa Pemberton continued to live at Gonzales for the next two decades, and was a familiar sight in her brougham, shielding herself from the hot sun with a tiny black parasol. She died on August 24, 1916. Six days later her son, Joseph Despard Jr., died of a heart attack, aged only 42. Like his father, he was a surveyor and engineer, and had been leading a pack horse on the Silver Mine trail, seventeen miles from Shawnigan lake, on the way to inspect an antimony property, when he collapsed.

Gonzales Farm was broken up following Theresa Pemberton's death. The remaining children continued to live on parts of the old estate. Frederick Bernard lived at the 10-acre "Mount Joy," at 617 Foul Bay Road, which was said to have the finest gardens anywhere. He carried on the Pemberton & Son real estate company, founded with his father in 1887; in his spare time, he was a crack shot and an avid hunter, and the long-time president of the Victoria Horticultural Society. According to his obituary, he originated the holly industry in Canada. "Mount Joy" was renowned for its thirteen tiled fireplaces and the heated conservatory with its own heating plant. Frederick died in November, 1947, aged 83.

Joseph Despard Pemberton, the squire of Gonzales Farm, held his attachment to mother England above all else. During the heated confederation debate in the late 1860s, he wrote in a letter to the editor that Americans were not really foreigners—at least, he said, they were no more foreign than Canadians. He was thereafter sharply criticized for his "Yankeephile" ideas.

"Gonzales," the English-style manor house of Joseph Despard Pemberton, on the huge property which stretched from the corner of Rockland and St. Charles all the way to the sea.

Frederick Bernard Pemberton ran his late father's Pemberton & Son land development company until his retirement in 1933. Like his brother-in-law Hugo Beaven, he was renowned for his skill as a gardener—the gardens at "Mount Joy," his estate on Foul Bay Road, were said to be as fine as any.

The house was sold and sat vacant for three years until March, 1953, when it burned to the ground in a spectacular blaze (it was in the process of being razed at the time). Like his father, Frederick and his wife Mary Ann Dupont (née Bell) had six children: two sons were killed in the Royal Flying Corps during World War I; two of the daughters, Mrs. Lancelot Duke and Mrs. H. Cuthbert Holmes, continued to live in Victoria.

The other children included Ada, who married Hugo Beaven and lived at "Arden" above the Oak Bay Beach Hotel (page 142); Susan Harriett, who married William Curbis Sampson and lived at "Molton Combe" adjoining the Beavens' property; W.P.D., who owned a house also called "Gonzales" on the Foul Bay Road; and Sophie, who married Canon Beanlands, for 25 years the rector at Christ Church (after his death she remarried and moved to England).

The original "Gonzales" manor house at Rockland and St. Charles was sold after Theresa Pemberton's death and used for years as the residence house of the Norfolk Girls School. Although the estate was largely subdivided then, there were still roads, like Gonzales between Despard and Foul Bay Road, which were part of the estate's driveways and private until the thirties. "Gonzales" was torn down in November, 1952—the demolition contractors found about five gallons of honey in hives within the walls.

The Pemberton & Son real estate company continues to exist. Joseph Despard Pemberton's will bequeathed money for the Pemberton Gymnasium and the operating theatre at Royal Jubilee Hospital. The Pemberton Chapel, adjoining Royal Jubilee's kitchen block, was a bequest of Theresa's.

The Dunsmuirs

Robert Dunsmuir was the ultimate Victoria capitalist in an era which almost unequivocally admired wealth and business success. He started with practically nothing in the employ of the Hudson's Bay Company, and ended as reputedly "the province's most important citizen," with a massive fortune and a castle on the Fort Street hill. By comparison, his son James was continually embroiled in political controversy as his employees became more militant and his motives in creating "stable" government and management became increasingly transparent. Together, the father and son did more to radicalize the working class, and bring issues like "landlordism" and working conditions into public debate and eventual legislation, than anyone else in the province's history. They also left the two grandest mansions: "Craigdarroch" and "Hatley Park."

The discovery of coal in the vicinity of Fort Rupert in the 1840s started a chain of events which was largely responsible for the prosperous economy of Vancouver Island. Boyd Gilmour and his nephew, Robert Dunsmuir, arrived on the coast in 1851, coalmining experts hired by the Hudson's Bay Company to exploit the Fort Rupert discovery. Dunsmuir, born in 1825 in Hurlford, Ayrshire, was both son and grandson of coal masters. He married Johanna White when he was 22, and (the story goes) promised her a castle if she agreed to accompany him to the far side of the world. They abandoned the Fort Rupert mines after a few years and moved to Nanaimo to help open up the coal mines which had been assayed by colonial surveyor Joseph Despard Pemberton. Dunsmuir remained there for the next fifteen years, operating mines for others, until he discovered some outcroppings of coal at Departure Bay in 1869. He sunk a shaft but was unable to locate the main coal seam; he continued to search until one day, under the roots of an upturned tree in the dense forest, he found it. The coal was of extraordinarily high quality, and he started Wellington Collieries there. Three Admiralty officers became interested in the mine for more than strategic reasons—the Esquimalt naval base also had to serve as a coaling station—and invested heavily in it. Dunsmuir bought out Admiral Farquhar and Captain Edgerton in 1878 and Lieutenant Diggle five years later. Diggle's original few thousand pounds of investment grew to nearly three-quarters of a million dollars.

Dunsmuir's new wealth was largely invested in Victoria's industrial enterprises, including the Albion Iron Works and the Canadian Pacific Navigation Co., but he was also the major backer and president of the Victoria Theatre. He agreed to build the Esquimalt & Nanaimo Railway in 1884, and was widely touted as the saviour of confederation for "giving the Island her railroad," even though his major purpose was to connect his coalfields at Nanaimo with the Royal Navy base at Esquimalt and the industrial centre at Victoria. He was elected MLA for Nanaimo in 1882, 1886 and 1888, and was President of the Council (government house leader). Leaving the management of the Nanaimo mines in son James's increasingly capable hands, Dunsmuir moved to Victoria and built a house called "Fairview" at the corner of Quebec and Menzies in James Bay. In the mid-1880s, he began to plan his baronial "Craigdarroch"

"Craigdarrock," the Residence of Mrs. Robert Dunsmuir, Victoria, British Columbia.

castle on a 27-acre estate between Fort Street and Rockland. As the castle neared completion, he suddenly lost his good health and died on April 12, 1889, aged only 63. "On the day of his funeral, from an early hour in the morning," noted a contemporary account, "the streets were thronged with people from every part of the province who had come to pay their last respects to the man who had done so much to promote the best interests of their common home."

He was an institution almost on the scale of a parallel government. Although his major coal sales were to San Francisco, he was able to convince the governor general, the Dominion Government, and the public that his motives and loyalties were entirely British, British Columbian, and Canadian—in that order. Thus, he bided his time until the governor general and the Dominion government practically begged him to construct the E&N railway, then he drove an amazingly hard bargain, including cash subsidies, tax relief, coalfields, and nearly two million acres of the best timberland on Vancouver Island. In order to ensure his access to the American market, via the Southern Pacific Railroad, he brought in the surviving "bonanza kings"—Stanford, Crocker and Huntington (Mark Hopkins was already dead), who from their Nob Hill mansions ran San Francisco and much of California almost as a personal fiefdom—as co-investors, but organized their joint venture so that he alone controlled its financial policy.

During the two decades after Robert's death, Joan Dunsmuir (his "relict" in the language of the time) lived on at "Craigdarroch" like an

Robert Dunsmuir and his castle, "Craigdarroch," on Fort Street. Dunsmuir died before the home was completed.

Hatley Park, Residence of Hon. James Dunsmuir, Victoria, B. C.

James Dunsmuir and his "Hatley Park" estate, at Royal Roads west of Victoria. It took nearly 100 gardeners to maintain the 650-acre grounds. The estate was split so many ways following the deaths of Dunsmuir and his wife that no one child could afford to maintain it.

aristocrat of an earlier era. The Winter brothers (page 131)—the premier coachmen in Victoria—regularly took the Dunsmuir girls, sometimes accompanied by a nurse in a blue and white uniform, in elegant, two-wheeled, single-horse traps to Dr. Pope's Queen's Academy at Rock Bay for their schooling; then, in full livery in a grand carriage with brass lamps, they took Mrs. Dunsmuir shopping and calling. As the years passed, the stories of the Dunsmuirs' wealth and position were embellished: in English Victoria, anyone who owned a castle *must* have been royalty. Writer Peter Stursberg recounted how the tour bus operators described "Craigdarroch" as the home of "Lord and Lady Dunsmuir," and humble Mrs. Cameron, the wife of the owner of the Westholme Lumber Company, was pointed out as "Her Grace" when she sat in the "Craigdarroch" garden.

None of the Dunsmuir daughters married anyone who amounted to much, but all their weddings were treated in the same breathless fashion. They all received large marriage settlements from the family fortune. In 1888, Emily married a "second son," Northing Pinckney Snowden, and received as a wedding gift "Ashnola" (later the Gorge Road hospital, with its five acres of waterfront property on the Gorge across from brother James's "Burleith."

Joan Dunsmuir's death in October, 1908, left the castle as a white elephant—the ultimate rich man's folly. Son James was away, and wasn't interested in it, as his Hatley Park estate was already under construction.

The castle had a large number of rather small rooms, and was on a scale too ostentatious even for most of Victoria's *nouveau riche* real-estate "boomers." Griffith Hughes, later the owner of the *Victoria Times*, purchased the castle and its grounds, but was forced to subdivide the latter into 144 lots. The castle was a giveaway, in a draw, to one of the purchasers of the new lots, the above-mentioned Mr. and Mrs. Cameron. Their mortgage was foreclosed after the 1913 economic collapse. The castle served as a convalescent home during World War One, then as the headquarters of the Victoria School Board and the Victoria School of Music. Its restoration was organized by newspaperman and Victoria historian, James K. Nesbitt, in the early 1960s.

According to the terms of Robert Dunsmuir's will, son James inherited the coal mines and shipping, and son Alexander got the E&N railway and the lucrative San Francisco sales agency. Alexander died in 1900, leaving James to control everything. The latter became deeply embroiled in the province's volatile political life, serving a brief term as premier (page 89). By 1902, when he had just passed his 50th birthday, he was working to consolidate his interests—he bought out the "bonanza kings" that autumn for $1,500,000, repelled a railway purchase attempt by the Liberal entrepreneurs MacKenzie and Mann of the Canadian Northern Railway, then sold the railway three years later to the Conservative CPR for $3,000,000. He became lieutenant-governor, following the retirement of Sir Henri Joly, but was constantly vilified in the legislature for his role as major employer and alleged importer of Orientals (page 57). Following bitter debate in the winter and spring of 1908, during which he was described as "an inhuman monster" and survived a no-confidence motion in the legislature, Dunsmuir left the province for a prolonged yachting cruise. He visited Kiel, in Germany, during a naval regatta, and had Kaiser Wilhelm as a guest on his yacht, then passed a lengthy visit at the Quebec Tercentenary celebrations on his way back. Meanwhile, his massive "Hatley Park" estate was being built on 650 acres above Esquimalt Lagoon. Rumours surfaced that he was attempting to sell his mines and other assets to a syndicate of English capitalists for $15 million. (The syndicate was the Canadian Northern's MacKenzie & Mann, and a price of $11 million was negotiated in 1910. A dispute over precisely what had been sold dragged through the courts until 1914—Dunsmuir maintained he hadn't sold his steamers and various bank balances, but he lost and had to pay $1.5 million damages.)

Dunsmuir retired to "Hatley Park" and lived out of the public eye until his death in 1920. His will left $3,597,583 to his wife, Laura, with the expressed wish that she divide it equally among their nine children. Thus, in a very non-English way, his fortune was divided up and diminished; following Laura's death in 1927, "Hatley Park" became a huge white elephant. The Canadian government picked it up in the Depression for $75,000—scarcely a fraction of the $4 million the house had cost to build. The estate became HMCS Royal Roads—a joint navy and air force facility—in 1941. It is now known as Royal Roads Military College. The impressive grounds, as with "Craigdarroch," are open to the public.

Samuel Nesbitt

Carberry Gardens, which angles south from Fort Street and connects to Pemberton Road just east of "Craigdarroch," is the old driveway into "Erin Hall," the Nesbitt family residence which burned down in July, 1962. The Nesbitts were one of the first successful families "in trade"—they owned a bakery. Samuel Nesbitt was "low Irish," and his wife came to the city on the bride-ship *Tynemouth*; thus, the "Crown Colony clique" sneered at their success and nicknamed the house "Cracker Castle."

Samuel Nesbitt made enough money in the California gold rush to open the bakery in Victoria in 1858. Four years later, on September 17, 1862, the *Tynemouth* docked at Esquimalt. Jane Anne Saunders, one of the passengers, married Nesbitt seven months later. The couple took up residence at "Holly Lodge" on Cormorant Street near Quadra. It was claimed that Nesbitt imported the first holly trees from England, and planted them there. Eleven years later, they purchased ten acres on the Cadboro Bay Road, high on the wind-swept hillside, and built "Erin Hall," a country villa "in the best tradition of an Irish manor house." The house, standing on a high rock outcropping, had a panoramic 360-degree view, from SaltSpring Island past Mount Baker to the Olympic Mountains and Race Rocks. It had double parlours, a black walnut staircase, five bedrooms with thirteen-foot ceilings, a library with marble mantels, and a six-foot balcony all around it. Beneath the house was a tank for 20,000 gallons of rainwater, "which may be raised to every room in the house."

The Nesbitts lost several children in infancy. Brother-in-law John Saunders, who managed Moore & Co.'s drug store on Yates, died in the house of a sudden illness in his 30th year. Samuel Nesbitt himself died at home in April, 1881, "after a wasting illness of two months." His widow carried on and expanded the bakery.

The most famous descendant was grandson James Knight Nesbitt (1908-1981), who was legislative reporter for the *Times* from 1936-45, and later wrote a long series of columns for the *Colonist* under the title "Old Homes and Families." He was a good popular historian, and knew many of the members of Victoria's pioneer families. "A nattily-dressed bachelor who disdained an auto, preferring to walk," Nesbitt lived on Pemberton Road, a few minutes from "Erin Hall."

(The Colonial Office's Edward Bulwer-Lytton and the Duke of Newcastle wrestled with the political problems of the time, but the Bishops of Oxford and London worried over the social problems. In February, 1862, the "cry from Macedonia" caused the formation of the B.C. Emigration Society, under the patronage of Baroness Burdett-Coutts. On April 17, 20

girls—the majority of whom were aged from twelve to eighteen—were taken from orphan asylums as "wives-to-be," trained in domestic service, and loaded onto the *Tynemouth* for the passage to Vancouver Island. The word quickly spread in Victoria, and when the small transfer-boats docked in front of the legislative buildings, "every square inch of ground was covered." The women were led through the dense crowd, marching two by two, to their temporary accommodations. "A certain proportion went quickly to the bad, and from appearances had been there before." Another bride-ship, the *Robert Lowe*, arrived the following January. The experiment was enough of a success that the Rev. Macfie wrote that "all who have conducted themselves properly have had offers of marriage, and have become participants in conjugal felicity.")

The Nesbitts' "Erin Hall," seen from the corner of Fort Street and Carberry Gardens, commanded a splendid view in every direction. It burned down in July, 1962.

The Angus Families

A number of relatives of Canadian Pacific Railway founder Richard B. Angus moved to Victoria before the turn of the century. He had encouraged his eleven siblings to move west and, according to nephew Henry Angus, had purchased land in the Rockland area "to settle his unmarried brothers and sisters there."

Richard B. Angus (1831-1922) had an extraordinary career, starting as a clerk with the Bank of Montreal and rising, in twelve years, to its general managership. Along with Donald Smith (later Lord Strathcona and Mount Royal) and George Stephen, Angus pledged all his personal wealth as collateral for the Canadian Pacific Railway construction at the point in 1885 when its credit was exhausted and it was in danger of collapse. He was a man of extraordinary ambition and energy, and maintained his company directorships and Bank of Montreal chairmanship until he was in his late eighties. (R.B., as he was universally called, could be somewhat imperious: he wrote a letter to his brother, Forrest, to accompany some photographs he was cleaning out of his house: "these are not first rate photographs," he wrote, "but they should be perfectly adequate for your house.")

Six of Angus's brothers and sisters took his advice (and possibly money) and moved to Victoria: James, Forrest, Kate, Margaret, Jessie and William. James Alexander Angus, who came in 1887, established himself as a wine and provision merchant in the firm of Angus and Gordon at Fort and Government streets. His first house in Victoria was at the triangle corner of Simcoe, Toronto and Menzies; he moved from there to "Ellesmere" at 1321 Rockland Avenue in 1889. He had five children: Lucy, Amy and James Alexander (Sasha) never married, and lived together at "Ellesmere" with their mother after the father's death in 1903; "Bella" (Mary Isabella) married Benjamin Tingley Rogers, the exceptionally wealthy founder of the B.C. Sugar refinery in Vancouver; Col. Richard Angus ran a wholesale automobile sales business called R. Angus & Co. Ltd. in Victoria. He was a colonel of the Fifth Regiment, Royal Canadian Artillery, and a member of Oak Bay council for 17 years before his death in 1950. (His second daughter Elizabeth married Alan Patrick Izard, and still lives in Uplands, where she has contributed to the formation of the Oak Bay archives.)

Bella's husband, the twenty-four-year-old B.T. Rogers, had come west from Montreal in 1889 with a letter of introduction and promise of capital from R.B. Angus and other CPR directors, with the intention of establishing a sugar refinery at the coast. James Angus "was adamant that he choose Victoria, and there was quite a row," but Rogers correctly decided that Vancouver, with its CPR connection and better port, would become the more important city.

Forrest Angus, who never married, lived in a house called "The Oaks" on Angus Place between Pemberton and St. Charles with his three sisters, including widow Kate (Angus) Rennie, and two of Kate's in-laws. Much of Forrest's working career was spent with the Bank of Montreal. His great-nephew David remembers him during visits always wearing a black skull cap and offering chocolate cookies.

William Angus became a commercial salesman, and married Mary Edith Dunckley, a "free thinker" (and author of a privately published book called *Chapters of Life*) who was the daughter of an editorial writer for the *Manchester Guardian*. William was rumoured to have been a drinker, and died quite suddenly in 1892. Their only child was Henry Forbes Angus, the noted economist whose defence of Japanese Canadians during the thirties and forties was considerably ahead of its time (page 57). (Henry Angus's best friend at Victoria High School was Frederick Wood, who married Beatrice, an actress and daughter of B.C. Sugar Refinery president and lieutenant-governor J.W. Fordham-Johnson. Fordham-Johnson was connected with the Angus family through Bella Angus's husband, as he was a long-time employee of B.C. Sugar. He started as an accountant in 1899, and was resident manager of the Vancouver-Fiji Sugar Company before 1910. He assumed the presidency on the sudden death in 1920 of B.T. Rogers' eldest son, Blythe Dupuy.)

R.B.'s youngest son, David James Angus (1875-1948), was said to be "a bit of a dilettante" in his youth in Montreal. He was light-hearted and handsome and took it easy for most of his life. His love for a Roman Catholic girl apparently scandalized his Presbyterian family, who promptly sent him on a world cruise. On his return, he married a more suitable girl, the daughter of a prominent Montreal lawyer. He was apparently on his honeymoon in Banff at the outbreak of World War I when, according to Henry Angus, he "suffered a complete breakdown and was sent to Victoria for an early retirement." He lived just up the street from the James Angus family at 1617 Rockland, and was active as a director of Royal Jubilee Hospital. He had a son, Dr. John Angus, who lived at the same address until his death, aged 60, in 1975. Another son, David, lives in Spain, and his daughter Peggy lives in Ontario.

Government House

Government House, the lieutenant-governor's enormous official residence set amidst nearly 30 acres of gardens on Rockland Avenue, is the third building on that site. The previous two vice-regal residences were gutted by fire—the first in 1899, the second in 1957.

The long-time nickname of Government House has been Cary Castle, after the builder and occupant of the first residence—George Hunter Cary. Cary arrived in Victoria in 1859 with "a carpetbag, a toothbrush, and six law books." He juggled his time among mining speculations, business ventures (including an attempt to buy and rope off Victoria's water supply at Spring Ridge), and politics—he was the first attorney general of the Colony of Vancouver Island. Cary bought property about as far out of town as one could in the 1860s—at the end of Belcher Road, "exposed to every wind that blows"—and built a house with a weird castlelike turret on the hillside overlooking Ross Bay and the Fairfield frog swamps. He resigned his attorney general's position abruptly in 1864—at the end of Governor Douglas's term—and returned to England, where he died two years later at age 35 of "softening of the brain."

Thus, when the new governor, Arthur Edward Kennedy, arrived in Victoria on Good Friday, March 25, 1864, Cary's little castle was vacant. There was no official governor's residence, as Douglas had lived at his own home on James Bay. (The early 1860s were a period of retrenchment and "little Englandism" at home. The Duke of Newcastle, who was responsible for colonial matters in the British government, had told the Vancouver Island legislature that it would have to be willing to pay salaries on a Civil List in the amount of £5,800 a year in order to retain a separate governor—separate, that is, from British Columbia's. The Assembly was unanimously opposed to the amount, and demanded an outright grant from England for the erection of an official residence.) Kennedy was enthusiastically received by the populace, as he had no connection with the hated Hudson's Bay Company. People also initially liked his suave and amiable manner and his talented and pleasant daughters, but they quickly came to dislike his rather superior view of the colony: Kennedy felt there were only two classes of people—loyal and disloyal. He considered the 800-strong Victoria Negro population, and the all-black Victoria Volunteer Rifles (the first military reserve organization in Victoria, formed in 1860 and nicknamed the "Africa Rifles"), to be loyal, which alienated the American element in Victoria. On his arrival Kennedy promptly took up residence in a downtown hotel and, as directed by the Duke, issued warrants to pay his own (£3,000) and the Colonial Secretary's salary. The rift between him and the Vancouver Island legislative council widened.

By the following April, Kennedy had tired of living in a hotel, and at Joseph Trutch's "Fairfield House," and decided to exercise his authority by purchasing the vacant Cary Castle. He borrowed $80,000 at twelve percent interest from the Bank of British North America, issuing a governor's warrant in defiance of the legislature's wishes. Half the money was for the purchase and renovation of Cary Castle; the other half was for salaries and "Victoria's indebtedness." A movement to have him recalled was started; on April 23, Leonard McClure made his memorable eighteen-hour speech in the legislature (page 44); W.F. Tolmie suggested that the ultimate solution would be the union of Vancouver Island and the colony of British Columbia, thus halving the cost of government; Kennedy refused to forward the legislature's resolutions to London; London, for its part, refused to intercede, advance any money, or give any direction; on May 21st, following a motion of the legislature demanding that Kennedy return the $80,000, the Bank shut off further credit to the colony. The situation was only resolved on June 11, 1866, when the bill to amalgamate the two colonies was introduced into the British House of Commons.

The Vancouver Island officials disliked Kennedy "in his official capacity and his family in their domestic capacity." As Union approached, when only one governor would be required, Benjamin Pearse put the general feeling into words: "I only hope 'Old Deportment' won't get the two colonies." Governor Seymour, who succeeded Kennedy, only moved to "Bleak House" under duress. Musgrave, his successor, enjoyed enormous popularity, as his mandate was to effect Confederation.

The lieutenant-governors who occupied Cary Castle following confederation were a mixed lot. Joseph Trutch (1871-6) was a respected Canadian politician and engineer who owned a lot of property in the Fairfield area; his wife apparently travelled to England and brought back larks, songbirds and thrushes for the gardens. Albert N. Richards (1876-81) was considered an ill-mannered Liberal carpetbagger, appointed by the hated MacKenzie Liberals in Ottawa; during the visit of Lord and Lady Dufferin, he was given no respect at all. That was not the case with the next lieutenant-governor, Clement F. Cornwall (1881-7), a direct descendant of a son of King John who had been made Earl of Cornwall. His "blue blood" connections made the visit of the Marquis of Lorne and Princess Louise (Queen Victoria's daughter) an occasion of appropriate pomp and good behaviour. Princess Louise, for her part, developed a curious attachment to the wind-swept Cary Castle grounds during her three-month visit, and described the place as "halfway between heaven and Balmoral." She had developed "an aversion to her husband" which, it was claimed, was due to the shock she suffered in a sleigh accident in eastern Canada in 1880, when "she was dragged by the hair for several minutes and lost one ear." She spent the time in Victoria happily shopping and wandering, leaving her husband (the governor general) to negotiate weightier matters, including the building of the Esquimalt & Nanaimo railway with Robert Dunsmuir. At the end of their visit, lame duck Premier Beaven made his wistful request that Princess Louise become the queen of an independent Vancouver Island.

Cary Castle burned to the ground on May 18, 1899; Lieutenant-Governor Thomas McInnes escaped with only the clothes on his back, and arranged to move into the vacant A.A. Green residence "Gyppeswyck" (now the Art Gallery). Rent of $50 a month was paid to the new owners, the Spencer family (who moved in late in 1903 following the re-erection of Government House). On October 1, 1901, the new lieutenant-

A patriotic tea party on the Government House grounds about 1914. Women's groups ceaselessly organized aid programs for the war effort under the patronage of Sir Frank and Lady Martha Barnard, the lieutenant-governor and "his gracious chatelaine." Lady Barnard, however, was the daughter of German-born Victoria brewer Joseph Loewen. On Saturday morning, May 8, 1915, news of the torpedoing of the liner Lusitania and the loss of 1,500 lives, including James Dunsmuir's son, hit the papers. That night, a mob sacked the Kaiserhof Hotel on Blanshard, the German club, and the business premises of Simon Leiser and Moses Lenz on Yates Street. Firemen refused to turn their hoses on the crowd. Two days later, a mob streamed up Rockland and threatened the lieutenant-governor and his wife. Soldiers were placed on guard around the grounds thereafter. Public meetings demanded the interning of all aliens, and anyone with a German name—like Victoria MLA H.F.W. Behnsen, whose son wanted to enlist in the Canadian Expeditionary Force—came under suspicion.

governor, Sir Henri Joly de Lotbinière, entertained the Duke and Duchess of Cornwall and York (later King George V and Queen Mary), Sir Wilfrid Laurier, and a host of other glittering worthies at the house.

The design of the new Government House was supposed to be chosen through an architectural competition organized by Premier Dunsmuir's government. According to biographer Terry Reksten, the winner of the competition was bamboozled out of the commission, allowing Victoria's two premier architects—Francis M. Rattenbury and Samuel Maclure—to share the work and fees. Rattenbury ended up doing the work (Maclure became ill) but, as with nearly everything he did on public commission, it ended up grossly over budget—$75,000 rather than "less than $45,000." An enquiry by Richard McBride's government in early 1904 placed some of the blame on the tastes of Sir Henri Joly, who had a lot of expensive panelling installed and a shower with a fancy array of pipes and taps. Nevertheless, architect Rattenbury was strongly criticized, too, especially as some marble ordered for Government House ended up in the kitchen of his house at Oak Bay. Rattenbury's reputation was preserved largely through the brilliant defence put up by his lawyer, Lyman Duff, for whom Rattenbury had designed a splendid house at 1745 Rockland Avenue.

Most of the lieutenant-governors before the turn of the century were men with connections to the British colonial office and the colonial "civil service" class. Later, they were more likely to be prominent provincial businessmen. They had a dull, ceremonial time of it by comparison with the wild dealings of their predecessors in the days of non-party politics. Provincial premiers after E.G. Prior were in much better control of the legislature—"rule by caucus" became the standard, and there remained almost no opportunity for a lieutenant-governor to influence events by "changing his advisers" (dismissing the government).

The early twenties at Government House were "a brilliant time," following the appointment of newspaperman Walter C. Nichol as lieutenant-governor. It was a period of almost continual afternoon teas, bridge and mah-jongg parties, dances "for the younger set," and glittering entertainments, the most memorable of which was the 48-hour visit of the Prince of Wales, travelling incognito as the Earl of Renfrew. The

Prince stayed at the Empress, used taxis to get around, played golf at Oak Bay and Colwood, and, informal in a dinner jacket, greeted 26 guests at a Government House dinner. Music was provided by Professor Paddy Heaton's Orchestra, and the Canary Cottage Orchestra of New York. Desserts were provided by L.C. Klitteng, "the world's greatest authority on Danish pastry, and the highest-priced pastry cook in the world, receiving $250 a day while working," whom Nichol had hired for Government House.

A typical example of the "younger married set" who frequented Government House parties during Nichol's tenure was architect Samuel Maclure's vivacious daughter Bobbie Mellin, married to Capt. A. de M. Mellin. She had been the heroine of the torpedoed S.S. *Leinster* in 1917, when she was accompanying her badly-wounded husband home from a hospital discharge in Ireland. Of the 500 passengers only 50 were saved, including Mrs. Mellin, who managed to save her husband by keeping him afloat on a raft though her collarbone was broken.

Nichol was awarded the Cross of the Legion of Honour in April, 1927 for his work in promoting better understanding between Canada and France. He made an $18,000 gift to a fund which allowed two UBC graduates each year to study at the University of Paris. Mrs. Nichol, the former Quita Josephine March Moore, died in 1968 at age 93. Nichol's daughter, Maraquita, married Mr. Rollo Mainguy, who went on to become Canada's naval chief of staff in 1951. His son, John Moore Nichol, served in the Royal Flying Corps in World War I, and died suddenly in Victoria in 1941, when he was only 43. Nichol retired to "Miraloma" at Sidney, a huge house built almost entirely of logs, where he lived until his death in December, 1928.

Government House burned again on April 15, 1957, destroying everything but the porte-cochère, which was not part of the original design—Lieutenant-Governor Dunsmuir had added it in 1909.

Sir Henri Joly de Lotbinière (1829-1908) was selected by Sir Wilfrid Laurier in June, 1900, to replace the fired Thomas McInnes as lieutenant-governor. Born in France, he was the son of a Huguenot, and became an Anglican. He was Minister of Inland Revenue in Laurier's first cabinet; in their youths, they had been among "les rouges"—young radicals opposed to the ultramontanes of the Quebec establishment. People in Victoria thought him "a gentleman of the old school."

Edward Gawler Prior, appointed lieutenant-governor in 1919, had been active in the federal Conservative party during the 1890s, including a stint as Minister of Inland Revenue in MacKenzie Bowell's and Charles Tupper's governments. He lived at "The Priory" at 729 Pemberton Road, which had six "sleeping apartments," a nursery, hot and cold running water in every room, and electric bells for summoning the servants. Its four acres of woods also had the last postern gate in Victoria, separating it from the eastern edge of "Duvals," before Pemberton Road was put through in the late 1950s.

The Barnards

Francis J. Barnard, the founder of the famous "BX" stagecoach service during the Cariboo gold rush years.

George Henry (Harry) Barnard

One of the homes directly across Rockland Avenue from the Government House grounds is "Duvals," the long-time residence of Harry Barnard. It was built in 1862, far out from the city with a lot of space for cows, horses, tennis courts and a scattering of oak trees, for Mrs. Elizabeth Miles, the widow of a Hudson's Bay Company official (two years later, she purchased Cary Castle across the street, when G.H. Cary returned to England, selling it the next year to Governor Kennedy). Mrs. Miles sold "Duvals" to Joseph Needham, when he took over as Chief Justice of Vancouver Island from David Cameron in October, 1865. Five years later, when Needham was appointed Chief Justice of Trinidad, he sold the house to Francis J. Barnard.

F.J. Barnard, following business reverses, had left Toronto for Victoria and the Cariboo in the spring of 1858, leaving his wife and young son Frank behind. For two years he worked as a wood chopper, trail clearer, and constable for the town of Yale—he once had to deliver a prisoner single-handedly to New Westminster by canoe. In 1860, he started a mail delivery business, carrying letters for two dollars and newspapers for one, *on foot* to Barkerville. In the winter of 1861-2 he started making trips between New Westminster and Yale, carrying mail. When the new Cariboo road opened that summer, he started the "BX"—Barnard's Express—with six-passenger, four- and six-horse express coaches. They caused quite a sensation with their springs, yellow running-gear trimmed with black, and red coachwork trimmed with white. He competed initially with Billy Ballou's Pioneer Fraser River Express. Later, he secured the government mail contract, and an excellent partner named Stephen Tingley, and ended with what was practically a monopoly on express shipping between Victoria and the Cariboo. In 1864, he carried $4,619,000 worth of treasure. He lost his shirt attempting to build a government telegraph line between Fort Edmonton and Cache Creek, a project he finally had to abandon without receiving a cent when the Dominion government changed in 1878. He became MP for Yale following Edgar Dewdney's appointment as Indian Commissioner, but was defeated by his future son-in-law, J.A. Mara, in 1886 (Mara had been Speaker of the B.C. Legislature since 1883, but resigned to go to Ottawa). Worn out by stress and anxiety, he had a stroke, and spent his last months helpless in his chair at "Duvals" until his death in 1889. His wife died a week later.

His first son, Frank Stillman Barnard, was elected in the Cariboo in late 1888 to replace Senate-appointee James Reid. Barnard served the Cariboo riding until he was defeated by Hewitt Bostock in the Liberal sweep of 1896. His Conservative credentials got him appointed to the lieutenant-governorship by Robert Borden in 1914. Following his term, he retired to "Clovelly" in Esquimalt (page 159).

George Henry Barnard was born in Victoria in 1868, twelve years after older brother Frank. When he was two years old, the family moved from their house on Pandora Street to "Duvals," where he lived for the next 84 years. "Harry" was on Victoria's city council in 1902, and was co-credited (with Capt. Troup of the Canadian Pacific Navigation Co.) with convincing both the Victoria citizenry and the CPR to come to terms on the building of the Empress Hotel. He was elected mayor in 1904, and, as one of the most prominent city Conservatives, easily unhorsed William Templeman in the 1908 election. His supporters gave him a torchlight parade through the city streets following his victory. He was re-elected in 1911—finally becoming part of the government—and took a Senate appointment in 1917. In an almost unprecedented move, he resigned his Senate seat in 1945, stating that he was too old to give the position enough time. He celebrated his golden wedding anniversary at "Duvals" on June 5, 1945, and died the following year, aged 86.

Henry Crease

Pentrelew Place, which extends south from Fort Street just west of the Victoria Art Gallery, marks the location of "Pentrelew," the estate of "the father of the bar" of Vancouver Island and British Columbia. Henry Pering Pellew Crease was born in 1823 into an upper-class Cornish family whose fortunes were declining. He took legal training, then followed his family to Canada West (Upper Canada before 1841) in 1849. He returned to England the following year to marry his betrothed, Sarah Lindley, the daughter of a professor of botany at the University of London. Crease then decided to emigrate to Vancouver Island, where he became the first barrister qualified to practice in either of the two west-coast colonies. A year later, in September, 1859, Sarah and her three daughters sailed for Victoria to join him.

The couple initially lived with surveyor Benjamin Pearse at "Fernwood Manor," moving to New Westminster in 1861 when Crease was appointed as first attorney general of British Columbia. He was fluent in six languages, and carried on an extensive private law practice in both cities as well as the gold-mining towns of the interior. At Union, in 1866, he was able to retain his position as attorney general, but had to move back to Victoria two years later when the capital was transferred from New Westminster. He was appointed to the British Columbia Supreme Court in 1870, as the first Puisne judge, and held the position till he retired 25 years later.

In the early 1870s, the Creases purchased property on Fort Street east of Cook, and set out to build a house in the fashionable Italianate style of Queen Victoria's Osborne House. Called "Pentrelew," translated from the Cornish as "house on land sloping two ways," it was ready for occupation in 1875.

With the approach of confederation, and rise to prominence of so many independence-minded Canadians, Henry Crease felt almost stateless—"a political pariah" he called himself. He believed his English education and background to be superior to anything Canadian (the Crease daughters were educated in Victoria, but the sons were sent to England)—as did his friends in the Vancouver Island "establishment," including Matthew Begbie, Peter O'Reilly, Joseph Pemberton, Richard Moody, W.J. Macdonald, and Clive Phillips-Wolley. He resented the way that his old friends and contacts in England were abandoning British Columbia to "the Canucks." Nevertheless, once Lord Granville and the colonial administration threw their support to the confederation movement, Crease put all his energy into British Columbia's new legal needs. He chaired the Royal Commission for the Revision of Laws of British Columbia prior to confederation, and the Royal Commission for Consolidation of the British Columbia Statutes in 1877, dovetailing B.C.'s colonial laws into the Canadian system. Many others in the old "Crown Colony clique" (like Chief Justice Needham) took transfers to British colonies in the tropics, or emigrated to Australia (like Needham, though, Crease was thwarted in his ambition to become Chief Justice of British Columbia, a position held

by Sir Matthew Baillie Begbie until Crease was too old to succeed him). Crease still felt that "dear old Victoria" was "a conquered country" about to be possessed by Canada. Canada, he wrote, seemed even more distant than "home" used to be. A lot of his complaining was due to pure snobbishness, and the loss of the old British social distinctions, leaving B.C. society "greatly changed for the worse." His old friend, Senator Macdonald, felt that the new Canadian and British Columbia political elite contained no one "that you would care to have for a friend, or to ask to your house."

Crease continued his work on the judicial circuit in the interior of British Columbia. In 1877, while riding between towns, he was thrown from his horse and badly hurt. He insisted on being carried in a litter from McDavie's Creek to Glenora to finish the assizes before seeking medical treatment in Victoria. In the great tradition of the English court, Crease was "blind" to the address of any wigless barrister, and maintained that standard even through the tradition-bashing 1890s. The wearing of wigs in court became an issue at the turn of the century. Egged on by barrister and former premier Joe Martin, the government eventually introduced and passed (in 1905) the "wig act"—forbidding the wearing of the customary official wig in all British Columbia courts (Puisne judge Denis Murphy noted that the wearing of toupees and "what used to be called ladies' swatches" didn't fall under the statutory ban).

Both Henry and Sarah Crease were accomplished watercolour painters, specializing in charming, English-style landscapes. Sarah's first ten watercolours of Victoria, painted in 1860, were included by her father in the "British Columbia Department of Canada" section of the International Exhibition in London in 1862. They were the first views of Victoria and Vancouver Island to receive any wide showing in England. Sarah's daughters, Mary and Josephine, also painted, and were active with the Island Sketch Club, which involved many ladies in sketching activities, small exhibitions, and teas. Many accomplished landscapes and views of Victoria scenes and houses were painted by the likes of the Creases, Sophie Pemberton, Josephine Woodward, and Samuel and Margaret Maclure.

"Pentrelew" was initially a comparatively modest brick house, but was expanded in 1890 with the addition of a three-storey campanile-style tower, dormer windows, and additional rooms—eventually it had eleven bedrooms, often all in use to accommodate the many visitors from England. Henry Crease retired from the bench and was knighted in January, 1896; he died in 1905 at age 82. Sarah lived on until 1922 (aged 96), sharing the house with three of her children—Susan, Lindley and Josephine. "Pentrelew" remained a little enclave of early Victoria life until the late thirties, when electric light was finally installed. The splendid grounds, extending south from Fort Street, were the site of many picnics and summer entertainments. Arthur Crease, the last surviving son (married to Helen, the daughter of Judge Tyrwhitt-Drake), said after the estate was

Sir Henry Pering Pellew Crease

Lady Sarah Crease in her "widow's weeds" on the circular driveway in front of "Pentrelew," at 1201 Fort Street, about 1907. Daughter Susan is visible in the garden to the left.

broken up in 1947 that "there was hardly an admiral in the British navy who hadn't, as a midshipman, climbed our cherry trees." The oaks behind the house were supposedly grown from acorns sent to Henry Crease by the English jurist Torrens, who had gathered them under the Tree of Liberty in the garden of William Pitt the Younger ("Under that tree, William Wilberforce the English emancipator pledged to work to free slaves all over the world"). Arthur Crease, a barrister, lived at "Ince" on Foul Bay Road—named after Ince Castle near Plymouth, which Henry Crease's mother had inherited. Old "Pentrelew" survived at 1201 Fort Street, much altered and painted white, as the Victoria Truth Centre. It was finally demolished in 1984.

Fairfield

Fairfield was an area of small farms and market gardens until the great land boom before the First World War. The western part adjoining Beacon Hill Park was originally part of Governor Douglas's Fairfield Estate; the eastern half, along Ross Bay and Gonzales Bay, was owned by Joseph Despard Pemberton and Isabel Ross—the widow of Fort Victoria's first factor, Charles Ross. Parts of Fairfield were later sold, as estates of around ten acres, bought by the likes of Joseph Trutch, Augustus Pemberton, and Robert Burnaby.

The Fairfield shoreline along Ross Bay was the best available site for a much-needed cemetery, as the Quadra Street "Pioneer Square" had been filled by the early 1870s. The government granted 47 acres near Ogden Point for a new cemetery, but memories of the recent smallpox outbreaks, and the deaths of over 30 Indians at an Ogden Point camp in 1862, were still fresh; as well, the land was to the windward of downtown. The government accordingly bought twelve acres at Ross Bay from Robert Burnaby for $300 an acre, and laid out a very picturesque, English-style cemetery. In the opinion of the time, which held that matters of life and death were best contemplated amidst birds, wildflowers and hedgerows, rural Fairfield was ideal. Thereafter, anyone who was in a hurry did best to avoid Fairfield Road, as custom demanded that any passerby stand still and solemn while the entire funeral procession passed (people later became considerably less respectful: a dubious record must be held by Angel Hotel owner Frederick Carne's funeral cortege in 1904, which was cut across twice by a mounted "hunting party" in full flight on a paper chase).

One of Fairfield's most bizarre incidents, the suicide of F. James Roscoe, occurred at his Ross Bay residence on December 20, 1878. Roscoe had been one of Victoria's MPs (Amor de Cosmos being the other), but had declined renomination for the September, 1878 election. (A number of Victorians had announced their candidacies, but when the news reached the city on September 18 that Sir John A. Macdonald had been defeated in his Kingston riding, all but Judah Phillip Davies and de Cosmos withdrew. Macdonald and de Cosmos were elected to the two Victoria seats on October 17.) "He had complained that he would eventually go insane," noted the *Colonist*, "but appeared to be getting over the idea." Partially dressed, with his feet entangled in some children's clothing, he had shot himself with a pistol shortly after breakfast. His body was discovered by his friend Alfred Fellows.

Another Fairfield curiosity involved the proprietor of the Five Points Barber Shop, J.A. Shanks, at Five Points on Fairfield Road at Moss Street. According to a story recounted by writer Bruce Hutchinson, Shanks was sued by the parents of a boy who had received an unusual haircut; the suit was reportedly dropped after the evidence (the hair) was lost. Shanks, a city alderman in 1925-6, is better remembered for his concern for the fate of *Ursus Kermodeii*, the white bear in Beacon Hill Park zoo.

Joseph Trutch, who owned a ten-acre estate surrounding "Fairfield House" at 601 Trutch Street near Fairfield Road, died in England in 1904. His property was subdivided two years later, precipitating other subdivi-

A croquet party in the summer of 1870 at Joseph Trutch's "Fairfield House": on the lawn, left to right, are John Trutch, Caroline O'Reilly and son Francis, Julia Trutch, Mrs. William Trutch, an unidentified man, Joseph Trutch and Kathleen O'Reilly. Built in 1862, the house was surrounded by a considerable estate of lawns and gardens. Collinson Street, running along the side of Matthew Begbie's property, provided an entrance driveway to the house. (Above right) Joseph Trutch was appointed surveyor-general of British Columbia by Governor Kennedy following J.D. Pemberton's sudden retirement in 1864. Pemberton had accompanied the new governor on the ship from England to Victoria, and resigned soon after; Kennedy had no official residence, so stayed at Trutch's home until he purchased Cary Castle. Trutch was chosen as the province's first lieutenant-governor in 1871 by Sir John A. Macdonald, as he was identified with neither the British nor the Canadian factions. Trutch promised Macdonald that B.C. wouldn't hold Canada to the letter of the railway clause in the confederation terms, a grave misjudgement which later almost resulted in B.C.'s secession.

(Above) William Bayliss, a hotel owner and butcher, built his Hollywood Grocery (next page) at Fairfield Road and Lillian Street in 1912 to serve the rapidly expanding Fairfield area.

sions, and suddenly Fairfield became a grid of streets. The frantic real-estate selling of the years until 1913 pushed the value of the little lots from $400 to $5,000. The area around the foot of St. Charles Street stayed quite rural through the twenties, when Hollywood Park was created on land formerly used by the gravel and stone bunkers of the Worswick Paving Co. The Hollywood Court, just east of Lillian Street, was designed for the new generation of Victorians who didn't want an ostentatious residence but needed a garage.

Thomas Shotbolt's "Hollywood," built on a 10-acre estate on Gonzales Hill. Shotbolt Road, south of Fairfield Road, was the estate's driveway. The house was built high enough so that, from the lookout tower, both Race Rocks and the Inner Harbour could be seen. Shotbolt (1842-1922) was one of three pioneer druggists in Victoria (along with Langley & Co., and Moore Bros.). He arrived from England in 1862 at age 20, and started his store on the south side of Johnson below Government Street. It became a centre for Leechtown and Cariboo gold rush gossip. Shotbolt and his wife lived in rooms above the drug store. On the completion of "Hollywood," Mrs. Shotbolt (a keen gardener who had formerly had to content herself with pots of flowers on the balcony) finally got her garden.

Three hundred real-estate firms jockeyed for business in Victoria in the years before the real-estate collapse of 1913. With a stable population of only 40,000, and most of the real growth occurring in Vancouver, the Victoria agents sweet-talked potential buyers of what was little more than frog-swamp—especially in almost-rural Fairfield. Little 60-foot lots ended up being worth $5,000. When many English investors withdrew their capital in 1912, the boom collapsed (page 91). Some of the Victoria salesmen were (left to right, above) Robert William Clark, a real-estate and investment broker with Bond & Clark of Trounce Alley; Robert Rubie Jones, an architect, builder and developer; Thomas C. Johnston, of Moore & Johnston at 632 Yates Street; (below) William Thwaites Williams, who had owned a clothing store but got quickly into the real-estate business with the City Land Co.; Victor A.G. Eliot, of the Western Dominion Land & Investment Co. Ltd.; Andrew H. Mitchell, a general contractor and "spec"-builder; and (picture on page 164) Arthur Currie, a schoolteacher who branched into real estate, then commanded the Canadian army overseas during the latter part of World War I. The biggest company of all was the B.C. Land & Investment Co. (page 33), at one time holding claims on half the land in the Victoria area. Many of the houses in Fairfield and Shoal Bay were prefabricated bungalows, erected by companies like C.G. Walsh's Victoria Bungalow Construction Co., and William Dumford & Son Ltd. The former built five- and six-room bungalows for $2,500 to $5,000, with one-tenth down and mortgages at seven or eight percent. "The landlords in B.C. have little terror for the majority of residents due to the system of deferred payments," said one advertisement. Dumford advertised that he employed "the exclusive services of a fully-qualified English architect." The California style, he said, was most favoured, and the one-storey bungalow plan "makes a strong appeal to the housewife."

George Winter

Coachman George Winter and a footman, awaiting the lieutenant-governor's pleasure at Cary Castle in the late 1860s. Later, when Winter had started his own business, everyone hired his carriages for special occasions, giving rise to the saying "he brought her in a Winter hack." (The expenses form below was submitted by auctioneer Judah Phillip Davies, following his attempt to gain one of two federal seats in the October 17, 1878 by-election. Davies lost to Sir John A. Macdonald and Amor de Cosmos.)

Victoria's elite always hired coachman George Winter for their special occasions. He had a great variety of coaches, hacks, traps, and even sleighs with bells for the occasional snowy winter day. An event was always that much more special when Winter, dressed in blue, brass-buttoned livery with a cockaded top hat, brought a polished équipage clattering up the driveway.

George Winter joined the British navy as a teenager and was serving on HMS *Bacchante* when it docked in Esquimalt harbour in 1861. Roused by stories of the Cariboo gold rush, he jumped ship, and didn't return to Victoria for several years. He managed to get a job as coachman for Governor Kennedy, and, with his new wife, the former Margaret Orrick, he moved into a cottage on the Cary Castle grounds. Dressed in his livery every day (with a young assistant as footman), he drove for Kennedy, and subsequently for Musgrave, and Trutch, Richards and Cornwall. By that time, he had started his own business and had moved his family to a cottage at Cook Street and Fairfield Road, across the fields from Judge Begbie's house.

In the 1890s, his son, George Jr., became coachman to James Dunsmuir at "Burleith" on the edge of Victoria Arm; his other son, Robert, was coachman to Judge Paulus Aemilius Irving. Society had changed enough after the turn of the century to make the Winters something of an anachronism, though people continued to hire the carriages for special events like weddings, funerals, and the Native Sons' ball. The popularity of the daring new motorcar finally put them out of business. George Winter Sr. died at his Ross Bay house in July, 1911, aged 72.

Sir Matthew Baillie Begbie

Judge Matthew Baillie Begbie is a legendary figure of the early years of British Columbia. He was the first judge of the Colony of British Columbia, and represented British justice throughout the mining camps and shack towns in the gold rush days from 1858 until confederation. He, Governor James Douglas, and the handful of Irish-born magistrates and gold commissioners like Augustus Pemberton, Chartres Brew, and Peter O'Reilly, ruled the wild colony. So significant was their contribution that, without the sheer force of their personalities, British Columbia would likely have become either another victim of American "Manifest Destiny," or at least as bloody as California, run by vigilantes and gangs. The law, and allegiance to the British Crown, were rather intangible and foreign concepts to the thousands of miners who turned British Columbia upside-down in the 1850s and 1860s. In addition, the Indians were understandably restive, and would likely have duplicated the maraudings so common in the American west if they hadn't been impressed with the fairness of the colonial justice system.

Begbie, like James Douglas, was a lowland Scot of somewhat humble background. He was born in Africa, either in Mauritius or near the Cape of Good Hope, in September, 1819, the son of a British army colonel. He was taken to England for his education, and showed great promise as a mathematician and later as a law student, articling at Lincoln's Inn, but was also something of a dilettante. He spent many summers wandering in Europe, sketching, and passing the evenings in the local hostelry. Regardless, he graduated from Cambridge in 1841 and was called to the bar three years later.

It was the period of English legal history best described in Charles Dickens's *Bleak House*. Begbie was moderately successful as a barrister, but lacked the contacts and the temperament necessary for great advancement. A former fellow student who possessed both—Solicitor General Sir Hugh Cairns—suggested to Colonial Secretary Bulwer-Lytton that Begbie had the qualities necessary to dispense British justice in the hinterland. Begbie was thus appointed as "A Judge in Our Colony of British Columbia" on September 2, 1858, and took his oath of office at Derby (Fort Langley) on November 29. His first action was to swear in James Douglas as the mainland colony's governor.

The legend of Judge Begbie during the gold rush years includes the slander that he was "the hanging judge." He actually had an aversion to murder trials and disliked passing the capital sentence, though it was claimed that Bulwer-Lytton hired him because he was physically capable of performing the hanging himself, from a branch of the nearest tree. Begbie was certainly unorthodox, and often flew into a rage at what he considered to be stupid, equivocating juries and lawyers. He didn't hear a case, "he ran it," and although he was well aware of the law and its precedents, he would often bend his own rules to see natural justice done. Dozens of stories circulated about Begbie: of travellers meeting him while he was on circuit, trudging along mountain trails "waist deep in snow"; upon receiving a threatening letter, he reads it out in court, "inviting the

writer to get on with the shooting." One story recounts that as he sat in a rocking chair on the verandah above a hotel's entrance, he overheard a group of "toughs" making a plan to shoot him as he rode out of town the next day. He went into his room and returned with a pail of night soil, which he emptied over the railing onto their heads. Thus, "the west was won" in a peaceful, law-abiding, uniquely Canadian way, helped by the law-abiding tendencies of the vast majority of the gold miners and their hangers-on.

His idea of justice was "that if a man insists upon behaving like a brute, after fair warning, and won't quit the colony, treat him like a brute and flog him." Unorthodox sentences—like one in the New Westminster assizes in 1866 for "private whipping" in addition to imprisonment of "a jail-bird well known to the police"—were well-suited to the spirit of the times, when, as the *Colonist* surmised, "scamps frequently visited the jail to be provided with wholesome food at the public expense in return for an indifferent day's labour." Begbie's judgements in civil actions, and his close identification with Governor Douglas and the "Crown Colony clique," made him unpopular with pro-mainland agitators like *Columbian* editor John Robson. Begbie's rows were legendary—John Robson was jailed for contempt of court, lawyer and future premier John Foster McCreight was disbarred (but immediately reinstated), and George Walkem's call to the bar was delayed for years. Walkem's running feud with Begbie, when the former was premier and attorney general, resulted in numerous contempt of court threats, and the passing of legislation by Walkem to ensure the government's control of procedural matters—specifically to clip Begbie's unorthodox wings.

Begbie became the first Chief Justice of British Columbia on March 29, 1870. He was knighted on November 26, 1874. In his later years on the bench in Victoria, he mellowed considerably and, though still Chief Justice, sat as presiding judge at county court, which often was little more than a small debts court. He apparently enjoyed the sittings hugely, and would let plaintiff and defendant argue practically to the point of trial by combat, then throw his head back, emit a low whistle, resume his judicial attitude and give his decision. One example recounted in a memoir by Judge Denis Murphy had two parties fighting over a five dollar debt. The arguments became so strenuous that a challenge was issued for physical combat outside. Begbie urged them to toss a coin; otherwise, he said, he would pay the five dollars himself. The two men dropped their fight.

Another of Judge Murphy's stories described how Murphy's father, living in Victoria in the mid 1860s, had wanted to travel to New York to marry his betrothed, but had lost all his money in the collapse of Macdonald's Bank. By chance, he met Begbie on Government Street, and found himself telling his sad tale. Begbie took him immediately into the Bank of British Columbia, and co-signed a promissory note for Murphy's trip.

Like many Englishmen of the time, Begbie remained a bachelor, content to flirt outrageously and behave gallantly with the ladies. Dressed in

The Hon. John Hamilton Gray's presence in Victoria was one of the results of Confederation— Prime Minister John A. Macdonald appointed him to the B.C. Supreme Court, although Gray had hoped to be speaker in the House of Commons. He was not a member of the B.C. bar, and didn't want to move west, as he resided in New Brunswick at the time. Many B.C. Tories who had hoped for patronage appointments were infuriated with Gray's elevation to the bench—as useful, in Justice Begbie's words, "as the 21st wheel on a coach." One probably apocryphal story, recounted by Judge Murphy, concerned a day when Gray was "busily engaged in obeying Voltaire's injunction to cultivate your garden." A messenger arrived from Justices Begbie and Crease, requesting Gray's presence to hear appeals. "What? Cease gardening on a beautiful day like this for the miserable pittance paid me as a judge?" he asked. Gray spent more than he earned, and left his widow practically penniless when he died on June 5, 1889. He is the only Father of Confederation buried west of Ontario (in Ross Bay Cemetery).

Sir Matthew Baillie Begbie lived in a modest, cottage-style residence on his property east of Cook Road, between Fairfield Road and Collinson Street. Once Begbie had decided not to return to England, he developed his gardens with herbaceous borders of stocks, phlox, honeysuckle, and foxgloves, had frequent tennis and badminton afternoons, and gave some of the best dinner parties in Victoria. Begbie mellowed considerably from his "hanging judge" persona in his final years, and enjoyed tramping across the Fairfield marshes, a little duck shooting, and good conversation and Madeira next to the coal fireplace in his library. He often walked to his friend Peter O'Reilly's house at Point Ellice for the evening.

Sir Matthew Baillie Begbie

a cape, with his Van Dyke beard and buttoned shoes, he strode about the downtown area, towed by a fan of cocker spaniels. His great passion was drama, and he bought and renovated one of the old Fort Victoria buildings for a theatre. He had been a judge for so long that, "like Queen Victoria and Browning's Pippa, no one could remember a time without him. Having lived thus long, there seemed no need (that he) should ever die." In his final illness (cancer), he was visited every night by his old friend Peter O'Reilly. The latter's diary recounts that, one night, Begbie told him not to stay long, as he didn't have much time left and wanted to make his peace with God. He died that night—June 11, 1894. His successor, Theodore Davie, resigned the premiership to become chief justice.

R.P. Rithet

Robert P. Rithet's grand "Hollybank" occupied a large part of the block of Humboldt Street just east of St. Joseph's Hospital. It was noted for its beautiful iron fence, six chimneys, holly trees and winding garden paths. During the 1890s, when Rithet was the toast of the town for having the foresight to build the Outer Wharves, there was a constant parade of carriages on the circular drive, ladies with embroidered parasols in the garden, tennis parties and political meetings.

Rithet was born in Ecclesfechan, Scotland, and left home at age eighteen to come to the New World. Like so many others who arrived in Victoria in 1862, he went into business instead of trying the worked-out Interior gold creeks. He got a job as bookkeeper for Sproat & Co. wholesale provisioners, and moved to San Francisco in February, 1869. But, on a return visit, he fell in love with one of retired Hudson's Bay Company factor Alexander Munro's three daughters. They were married on October 27, 1875. Rithet then formed a prosperous partnership with Andrew Welch in Victoria.

Welch, Rithet & Co. were agents for the Moodyville Sawmill on Burrard Inlet, and imported groceries and liquors into British Columbia. They were especially active in Hawaii, importing sugars into North America—Rithet was consul-general for Hawaii in Victoria during the period when Hawaii was an independent country with its own queen. They built the Outer Wharf in James Bay in the early 1890s, so that for the first time ocean-going ships like the CPR *Empress* liners could actually dock at Victoria (large ships couldn't manoeuvre into the Inner Harbour). Rithet also was involved in other business projects, including an abortive attempt with engineer and Standard Time inventor Sandford Fleming to lay a telegraph cable across the Pacific (they attempted to erect a staging area on an uninhabited island near Hawaii, but were chased off by a U.S. cutter). He was Victoria's mayor in 1885, when the issue was drainage, and campaigned on the slogan that the city "must be drained of its filth or it will be drained of its wealth and populace." He served a term as MLA, supporting Premier Turner until 1897.

A change in the Canadian sugar tariff in 1891 allowed Rithet to import sugar directly from China, at a price below that possible at the new B.C. Sugar Refinery in Vancouver. Rithet bitterly resented B.T. Rogers's decision to establish the sugar refinery in Vancouver, instead of in Victoria, and fought stubbornly for three years to put the Vancouver establishment out of business (B.T. Rogers's uncle was Victoria merchant James Angus,

a business associate of Rithet's; most of Rogers's backing was from James Angus's brother—R.B. Angus of the CPR and the Bank of Montreal; to add insult to injury, B.C. Sugar's president was James Angus's older brother, Forrest). Rithet imported Chinese sugar from Butterfield & Swire in Hong Kong, and threw it on the B.C. market at a loss. He then, according to Rogers's widow, approached B.C. Sugar with a market-splitting and price-fixing arrangement, which was rejected by the Vancouver establishment. Rogers travelled to Hong Kong in an effort to reach a settlement, but had little luck. The Vancouver vs. Victoria sugar battle continued through 1894—at one time, Vancouver papers warned consumers not to use Chinese sugar because of the smallpox germs that might come on it; later, advertisements printed magnified photographs of bugs, allegedly found in the Chinese sugar. Finally, Rithet gave up the fight.

The Rithets had three children: Edward died in his youth; Jack was an excellent athlete and one of the big tippers of caddies at the Victoria Golf Club, but was rumoured to be a drinker and didn't take over his father's firm; Gertrude married Lawrence Genge, an accountant with Welch & Rithet, who did. The family owned the 730-acre Broadmead Farm—also called Rithet's Ranch—near Royal Oak on the Saanich road. After her husband's death, Elizabeth Rithet was a familiar sight, dressed in black and being driven in her black electric car with its white-spoked wheels and little flower arrangements in the windows.

(Next page) Looking east past the Rithet's "Hollybank" to their daughter and son-in-law's house, now the stylish Beaconsfield Hotel at the corner of Humboldt and Vancouver streets. The Rithets owned the eastern half of the block bounded by Humboldt, Vancouver, Collinson (Fairfield Road in that block was added later as a traffic expediter), and Rupert (now Quadra). A two-storey barn and a number of outbuildings and paddocks occupied the acreage behind "Hollybank" at 952 Humboldt; daughter Gertrude Genge's house was built at the eastern end of her parent's property (at 998 Humboldt) as a wedding present in 1904. Lawrence Genge, and later his son J.R. Genge, took over the operation of R.P. Rithet & Co. Ltd. after Rithet's death in March, 1919. The curious half-width block across Humboldt from "Hollybank" resulted from a small stream which, at high tide, created a shallow canoe route between Ross Bay and James Bay. Both Mrs. Rithet and Gertrude enjoyed riding across the meadow below their house and through Beacon Hill Park to the sea. Their cow grazed along the edge of the creek. "Hollybank," with its many holly trees, was demolished in July, 1953, not long after Mrs. Rithet's death. A piece of the iron fence was saved, and placed in the Provincial Museum grounds around a cherry tree which grew from the Black Prince cherry stones planted there in 1854 by James Douglas. The house's stable was the second last one left in Victoria—the last one being the J.H. Todd stable on the north side of Johnson between Quadra and Vancouver.

Robert Patterson Rithet

Elizabeth Jane Munro was tall and slender and favoured black silk gowns; she was a sensational bride at age 22 for the up-and-coming businessman R.P. Rithet. She outlived her husband (by 33 years) and all her children, and died a week after her 99th birthday in 1952 at "Hollybank"—built for her as a wedding present in 1875.

Oak Bay

Until the streetcar line was opened in the early 1890s, Oak Bay was so far from town that it was only suitable for farming and summer camping. There were at first only four owners: William Henry McNeil owned the land bounded on the south by Shoal (now McNeill) Bay, and on the other three sides roughly by the Oak Bay boundary at Gonzales Hill, McNeill Avenue, and the golf links; the land to the east and north of it, all the way to Bowker Creek by Glenlyon School, was part of Joseph Despard Pemberton's Gonzales Farm; north of that, John Tod owned the land to the Uplands Farm boundary (Tod's house, dating from about 1851, still stands at 2564 Heron Street, and the Cadboro Bay Road originally had the sole purpose of connecting it with the city); Uplands Farm, like Beckley Farm in James Bay, was owned by the Fur Trade Division of the Hudson's Bay Company.

Oak Bay began to open up around 1890, after J.D. Pemberton laid out and graded Oak Bay Avenue through his farm and presented it to the city. The Victoria tramway company had barely been in operation for a year when, on February 21, 1891, it agreed to extend streetcar service from Fort Street down the hill along Oak Bay Avenue to the beach (an earlier line from downtown continued from Fort Street along the Cadboro Bay Road to Royal Jubilee Hospital). The tramway company had been approached by a group of real estate developers under the name of the Oak Bay Land & Improvement Company, who had purchased some of Pemberton's land, and were willing to offer a cash and land bonus for regular streetcar service. The new line opened on July 1, 1891, making it possible for people to commute between the new suburb and the city. The rural nature of the line caused the tramway company some difficulties, especially with animals wandering loose and sometimes lying across the track at night. One accident quoted by railway historian Douglas Parker involved a stray, blind-in-one-eye horse rushing into the oil-fired headlight of a streetcar on a March evening in 1893. The horse did considerable damage both to itself and the streetcar, and had to be shot the next morning.

Oak Bay became a tourist destination following the June 8, 1893 opening of the Mount Baker Hotel at the beach. A grand dance in a ballroom decorated "with festoons of wreaths, inset with red berries and flowers," was so successful as to make the *Colonist* enthuse that the hotel "is a delightful place to have a trip to in the summer—very convenient, cool and comfortable." The lower balcony, lighted with Chinese lanterns, was in constant use as a promenade, but the upper one attracted a cool, stiff breeze which made it not so well patronized. "The cold collation served was capital," said the *Colonist* reporter, meaning that the food was good. A lot of the credit went to hotel manager J. Alexander Virtue, formerly of the Hotel Vancouver. Discussion revolved around whether people "would care to go out that far, just for an evening party," but the regular service on the streetcar solved the problem. This new accessibility, and the fashionable interest in Oak Bay, contributed to the swift decline of the Dallas Hotel near Ogden Point. Before long, the Mount Baker had an international reputation, especially with British travellers stopping over from the Orient on their way back to England. The Duke and Duchess of Cornwall and York, later King George V and Queen Mary, stayed there during their visit to Victoria in the autumn of 1901. The hotel burned to the ground in 1902; it was superseded by the Rattenbury-designed Oak Bay Hotel, renamed and remembered for years as the Old Charming Inn.

The scenery along the waterfront attracted the attention of English writer Rudyard Kipling, who visited Victoria with his bride in April, 1892, and stopped over again in 1907. On his second visit, he was driven along the waterfront by motorcar, sharing in a ritual dating back decades to the *en masse* horse and carriage excursions of Sunday afternoons.

The beach provided a cool, clean respite from the soot and noise of downtown in the summertime. Families fleeing the heat and grime (and the smallpox) of the early 1890s camped for weeks at a time on the beach. By 1905, Oak Bay had a permanent population of about one hundred families but retained, with its piggeries, open ditches, and wind-blown dust, a decidedly rural character.

Another attraction for Victorians was the establishment, in early 1895, of the Oak Bay recreation park (now Windsor Park at Windsor Road and Oak Bay Avenue). Built as a "feature destination" by the tramway company to increase ridership on the Oak Bay line (much as Gorge Park was, a decade later), the park had a bicycle racing track, a lacrosse field, and a grandstand seating 2,000. Concerts by the Royal Arthur band and promenades on the pathways throughout the fenced, eleven-acre park were widely advertised.

One of the first wealthy residents was famed architect Francis Rattenbury, whose designs for the legislative buildings, the Empress Hotel, Government House, and some of the Canadian Pacific Railway's mountain resorts had given him financial freedom. He started building a home on five acres of land just north of the Mount Baker Hotel in 1899, a year after he married. Other Victorians, including Beaumont Boggs, Samuel Maclure, John Shallcross, and William Oliver, bought property along the beach and built substantial homes.

The afore-mentioned Oak Bay Land & Improvement Company had been formed in 1891 with 3,000 shareholders each paying $100 for a share. Their intention was "to attract a good class of residents." Steamers were to dock in the bay, and other attractions—like regular balloon ascensions in front of the Mount Baker Hotel—were destined to make it "one of the most beautiful and popular resorts" in the province. The leaders of the Improvement Association tried to arrange an amalgamation of Oak Bay with Victoria, then petitioned the Provincial Secretary for incorporation as a separate municipality. This was finally arranged on July 2, 1906. The new Corporation of the District of Oak Bay wanted to avoid "the expense and annoyance of an election," and to that end ensured that only enough names were nominated for councillors and reeve to fill the available seats. William Oliver became the first reeve, and architect Rattenbury sat on the first council.

William Alfred (Bill) Scott, "the lighthouse philosopher," visited Victoria in 1939 and, when he returned after three years in a Japanese P.O.W. camp in North China, bought a guest house at 1026 Newport Avenue in Oak Bay. Born in England in 1898, he went to China in 1919 as a lighthouse reconstructor. He gained a reputation as one of Victoria's prize eccentrics, his antics including challenging political opponents to a singing debate, and welcoming Pierre Trudeau to Victoria in 1971 dressed as Diogenes, complete with a table lamp. He died in Maui in 1979; his will left money to the University of Victoria for Norman Bethune and Mao Tse-Tung memorial awards.

Included in Oak Bay municipality was the Willows Fairground, Lester Patrick's arena at the corner of Cadboro Bay Road and Epworth, and the Oak Bay racetrack, all owned by "Victoria interests." The racetrack became a particular issue: the 60 days of racing approved by the City of Victoria for the track in 1911 "shocked" Oak Bay. The buildings on the fairgrounds, including the racetrack, burned in 1948. The land was bought by Oak Bay municipality, which subdivided it and sold the lots to builders. Today, not a trace of the old fairground remains.

No such annoyances ever disturbed Uplands. The 450 acres of the Hudson's Bay Company's old Uplands Farm—rolling land above Cadboro Bay—were purchased in 1907 by a syndicate of Winnipeg and Victoria capitalists for the development of an exclusive suburb. The entire property was sold in 1911 to the Compagnie Franco-Canadienne, which formed a subsidiary called Uplands Ltd. An agreement was struck with Oak Bay municipality to zone the area for houses having a minimum price of $5,000 (or at least half of the purchase price of the lot, whichever was greater). Lots averaged one acre, and no apartments, hotels or commercial buildings were permitted. The company developed a series of looping cul-de-sacs with roundabouts, underground wiring, distinctively modern light-standards, 66-foot-wide asphalt-paved roadways, boulevards, and stone gates at each end of the development on Beach Drive. Uplands was very similar to Shaughnessy Heights, the prestigious development created by the Canadian Pacific Railway in Vancouver a few years previously. It even employed the same paving contractor, Miles Cotton.

OAK BAY HOTEL

Samuel Maclure, the architect whose beautiful homes dominate the Foul Bay Road, Rockland Avenue, and Oak Bay areas. He was the first white child born in New Westminster, in 1859, and worked first as a telegraph operator before devoting himself fully to painting and architecture. He was a natural artist with a love of nature and beauty which showed up in different ways in his paintings and his buildings—he had an extraordinary gift for fitting houses into the landscape. Both he and his wife Margaret were accomplished watercolourists. They had three daughters. Maclure died in August, 1929, at his Oak Bay home.

The first house was the immense "Riffington" on a considerable acreage along the beach at 3175 Beach Avenue. The Royal Victoria Yacht Club purchased land on the site of the old slaughterhouse at Cadboro Bay. Unfortunately, Uplands was barely off the ground before the economic crash of 1913. Most of the lots weren't purchased and built on until the twenties or the thirties, by which time society had changed—very few had the income they had before the First World War (income tax had been introduced), and the new attraction was mobility—not the servant problems and responsibility of a large estate.

The Oak Bay Hotel, at the corner of Windsor Avenue and Beach Drive, was completed in 1907 at a cost of $15,000. It was a popular summer resort during the 1920s, when grass and thistles still grew in the open ditches and Beach Drive was still dirt. In the 1930s, it was called the Oak Bay Apartments. In 1937, Miss Jane M. Ewing bought it for about $60,000, and changed its name to the Old Charming Inn. Born in Scotland, she came to Victoria after World War One and worked for her sister, Mrs. F.M. Armour, managing the Cadboro Bay Hotel, then opened the Small Charming Inn at 1456 Beach Drive in the early thirties. Many guests stayed at the Old Charming Inn for years, including Sir Charles Bell, who hung the walls of his room with satin Tibetan panels while writing a book on Tibet. Miss Ewing hung Scottish calendars on the staircase, one for each year since 1937. The Old Charming Inn was demolished in July, 1962, and replaced by the "Rudyard Kipling Apartments," a highrise which was advertised to have lockers in its basement equipped with blast doors, kitchens and bathrooms "to make them effective as bomb and fallout shelters." When Rudyard Kipling was staying at the old Mount Baker Hotel on the beach there, he wrote of Oak Bay that: "you must take all that the eye admires most in Bournemouth, Torquay, Isle of Wight, The Doon, Sorrento and Campo Bay; all reminiscences of the Thousand Islands, and arrange the whole around the Bay of Naples with some Himalayas for background."

Francis M. Rattenbury

Francis M. Rattenbury's house at 1701 Beach Drive, now the Glenlyon Boys School, about 1900. Rattenbury is possibly the insouciant, moustachioed young man at the front door.

Francis Mawson Rattenbury was Victoria's most celebrated architect at the turn of the century; subsequently, he became Victoria's most celebrated murder victim in a sordid love triangle involving his youthful second wife and their chauffeur. He was described as hot-headed, opinionated, bad-tempered, and devious, and his children disliked him. He was also tall, handsome and forceful—and a superb architect until he began to dissolve into self-pity and drink in the twenties. In his heyday, he designed the legislative buildings and the Empress Hotel, giving Victoria its distinctive and dramatic Inner Harbour profile.

Rattenbury was born in Leeds in 1867, the grandson of a preacher. His relatives were active as architects in Bradford, but Rattenbury saw only narrow horizons in that provincial town and, after completing his architectural apprenticeship, set out for the new world shortly after his 24th birthday. He moved west to Vancouver, where he responded to the newspaper advertisements for the legislature design competition, entering a sketch which he shrewdly signed "B.C. Architect." On March 15, 1893, he received a telegram with the words "accept congratulations—come to Victoria by tomorrow's boat if possible." He moved into the Driard, embellished his almost nonexistent past accomplishments, and proceeded to

create an unforgettable monument on the James Bay shore. The Rattenbury legend had begun.

Rattenbury went from strength to strength, investing heavily in Klondike transportation schemes, designing landmarks like the Bank of Montreal on Government Street, the new Government House, the Empress Hotel, the Oak Bay Hotel, and a number of fine houses in the Rockland area. He severed his connection with the CPR in December, 1906, and threw all his energies and assets into Charles Hayes' Grand Trunk Pacific Railroad. He designed terminal facilities and tourist accommodation for Prince Rupert, and invested heavily in land all along the line in northern B.C. When the crash came in 1913, he lost heavily. His career foundered, and only picked up again briefly in the early twenties when, in partnership with Percy James, he designed the CPR Steamship terminal on Belleville Street and the Crystal Gardens amusement centre behind the Empress.

At the dinner in the Empress, on December 29, 1923, following the successful passage of the Crystal Gardens tax-relief referendum, Rattenbury met Alma Victoria Clarke Dolling Packenham. Twice widowed, 28 years old, beautiful, a "flapper" with a sequined headband, and a talented *pianiste*, she was in sharp contrast to his slightly dull first wife Florrie, whom he had married in 1898 after an on-again, off-again courtship, six months before their first child was due. Rattenbury's affair with Alma in their "trysting palace" on Niagara Street quickly became public gossip; her immorality was due to cocaine, people whispered, as was Rattenbury's erratic, wilful and quarrelsome behaviour. He became ever more cruel to Florrie, cutting off the heat and light in the Oak Bay house and flaunting his paramour about Victoria. Florrie sued for divorce in January, 1925, by which time Alma had taken to calling herself Mrs. Rattenbury. Social outcasts, Rattenbury and Alma left Victoria in late 1929 for England.

Their new life in their Bournemouth villa deteriorated as Rattenbury became increasingly besotted by drink, demoralized by his resulting impotence, and impoverished by collapsed land dealings. Alma started an affair with their simple-minded, 18-year-old chauffeur, George Percy Stoner. The latter became enraged at what he thought was a reconciliation between Alma and Rattenbury, and killed the dozing, drunken architect with a wooden mallet on March 24, 1935. Stoner was sentenced to death on May 31, following a sensational trial. Alma committed suicide on June 4, stabbing herself and then drowning in the Avon River. A campaign—like several in England at the time against capital punishment—gathered 300,000 signatures to a petition claiming that Stoner had been led astray by an older woman. His death sentence was commuted on June 25.

Sir Charles Hibbert Tupper

Sir Charles Hibbert Tupper, until the mid-twenties the moral conscience of the B.C. Conservative party and one of Victoria's prominent lawyers, lived at 1587 York Place in Oak Bay. His celebrated switch of allegiance to the Liberal Party in the 1916 election was national news, helping to topple the McBride-Bowser regime and initiating a series of recriminations which poisoned party politics for decades.

Tupper's father was Sir Charles Tupper, Bart. (1821-1915), a Nova Scotian who figured prominently in the political discussions preceding confederation, then entered Sir John A. Macdonald's Conservative government. He was an early supporter of the Canadian Pacific Railway, pulling the political strings in the House of Commons and dealing with English capitalists to ensure the project's completion. He became prime minister of Canada on May 1, 1896—the last of a hapless group of four Conservatives who fought among themselves and with their caucus in their attempts to govern the country. On July 8, 1896, Wilfrid Laurier defeated Tupper, giving him the shortest term as prime minister in history (until John Turner in 1984). He was the last surviving Father of Confederation.

His son, Charles Hibbert Tupper, entered parliament in 1882 at age 27, and became Minister of Fisheries in his father's cabinet. He worked diligently on the Bering Sea sealing treaty for which he was knighted by Queen Victoria. He applied to the B.C. Law Society for admission to the Supreme Court as a solicitor; then brought his family to live in Victoria following the collapse of his father's government.

Tupper was an advocate of party politics, believing that it would result in reduced corruption and more stable government, and he worked hard in support of Richard McBride when the latter decided to campaign as a Conservative in the 1903 election. Shortly thereafter, though, Tupper began to feud openly with McBride and the Conservative Party. He "smelt a rat" on the deal McBride concocted with the promoters of the Grand Trunk Pacific terminus at Prince Rupert; and again in 1909 when the deal with the Liberal promoters of the Canadian Northern Pacific Railway was an election issue. He considered the latter "a reckless investment" made without proper guarantees, but his response was almost apoplectic over "the raiding of the provincial treasury" in 1912 for the PGE Railway (now B.C. Rail). In August, 1914, when the Canadian Northern's credit collapsed in London, Tupper wrote that he could get only a "melancholy satisfaction" from being proved right.

However, Tupper's arch-enemy, William J. Bowser, then became premier, following McBride's resignation. Tupper was so incensed that he publicly took to calling Bowser "the little Kaiser." World news in late 1914 was dominated by the invasion and pillaging of Belgium by Germans, who had violated Belgian neutrality, claiming the military "necessity" of annihilating France; Tupper drew a parallel with Bowser, who had said "it is necessary to grease the palm of an Indian" in order to get title to the Songhees reservation on the Inner Harbour. Tupper went so far as to describe Premier Bowser as "the embodiment of Prussian 'kultur'," and proceeded to campaign actively for the Liberal party, a switch which helped defeat the Conservatives.

Tupper's old-line Conservative clients, however, were injured economically by the new Liberal government's introduction of Prohibition. Tupper launched lawsuits on their behalf, arguing that their liquor interests deserved compensation for being put out of business (page 95). He was a leader of the Moderation movement which eventually put the liquor importers back in business. In the early twenties, he was active in the renegade Tory part of the Provincial Party movement which set out to dump the tenacious Bowser, who had managed to hang onto the party leadership even though the Conservatives had been out of power for more than half a decade. Tupper finally got out of politics after the 1925 election, and died at his Oak Bay home two years later.

His son, Sir James MacDonald Tupper of Vancouver, a former assistant commissioner of the RCMP, inherited the Baronetcy following the 1962 death of yet another Sir Charles Tupper in Toronto. Another of his sons, Reginald Hibbert T. Tupper (1893-1972), was a Vancouver lawyer who had been severely wounded as a machine gunner at Ypres in 1915. Like his father, he took on widely publicized cases, and argued against government control of the legal and medical professions and the "dictatorship of the CBC" during the 1940s. He is best remembered for chairing the Royal Commission that investigated Vancouver police force corruption in 1955 and convicted Police Chief Walter Mulligan of accepting bribes.

Sir Charles Hibbert Tupper, the "renegade Tory" of the first two decades of this century, with his father Sir Charles Tupper Bart., the former prime minister and one of the Fathers of Confederation, about 1915.

Sir Clive Phillips-Wolley

"Woodhall," the Phillips-Wolley estate on Clive Drive, just above the beach north of Oak Bay Avenue.

Sir Clive Phillips-Wolley

Clive Phillips-Wolley first saw Victoria on a stopover during a world tour with his wife in the mid-1880s. He was instantly taken with the rocky outcroppings, Garry oaks and wildflowers, and he purchased sixteen acres above Oak Bay beach—roughly from Monterey Avenue to the beach, with Clive Drive as the driveway north of Oak Bay Avenue. He then arranged for the building of an Elizabethan-style house, and sent for his belongings, his children, and their governess from England.

Born Edward Clive Oldnall Long Phillips, he had inherited the Wolley estate in Shropshire, and changed his surname accordingly; he named his Victoria estate "Woodhall" after his ancestral home. He had been British consul at Kertch, Russia, was a good amateur boxer, an expert big-game hunter and later a good friend of Theodore Roosevelt, but primarily he occupied himself writing poetry. He was likened to Kipling, and indeed was *the* poet to sing the praises of the Empire in the years just before World War I (he was a descendant of Lord Clive, who established British rule in India). His sense of adventure took him around the world, and while in British Columbia he wrote Robert Service-like rhyming verses, such as "Gold, Gold in Cariboo." He also dabbled in newspaper work, and owned the *Nelson Miner* for a time; he was editor of *The Province* for four days, but quit in disgust over its lack of a definite philosophical direction.

Phillips-Wolley's motto was "those who cross the seas change their sky but not their mind," a maxim he followed to the letter. It was inscribed in Latin above the doorway at "Woodhall." His house and all its furnishings were in the English style; his friends were the stalwarts of the old colonial administration, like Crease and O'Reilly. He was knighted in 1915 for his patriotic poems (such as "The Sea Queen Awakes"), his Coronation Hymn, which he wrote for the new King George V in 1911, and his war work, including the organization of the Victoria branch of the Federated Navy League of B.C. The latter was one of the staunchest voices for Admiralty control of the Imperial fleet, rather than an independently-commanded Canadian navy, during the great naval debate of 1911 and 1912.

He moved in the First World War years to "The Grange" at Somenos. His only son, Lieut.-Comm. Clive Phillips-Wolley, died late in 1914 in the sinking of the HMS *Hogue* in the North Sea. Sir Clive died in July, 1918, aged 64; Lady Phillips-Wolley died two years later. "Woodhall," the house on Clive Drive, was later occupied by Dr. and Mrs. Herman Robertson—he the son of the former Supreme Court justice, she one of the five Loewen daughters.

Hugo Beaven

Hugo Beaven and his wife Ada (née Pemberton) at "Arden," their rambling cottage at Beach Drive and Margate Avenue in Oak Bay. The Oak Bay Beach Hotel, the last of Victoria's seaside hotels, is more or less across the street. It was built in 1927 by Major Merston, the retired head of the Vancouver Island Corps of Commissionaires.

The image of a Victoria gardener as an Englishman in paradise was exemplified by Hugo Robert Beaven, probably the city's best rose gardener of the 1910s and 1920s. The Beavens' old-world cottage "Arden," on Beach Avenue behind the Oak Bay Beach Hotel at Margate, had about 2,000 different roses in the garden. Beaven only exhibited roses which he bred himself, created from the 800 stock plants in the garden. His advisor was Alex Mitchell, the gardener at Government House.

Beaven was the eldest son of former B.C. premier Robert Beaven. He joined the Bank of British Columbia as a youth, then moved to the Canadian Bank of Commerce, retiring from there in 1927, following 42 years of service. His sister became Viscountess Churchill. In 1902, Beaven married Ada Georgina Pemberton, the daughter of the late Joseph Despard Pemberton, who had grown up "snipe hunting amongst the lupins" on Gonzales Farm. After Theresa Pemberton's death in 1916, the Beavens inherited a portion of the estate and built "Arden" soon after.

Following Beaven's death at age 69 in March, 1937, his wife donated the land and furnished the plants for the Ada G. Beaven Memorial Rose Garden in Windsor Park at Newport and Currie Road. Mrs. Beaven continued to live at "Arden" until her death at age 91 in 1958. The Oak Bay Native Plant Garden occupies part of the "Arden" site.

"Riffington," at 3175 Beach Drive, was the first house in Uplands. Built in 1913 on what was then called Shore Road between Rutland and Lansdowne Road, it was owned by Andrew Wright, the manager of the Lansdowne Floral Gardens Company. It was later occupied by the U.S. consul, then by Hubert Wallace, the brother of Lieutenant-Governor (1950-55) Clarence Wallace. Wallace bought "Riffington" and moved to Victoria after his family's Burrard Drydock Co. bought out the Yarrows shipyard in Esquimalt in April, 1946. Hubert was named Yarrows' vice-president and managing director, while his older brother "Clarry" retained control, as president, of both Yarrows and the main shipyards in North Vancouver. The Wallaces' connection with shipbuilding started in 1894, when their father, Andrew, started building fishing boats on False Creek. In the early days of Uplands, the nearest neighbour to "Riffington" was the Royal Victoria Yacht Club a half-mile down the road. Beach Drive, "out in the country" in Uplands, was a popular lovers' lane, possibly due to the proximity of the dances for the "young set" at the yacht club.

The Willows Hotel, at the corner of the Eastdowne Road and Cadboro Bay Road, was the second building in Oak Bay. It was built in 1864, two years after Governor Douglas finally got his way and extended the Cadboro Bay Road through John Tod's property all the way to the Uplands farm and Cadboro Bay. The hotel was a popular roadhouse for people riding or driving on Sundays—a suitable turn-around spot on a day's picnic in the country. An omnibus service was also available on Sundays for pic-

nickers. As the city expanded around it and past it, the hotel did a roaring business as the only liquor outlet in the vicinity, especially during World War I, when troops were bivouacked and trained at the Exhibition grounds nearby. Alex Lipsky, the proprietor during the war years, was put out of business by Prohibition in 1917. The hotel became "Cranleigh House" school between the wars, then was converted to a four-plex before its demolition in 1968.

The little house at 2564 Heron Street in Oak Bay is probably the oldest house west of the Great Lakes. It was built in 1851 by retired Hudson's Bay Company trader John Tod, whose Willows Farm occupied all of Oak Bay between Bowker Creek and the Uplands farm. Tod was 59 when he retired to Victoria—he had first left his native Scotland in 1808 to work at York Factory, and later ran Fort Kamloops. In his old age, he was tall and gaunt "with a mouth like the new moon" and his hair always "standing at attention." On cold days, he wore a cap with large ear flaps. He could often be seen, with an old bay hitched to his buckboard wagon, bouncing his way up the Cadboro Bay Road to the Willows Hotel for a drink. He had two "country wives" (Indian women with whom he lived without benefit of clergy)—the first one went crazy, but the next outlived him. When children visited him, he gave them milk and fruit, and played his violin for entertainment. He had a reputation as something of a spiritualist.

The house gained a lot of notoriety, long after his death in 1882, when it appeared to be haunted by a poltergeist. The first stories said that an antique chair would suddenly rock, cupboard doors swing, cellar doors open, and sudden draughts cause cats to snarl and spit. Finally, in 1952, when owner Col. T.C. Evans was digging a hole in the back yard for an oil tank, he discovered a skeleton buried in quick-lime. It disintegrated quickly when it was exposed to the air, frustrating any attempt at identification. At that point, the haunting ceased. The stories, however, didn't, and later versions featured more aggressive poltergeists and skeletons discovered in the basement.

The Fairgrounds

The only trace remaining today of the old Exhibition grounds in Oak Bay is in the name of Fair Street, between Epworth and Eastdowne just north of Cadboro Bay Road. The grounds used to occupy the irregular rectangle bounded roughly by Henderson, Fair, Eastdowne and Neil streets. They were purchased by the Municipality of Oak Bay in 1948, then divided and sold as small suburban building lots.

The British Columbia Agricultural Exhibition was first held in 1861. Winners of early prizes for produce and animal husbandry included the noted farmers of the early colonial period: William Tolmie of "Cloverdale," John Work of Hillside Farm, Thomas Skinner of Constance Cove Farm, and Kenneth McKenzie of "Craigflower." Land was purchased from Governor Douglas just east of Beacon Hill Park (the site of the town's racetrack), and a forty- by sixty-foot, two-storey exhibition building was erected. On alternate years, the fair was held in New Westminster. Numerous examples of new technology were introduced here to British Columbians during the early 1860s, notably a method of hermetically-sealing tin cans which revolutionized the preservation of fish and produce. By the late 1880s, the Agricultural Society had decided to hold annual exhibitions on the Island and wanted to expand their Beacon Hill property, but a simmering dispute over the fair's encroachment on the park caused the directors to look elsewhere for land. Thus, they decided to purchase land near the Willows Hotel, at what was called the "driving park."

In 1890, a by-law was presented to Victoria's ratepayers to raise $25,000 towards the $45,000 cost of an exhibition building. It passed, and the building—"one of the handsomest pieces of architecture on the Pacific Coast"—was finished in 65 days. The main exhibition building displayed agricultural and manufactured products, plus merchants' displays, on the main floor; above, running around the interior of the building, were two broad galleries: one exhibited horticultural displays and ladies' "fancy work," while the other was used for the art department. Stock and poultry occupied smaller buildings nearby. The Exhibition lasted for a week during the fall, "music is discoursed by Professor Pferdner's orchestra, races and sports of all kinds consume the day while the display of fireworks in the evenings is worthy of especial note." The half-mile race track was said to be the best on the coast, and fans passed pleasant afternoons at the bar in the Willows Hotel. The racetrack was reputedly built by John Bowker, the grandson of John Tod's second daughter Mary (Mary Tod Island, immediately off Rattenbury's old house at Oak Bay beach, is the namesake of Mary).

David R. Ker, the Agricultural Society's president, approached the National Electric Tramway & Lighting Co. in April, 1891, to get an extension built to the newly opened Fort Street-Royal Jubilee streetcar line. An agreement on terms was finally reached in mid-August and the line was ready to go in late September, in time for a well-advertised gun tournament. The cars stopped in front of the Willows Hotel at Eastdowne. Passengers had to pay an extra five cents to travel past the city limits at Foul Bay Road to the Exhibition grounds.

The Agricultural Society had originally purchased only six acres, but the fair expanded so that by 1907 they had bought 60 acres. On December 27, 1907, the main building was destroyed in a spectacular fire, but was rebuilt. The grounds were used for troop training for the Victoria regiments of the Canadian Expeditionary Force during World War I. The Exhibition was revived after the War, and in the thirties the buildings were used as a movie studio—128 "B" movies were cranked out, including ones reputedly starring Rita Hayworth and some young, female Dunsmuirs. The Horse Show and Industrial Buildings burned down in 1944, four years before the land was subdivided.

The Willows was also a centre for ice hockey. In 1911, Lester and Frank Patrick sold their lumber interests in Nelson for $300,000 and decided to build hockey arenas in Victoria, Vancouver and New Westminster, using the fledgling artificial ice technology. Lester, then 27, paid land-boom prices of $10,000 for lots at the corner of Cadboro Bay Road and Epworth Street, just southwest of the race track, and built a $110,000, 420-seat wooden arena. It opened on January 2, 1912 with Lieutenant-Governor Paterson facing off the puck in what was the first professional hockey game ever played on artificial ice (New Westminster beat Victoria 8-3).

Later that year, Patrick brought a National Hockey League all-star team west to play against his Coast All-Stars. The following year, his Victoria Aristocrats won the coast championship, then played and defeated the eastern champions in Quebec. After the war, he renamed his "cinderella team" the Victoria Cougars. In 1925, the Cougars included Frank Frederickson, "Happy" Holmes, Frank Foyston, Jack Walker, Slim Halderson, Clem Loughlin, Harry Meeking, "Gizzy" Hart, Gordon Fraser, and "Jocko" Anderson. They took on the Montreal Canadiens (which included hockey immortals Howie Morenz, Aurele Joliet, Georges Vezina and Sprague Cleghorn) that spring and beat them 3-1 to win the Stanley Cup.

Soon after, some of the Western Hockey League owners, including Patrick, agreed to sell their teams to eastern interests. The Victoria Cougars became the Detroit Cougars in the 1926-7 season. The name was changed to the Red Wings the following year. Patrick's Oak Bay arena burned down in 1929. Hockey started up again in 1942 in the converted Horse Show Building on the Exhibition grounds. Later, with the construction of the Memorial Arena on Blanshard, hockey moved downtown. Lester "The Silver Fox" Patrick hung onto the Oak Bay property until 1954, when prices had climbed back to their 1911 levels. He died in 1960, aged 76.

The racetrack and main exhibition building at the Fairgrounds at the Willows, on the Cadboro Bay Road, in 1902.

David R. Ker of Brackman & Ker Milling Co., was president of the B.C. Agricultural Association, and raised the money to move Victoria's fall fair to its new home on the Cadboro Bay Road in Oak Bay in the late 1880s.

1902.

Point Ellice

Montague William Tyrwhitt-Drake (1830-1908) was a descendant of a brother of Sir Francis Drake. Trained as a solicitor, he abandoned his Hertfordshire home for the Cariboo gold fields in 1859, then had a brief legal partnership with Attorney General G.H. Cary and served a term as mayor of Victoria in 1877. He was Canadian counsel for Victoria's sealing schooners seized by the U.S. in the early 1890s, was appointed to the bench, and retired in 1904 to his Point Ellice home.

The view from J.H. Turner's house, on Pleasant Street just north of Bay, in the 1890s. The shoreline of Victoria West, though still a part of the Songhees Indian Reservation, had been leased by numerous sealing operations, boathouses, and boat-building firms. The old E&N railway bridge crossed the harbour just north of the current Johnson Street bridge. The view is now blocked by the Victoria Machinery Depot buildings, which occupy the slope above the water where the old Victoria Sealing Co. warehouses stood.

The Point Ellice area offered its few residents fine views and boating in the Upper Harbour area. Although the area is now heavily industrial and has been since the turn of the century, it was once an attractive place to live. "Point Ellice House," the former residence of Peter O'Reilly, on Pleasant Street just north of the Point Ellice bridge, is the only survivor from that period.

The first Point Ellice bridge opened in 1861, providing a link to Victoria West and Esquimalt via the Old Esquimalt Road (the current Johnson Street bridge was built in the early 1920s, replacing an 1888 one which first allowed E&N Railway trains across the Upper Harbour into Victoria City). In the thirty years between 1861 and the arrival of the Number Four Esquimalt streetcar line in 1891, four families built large houses on properties on Pleasant Street. On the water side, going north from Bay Street, were the houses of Captain William Grant, Judge Montague Tyrwhitt-Drake, and Peter O'Reilly. On the other side of the street, occupying the block bounded by Bay, Pleasant, John, and Turner, was the house of businessman and politician John Herbert Turner.

Captain Grant was a sealer, and a friend of Captain Victor Jacobson of West Bay. His house, with its elaborate mansard roof, lookout tower, widow's walk and exotic gingerbread, was almost identical to Jacobson's house. Grant was connected with the Victoria Sealing Co., which had offices, storage sheds and a wooden wharf directly across Bay Street from his house (now the Victoria Machinery Depot yards).

The oldest part of Peter O'Reilly's much-expanded house was built in 1861. O'Reilly, like the Pembertons, was a well-born Anglo-Irishman

with a taste for adventure; he was appointed as a gold commissioner by Governor Douglas on the recommendation of Secretary of State Edward Bulwer-Lytton. Following his arrival in Victoria in 1859, he moved to the mainland and served as magistrate, gold commissioner, high sheriff, and county court judge at various locations in the province. Like the rest of the "Dublin castle gentry," O'Reilly was as tough as nails, and kept law and order in the face of some concerted opposition (he was quoted by historian Margaret Ormsby as having said, on his arrival in the Kootenays: "Now, boys, there must be no shooting, for if there is shooting there will surely be hanging!"). Like Henry Crease, he settled and invested in New Westminster and was unhappy about the move of the colonial capital to Victoria in 1868. He married Caroline Agnes Trutch, the daughter of the Colonial Surveyor. The couple thought it best to move to Victoria before the birth of their second child, so Caroline could have closer contact with her mother. Accordingly, on December 12, 1867, they moved into the house at Point Ellice. They had four children, who were grown but unmarried when the O'Reillys left Victoria in 1899 to seek medical treatment in England for Caroline's worsening health. She died as they arrived in England. O'Reilly returned to Victoria and spent six years

John Herbert Turner

Peter O'Reilly

Joseph James Lemon had a sash and door plant which was more typical of the Rock Bay-Point Ellice area than were the houses of O'Reilly and Turner. Born in New York in 1856, he quit school at sixteen and worked his way across the U.S., building grain elevators for the Union Pacific. He built the Northern Pacific railway station at Tacoma, before coming to Victoria in 1887. Lemon, Gonnason Company Ltd. employed 140 men, and made window sashes for the Empress Hotel and the Sayward and Pemberton buildings.

KLUCKNER 1985

Peter O'Reilly's grand "Point Ellice House," now restored and open to the public, occupied some beautiful acreage above the Upper Harbour. The gardens surrounded a lawn tennis court and croquet grounds. There were several outbuildings, including a barn with stables, a carriage house, greenhouse, and a boathouse on the water below. Prime Minister Sir John A. Macdonald was fêted there in 1886—one of the few times he visited Victoria, although he was the local Member of Parliament from 1878-82.

puttering about in his garden until he died in 1905 at age 77. He was the last survivor of the colonial civil servants hired by Governor Douglas.

John Herbert Turner's house across the street was comparatively modest, although its attached greenhouses and verandahs gave it a rambling look. The house faced Pleasant Street, but was built to take advantage of the spectacular view down the harbour, all the way to the legislative buildings framed by the Olympic Mountains. Turner moved from England to Charlottetown where he became a wholesale merchant; he married the beautiful Elizabeth Eilbeck in 1860 and two years later, when he was 29, set off for Victoria. He founded the forerunner of the large and prosperous Turner & Beeton Company, a general importer and clothing manufacturer, in 1865. He had a retail store called London House, offering millinery and fancy goods, on Government Street, and tried the produce business on Langley Street with future cannery-magnate J.H. Todd. The Turners loved horticulture—the gardens were notable even in garden-mad Victoria, and Mrs. Turner was one of the few wealthy white

women actually to get down and dig in a garden in the 1890s. Later, when they lived in England, they bought a house at Richmond in order to be close to the Kew Gardens.

Following his defeat as provincial premier in 1898, Turner took the opportunity, on the retirement of his old friend and partner H.C. Beeton, to go to London as the province's agent-general. He did an admirable job, and there was a storm of protest when ex-premier Sir Richard McBride elbowed him aside in 1916. McBride died the next year, and Turner, though of greatly advanced age, took the position over again and continued to attract orders for B.C. industry until his retirement in August, 1918. He died in December, 1923, aged 90. His wife had predeceased him by five years.

The four elegant Point Ellice houses formed a tiny oasis in the midst of a sea of heavy industry. Even before the First World War, the Upper Harbour and Selkirk Water were ringed with lumber operations, including J.A. Sayward's Rock Bay Sawmills at Store and Pembroke, and the Lemon & Gonason Sash & Door Co. on the other side of Rock Bay at Orchard and Government. Further along Pleasant Street from Turner's was the Moore-Whittington Lumber Co. and Joseph Leigh Sash & Door. On the north side of Selkirk Water was the huge B.C. Forest Products mill, then called the Cameron Lumber Co.

The Point Ellice Bridge Disaster

The wreck of streetcar number sixteen, in which 55 people died on May 26, 1896, when the Point Ellice bridge's centre span collapsed. The photograph looks across the Upper Harbour to Victoria West, from the shore near Captain Grant's little boathouse, visible behind the tram.

Queen Victoria's birthday on May 24th was the big picnic and regatta day in Victoria. Races and novelty events were held at the Gorge, involving everyone from native Indians in canoes to the Royal Navy's "bluejackets" to amateurs from the James Bay Athletic Association. The mansions along the waterway opened their doors and served strawberries and cream and tea. Everyone in Victoria attended. Such was the case on Monday, May 25, 1896—as that year the Queen's birthday fell on the Lord's Day.

The next day, the Tuesday, was also "Queen's weather," and was to feature a "sham battle" at Macauley Point. Military manoeuvres such as this, held some years at Beacon Hill Park, were a popular attraction, featuring the firing of the big defence guns, marching, bands, and military pageantry. Thousands piled into carriages and streetcars to get there. Streetcar Number 16, operated by the Consolidated Railway & Light Co., was supposed to carry only 60 people, but had 142 crammed into it, hanging from the sides, and even sitting on the roof. It left Cambell's corner at Yates and Government Street at about two p.m. Part way across the first of the 150-foot-long whipple-trusses which made up the centre section of the Point Ellice bridge, it broke through and plunged to the bottom of the harbour. Buggies with their horses, pedestrians, and a cyclist went with

it. Fifty-five were killed, and another 27 injured. Most of the dead were either killed by the impact of the streetcar, hit by pieces of the bridgeworks which came down on top of it, or drowned. All that day, on Capt. Grant's front lawn, "there reposed two long lines of dripping, inanimate figures."

Victorians were staggered at the scale of the tragedy. Everyone knew somebody who had died in the streetcar. The bridge was only eleven years old and had been built by the reputable San Francisco Bridge Company, which had constructed a number of bridges in Vancouver and Victoria. It had been closed four years earlier, in June 1892, when the City Engineer declared it unsafe for anything other than pedestrians. Test holes had been bored to check for rot—and not refilled, causing some rot on their own account. An inquiry concluded that the bridge had collapsed due to the rotting of one structural member, owing to water entering the holes required for the iron reinforcing rods. Blame was placed equally on the City, for not inspecting the bridge properly, and the streetcar company, for running a grossly overloaded streetcar across it. The lawsuits continued for years. Bankruptcy followed for the streetcar company, leading in April, 1897, to the purchase of its assets by a group of English capitalists and the formation of the B.C. Electric Railway Co.

Esquimalt

Looking west along Esquimalt Road toward the Naval dockyard area after 1904, with a party of Royal Navy "bluejackets" marching to the beat of their band. The streetcar is at its terminus opposite St. Paul's Church, which had been moved in 1904 to its current site at Grafton Street and Esquimalt Road. It was originally erected in late 1866 by Thomas Trounce on a level spot practically on the seashore below Signal Hill. As it risked damage from the heavy gales there, and from the firing of the heavy guns atop Signal Hill, it was moved. Mrs. C.E. Pooley, whose marriage was the second one held at the church's original site, laid the foundation stone at the new location.

Richard Wolfenden, apprenticed to a printer in his teens, arrived in Esquimalt in 1859 with the Royal Engineers. A crack shot, he became an Instructor of Musketry, but also printed the proclamations of the Colonial Government for Colonel Moody. In 1863, he was appointed to the position later called Queen's Printer, and held it until his death in 1911, aged 75. He lived at "Ackholme," at 125 Menzies Street in James Bay.

British military officers who visited Vancouver Island in the 1840s were unanimous in their opinion that Fort Victoria's site had been chosen by Governor Douglas solely for its agricultural advantages. By contrast with Victoria's intricate entrance via the Inner Harbour, Esquimalt Harbour was accessible under sail by Her Majesty's warships. As well, it had a good supply of fresh water nearby, at the mouths of Craigflower Creek and Mill Stream.

The possibility of war with the United States over the Oregon Territory brought several British warships to Vancouver Island in the summer of 1846, including the sailing frigate HMS *Fisgard*, the barque HMS *Herald*, the brig HMS *Pandora*, and the steam paddle-sloop HMS *Cormorant*. The *Fisgard* and the *Pandora* spent the summer of 1846 doing a comprehensive survey of Esquimalt harbour. Over the next couple of decades, Royal Navy ships operating from there supervised the movement of thousands of gold-seekers between Victoria and the mouth of the Fraser River (the "highway" to the gold fields), showed the British flag in the San Juan

Islands boundary dispute, and created a small naval establishment at Duntze Head. Finally, on June 29, 1865, the permanent naval base of the Royal Navy's Pacific Squadron was transferred to Esquimalt from Valparaiso, Chile. Almost immediately, the little community of civilians established outside the Dockyard on the narrow neck of land between it and Signal Hill began to expand. The next year, the foundation stone was laid for St. Paul's Church. Both land fortifications and naval buildings were erected. A drydock, the predecessor of the modern one at Skinner's Cove, was built on the Constance Cove side of Duntze Head as one of the terms of B.C.'s entry into confederation.

Meanwhile, much of the balance of the "peninsula"—the land comprising Esquimalt and Victoria West extending from the quarter-mile-wide portage between Thetis Cove and Portage Inlet—was divided into three farms for the Puget Sound Agricultural Company, a branch of the Hudson's Bay Company's fur-trade division (map, page 158). Communication with Victoria was by small boat, a risky business in bad weather. Early in 1852, three navy men lost their lives when their craft overturned in the rough sea and they became entangled in the floating kelp along the shoreline. Accordingly, Captain Kuper and Gunnery Lieutenant John Moresby of the HMS *Thetis* resolved to break a road through from Esquimalt to the Songhees village across the Inner Harbour from the fort.

Esquimalt today is still dominated by the navy—the Canadian Navy, which took over the Royal Navy installations when it was founded in 1910. The Esquimalt "village" is still only a few blocks of shops and pubs near the naval base around Constance Cove. Writer Leigh Robinson noted in the late 1940s that "we pass on our roads comfortable homes in attractive gardens, cheek by jowl with tiny cabins. Strangers ask us why we tolerate those disreputable shacks. We answer that we like 'our cabins.' They are part of our past. Old sailors and soldiers live in them, old pensioners who can talk of days and battles long ago. They gather their firewood from the beaches, tend their small garden plots and give you a cheery greeting as you pass. To us those tiny cabins are part of the atmosphere of Esquimalt, as much a part as its beautiful shoreline."

Victoria West became a popular spot to live after the first Point Ellice bridge was constructed in 1861. The area along Victoria Arm, east of the Gorge bridge, was particularly fashionable in the two decades before the First World War. The Gorge Road area today is lined with tourist motels.

The Gorge

The Gorge part of Victoria Arm was first explored by Roderick Finlayson in the summer of 1847. He was looking for a sawmill site and water-power source, and ended up choosing Mill Stream above Parson's Bridge. A bridge consisting of a single tree was thrown across the Gorge soon after; boating outings up Victoria Arm became popular, and many Victorians rented canoes from McIntosh's boathouse on the Inner Harbour. By the 1890s, several fine houses had been built along the banks of the Gorge, each with floats and boathouses. The Queen's birthday on May 24th became the occasion of the annual Gorge regatta, with canoe races and greased pole climbings and the big houses along the shore thrown open to serve strawberries and cream and tea.

At the Gorge, Victoria, B.C.

Observation Car, Seeing Victoria, B.C.

The B.C. Electric Railway's Number Five "Gorge" streetcar ran through Victoria West, along Craigflower Road and Tillicum to the company's Gorge Park. Swimmers went to "the pay" (an exclusive pool costing a dime) or "the free" (the public bathhouse east of the bridge). Gorge Park opened July 26, 1905. Eight years later, the Japanese Tea Gardens opened, followed a month later by a scenic railway. Observation car 123—similar to the ones in Vancouver—gave tourists a three-hour sightseeing ride, visiting Oak Bay, Esquimalt, and the Gorge, for 50 cents.

Edgar Fawcett

Dingley Dell, off Selkirk Avenue, marks the two-acre property of Australian writer Edgar Fawcett, who named his house there "Dingley Dell" after Dickens' Mr. Wardle's home. Fawcett (1847-1923) was, like Arthur Fellows' wife, a relative of Sir Rowland Hill, the inventor of penny postage. He was a great contributor to the newspapers, and his book "Some Reminiscences of Victoria" is one of the most colourful pictures of life as a "fifty-eighter."

P.R. Brown

Percival Rideout Brown was a Nova Scotian who came to Victoria at age 20 in 1875. He started work with W.P. Sayward in the sawmilling business, then started selling real estate with B.C.L&I. He built "Birchwood," just west of "Burleith" at about Arm Street on the Craigflower Road, in the mid-1890s. His daughter married B.C.L&I salesman Arthur Wolfenden, the son of the King's Printer.

Victoria Phoenix Brewing Company founder Joseph Loewen (1832-1903) lived at "Rockwood," just west of Tillicum on Gorge Road. (His copper-roofed brewery, later the Lucky Lager and Labatt's operation, was a downtown landmark.) Two of his six daughters were singers of note; of the others, Martha became Lady Barnard, and Eva Mrs. Edward Prior.

Victoria Gardens

There were several early roadhouses and resorts along the Gorge, including The Retreat, Mrs. Marshall's, and Victoria Gardens. Couples passed pleasant evenings in little boats on the Arm, or danced under the moonlight and the Chinese paper lanterns.

The Yates Estate

The land from Gorge to Burnside between Tillicum and the city limits at Harriet Street was owned originally by James Yates (1819-1900), who came to Victoria in 1849 as a Hudson's Bay Company clerk. After eighteen months, and a brief stint absent without leave in California, he purchased his discharge, and worked thenceforth as a trader. He took his family back to Scotland in 1860, returned from 1862-64 to put his affairs in order, then left again to reside in Portobello, a suburb of Edinburgh. His son James Stuart Yates (1857-1950) lived near Victoria on Millstream Road throughout his life and was a practising lawyer for 62 years. Lots in the old Yates Estate, also called "Craigilea Farm," were put on the market by B.C. Land & Investment Co. in 1908, at prices from $100 to $500 each.

David McEwen Eberts (1850-1924), a Conservative lawyer and speaker of the legislature, lived at "Hopedene," built by R.B. McMicking between Wascana and Earl Grey on the Gorge.

Three other residents of Gorge Road before the First World War were William Ridgeway Wilson, Thomas Ellis, and Charles William Ringler-Thomson. Col. Wilson lived just west of Baker's "Sissinghurst." Born in China in 1863, he became a prominent Victoria architect, and designed the Bay Street Armouries. During the First World War, he commanded the Vernon prisoner-of-war camp. He died in Victoria in 1957. Thomas Ellis was a great cattle rancher in the Penticton area. He arrived in the early 1860s with the intention of looking for gold but ended up with a 40,000-acre ranch north of the Similkameen River. He retired to "Winona" at 101 Gorge Road, where he died in December, 1918, aged 73. Charles Thomson (1827-1916) built the "Dingle House" east of "Sissinghurst" around 1880. Like his neighbour Ellis and friend Hewitt Bostock, he was a cattleman (though he was the French-educated son of a London solicitor), and was part-owner of the Douglas Lake Cattle Company near Nicola.

James Dunsmuir's "Burleith" estate occupied the land between Burleith Crescent and Sunnyside Avenue along the Gorge.

"Sissinghurst," now the five-acre grounds of the Gorge Road Hospital, was originally called "Ashnola" when built by Robert Dunsmuir for his daughter Emily and her new husband Northing Pinckney Snowden. It was later occupied by Edgar Crow Baker (1845-1920), who was originally the Victoria accountant for the Hastings Sawmill Co. and later organized the Victoria & Esquimalt Telephone Co. and the pilotage system in B.C. He also served as a Conservative MP and MLA. The old red-brick home was demolished in 1971.

Premier Richard McBride had made a number of investments which paid off in the boom before 1913, so he could afford to move to 219 Gorge Road.

Kenneth Mackenzie

Number 236 Gorge Road was a property called "Caberfeigh," occupied by the accident-prone Kenneth Mackenzie and his wife Anne. Mackenzie was the son of the Kenneth Mackenzie who came from Scotland to run Craigflower Farm for the Puget Sound Agriculture Co. On several occasions he was knocked insensible in falls from horses and in farming accidents, before retiring to Gorge Road.

The Royal Navy

The survey of Esquimalt harbour in 1846 was part of a general strategic mapping and wartime preparation by the British navy. Many of the names on the Esquimalt shoreline are of crew members of the HMS *Fisgard*. Fisgard Island, with the famous Fisgard Lighthouse, guards the port-side entrance to the harbour. Rodd Hill, immediately behind the lighthouse, is named for John Rashleigh Rodd, the ship's first lieutenant. Duntze Head, on the starboard side, is named for the ship's captain. The first naval buildings were erected there, on land later called H.M.C. *Dockyard* and now called DND Signal Hill. Lang Bay, the easternmost dent of Esquimalt Harbour where the Yarrows Number One shipyard is located, took its name from the *Fisgard*'s Fourth Lieutenant, Edward Lang. And so on.

Once the Oregon Treaty was signed in June, 1846, making the 49th parallel the United States' northern boundary, naval activity declined in the Esquimalt area. The headquarters of the Royal Navy's Pacific Squadron were afloat in Valparaiso harbour in Chile—a strategic location due to revolutions in Chile and Peru and the threat to British commercial activities from the Royal Spanish Navy. In 1854, Britain and France went to war against Russia, and the disastrous attack by their fleets against Petropavlovski on the Kamchatka peninsula left 200 of their men wounded. All had to be taken to the nearest hospital, in San Francisco. The following year, a second assault was planned, and Governor Douglas was requested to erect a temporary hospital at Esquimalt for the use of the fleet. Douglas reserved seven acres on Duntze Head, and built three huts there for the purpose. It turned out they weren't needed, as Petropavlovski had been deserted by the Russians. Three years later, a group of Royal Engineers under the command of Lieut. Col. John Summerfield Hawkins arrived to survey the western boundary between the United States and mainland British Columbia. They erected some huts on the land between Lang Cove and Skinner's Cove (now the Dominion Graving Dock site). Various ships of the British fleet used Esquimalt harbour during the late 1840s and 1850s; and the Royal Navy's "bluejackets" became a regular part of the Victoria scene, and their officers a desirable adjunct to the colony's entertainments.

The rather placid little naval base became quickly more serious and strategic during the San Juan dispute in the mid-1850s. The Oregon Treaty had not plotted the boundary through the maze of islands in the Gulf of Georgia. The dispute came to a boil over the shooting of a farmer's pig on San Juan; a joint commission was appointed to investigate and settle the question, but meanwhile several warships were dispatched to Esquimalt, including the Pacific Station's flagship HMS *Ganges*, and the ultramodern screw corvette HMS *Satellite*. (The decision was made in favour of the American position by arbitrator Kaiser Wilhelm in 1872.) The naval dockyard installations expanded: the "Crimean huts" were taken over in 1857. One of the huts was converted into a residence for the Naval Storekeeper—it was torn down in 1885 and replaced by the "Dockyard House," now the "Admiral's House." The other two huts were in use until the 1930s, but were demolished in the rapid construction period of the Second World War.

On June 29, 1865, Esquimalt was named as the permanent naval base of the Pacific Squadron. The move was a popular one with the naval officers who had been living afloat at Valparaiso on the old frigate *Nereus*. Houses began to occupy the naval base end of Esquimalt Road, and St. Paul's church, designed by Thomas Trounce, was erected in 1866. The military fortifications were expanded in 1877, when it looked again as if Britain and Russia might go to war. Earthworks and gun emplacements were built along the shoreline from Duntze Head to Beacon Hill. By that time, the Royal Navy had advanced technologically into the steam age, and Esquimalt was one of a dozen world-wide coaling stations necessary to maintain the Empire on which "the sun never set."

The 1870s were the heyday of the age of sail at the Esquimalt naval base. Most memorable was the arrival, on April 15, 1870, of the Flying Squadron. Already there were Admiral Farquhar's flagship *Zealous* and three other sloops of war in the harbour; shortly before Sunday noon, a message flashed from Race Rocks light that the squadron was in sight. As the *Colonist* described it: "A breeze sufficiently strong to fill every inch of canvas was blowing, and as the vessels rounded the rocks, the townspeople flocked to adjacent hills and points to witness the grand, picturesque sight. Off Albert Head four of the ships were abreast, tall, stately and majestic, with the bright rays of the sun falling full upon their snow white sails and the stiff breeze bowling them swiftly on towards Esquimalt." There followed two weeks of celebrations in Victoria, including regattas, dances, picnics, a luncheon on the flagship, horse-races for the "bluejackets" on the track at Beacon Hill park, and a 168-gun salute by the fleet.

The "bluejackets"—naval seamen—wore a simple blue uniform, brightened in summer with a beribboned straw hat with the brim turned up. Their arrival was usually marked by a pub-crawl through Esquimalt, then a ride on the Number Four streetcar to Victoria for another one. Old-timers remembered them as "wonderful sports," always looking for a laugh, prepared to joyride in a hack or serenade any pretty girl or join in a football (rugby) game against the local school teams. The officers often held big balls in the "sail loft" at Esquimalt. Many a well-born Victoria girl (and her parents) dreamed of marriage to a dashing officer, many of whom would come into money, and nearly all of whom represented a potential escape from the isolation of Vancouver Island.

The Esquimalt naval station expanded in earnest in the 1880s and 1890s. Red brick buildings began to fill the Naval Dockyard area, the drydock was finally completed, and William Fitzherbert Bullen established a ship-building and repairing operation under the name of Esquimalt Marine Railway Company (changed in 1898 to the B.C. Marine Railway when he opened a plant in Vancouver) on the south side

The first buildings of the Esquimalt naval establishment on Duntze Head were three wooden huts intended as temporary hospital facilities during the Crimean War in the 1850s. They were never used as such, for the second attack on Petropavloski caused no casualties. This photograph, taken between 1866 and 1869, was part of Admiral Hastings's album.

sabre-rattling. The greatest feature of the parade there was the procession of British-style redcoats, causing a bystander to remark: "That's magnificent marching—I wish our men marched like that!"

Between 1895 and 1898, the three batteries at Fort Rodd Hill were constructed. The guns in the Upper and Lower batteries fired 100-pound shells a distance of nearly two miles. Belmont Battery was designed to shoot apart any small torpedo boats attempting to zip into Esquimalt harbour. Submarine nets, searchlights, and a minefield, along with rapid firing guns and 40 mm Bofors antiaircraft guns, were installed through the years as different attackers and newer technology created new threats. All the British troops left in 1906, and the coast defences were manned by Royal Canadian Artillery men until Fort Rodd was declared obsolete in 1956.

In 1910, with the creation of the Royal Canadian Navy, the British navy withdrew from Esquimalt. The Canadian government stationed the antiquated HMCS *Rainbow* there, but as the world moved closer to war, military authorities began to be more concerned about the state of the coast's defences. The old sunken shore-batteries at Macauley Point and Finlayson Point, and most of the reserve regiments' small arms, lacked ammunition. In August, 1914, when war broke out, Victoria was illprepared to defend itself. The German Admiral Von Spee's China squadron went on a sustained looting mission around the southern Pacific, and the feeling in Victoria grew to an absolute certainty that these supermodern cruisers would attack and sack both Victoria and Vancouver.

Premier McBride grew increasingly alarmed. As luck had it, the Electric Boat Co. of Seattle had been building two submarines for the Chilean navy. The chief of the Chilean Naval Commission, Captain Charles Plaza, refused to accept them as they were "overweighted, which is considered a serious defect in submarine craft." The Seattle builder, J.V. Patterson, proposed to dispose of them "owing to the Chilean government not being able to pay for them," and approached McBride in the Union Club in early August (Plaza, in a letter published in the *Vancouver Sun* on February 9, 1916, threatened to sue Patterson for his "false statements"). McBride acted fast, buying the subs and writing the government cheque himself. He then had them spirited away from the Seattle shipyard before too many questions were asked about U.S. neutrality. "To even so bold a man as our Premier (W.A.C.) Bennett," wrote J.K. Nesbitt in the 1950s, "it has never occurred to buy warships." The transaction was so swift that few Esquimalt naval people were informed, and the submarines were nearly shelled by the Fort Rodd Battery. Originally named *Iquique* and *Antofagasta*, they were renamed *McBride* and *Patterson* by the senior naval officer at Esquimalt. Two days later, B.C. handed its navy over to the Dominion government. The subs—renamed again the *CC-1* and *CC-2*—escorted troop ships from the Island to the mainland, then served the balance of World War I on the east coast. Victoria was never attacked in either war.

of Lang Cove. Bullen's company was sold in January, 1914, to Sir Alfred Yarrow, who had earlier founded the famed shipbuilding yards on the Clyde. His second son, Norman, took over the management of Yarrows in Esquimalt, and later bought the Yarrows building at Fort and Broad streets in Victoria. A second yard—Yarrows Number Two—was built on the other side of Constance Cove in 1941, and produced a remarkable number of frigates and corvettes for the Royal Canadian Navy. A new, larger graving dock had been built across Constance Cove from the old naval dockyard—one of its tasks was the conversion in February, 1942, of the enormous liner *Queen Elizabeth* into a troop carrier.

The permanent army establishment in Victoria dates from 1887, when "C" Battery of the Royal Canadian Artillery under Major James Peters moved into the old Agricultural Building east of Beacon Hill park. The first part of Work Point barracks was completed in 1890; "C" Battery moved there, but following a new British-Canadian agreement in 1893 was relieved by an Imperial Garrison of Royal Marine Artillery and Royal Engineers. In 1898, Victoria's famous 5th Regiment (reserves), under the command of Colonel E.G. Prior, visited Seattle for a little pageantry and

The Drydock Scandal

A great many ships were damaged and lost on the uncharted rocks and reefs along the western coastline. In the 1850s and 1860s, damaged ships had to limp all the way to Mare Island at the San Francisco navy yards for drydocking and repairs. Recognizing a need, Rear-Admiral Hastings in 1867 ordered a study on the best location for a drydock; Lang Cove was chosen, but nothing was commenced before B.C. entered confederation in 1871. The eventual location became the north side of Duntze Head, in the Naval Dockyard area.

There was intense interest, at least in the Victoria area, in the construction of a proper dry- or graving-dock. It was included, as Article XII, in the Terms of Union of the colony of British Columbia with Canada, though not nearly as important in the public mind as the construction of a transcontinental railway.

Article XII guaranteed the interest for ten years at five percent on the cost of the drydock, which was not to exceed £100,000. Premier de Cosmos, in order to ease the province's financial woes, arranged in 1873 to change Article XII to an outright grant of £30,000, payable on completion of the project. Unwisely, he neglected to notify the public. When the change was leaked, it "excited the people," and on Saturday evening, February 7, 1874, a crowd of 800 rallied to demand no relaxation in the Terms of Union (the fear being that, once one clause was altered, the Dominion would find a way to weasel out of its railway obligation). On the Monday, the mob re-formed, and invaded the legislative gallery, "hooting, yelling, shouting and cursing," and drove Speaker Dr. Trimble from his chair. De Cosmos hid, then quickly resigned and went to Ottawa, where he was also Victoria's MP (page 84). George Walkem took over the government.

Walkem was almost immediately in political trouble over the drydock's cost, which was estimated at $500,000, especially with the mainland MLAs, whose constituents needed roads and bridges and who said the dock was a luxury. He went to England, and got the grant raised to £50,000—nearly $250,000. Contracts were let, but construction hadn't started when Walkem resigned in 1876. The new Elliott government then had to negotiate the drydock's dimensions with the Admiralty Lords, who demanded it be built to a size beyond anything required for commercial purposes. Thus, the value of the £50,000 grant was almost negated. Elliott approached the Dominion government, and found to his horror that the £50,000 was considered by the latter as a loan, not a gift. He then attempted to turn over the partly completed drydock to Ottawa, on condition they complete and operate it. Elliott was defeated, and Walkem became premier again before Ottawa had a chance to refuse.

The issue dragged on until October, 1880, when the new Conservative federal government of John A. Macdonald agreed to make the £50,000 a grant. New contracts were let by Walkem, but by this time the cost had ballooned to $620,000. The original estimates included only 100 tons of cement, costing about $3,500, but by early 1882 it was evident that between 4,000 and 5,000 tons of cement would be required, pushing the cost

PABC 12130

The old Admiralty Graving Dock at Duntze Head in Esquimalt.

up another $150,000. The mainland members in the legislature forced an inquiry, which reported on March 28 that between 6,000 and 7,000 tons of cement would be required. This cost overrun, now nearly one-quarter of a million dollars, was attributed to mismanagement "and a great want of business ability." The reading of the report "was followed by a scene." Following three days of furious debate, Walkem's government was defeated on the Speaker's vote. Walkem hung on until appointed to the Supreme Court on May 23. The drydock was finally completed and opened on July 20, 1887, sixteen years to the day after confederation. Young Kathleen O'Reilly cut the blue ribbon, and the drydocking of the HMS *Cormorant* was part of the ceremony.

Captain Jacobson

(Above) Captain Victor Jacobson's old sternwheeler Distributor *was moored in front of his big house on Head Street during the twenties and thirties. He lived on it, preferring the rocking of the waves and the coal stove in its cabin, and rented the house out. (Right) Jacobson and his wife Mary Ann McLear around the time of their marriage. Jacobson was known for his great strength and huge hands—he had to get white gloves custom-made in order to attend a Government House ball.*

The big blue and white house at 507 Head Street on West Bay in Victoria West was built by Captain Victor Jacobson, one of the leaders of the Victoria sealing industry. It was the centre of wintertime socializing amongst the sealers, and many all-night parties were held in the sail loft on the wharf below the house, and, later, in the old sternwheeler which Jacobson moored there and lived on during the twenties and thirties.

Born in Finland, Jacobson went to sea at seventeen, and came to Victoria in 1880, when he was 21. He first went sealing three years later. In November, 1888, he married Mary Ann "Minnie" McLear; together, they travelled up the west coast picking Indians for the sealing crews. Their most famous ship was the *Eva Marie*, named after their daughter (later married to Capt. Harold Sweeney of 1657 Hollywood Crescent). It was the only three-masted sealing schooner in Victoria—110 feet long with an eighteen-foot beam. Jacobson bought it for $250 in 1902, and sailed it until pelagic sealing finally shut down in 1911. His best year was the winter of 1904-5, when the Japanese were at war with Russia. The shortage of furs pushed the price up, and Jacobson made $40,000.

The "Big House" at 507 Head was built in 1893; before the First World War, Jacobson rented it out and moved into his sail loft on the wharf. In 1913, he bought the old sternwheeler *Distributor*, which had been used for Grand Trunk Pacific railway construction on the Skeena River, at an auction at Turpil's Ways (now the Victoria Machinery Depot at Point Ellice). He had its engine and paddlewheel stripped away, and towed it to his wharf in front of the sail loft at West Bay. He lived on it until his wife died in 1942, then moved in with his daughter and son-in-law. The *Distributor* was towed away after a few years, and broken up and burned on an Esquimalt beach. The sail loft on the wharf was demolished soon after.

Jacobson had spent part of his retirement, in 1935 and 1936, restoring Captain Voss's "Tillicum"—the canoe which sailed around the world in 1904—outside the Crystal Gardens. The "Tillicum" was later moved into Thunderbird Park, and now is installed in the Maritime Museum. Jacobson died in September, 1949. The house on Head Street was restored in 1974 by Mr. and Mrs. C.V. Laurenson.

The Puget Sound Agricultural Company

Most of the Esquimalt and Colwood area was occupied by four farms of the Puget Sound Agricultural Company, a subsidiary of the Hudson's Bay Company formed in 1840. Before these farms were established, the HBC's farming activities were centred around Fort Vancouver, on the Columbia River near the site of modern Portland, Oregon. Since its founding in 1825, Fort Vancouver had developed a lush 3,000-acre farm, producing huge quantities of wheat, barley, oats, peas, fruit, meat, and dairy products for trade. Two years later, the site of Fort Langley was chosen, also for its agricultural potential. The availability of so much food aided the trade in lumber, fish, sugars and furs with the Russians in Alaska, the Hawaiians, and occupants of the more established parts of North America.

In 1846, the Oregon Treaty ceded all the territory south of the 49th parallel to the Americans. By this stroke, the PSAC lost its most prosperous farm, and it couldn't make up the lost production with only Fort Langley, Uplands, and the dairy operation outside Fort Victoria's palisades. Thus, it decided to develop the four Esquimalt-area farms: Viewfield, Colwood, Constance Cove, and Craigflower.

(The Hudson's Bay Company and the PSAC complained bitterly about the loss of their seventeen Oregon bases, though as Captain Courtenay of the HMS *Constance* wrote in the summer of 1848, the HBC "would continue to trade and bicker with the Americans in Oregon as it was so profitable," and would "cry wolf until, like the shepherd's boy in the fable, they are not listened to." The "Hated British Company" was harassed unmercifully by American settlers in Oregon. American revenue cutters seized trading ships, like the *Albion*, for cutting 42 spars in a deserted cove after attempting to find someone to buy them from, and the *Cadboro*, for "smuggling" into Nisqually. Peter Ogden and James Douglas of the HBC filed a compensation claim in 1847 with the American government, seeking £74,766 for loss of trade and abandonment of the bases. In 1857, they filed another statement, this time for £466,600. This was further expanded in 1865 to over £1,000,000, by including losses of trade, cattle and rents. Historian F.W. Howay noted that "in any claim for damages, the HBC could never be accused of omitting anything." They were finally awarded $650,000 by the American government in 1865. Earlier, when the HBC returned the Colony of Vancouver Island to the Crown, it received £57,500 from the Colonial Office, and kept the Fort Victoria property, the Uplands, Beckley and four Esquimalt farms, and miscellaneous other properties. "If the company did not make a success of the Colony," noted Howay, "it certainly did of the negotiations.")

Viewfield Farm, in 1850, was the first PSAC farm in Esquimalt. It covered 600 acres from "Kanaka Bay," just east of the Naval Dockyard area on Duntze Head, to West Bay, from a line just north of the Old Esquimalt Road. Donald Macauley, a Scot who had been employed by the HBC at Fort Simpson, was hired to manage the farm. His eldest daughter, Mary,

The first School House erected in British Columbia in 1853. The material for its construction was imported from England by the Hudson's Bay Co.

A postcard of Craigflower School, across the Gorge Waters from Craigflower Manor. The card's caption is inaccurate, as only the locks and hinges were imported from England. The lumber was sawn at Mill Stream, and construction done by the tradesmen at Craigflower farm. The schoolhouse was part of the little community which sprang up at Craigflower in the early 1850s; it had rooms upstairs for the teacher and boarders from the other Puget Sound Agricultural Company farms nearby. Classes were held in the building until 1911.

married William McNeill, who owned a 200-acre property on McNeill, or Shoal, Bay near Gonzales Point. Flora, the second daughter, married John Tod's son James. Viewfield Farm only lasted about ten years, and only 35 of its 600 acres were improved. In 1854, it had a population of fourteen, including nine children, and produced a little mutton and wool. Macauley drowned in Esquimalt harbour in 1868. A cattle ranch later occupied the land; one account mentions a moss-covered snake fence seven or eight feet high, surrounding a corral, in which long-horned cattle grazed until driven to the slaughterhouse at Craigflower Farm. Much of the land there was covered with war-industry workers' housing and army buildings when the Macauley and Work Point military bases were expanded in World War II. Immediately to the west of the old farm site was the "Kanaka Ranch," a small settlement of Hawaiian Islanders imported as cheap labour for the PSAC's farm.

Colwood Farm was established in 1851 by the haughty Captain Edward Edwards Langford, a distant relative of Governor Blanshard who had been appointed by the PSAC in London. The Langfords were the first white family to arrive at Fort Victoria directly from England. Langford took an instant dislike to the Hudson's Bay Company and its officials, due to the "inadequate preparation" for his family's needs—a single-roomed log hut inside the fort (Langford was used to better, as he owned a 200-acre estate called "Colwood" in Sussex). Colwood Farm occupied 600 acres on the Esquimalt harbour south of Mill Stream, including part of the land now occupied by Colwood Golf Course. The new "Colwood," with windows and chimney bricks from England, was built just south of the entrance to the golf course, and another eleven dwelling houses for the farm's occupants were soon erected (Langford had brought his own farm hands with him from England). Colwood Farm was wellrun and prosperous: the 1854 census noted that 190 acres of timber had been cleared, and 30 people, 13 horses, 9 milch cows, 8 working oxen, 14 other cattle, 523 sheep, 97 swine and 80 poultry lived there. As well, wheat, oats, and peas were grown.

Captain Langford was used to the democratic ways of England, and rebelled against Governor Douglas, who was personally able only to "rule but not reign." Langford's attempts to involve himself in the colony's public affairs were stymied by the machinations of the Hudson's Bay Company clique, which controlled all the land purchases, and by Governor Douglas's brother-in-law David Cameron, who was the Chief Justice of Vancouver Island. Like Capt. Colquhoun Grant, an independent settler who had arrived in 1849 and settled in Sooke, Langford found the best Victoria-area farmland reserved for the HBC and its officers. Langford and his family returned to England in 1861.

Constance Cove and Craigflower Farms were managed respectively by Thomas Skinner and Kenneth Mackenzie, who came to Victoria with their families on the *Norman Morison*, arriving after a five-month journey in January, 1853. Skinner had been with the East India Company, and MacKenzie was a Scottish farmer; they arrived with 25 families of farm labourers and tradesmen. Both farms had to be hacked out of the forest.

The Skinners built their house, called "Oaklands," on the grassy southern slope overlooking the present site of the Dominion Graving Dock. The house was single-storeyed with two gables, surrounded by a trellis-fenced garden full of Mrs. Skinner's English flowers. The MacKenzie's "Craigflower" house was nearly two miles away through a woodland trail. Below "Oaklands," on the shore of what was Skinner's Cove before the Graving Dock was built, were two masonry storage houses for the PSAC farms' produce. Ships loaded beef, flour, butter and vegetables there for trading in Alaska and elsewhere. The warehouses were demolished in 1924 when construction commenced on the Graving Dock. Constance Cove Farm was the first butter-producer in the Vancouver Island colony. The area where "Oaklands" stood still contains vestiges of the parklike scattered oak groves of the early years, but was built up with shipyard workers' housing in the early 1940s.

"Craigflower," originally built in a maple grove, is the only one of the four farmhouses still standing. It was a "manor house" compared with the tenant farmers' cottages on the PSAC farms. Built with the materials at hand, using tools brought from England on the *Norman Morison*, "Craigflower" became a regular gathering spot for admirals, the Governor, and the other "squires" of Esquimalt. It was named for the English farm of Andrew Colville, the HBC's governor from 1852-6. Strategically located at the crossroads of Admirals Road, Craigflower Road, and the Goldstream & Sooke Road, it provided beef, flour and sawn lumber to the surrounding community. By the end of 1854, there were 30 children under the age of fifteen, so a schoolhouse was built across the Gorge Waters from "Craigflower." The enterprising Mackenzie built brick ovens to supply bread and hardtack to the Royal Navy ships in Esquimalt harbour, then branched out in the Gold Rush period in 1858 into the production "at San Francisco prices" of pilot bread which "will not be damaged by salt water." He also bought acreage on Dallas Bank, on the north shore of Constance Cove, and built "Maplebank," a comfortable house which he leased to Admirals Denman and Hastings. The trail between this house and "Craigflower" became Admirals Road. Mackenzie's "Maplebank" was offered for sale to the Admiralty, then taken over by the HBC It was destroyed by fire in 1910.

Once the HBC lease on Vancouver Island was cancelled and the colony turned back to the British crown in 1859, the four Esquimalt farms became increasingly difficult to operate. No successor of the calibre of James Douglas, who was forced to resign his HBC connections when he became governor of British Columbia in 1858, came forward to manage the HBC operations. Craigflower Farm was subdivided in 1866; the others were eventually leased and broken up. Most of the PSAC farmland which still remained in the HBC's control was relinquished to Esquimalt for unpaid taxes in 1934.

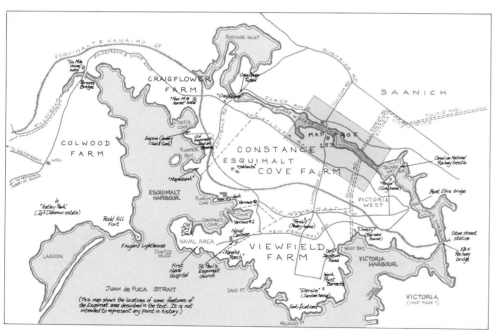

The view from the front garden at "Clovelly," looking across to Work Point.

John Jardine made a great success of his Victoria house-painting business. He purchased two pieces of land from the Hudson's Bay Company in 1901: the first was a ranch in Langley, where a B.C. Electric interurban station was named for him; the second, a piece of the old Viewfield farm, became the site of his commodious residence "Ellerslie," on the waterfront on Anson Street, now part of the expanded Work Point barracks.

Born in Dumfriesshire, Scotland in September, 1854, he quit school to apprentice as a house painter with his brother's firm, then left for North America, establishing himself in St. Paul when he was 26. Four years later, he moved to Victoria, where he painted houses when not dabbling in politics. His interest in the harbour led him to join the Board of Trade and (unsuccessfully) contest a city council seat—he proposed a breakwater from Ogden Point to Brotchie Ledge, which was eventually built further east during the First World War years to shelter the Ogden Point docks. He ran for the Liberal party and was defeated by fifteen votes in Esquimalt riding in the 1903 election, He was elected four years later, and sat with H.C. Brewster, the only other Liberal in the legislature.

Jardine and Brewster couldn't agree on who was to be Liberal leader, though Jardine seemed only to have the backing of himself. Jardine's split with the Liberals became deeper, until one day he rose in the legislature and "exposed the skeletons in the Liberal closet and mercilessly rattled the dry bones." He described how he had developed "a deep-rooted contempt for Liberalism," and with his voice becoming increasingly strident, told how the "Brewster-Templeman rump" of the party had humiliated him during Sir Wilfrid Laurier's recent visit, refusing him even an introduction to the prime minister. Then, he said, Templeman (the Victoria *Times* founder and federal Minister of the Interior) had "shoved his fist in my face" in the public works office of the legislative buildings. As he described his "victory" in the ensuing fisticuffs, his gestures became wilder and the Conservative majority's fascination greater. Finally, Brewster got a chance to speak, and rose with great dignity to say that "today is Monday, and Monday is always wash-day." The Esquimalt Liberal association, led by Templeman's niece's husband C.J. McIntosh, asked Jardine to resign. The next year, Jardine supported Premier McBride's railway-policy. In the 1912 election, the Esquimalt Liberals ran M.B. Jackson, who was defeated by Harry Pooley. Jardine's reward for his humiliation of Brewster was an appointment by McBride to a five-member Labour Commission, which reported to the Legislature in 1914. A contemporary biographer described Jardine as "never narrowly partisan, (but preserving) a commendable independence of view." He thereafter stayed out of politics, and died on October 15, 1937.

John Jardine

F.S. Barnard

"Clovelly," the Barnard home on the shoreline below the Esquimalt Road at Barnard Street.

Charles Edward Pooley (1845-1912) arrived in Victoria in 1862 with the intention of seeking gold. Instead, he became registrar general of the Supreme Court, and travelled all over British Columbia with Judge Begbie, before being called to the bar in 1877. Later, he was A.E.B. Davie's law partner, and took over all the Dunsmuir family's legal business in the 1880s. He served as Speaker and president of the council in most of the governments of the 1890s, and was a senior executive with the Esquimalt & Nanaimo Railway, Esquimalt Water Works, and the Colonist newspaper. He lived at "Fernhill" on Lampson Street above the Esquimalt Road (demolished 1937). His son Harry was B.C. attorney general from 1928-33.

Frank Stillman Barnard, the son of Cariboo freighter F.J. Barnard and older brother of Victoria lawyer and Senator Harry Barnard, lived at "Clovelly" on West Bay, just east of the the boundary between Esquimalt and Victoria West. Little Barnard Street, which runs for a few hundred feet south of the Esquimalt Road, was the driveway into his property.

The Victoria electric streetcar system of the early 1890s was an outgrowth of Frank Barnard's Victoria Transfer Company, which had its stables behind the original Union Club at Broughton and Broad (now Eaton's parkade), and ran an hourly, horse-drawn omnibus service for a ten-cent fare from Humber Green (The Fountain) to the Outer Wharf, and from Fort and Yates to the Point Ellice bridge. The omnibus service was superseded by electric trams in February, 1890. The Victoria Transfer Company survived until the twenties as a livery and haulage business; the old, rat-infested stables became the depot for Sam Matson's Vancouver Island Coach Line. Barnard, with his friends in the real-estate-oriented Vancouver Improvement Company, was also an investor in Vancouver-area streetcar systems (Union Street there used to be called "Barnard"). Following the collapse of the Consolidated Railway and Lighting Company in late 1896, Barnard was instrumental in attracting English capital to British Columbia for the formation of the B.C. Electric Railway Company, and ran it for several years thereafter. He served as Conservative MP for the Cariboo in the 1880s and early 1890s, and was appointed lieutenant-governor in 1913.

Barnard married Martha Loewen, the daughter of Victoria Phoenix Brewery owner Joseph Loewen. The couple lived briefly at "Rockwood," the Loewen home on the Gorge, before "Clovelly" was completed in 1894. Barnard died in 1936, and "Clovelly" was demolished in 1960, ostensibly for the construction of a new RCMP building. Apartments now cover part of the grounds, but the land along the rocky shore at the bottom of Barnard Street has become an attractive park with a good view of Work Point, James Bay, and the Olympic Mountains.

The Esquimalt & Nanaimo Railway

Victoria was supposed to be the terminus of Canada's first transcontinental railway; with that promise of prosperity, the residents of Vancouver Island voted to forsake their colonial status and join Canada in 1871. The railway was to have come through central British Columbia, down Bute Inlet, across the islands and channels north of Campbell River in the Strait of Georgia—though no-one had ever built bridges that long before—then down the Island through Nanaimo to a terminus at Esquimalt hárbour and Victoria. The southern end of Vancouver Island was the logical location of a terminus, as it was the only part of the province with any substantial number of voters. Thus, in June, 1873, Esquimalt was named the terminus in "a flagrant bribe to the voters of Victoria." Premier George Walkem's political machinations (pages 84 and 85) to force Canada to start the railway practically tore confederation apart; the "Carnarvon Terms," including an immediate start on a railroad between Esquimalt and Nanaimo, were negotiated to keep British Columbia happily within confederation. Despite this, the Canadian Senate felt that the E&NR was an absurdity, and refused in March, 1875, to pass the bill authorizing its construction.

When Prime Minister Sir John A. Macdonald was defeated in his Kingston, Ontario riding in the 1878 election, he took the opportunity to run in a by-election in Esquimalt, where he was easily elected, and briefly showed his gratitude by promising to again name Esquimalt as the terminus. He explained his about-face of October, 1879, by claiming that American commercial expansion via the Northern Pacific Railway and Imperial strategic concerns made the Burrard Inlet route—and thus the creation of Vancouver as the province's commercial centre—necessary.

Vancouver Island voters still wanted a railway which was part of the transcontinental system, to ease them out of the depression which had stifled business for most of the 1870s. During the autumn of 1882, Canada's governor general, the Marquis of Lorne, threw all of his diplomatic skills into convincing the coy Robert Dunsmuir to build the line. (A representative of the Canadian Pacific Railway syndicate had visited Vancouver Island in February, 1882, to examine the route from Esquimalt to Nanaimo, and told the Dominion government they weren't interested in building or operating it.)

Dunsmuir put together a syndicate including Vancouver Island investor John Bryden and the surviving three "bonanza kings" of the Southern Pacific Railroad—Charles Crocker, Leland Stanford and Collis Huntington. He had arranged the syndicate so that he put up only a fraction of the capital but still controlled the nomination of a majority of the railway's directors. He then announced to the Marquis of Lorne that he would build the railway, but set some extraordinary terms, including the granting of coalfields, construction subsidies, tax relief, and nearly two million acres of Vancouver Island. Premier William Smithe, who defeated Walkem's crony and successor Robert Beaven, introduced the necessary legislation in early 1883 to hand the land over to Dunsmuir's E&NR syndicate. The contract was signed on August 20, 1883.

Most people in B.C. thought that Smithe's policy of granting land to capitalists to stimulate construction of public works was worthwhile. The province had few assets other than land, and little ability to raise money through taxes, as there was little business to tax (personal income tax was first levied as a temporary war-financing measure in 1917). A grant of 6,000 acres on Burrard Inlet the following year to the CPR was the "incentive" for the railway to build its terminus at the little town of Granville, where it probably would have built anyway. The CPR used the land to develop most of the downtown and west side of the city of Vancouver. Most of the other land grants made by Smithe and successive governments over the ensuing decades to speculative pipe-dream railroad entrepreneurs amounted to nothing.

Many doubted whether the E&NR could ever be built. The Malahat grade was said to be impossible. Dunsmuir hired John Robson's brother-in-law Joseph Hunter as chief engineer, and supposedly gave him these brief directions: "You are instructed to build a railroad from Esquimalt to Nanaimo." Prime Minister John A. Macdonald drove the last spike on August 13, 1886.

The service originally ran from Russell's station in Esquimalt, near the modern Victoria West station at Catherine Street and Esquimalt Road. A train left at 8 a.m. and arrived in Nanaimo at 11:40 a.m., then left for the return journey at 2:00 p.m. Islanders were thrilled with the speed and comfort. Agriculture became more profitable, settlement was stimulated, and the old isolation of the little communities ceased. An extension was built to connect Dunsmuir's new Wellington mines with the main line in 1887. The next year, a bridge was thrown across the Inner Harbour at Johnson Street, and a masonry station and several freight sheds were erected on Store Street, just north of Johnson.

The E&NR was a closed, private company, and issued no public stock. It wasn't directly profitable—although it made the Dunsmuir mines profitable—until James Dunsmuir added a ferry link between Vancouver and his Ladysmith mines. This re-stimulated the CPR's interest in the system, and Dunsmuir sold out in 1905 for $3 million.

A number of attractive resorts were established on the E&NR line before the First World War. At mile eleven, the Goldstream Hotel was a popular drinking and picnicking spot for Victorians. Further north, the trains climbed the Malahat—a trip at least as far as Malahat Station was "a must" for visitors, and many continued further for a view of the spectacular trestles and canyons between there and Duncan. Weekenders and picnickers flocked to the resort hotels at Shawnigan Lake (the Strathcona Hotel) and Cameron Lake. Tourist use of the line declined in the early twenties, due to improved roads in the area and more widespread automobile use, but the main line was still busy with freight, and was extended northward during the McBride years. It eventually reached Courtenay, but never achieved the great ambition of crossing the Seymour Narrows to the mainland.

William Smithe, the premier of B.C. whose land deals brought the E&NR into existence and gave much of Vancouver to the Canadian Pacific Railway.

Prime Minister John A. Macdonald's national railway policy was the last hope for Victorians who wanted the transcontinental railway to terminate at Esquimalt. When he was defeated in his Kingston riding in the 1878 election, Victoria voters offered him a safe seat in a by-election. Late in the year, he restored Esquimalt as the terminus (though his predecessor Alexander MacKenzie had said it was impractical), then promptly contradicted himself by affirming the Fraser River route which eventually created the City of Vancouver.

The entry of the first E&N train into Victoria in March, 1888, was a tremendous event for Victoria, but something of an anticlimax after the completion less than a year previously of the transcontinental CPR line into Vancouver. Victoria held onto its dreams of a direct rail link with the mainland until the First World War years.

Peter Curran Dunlevy (1833-1905) was born in Pittsburgh, and came west to the Cariboo in 1857. After establishing a chain of trading posts in the Peace River district, he bought and ran a large cattle ranch at Soda Creek. He claimed to have conceived the idea of the Victoria Terminal & Sidney Railway, and used his influence to get a charter for the similarly ill-fated Nelson-Fort Shepard Railway in the Kootenays.

Taxation of the 1,900,000-acre E&NR land grant became an issue in the mid-1940s. It was a massive piece of the island—all the land east of a line running northwest from a point on the Pacific coast west of Victoria, through Alberni Inlet and Sproat Lake to Upper Campbell Lake, then on a right-angle to Campbell River. The land had been handed over by B.C. to the Dominion, which had given it to the E&NR syndicate as part of the railway deal. The agreement was made that none of the resources in the land grant could be taxed, unless sold or used by the company for other than railway purposes. Later, on April 7, 1887, the province decided to put a royalty on all timber sold in the province.

The Sloan Commission on Forestry in 1945 had recommended that the timber cut within the railway belt be taxed. The Commission pointed out that one-third of the total timber cut in B.C. came from the E&NR grant, that more than $14 million worth of timber had been sold by the E&NR since 1905, that an estimated $17-$24 million worth remained, and that the E&NR was paying only taxes of only $10,759 on all its operations within the railway lands. CCF Opposition leader Harold Winch took up the issue, and pressured the provincial government to take the E&NR to court. The railway's defence, presented by J.E. McMullen, was that the land deal "was part of the bargain of confederation." B.C.'s case was presented by former Attorney General J.W. deB. Farris. Following months of wrangling, a clear decision came from the Appeal Court in June, 1947, that B.C. could legally tax all railway belt lands "not specifically used for railway purposes." The railway appealed to the Supreme Court of Can-

ada, which reversed the Appeal Court's decision on June 25, 1948. B.C. then proceeded with its case to the Privy Council in London, and opened arguments the following June 27. On November 2, the B.C. government won—the Privy Council said that no contract existed between B.C. and the E&NR over the railway. Premier Byron Johnson hailed it as an important victory. However, the Privy Council also ruled that because there was an agreement between B.C. and Ottawa, and between Ottawa and the E&NR, any tax levied by B.C. might be disallowed by Ottawa. In 1950, the right of appeal by Canadians to the Privy Council was discontinued. Thus, the decision of the Canadian Supreme Court would be final, and not necessarily subject to the precedent set by the earlier decision. The B.C. government found itself in a conundrum, as it would likely be in breach of contract with Ottawa if it attempted to tax the E&NR. It decided to try anyway, and Finance Minister Anscomb introduced a bill to tax the railway lands in March, 1950. The E&NR petitioned Ottawa for disallowance, but lost on December 30, 1950. The decision was worth, at the time, about $6 million a year in new revenue.

Like most passenger train systems in Canada, the E&NR suffered declining traffic after the fifties. Repeated attempts by the railway to discontinue its Victoria-Courtenay "Dayliner" were always blocked, and the service still operates under the VIA Rail banner. The old Store Street station was demolished in 1972, to improve auto access to the Johnson Street bridge.

Arthur Currie

Arthur Currie arrived in Victoria in the mid-1890s to teach school at Boys' Central. He spent most of his spare time as an active reservist with the old 5th Regiment, part of the Esquimalt garrison originally under Col. E.G. Prior. Later, he became the regiment's colonel, camping at Beacon Hill Park and Macauley Point and organizing the sham battles and parades which were such a part of Victorian public holidays. He quit teaching in 1900, and went into real estate with J.S.H. Matson.

When the First World War broke out, the first troops to leave Victoria for the Valcartier camp were from the 5th B.C. Regiment. A few weeks later, the Gordon Highlanders (50th Regiment) left, commanded by Currie. He became field commander of the Canadian Army First Division on September 13, 1915, and held the position until he was promoted to Commander of all Canadian forces on the Western Front in June, 1917. He ended the war as one of Canada's greatest heroes.

Currie was 6'4" and 240 pounds and dragged a canvas bath around France with him. According to a contemporary chronicler, he disliked "tomatoes, politicians, movies of the Americans capturing Vimy Ridge, crème de menthe, Turkish cigarettes, and waist cords in pyjamas." He was well-received on his return to Canada, but lacked the personal magnetism of Haig and Allenby in England or Pershing in the U.S.A. (only Pretoria Day in 1902, and the visit of the Prince of Wales in 1919, roused Canadians into spontaneous demonstrations of great affection). In Victoria, he received a silver tray from Premier John Oliver, and a banquet and public reception at the legislative buildings on February 6, 1919.

On March 4, General Sir Sam Hughes, Prime Minister Borden's erratic war minister, denounced Currie for the "undue sacrifice of men to win victories." He detailed how Currie had ordered an attack at Mons, with heavy loss of life, four hours before the eleven o'clock Armistice on November 11. Other Canadian officers including Lieut.-Col. W.W. Foster of Victoria and British generals swiftly came to Currie's defence. Hughes was considered by many at that time to be suffering from a mild paranoia, so the matter was quickly forgotten. Currie accepted the vice-chancellorship of McGill University, and moved from Victoria to Montreal.

Currie's record was again challenged, in an article in the Port Hope, Ontario *Guide* of June 13, 1927. F.W. Wilson and W.T.R. Preston claimed that the Armistice Day attack on Mons had been undertaken to glorify the military authorities, and that Currie had falsified military records. Currie sued for libel, and the trial in Cobourg, Ontario attracted nationwide attention and rattled a number of wartime skeletons for weeks. Currie was exonerated, and received $500 damages and costs. He died on November 30, 1933 in Montreal, aged only 57.

A.W. Currie, photographed in 1912 while he was still a real-estate agent and military reservist.

Andrew Gray's magnificent "Roslyn," at 1135 Catherine Street on Victoria Arm. Gray, with his partner Joseph Spratt, founded the Victoria Machinery Depot, which manufactured machinery and acted as an agent for many of the big eastern boiler and engine manufacturers. VMD in its early years built complete fish cannery outfits, locomotive boilers, and rails for the National Electric Tramway & Lighting Company.

WHEN YOU'RE A LONG, LONG WAY FROM HOME (2).

When you're a long, long way from home, it makes you feel like you're alone,
It's hard to find a pal that's true, that you can tell your troubles to,
And when you send a letter home, your mother's voice rings in your ears,
And then you cross the t's with kisses, what a strange world this is!
Then you dot the i's with tears, and all the sunshine turns to gloom
When you're a long, long way from home.

BY ARRANGEMENT WITH MESSRS. FRANCIS, DAY & HUNTER, THE PUBLISHERS OF THE MUSIC.
BAMFORTH COPYRIGHT

Saanich & Beyond

William Fraser Tolmie (1812-1886) was a Hudson's Bay Company physician, explorer, farmer, cattle breeder, and legislator. He married fellow farmer John Work's eldest daughter Jane. He gained recognition as an ethnologist and historian, and learned the vocabularies of a number of Indian tribes, published in 1884 in collaboration with Dr. G.M. Dawson.

By the turn of the century, a network of roads and railways connected outlying farms and communities to the City of Victoria. The modern expansion of Greater Victoria, especially since the Second World War, has swallowed up many of the farms of the colonial period. John Tod's "Willows" and the Uplands Farm are part of suburban Oak Bay. The four Puget Sound Agricultural Company farms in Esquimalt and Colwood have disappeared almost without trace. The Yates farm north of the Gorge was subdivided in 1908. The huge Rithet ranch in Royal Oak was subdivided in the early 1950s. And so on.

One of the most famous farms was "Cloverdale," the 1100-acre property of Dr. William Fraser Tolmie in Saanich just north of Victoria's downtown. Tolmie was born in Inverness in 1812, and completed his medical training at Glasgow University when he was barely 20. He joined the Hudson's Bay Company as a surgeon, and arrived at Fort Vancouver on the Columbia River in 1833, after a brief stay at the company trading post at Honolulu. Before moving to Victoria permanently in 1859, he was a member of exploration parties on the coast which established Fort Simpson, discovered the coal seam which brought Robert Dunsmuir to B.C., and climbed Mount Rainier. He retired to "Cloverdale" in 1870, and bred cattle and horses until his death in December, 1886. He had married Jane

"Benvenuto," the home of Mr. and Mrs. R.P. Butchart, in the 1920s. The house had a tiled swimming pool, a bowling alley, and a room full of mechanical and clockwork toys which Mr. Butchart had collected on his world travels. He loved gadgets, and kept an electric organ, which also played phonograph records, on the sun porch.

Residence of R. P. Butchart, Victoria, B. C.

Work, a daughter of "Hillside" farm owner and retired Hudson's Bay Company factor John Work, in 1850. They had seven sons and five daughters, including Dr. Simon Fraser Tolmie, a veterinarian who was premier of British Columbia from 1928-1933. All of the children remained residents of Victoria.

Travellers heading towards Sooke or Nanaimo by road went along the Craigflower Road, through Victoria West and Esquimalt and past Craigflower Farm. The first hotel they reached was Four Mile House, which still stands today on the Island Highway in the suburb of View Royal. Four Mile House was an outgrowth of the farm of Peter and Elizabeth Calvert, who had originally come to Victoria to help establish Craigflower Farm. In the early 1860s, Mrs. Calvert began to accept "PG's" (paying guests) to help with the bills, and was such a successful landlady that they were able to purchase the Parsons' Bridge Hotel two miles further along the Sooke Road, at Mill Stream.

Parsons' Bridge dates from 1850, when William Parsons arrived to work at the sawmill which Roderick Finlayson had established two years before. Parsons built the bridge, and established the hotel there in 1855. Mill Stream was the source of fresh water for the British Navy in the early years. The two hotels were also watering holes—both suffered financially during Prohibition, but prospered after Victoria rejected the Local Option liquor vote in the late twenties. Anyone with a motorcar could easily make the trip to Four Mile or Six Mile House for a drink.

A couple of miles further, at the modern site of the Colwood shopping centre, a road branched off to the west towards Goldstream and, after the opening of the Malahat in the early Twenties, Duncan and Nanaimo. (The number of autos in B.C. had grown from 2,000 in 1911 to 28,000 in 1920, 11,000 of which were on Vancouver Island. The Pacific Highway Association's A.E. Todd estimated in 1916 that 10,000 families in motor cars would visit the province, spending $15 million in a single season.)

The Goldstream Hotel, built on the Goldstream River about eleven miles from Victoria, was "the terminus of pleasure seekers on perhaps the most beautiful drive around Victoria," according to an 1890 advertisement. By that time, Goldstream House was managed by American James Phayer, "an ardent sportsman who is always willing to accompany his guest on a hunting expedition." The manicured hotel grounds extended into a thousand-acre property reaching down to Langford Lake, and guests were invited to help themselves to the trout, grouse, deer and bear in the thick woods. Once the E&N Railway opened in 1886, picnickers flocked there (Goldstream was the second station, after Langford, once the train began its climb out of Esquimalt). The "Goldstream Special," a collaboration of Phayer and the E&NR, offered a round trip for 25 cents, and band concerts and other entertainments were provided at the hotel. The hotel burned down in the mid-1930s, but was rebuilt.

Other railway excursionists with a penchant for hunting used the Victoria Terminal & Sidney Railway to get into the Saanich countryside for an afternoon's sport. The VT&SR was established in 1894 as part of James

"Cloverdale," the Tolmies' stone farmhouse surrounded by 1,100 acres of prime farmland on the Victoria-Saanich border. Built in 1860, the house stood at 978 Cloverdale Avenue west of Quadra—exactly three miles north of City Hall. It was surrounded by the original acacia trees imported by Tolmie from Fort Vancouver, and had a remarkable English ivy, with an eight-inch-diameter trunk, growing on its front façade. Even in the early thirties, it was called "the garden of Canada" and famed for its Holsteins. The last 225 acres of the original property, called the "Braefoot Farm," was subdivided in 1933 into hobby-farm plots called Saanich Delta Manor. Following S.F. Tolmie's death in 1937, the house's contents—some of which had come around the Horn in the 1860s, were auctioned; many went to museum collections in Oregon and Washington, due to the historical interest there in W.F. Tolmie. The house spent its final years as a multiple dwelling, then was demolished in 1962.

Jerome Hill's massive campaign to pull Canadian business away from the CPR to his Great Northern Railway system. The GN's expansion north-ward, due to a supposed feud between Hill and the CPR's directors, began in 1891 when the New Westminster & Southern was built from White Rock to Brownsville, across the river from New Westminster. A ferry service was established to connect the VT&SR's Sidney terminus to the mainland, just north of Tsawwassen. The local president of the VT&SR was future Lieutenant-Governor Thomas W. Paterson. A station was built as part of the city's market building on Cormorant just west of City Hall. It was abandoned in 1910, when a more modest terminus was built on Blanshard Street. The VT&SR was something of a joke—no one seemed to know whether it really wanted to provide a good service, or whether it was just intended to "show the flag" for the GN on Vancouver Island. It was quickly named the "Cordwood Limited," and was most popular with hunters on Sunday mornings. Merchant Henry Young's son Louie recalled that in the hunting season the train was "jammed with hunters who got off every quarter of a mile from Victoria to Sidney." Similarly, on the E&NR there were often "five coaches full, going up the line and getting off at various places. On Sunday night coming in, the baggage train on the E&N Railway was full of deer."

The B.C. Electric Railway started into competition with the VT&SR before the First World War, running a smart interurban service from a terminus on Douglas Street opposite City Hall to Deep Bay at the northern end of the Saanich peninsula. Like its companion service between New Westminster and Chilliwack on the mainland, the Saanich interurban meandered through the countryside, stopping to pick up produce and milk from the many farms scattered along the line. The BCER began an advertising campaign in England, hoping to induce new settlers (and customers) to immigrate and take up some of the land it had purchased. The campaign had barely commenced when the economy crashed in 1913, followed a year later by the declaration of war. Business was crippled, and over the ensuing years ridership and service suffered. The VT&SR felt the pinch, too, and collapsed in 1919. The Canadian National system further plugged the system by starting a rail line in the early twenties to Patricia Bay. The BCER interurban system struggled along, though by the early twenties much of its business was tourist excursions to the Butchart Gardens at Tod Inlet. Fifteen trips each way were offered daily, and the scenic journey took less than an hour and a half. Freight continued to decline, as farmers and businesses found trucks more convenient and less expensive than delivering goods to the interurban stations. The BCER's Saanich line was closed down in 1923.

Butchart Gardens has been an international attraction since the early 1920s. Robert Pim Butchart started his working career in his father's hardware business in Owen Sound, Ontario. When he was 32, in 1888, he became interested in the fledgling Portland cement industry, and opened the Owen Sound Portland Cement Company. In 1904, he moved to Vancouver Island, and bought land at Tod Inlet, where there were extensive limestone and clay deposits which were ideal for making Portland cement. The industry achieved spectacular growth, due to the use of reinforced concrete in the construction of the modern, tall buildings made possible by the recent introduction of electric-motored elevators. As well, the boom in automobile use created a need for paved roads: by 1916, there was 60 times as much paved road in North America as there had been seven years before.

Butchart's cement plant left an almost lunar landscape of abandoned quarries along Tod Inlet. The Butcharts were avid gardeners, and had fine gardens surrounding "Benvenuto," their nearby house. In an inspired moment, they decided to reclaim the quarries by planting gardens there. (The story has been romantically embellished many times: some give the credit to Mrs. Jennie Butchart, some to Robert, some to both of them, and others to their daughter Jenny (1884-1971)—Princess Chikhmatoff by her second marriage. Still others say the *real* credit belongs to the gardeners: W.J. Westby and his father, who developed the first sunken

garden around 1913, using Chinese labour and horses otherwise occupied loading the cement boats; Arthur Robillard and his son Raoul, who supervised the installation of the Alpine Garden from 1919-22; Alfred Shiner, Archie Nicholls, Bob Ballantyne, and others.) Robert Butchart was made a freeman of the City of Victoria in 1928. He died in October 1943, seven years before Jennie. Butchart Gardens celebrated its 50th anniversary, with a new night-time illumination system and a dazzling series of outdoor symphony concerts, in May, 1954.

Butchart Gardens was only one of the attractions sought out by tourists. Showing them around has been a major Victoria business since the turn of the century. C&C Transportation (standing for Cameron & Calwell) had a depot at 906 Government Street, and their open-topped blue and white buses were a familiar sight around the city. Vancouver Island Coach Lines was founded in 1928 by the Matson family. The most famous of the tour bus operators was a wise-cracking booster named George "Rebel" Mowat. Mowat was a legendary character, much loved by newspapermen for his wild gimmicks and promotions. His nickname "Rebel" was supposedly given to him during his school days at South Park; it became so accepted that a "MacLean's" magazine story in 1954, showing him conducting a group of tourists around Butchart Gardens, called him simply Rebel Mowat. Born in 1903 in Brooklyn, he started driving a bus when he was nineteen. He said he had four hobbies, "talking, talking, talking and tropical fish." A fifth hobby was probably baseball, especially his Cox's (or Coxey's) Army novelty team, which played comedy games at Beacon Hill Park during the late thirties to raise money for charity. Named for team-member Bill Cox, they played in wild costumes (in one game dressed as Zulus) for crowds which grew to an estimated 10,000 by the outbreak of the Second World War. Famous sports figures took part, including hockey player Lester "Silver Fox" Patrick, world welterweight champion Jimmy McLarnin, and cyclist Torchy Peden. Mowat drove Gray Line sightseeing buses for 46 years. He retired in 1968, and set off on a world tour with his wife. He died suddenly in Ireland, not long after he left Victoria.

Nellie McClung (1873-1951) retired to a "two-acre bulb farm" called "Lantern Lane" on Ferndale Road in Gordon Head. She was a tireless crusader for causes like women's suffrage, temperance, and international peace. Her most famous novel was Sowing Seeds in Danny, *which went through seventeen printings in her lifetime. A long-time supporter of MacKenzie King, she broke with the Liberals in 1935 over their refusal to enfranchise native-born Orientals, though she retained her position as Canadian delegate to the League of Nations. Her prescription for happiness was that "husband and wife develop their own individualities, without impinging on each other." She used to joke that she had early recognised her Bible-class teacher as an excellent prospective mother-in-law, because her son had red hair—McClung's favorite colour. "I went to the store where he was employed and purchased a fountain pen with my last three dollars. He had no chance to escape after that."*

George "Rebel" Mowat, one of the best-known tour guides and bus drivers in Victoria.

Nanaimo & The 1913 Riots

Nanaimo's relationship to Victoria during the heyday of coal was like a fairy tale of an ugly stepdaughter and a cruel stepmother, without the happy ending. A lot of Victoria's prosperity, and the grace and elegance made possible by it, was due to the mining of coal by Dunsmuir-related interests at the Wellington Collieries at Nanaimo, the Extension mines, and the Union Collieries at Comox. The rise of the working class and socialist-type politics on Vancouver Island can be directly traced to the relations between the Dunsmuirs and the miners—the closest thing to the capitalist vs. labour organizer model which so poisoned the affairs of men like John D. Rockefeller in the United States. Once coal began to lose its importance to oil during the twenties and thirties, the Vancouver Island mines declined.

The development of Esquimalt as a naval station was made possible by the huge quantities of coal in the Nanaimo area. Robert Dunsmuir came from Scotland to B.C. in the early 1850s to develop coal mines for the Hudson's Bay Company (page 118). In 1864, the Harewood Coal Company was founded by Horace Douglas Lascelles and bought out the HBC's Nanaimo coal fields. It started operations with Robert Dunsmuir as resident manager. Vancouver Island Governor Kennedy described Nanaimo as "the future Newcastle of the Pacific," and used his influence to get the Royal Navy base moved north from Valparaiso. He suggested there was enough coal there to supply a merchant fleet trading throughout the Far East and India. Nanaimo thus graduated from being a Hudson's Bay Company fort, with bastions identical to those at old Fort Victoria, to a company town. In 1868, when the Assembly of British Columbia met to decide on the final location of B.C.'s capital, Nanaimo sided with New Westminster against her "cruel stepmother" Victoria.

Relations between the owners and the miners were at best polite. The Vancouver Island mines had difficulty competing with the Bellingham mines for the San Francisco market. A reciprocity treaty had been negotiated between Britain and the U.S. in 1854, but it didn't apply to Vancouver Island, so the imposition of an American coal tariff caused a severe depression in the 1860s. When the San Francisco coal tariff was increased to $1.28 a ton in 1870, the owners attempted to cut the miners' wages by 12½ cents a ton. The miners struck, arguing that the imposition of the B.C. tariff on Vancouver Island since 1866 (when Vancouver Island lost its free-port status) had increased their living costs (the *British Colonist* saw this as yet another argument for confederation, as Canada would have the clout to negotiate a good reciprocity deal for B.C.).

The workers became radical during the 1870s on the issues of (so-called) landlordism and Chinese exclusion. The Dunsmuirs' increasing ostentation was in sharp contrast to the mean, grimy lives of the workers and their families near the pit head at Wellington. The miners struck again on February 3, 1877, and stayed out until April 28, when Dunsmuir's influence finally persuaded the Royal Navy to dispatch the HMS *Rocket*, loaded with 90 militiamen, for a show of force in Nanaimo. Two years later, on April 17, a dozen miners were killed in an explosion in

Wellington Collieries.

Increasing concerns with safety at the mines coincided with Robert Dunsmuir's decision to enter politics. Dunsmuir was elected as the member for Nanaimo in 1882, then again in 1886. In July, 1884, an explosion at South Wellington killed 23. The Miners' and Mine Labourers' Protective Association was formed to fight for the eight hour day, union recognition, and Chinese exclusion. Much of their program was prompted by the success of workers in Australia, where the "eight hours of work, eight hours of recreation, and eight hours of rest" theme had gained a lot of support. The miners struck again in 1890: as in the 1877 strike, miners were arrested for attempting to stop strikebreakers (or "blacklegs," as they were then called), and Judge Begbie ruled in favour of the strikebreakers' rights to work.

A new breed of politician representing workers' interests emerged in the Nanaimo area. Most significant was the election in July, 1898, which sent mine manager John Bryden from Nanaimo North riding and MMLPA representative Ralph Smith from Nanaimo South to Victoria. Two years later, James Dunsmuir (Robert's son) was elected in Nanaimo South and became premier, while Smith was elected for Nanaimo City. That year, there was another disaster, this time at Union Mines, and strikes elsewhere by salmon fishermen and Canadian Pacific Railway machinists. The MMLPA became more radical and moved away from its moderate Trades & Labour Congress affiliation; it was too radical for Ralph Smith, who resigned his provincial seat and ran federally as a Liberal. "Theoretical socialist" James Hurst Hawthornthwaite was chosen in the subsequent by-election.

Hawthornthwaite was returned in the 1903 election which brought Richard McBride's Conservatives to power. He had company, as the Newcastle riding elected socialist Parker Williams. The two held a sort of balance of power with McBride, and used it to get Eight-Hour Day legislation discussed (a companion to the recent Workers Compensation Act) against bitter opposition from the press and business groups. A statement from the provincial Socialist party convention in December, 1904, indicates the tone of much of the debate: "the two great wings of Capitalism, the Conservative and Liberal parties, stand for the perpetuation of the Capitalist system of production, the continuation of wage slavery, and the exploitation of human labour by the master class." Hawthornthwaite denounced Dunsmuir's Wellington Colliery manager as "an ordinary thin-lipped labour skinner." Dunsmuir threatened to close the mines if the eight-hour day was brought in; the mines were closed anyway for nearly five months in 1905 by strikes. Hawthornthwaite then turned on Dunsmuir, who was by that time lieutenant-governor, charging that, because he employed Orientals in his mining operations, he had refused his assent to a unanimously passed B.C. resolution to limit Oriental immigration. Hawthornthwaite repeatedly made motions for the removal of Dunsmuir, and was repeatedly ruled out of order by Speaker D.M. Eberts, as "no member shall be allowed to speak disrespectfully of the

James Hurst Hawthornthwaite was elected as a Socialist to represent Nanaimo in the legislature after Ralph Smith's departure into the Liberal fold. His loyalty was questioned when he was named in 1916 as the only English-Canadian member of the Board of the Vancouver & Nanaimo Coal Company—the balance of the board being German-Canadian. He apparently then fell out of favour with his supporters, and was not re-elected in 1916. He ran in a 1918 by-election in Newcastle, and was returned with a large majority as a "Bolsheviki" spokesman who claimed to know and respect Lenin.

Parker Williams, the socialist MLA from Newcastle.

Results of the 1913 riot at Extension—a flattened, burned automobile and ransacked buildings.

Ralph Smith represented the Nanaimo riding at the turn of the century, then entered federal politics as a Liberal. He ran again provincially in a Vancouver riding in 1916 as a Liberal, was elected, and became minister of finance briefly before his death. His widow Mary Ellen Smith won the by-election to replace him, becoming the first woman elected in B.C. She was appointed to the Cabinet in December, 1920, as a minister without portfolio (the first woman so to serve in the British Empire). She resigned the following November, claiming that she had wanted to work for the interests of women and children, but in reality was "in the unfortunate position of having to assume responsibility for the acts of the Government without being in a position to criticize or advise."

PABC 8960

Sovereign or His Representative."

The Nanaimo mines unrest climaxed in 1913, by which time Dunsmuir had sold all his collieries and operations to the MacKenzie & Mann (Canadian Northern Railway) syndicate. Labour unions had made tremendous strides since the turn of the century: there were 70 recognized unions with 11,827 members, and socialism as a political creed had been endorsed by 37 of them. The Provincial Federation of Labour meeting in Victoria from January 13-17 focused its attentions on the coal mines. Resolutions included a higher standard of technical knowledge for coal mine inspectors, a six-hour day underground, no piece work, a $4 a day minimum, no Oriental labour, and no one under sixteen down the mines. The previous September, scattered labour interruptions had begun "as a sort of collective holiday" when a miner named Mottishaw was dismissed by Canadian Collieries Ltd. at Cumberland (the Union Mines). The issue over which he was dismissed was evidently his insistence on adherence to safety procedures.

On May 2, 1913, 200 Nanaimo miners were ordered off the job "by their Seattle United Mine Workers union headquarters," according to a contemporary report. They "made things so unpleasant" that 2,300 non-affiliated miners also struck. Soon, 8,000 men were off the job, and all the Vancouver Island collieries were shut down, while all the miners in Washington State were working overtime. (The first "reasoned" accounts of the Nanaimo riots came out in 1914, by which time Canada was at war with Germany, and the U.S.A. wasn't. Much of the blame was placed on agitation by Bolsheviks or Americans, or on UMW leader John L. Sullivan attempting a power-grab for his loyal American workers, or on pro-

German agitators who used the miners as pawns and wanted to disrupt the B.C. economy. No blame was placed on the poor working conditions and lack of safety; the only local issue which could have motivated the workers, said the accounts, was the universal loathing of Oriental strikebreakers.)

After three weeks of seething discontent, the rumour that MacKenzie & Mann was bringing Chinese and Japanese strikebreakers to Nanaimo, Extension and Cumberland touched off the powderkeg. A mob of 1,000 took possession of Nanaimo on August 11. A constable was shot and the chief of police stoned, and the wives and families of men still working were driven out of their houses and into the woods. Explosions demolished some mine buildings and collapsed pitheads. Although wild looting and rioting continued, the strikers claimed they could preserve the peace if left unmolested by "that spawn of filth"—the militia and the Special Police. Nevertheless, acting Premier Bowser dispatched 400 militia from Victoria on the 14th, after a police force detachment of 25 had been driven off the Nanaimo docks back onto their steamer. "Now that we are in the field," he said, "we intend to stay to the bitter end." Arrests totalled 217, including MLA John Place, and "bloodcurdling" evidence was presented to the magistrates. J.J. Taylor, the vice-president of the B.C. Federation of Labour, was sentenced to two years in B.C. Penitentiary.

The strike dragged on into the new year. Two hundred militia remained in the Nanaimo district (becoming increasingly unhappy, as Bowser refused them extra pay). Sentencing of miners continued through March, though most were suspended. In June, the octogenarian anarchist "Mother" Jones visited Vancouver Island, and announced at a Nanaimo meeting that "if the capitalists rob us to buy guns for their hired assassins, we will have to buy guns ourselves." Her call-to-arms was scarcely heard over the call-to-arms in Europe—the strike was formally called off August 20, a fortnight after war was declared, and all the imprisoned miners were released.

Towards the end of the First World War, B.C.'s industrial unions became even more radical. The first Canadian general strike was held for 24 hours on August 2, 1918, to honour the memory of "Ginger" Goodwin, a labour organizer killed by police at Comox.

The attempts to organize a class struggle under the O.B.U. banner failed by the early 1920s (page 94). Subsequently, the rise of the Cooperative Commonwealth Federation (now the NDP) out of the agricultural protest movements of the twenties created a left wing political alternative capable of attracting broader political support.

Appendix I: Flowers & Plants

Many accounts of life in early Victoria mention the profusion of wild-flowers amidst the scattered Garry oaks and arbutus trees. Their subtlety is often overpowered by the vivid colours of modern gardens. I included typical Victoria wildflowers in some of the paintings, including the following:

Page 9 in high summer—(left to right in the foreground) Indian plum bush; a purple honeysuckle vine straggling onto the road; yellow-flowered common St. Johnswort and blue-flowered "Blue Sailors"; a blackberry vine spilling over the fence; yellow-flowered, dandelion-like hairy cat's ear on the roadside; and, purple-flowered Douglas aster. Page 13 in late May—blue-flowered camass; tall, purple-flowered Indian consumption plant; yellow-flowered, brown-eyed woolly sunflowers; and yellow-flowered spring gold. Page 76 in April—blue-flowered camass; clumps of purple satin-flowers; three pink sea blush on a mossy rock; a clump of yellow violets in the grass; and, on the right, a few pink peacocks and blue wild hyacinths. Page 106 in April—a field of white Easter lilies, and the pink plumes of the hardhack bush; underneath the fence in the cool shade are a few vanilla leaf or sweet after death plants, which were often gathered, dried and hung in rooms in the belief they would repel flies. Page 143 in April—yellow-flowered broom growing on the rocks. Page 145 in late May—camass, yellow-flowered gumweed, and trillium. Pages 160 and 161 in early March—purple satin-flowers and daffodils scattered among the grass.

Victoria's gardens in the last century featured flowers and plants which are less in fashion today. The paintings throughout the book include the standard flowers of Victorian English gardens—stocks and phlox, different types of lilies, violets, Canterbury bells, foxgloves, delphiniums, poppies, flag irises, sweet william, heliotropes, snapdragons, pinks, daisies, and shrub roses. English gardens of the period (as in the photograph on page 142) featured herbaceous borders—clumps or rows of increasingly-large flowers, backed by tall foxgloves or delphiniums and sometimes a stone wall or privet hedge. The flowers in the paintings grow in our own back garden, and were painted in the summer of 1985. Darlene Sanders gave me valuable advice on old English garden fashions—especially in roses.

A tremendous number of early Victoria residents were avid gardeners. Two of those mentioned in the text were Pembertons: Frederick of "Mount Joy" on Foul Bay Road, and Ada (Beaven) on Beach Drive. Bedding plants and seeds were available at a number of nurseries in the Victoria area. The Mitchell & Johnson nursery was established in 1864 on seven acres at the southwest corner of Fort and St. Charles streets. The Invertavish nursery at the southeast corner of Southgate and Rupert (now Quadra Street), now part of Beacon Hill Park, was started by G.A. McTavish and later purchased by former Belmont saloon manager Thomas Flewin; its greenhouses collapsed after the 1916 snowfall, and it was abandoned thereafter. The P.T. Johnston Nurseries on lower St. Charles Street in Fairfield, near the A.J. Woodward greenhouses (painting, page 129) supplied the shrubberies for Thomas Shotbolt's "Hollywood." Richard Layritz's nursery was near the Wilkinson Road interurban stop.

A few well-known Victoria gardeners not elsewhere mentioned in this book were Mr. Naysmith, the head gardener for the legislative buildings; Alfred Green, who maintained J.A. Sayward's five-acre estate with a group of Chinese assistants; Norman Rant, who established the Rockhome Gardens on north Quadra Street about 1920; Horace Whiteoak, who did plantings and rockwork at Spencer Castle, held spring shows at the Willows fairgrounds, and wrote monthly notes for the Victoria Horticultural Society under the *nom de plume* "Quercus alba"; and, Fred Saunders, the Empress Hotel's head gardener in the 1940s, who developed the Empress poppy, a seven-petalled Shirley poppy which was bred in various shades of pink. The erection of "Spencer Castle" at 2906 Cook Street in 1913, and the development of its rock gardens a few years later, heralded a new appreciation of native plants and the rocky, rugged landscape. Victoria's rock and alpine gardeners formed a society in 1921.

The yellow-flowered broom which is so common throughout Beacon Hill Park and on vacant land around Victoria is not a native plant. It is an escapee, first brought to Vancouver Island in late 1850 by Captain Colquhoun Grant, who was given some of the seeds by the British consul in the Sandwich Islands (Hawaii) and planted them in front of his house.

Appendix II: Bibliography

Major sources of printed material were the *Victoria Colonist* and its predecessors, and the *Victoria Times*, preserved on microfilm at the library of the University of British Columbia, and in selected clippings in the Provincial Archives of B.C. in Victoria, the Victoria City Archives, and the Matthews Collection in the Vancouver City Archives.

The books and pamphlets below are listed in chronological order.

Victoria The Queen City (Ellis & Co., "The Colonist," Victoria) 1891.

The Year-Book of British Columbia (and Manual of Provincial Information) (Queen's Printer) by R.E. Gosnell, 1897, revised 1911 and 1914.

The Canadian Annual Review of Public Affairs (Toronto) by John Castell Hopkins, 1905 through 1934 editions.

British Columbians As We See 'Em (Newspaper Cartoonists' Association of B.C.) 1911.

British Columbia, (London) by Henry J. Boam, 1912.

British Columbia (S.J. Clarke Ltd. Winnipeg) by F.W. Howay and E.O.S. Scholefield, 1914.

British Columbia Pictorial & Biographical (S.J. Clarke Ltd. Winnipeg) 1914.

The Western Recorder (Metropolitan Church of Victoria) 1934.

Edible Wild Plants (Collier Books) by Oliver Perry Medsger, 1939.

The Book of Small (Clarke, Irwin & Company) by Emily Carr, 1942.

British Columbia & The United States (Ryerson Press, Toronto) by F.W. Howay, W.N. Sage, and H.F. Angus, 1942.

The House of All Sorts (Clarke, Irwin & Company) by Emily Carr, 1944.

Growing Pains (Clarke, Irwin & Company) by Emily Carr, 1946.

Esquimalt (Quality Press Printers, Victoria) by Leigh Burpee Robinson, 1948.

Trees, Shrubs & Flowers to Know in British Columbia (J.M. Dent & Sons) by C.P. Lyons, 1952.

The Union Club of British Columbia by P.L. Bissley, 1956.

British Columbia—A History by Margaret A. Ormsby, 1958.

British Columbia—A Centennial Anthology (McClelland & Stewart Limited) ed. Reginald Watters, 1958.

Victoria Historical Review (Flynn Engraving & Publishing Company, Victoria) by James K. Nesbitt, 1962.

Victoria R.I. (Pan Books) by Elizabeth Longford, 1964.

Those Were The Days (Peter Martin Associates Limited, Toronto) by Peter Stursberg, 1969.

Politicians of a Pioneering Province (Mitchell Press, 1969) by Russell R. Walker, 1969.

Victoria (Quality Press) by Harry Gregson, 1970.

This Old Town (City of Victoria Heritage Advisory Committee) 1975.

Come Give A Cheer! One Hundred Years of Victoria High School (Victoria High School Centennial Celebrations Committee) by Dr. Peter Lawson Smith, 1976.

A Victorian Tapestry (Aural History Program, Provincial Archives, Victoria) ed. Derek Reimer, 1978.

Rattenbury (Sono Nis Press) by Terry Reksten, 197 .

This Old House (City of Victoria Heritage Advisory Committee) 1979.

Sacred Places (Douglas & McIntyre) by Barry Downs, 1980.

The Modern Room (Provincial Archives) by Edythe Hembroff-Schleicher, 1981.

The Crease Family Archives (Provincial Archives) by Christina B. Johnson-Dean, 1981.

No Horsecars in Paradise (Railfare/Whitecap) by Douglas V. Parker, 1981.

Arches in British Columbia (Sono Nis Press) by Chuen-yan David Lai, 1982.

Ross Bay Cemetery (Heritage Architectural Guides, Victoria) by John Adams, 1983.

Victoria Landmarks by Geoffrey Castle and Barry F. King, 1985.

The Story of the B.C. Electric Railway Company (Whitecap Books) by Henry Ewert, 1986.

Index

Italics indicate principal reference, where applicable.

Adelphi stand 34
Alaska 10, 20, 79, 80
Albion Iron Works 37, 112
Alexander, R.H. 67
Anderson, A.C. 16
Angel Hotel 12, 56, *58*
Angus, H.F. *57*, 97, 98, 121
Angus, James 70, *121*
Angus, R.B. 121
Anscomb, H. 98
Anti-Blue-Sunday League 70, 71
Anti-Oriental legislation 57, 90-1, 168-9
Arcade Block 52-3, 61
"Arden" 142
"Armadale" 104
Army & Navy Veterans' Clubs 95
Atlas Iron Works 112
Aviation 77, 90, 108

Baker, E.C. 62, 67, 153
Baker, James 62
Ballou, Billy 40, 125
Bank of British Columbia 21, 25
Bank of British North America 40, 122
Banks *see also* Currency
Barnard, Francis J. 122
Barnard, Frank S. 39, 42, 47, 77, 80, 122, *161*
Barnard, G.H. 46, 68, 125
Baseball, 58, 167
Bayliss, William 128
Beacon Hill Park 15, 16, 102, *110*, 146
Beaven, Hugo 142
Beaven, Robert 44, 84, *85*, 87, 88
Beckley Farm 102
Beeton, H.C. 149
Begbie, Matthew 21, 35, 42, 62, 66, 70, 84, 85, 86, 87, 99, *132-3*, 168
Bell-Irving, Henry 89, 95
Bennett, R.B. 97
Bennett, W.A.C. 79, 81, 87, 98
Benson, Dr. Albert 15, 28
Birdcage Walk 24, 81
Birdcages 33, 81, *82*, 102
Blacks (American Negroes) 99, 122
Blanshard, Richard 16, 20
Borden, Robert 90, 91, 94

Bostock, Hewitt 114
Bowser, W.J. 29, 57, *90-93*, 94, 95, 140, 169
Brackman-Ker Milling Co. 77, 79
Brew, Chartres 99
Brewster, H.C. 29, 91, *92-4*, 160
Britain 10, 15, 16, 20, 21, 42, 46, 57, 79, 80, 84, 85, 90-1, 96, 168
British American Paint Company 2, 77, 109
B.C. Agricultural Exhibition 146
B.C. Electric Railway Company 39, *47-9*, 74, 152, 161, 167
B.C. Land & Investment Company 33, 113, 130
B.C. Telephone Company 67
Broadmead Farm 134
Brothels 34
Brown, P.R. 152
Bryant, John 64
Bryden, John 86, 168
Bullen, W.F. 154
Bulwer-Lytton, Edward 19, 20, 99
Burdett-Coutts, Angela 70, 72, 120
"Burleith" 119, 153
Burns, Flora Hamilton 104
Bushby, Arthur 40
Butchart, R.P. 80, *165*, 167

C&C Transportation 167
Camass 11, 12
Cameron, David 20
Campbell, Frank 34
Canadian Northern (National) Railway 47, 78, 90, 91, 92, 93, 140
Canadian Pacific Navigation Company 68, 75, 77-8
Canadian Pacific Railway Company (*see also* Steamships) 12, 54, 68, 77, 86, 89, 119, 140, 162-3
Carey, J.W. 62
Cariboo 11, 84, 85
Carnarvon Terms 84, 85
Carr, Emily 19, 32, 39, *107*
Carr, Richard 34, 36, 102, 107
Carrall, R.W.W. 26, 104
Carter-Cotton, F. 86, 87, 88
Cary, G.H. 23, 33, 122
Cary Castle *see* Government House
Catton, J. Maurice 46
Chapman, J.H.A. 110
Charles, William 20

Chinese 11, *54-7*, 58, 71, 75, 105, 168
Churches *70-1*:
Church of England/Christ Church 10, 70
Metropolitan Methodist (United) 52, 61, 70, 71
St. Andrew's Catholic 66, 70
St. Andrew's Presbyterian 70
St. Paul's Esquimalt 151, 154
Reformed Episcopalian 10, 19, 70, 71
Churchill, Winston 90, 91
City Hall 23, 62-3
"Clovelly" 125, 160-1
"Cloverdale" 165-6
Coal 118, 154, 168-9
Collins Overland Telegraph 67
Colonist, The British (newspaper) 24, 29, 38, 44, 52, 67, 84, 86, 87, 88, 95
Confederation 11, 22, 24, 25, 26, 84, 128
Connolly, William 18, 19
Conscription 94
Cook, Capt. James 10
Cooke, Rev. A.E. 91
Cooper, James 20, 24, 30
Cooperative Commonwealth Federation 97, 98, 169
Cornwall, Clement F. 85, 104, 122
Courtenay, Capt. G.W. 14
"Craigdarroch" 49, 113, 118-9
"Craigflower" 158-9
Crease, Henry P.P. 24, 25, 49, 75, *126-7*
Cridge, Edward 10, 19, 70, *71*, 99
Crystal Gardens 51, 69
Currency 102, 104
Currie, Arthur 130, 164
Customs House 29

Dallas Hotel 77
Davie, A.E.B. 42, *86-7*
Davie, C.F. 86
Davie, J.C. 86
Davie, Theodore 17, 42, 75, *86-7*
Davie Fulton, E. 86
Davies, Judah Phillip 128, 131
Davies, Rev. Clem 71
Davis, E.P. 46, 93
De Cosmos, Amor 19, 24, 25, 26, 38, 44, 46, 84, 128, 156
Deluge Company 39
Demers, Rev. Modeste 70
Depression (1913) 91
Depression (1930s) 42, 69, 96-7

"Dingle House" 153
"Dingley Dell" 152
Doig, David 40
Dominion Trust Company 92
Dougall, John 37, 112
Douglas, Amelia 18
Douglas, James 11, 14, 16, *18*, *19*, 20-3, 26, 28, 32, 70, 81, 104, 154, 158
Douglas Gardens 18, 68
Driard Hotel 26, 35, 52
Duck, Simeon 84
Duff, Lyman 124
Dufferin, Lord & Lady 85
Dumbleton, Henry 113
Dumford & Son 130
Dunlevy, P.C. 163
Dunsmuir, James 57, 88-9, 90, *118-9*, 162, 169
Dunsmuir, Robert 35, 44, 86, *118-9*, 162, 168
"Duvals" 113, 124, 125

Eaton's 52
Eberts, David M. 20, 90, 153
Edward VIII, King 44
Electric Railway *see* Streetcars
Elliott, A.C. 84, 85
Ellis, Thomas 153
Emery, Bert 51, 74
Empress Hotel 51, 64, *68-9*, 78, 109
"Erin Hall" 49, 113, 119
Esquimalt 14, 17, 21, 24, 28, 95, *151-164*, 168
Esquimalt & Nanaimo Railway 85, 86, 118, *162-3*, 165, 167
Esquimalt Graving Dock 23, 25, 84, 85, *156*
Evans, Rev. Ephraim 70
Evans, Coleman & Evans 75, 78, 80

Fan Tan Alley 54-6
Fairfield, 12, *128-135*
"Fairfield House" 128
Fairgrounds, Oak Bay 146-7
Farris, J.W. deB. 93-5, 163
Farris, Mrs. J.W. 91
Fawcett, Edgar 152
Fellows family 24, 128
Fenians 66
"Fernwood Manor" 126
Ferries (*see also* Steamship Services) 69, 90
Fifth Regiment, Esquimalt Garrison 164
Findlay, Walter 94
Finlayson, Roderick 12, 14, 20, 23, 62, 152

Firehalls, 39
Fires 40, 49, 52, 53
Flumerfelt, A.C. 92, 93
Foley, Stewart & Welch 93
Fordham-Johnson, J.W. 121
Fort Rodd Hill 155
Fort Vancouver 10, 12, 14, 15, 18, 23, 158
Fort Victoria 10-29, 32
Four Mile House 165
Freezy, Chief 28
Fry, John 56, 58
Fulton, F.J. 86, 90

Galpin, Thomas 33
Gardiner-Vrooman, John 54
Garesche, Francis 104
Genge, Lawrence 134
George V, King 83, 136
German club 38, 122
Gibson, W.W. 108
Gold Rush 11, 20, 21, 22, 23, 32, 40, 44, 54, 60, 84, 99, 132, 148, 151
Gold Seal Liquor Company 36, 94
Goldstream Hotel 165
Golf 69, 137
"Gonzales" 116-7
Goodacre Lake 110
Goodacre, Lawrence 68
Gorge 12, 150, 152-3
Government House 113, 122-4, 131
Grahame, J.A. 21
Grand Trunk Pacific Railroad 28, 78, 90-1, 139
Grant, Colquhoun 17, 170
Grant, John 62
Grant, William 148
Gray, Andrew 37, 39, 47, 164
Gray, John Hamilton 132
Great War Veterans' Association 83, 93, 94, 95
Green, Alexander Alfred 114
Green, Alfred 170
Green, R.F. 28, 77, 90
"Gyppeswyck" 113, 122

Hall, Ernest 58
Hall, Lewis 32
Hamersley, A. St. George 75
Harris, Thomas 32, 110
Hart, John 92, 97-8, 100
Hastings, Oregon Columbus 110

"Hatley Park" 118-9
Hawaii, 10, 11, 16, 134
Hawthornthwaite, J.H. 57, 90, 94, 168-9
Helmcken, H.D. 26, 28, 29
Helmcken, J.S. 14, 16, 18, 20, 24, 25, 26-7, 28, 70
"Helmcken House" 19, 26, 81
Henderson, Stuart 94
Hett, J.R. 85
Hibben, Thomas Napier 38, 70, 110
Hibben-Bone Block 32, 38
Higgins, D.W. 35, 44, 47-9, 87
Hillside Farm 30
Hinchcliffe, Joshua 96
Hockey, Ice 146
Holland, Cuyler Armstrong 33
"Hollybank" 134
"Hollywood" 130
Hollywood Grocery 128
"Hopedene" 153
Horse racing 110, 146
Hudson's Bay Company 10-25, 77, 136, 158, 159, 168
Hunter, Joseph 47, 102, 162
Hutchinson, Bruce 12, 128

Indians (see also Songhees) 11, 15, 19, 25, 36, 57, 75
Industrial Workers of the World 92, 94
Inner Harbour 12, 77-80
Irving, Captain John 38, 77, 78
Island Arts & Crafts Society 107

Jackson, Robert E. 86
Jacobson, Captain Victor 79, 157
James Bay 12, 18, 19, 32, 33, 64, 102-111
James Bay bridge 33, 81, 102
James Bay mudflats 10, 39, 68, 72
Japan & Japanese 57, 79, 80
Japanese Tea Gardens 152
Jardine, John 91, 160
Jeune Brothers 108
Jitneys 49
Johnson, Byron "Boss" 80, 98, 163
Johnson Street bridge 58, 71, 80, 148
Joly de Lotbiniere, Henri 89, 119, 124
Jones, Jimmy 96
Juan de Fuca Strait 14

Kaiserhof Hotel 38, 122
Kanaka Row 34, 39
Kane, Paul 12
Kennedy, Arthur Edward 21, 25, 26, 122, 168
Ker, David R. 79, 146
Kidd, George 49, 96, 97
Kipling, Rudyard 136, 138
Kingham, Joshua 94

Labour see Unions
Laing, Freddie 75
"Lan Dderwan" see "Gyppeswyck"
Land development 23, 40, 128, 130
Langford, E.E. 17, 19, 158
"Laurels", The 113
Laurier, Wilfrid 88, 90, 91, 94
Leech, Peter John 102
Lefevre, Dr. Matthew 87
Legislative Buildings 19, 32, 81-3, 86, 87, 92
Lemon, J.J. 149
Lim Bang 57, 62
Liquor 20, 36, 58, 77, 91, 92, 94-5, 96, 99, 100
Loewen, Joseph 122, 153
Lord's Day Alliance 70
"Loretto Hall" 109

McBride, Sir Richard 87, 89-93, 94, 140, 153, 155
McClung, Nellie 167
McClure, Leonard 44, 122
McCreight, John Foster 44, 84, 85, 132
Macdonald, Alexander Davidson 102
Macdonald, John A. 22, 85, 149, 162
Macdonald, M.A. 29, 92, 93, 94
Macdonald, W.J. 42, 102, 104, 113
McGeer, Gerry 94
MacGill, Helen Gregory 91
McInnes, Thomas 87, 88, 122
McIntosh, McGregor 90, 91
MacKay, Hugh 79
McKelvie, B.A. 83
MacKenzie, Kenneth 153, 159
MacKenzie King, W.L. 56, 93, 96
McLarnin, Jimmy 167
MacLean, J.D. 95, 96
MacLean, Malcolm 75
McLoughlin, John 10, 15, 18
Maclure, Samuel 51, 124, 136, 138
McMicking, Robert 38, 67, 153
McMullin, J.H. 99, 100

McNeil, W.H. 136
McPherson Theatre 35
MacRae, A.D. 93, 95
Mainguy, Rollo 124
"Maplebank, 159
Manson, Alexander 99
Mara, J.A. 67, 125
Marchant, William 70
Marquis of Lorne 85, 122
Martin, Joseph 88-9, 94, 126
Matson, J.S.H. 29, 164
Maynard, Hannah 110
Mayne, Captain 21, 30
Mill Stream 152, 165
Milne, A.R. 79
Milne, G.L. 47, 105
Moderation Movement 95
Moody, Richard Clement 99
Moody, Sewell P. 34
Morley, Alfred J. 32
Morris, E.A. 32, 47
Mount Baker Hotel 136
"Mount Joy" 116
Mowat, George "Rebel" 64, 167
Musgrave, Anthony 25, 26, 40, 104

Nanaimo 10, 20, 75, 78, 84, 85, 90, 91, 162, 163, 168-9
National Electric Tramway & Lighting Company 39, 47
Navy League 141
Needham, Joseph 125
Nesbitt, James K. 30, 37, 119, 120
Nesbitt, Samuel 36, 120
New England Hotel 34, 64
New Westminster 11, 25, 75, 84, 85, 99
New Westminster Southern Railway 39
Nichol, Walter C. 114, 124
Nicholas, B.C. 46
North, Christopher Roland (Joe) 58
North West Company 10, 15
Northwestern Creamery 40, 62

Oak Bay 12, 136-147
Oak Bay Beach Hotel 142
Oak Bay Hotel 138
Ogden, Peter Skene 15, 158
Ogden Point docks 77
Old Charming Inn 138
Oliver, John 91, 93, 94-5
One Big Union 94

Oregon (& Oregon Territory, includes the modern State of Washington) 10, 12, 14, 20, 151, 158
O'Reilly, Peter 133, 148, 149
Owens, Robert 100

Pacific Club 42, 72
Pacific Great Eastern Railway 93, 95, 96
Pantages, Alexander 35
Park Hotel 107
Parson's Bridge Hotel 165
Paterson, T.W. 46
Patrick, Lester 146, 167
Pattullo, T.D. 19, 83, 96-8, 137
Pearse, Benjamin W. 25, 32, 126
Peden, Torchy 167
Pemberton, Augustus 33, 49, 70, 99
Pemberton, Frederick B. 116, 117
Pemberton, Joseph D. 20, 23, 24, 25, 32, 113, 116, 136
Pemberton-Holmes building 33
Pendray family (& soapworks) 67, 72, 92, 109
"Pentrelew" 113, 114, 126-7
Phillips-Wolley, Clive 141
"Pig War" 11
"Pinehurst" 102, 105
Pither & Leiser Ltd. 35, 36
Plimley, Tom 53, 64, 108
Point Ellice 148, 149
Point Ellice bridge disaster 39, 47, 150
"Point Ellice House" 148-9
Police, Victoria 56, 69, 71
Politics, Provincial & Federal 57, 81-98
Poodle Dog 32, 51
Pooley, C.E. 42, 46, 85, 86, 161
Pooley, R.H. 42, 97, 160
Porter, R.J. 58
Post Office 40
Powell, Dr. I.W. 26, 104, 105
Prince of Wales (later Edward VIII) 124
Princess Louise 85, 122
Prior, E.G. 24, 35, 89, 124, 155, 164
Prohibition 34, 70, 71, 77, 91, 92, 94-5, 140
Province, Victoria Weekly (later Vancouver Daily) 46, 87, 96, 114, 141
Provincial party 93, 95, 140
Provincial Police 96, 99-100
Puget Sound Agricultural Company 10, 17, 151, 158-9
Puget Sound Navigation Company 78, 79

Queen's Printer Bookstore 102
Queen Victoria 16

Radio 71, 95, 97
Railways (miscellaneous) 11, 84-7
Rattenbury, F.M. 43, 68, 83, 124, 136, 139
Reciprocity (trade with U.S.A.) 46, 91, 93
Redfern, C.E. 62
Reed, Kate 69
Reifel, H.F. 96
Rhodes, Henry 10, 85
Richards, A.N. 122
"Riffington" 143
Riley, George 46
Ringler-Thomson, Charles 153
Rithet, Elizabeth 72, 134
Rithet, R.P. 10, 12, 35, 36, 134
Rithet's Outer Wharves 36, 77, 79-80, 134
Robertson, A.R. 85
Robillard, Arthur 68, 167
Robson, John 19, 26, 44, 57, 84, 86, 102, 132
"Roccabella" 10
Rockland, 12, 113-127
"Rocklands" 113
Rogers, B.T. 121, 134
Rogers, C.W. 64
Rogers, Jonathan 94
Roosevelt, F.D.R. 97
Roscoe, F.J. 128
Ross, Charles 14, 23
Ross Bay Cemetery 19, 128
Rowell-Sirois Commission 57, 98
Royal Bank building 32
Royal Canadian Artillery 155
Royal Canadian Navy 91, 151, 155
Royal Jubilee Hospital 117
Royal Navy 16, 17, 91, 127, 151, 154-5, 156, 168
Royal Victoria Yacht Club 138
Russia 10, 20, 79, 80, 154
Russian-American Fur Company 20

St. Ann's Academy 10, 70
St. Joseph's Hospital 10, 70
Salmon (& fishing industry) 12, 15, 57, 92, 146
Saloons 21, 32, 34
Sanders, A.F. 68
San Francisco 10, 11, 20, 154, 156, 168
San Juan Islands 11
Schools 77, 158
Scott, W.A. "Bill" 136
Sealing 79-80, 140, 157
Seattle 75, 92
Sehl, Jacob 112
Semlin, C.A. 88
Seymour, Frederick 21, 22, 25
Shakespeare, Noah 40, 71
Shanks, J.A. 128
Shanks, Richard "Pop" 100
Shanks, Robert Hugh 33
Shaughnessy, Thomas 68
Shotbolt, Thomas 47, 130
Sipprell, Rev. W.J. 58, 71, 95
"Sissinghurst" 153
"Six Mile House" 165
Skinner, Thomas 159
Sloan Commission 163
Smallpox, 75, 86, 134
Smith, Donald 21
Smith, Mary Ellen 91, 169
Smith, Ralph 168, 169
Smithe, William 85, 86, 162
Snow 47, 74
Snowden, Northing Pinckney 119, 153
Social Credit 98
Songhees Indians 14, 26, 28-9, 90, 92
Sooke 14, 17
Spencer, David (& store) 35, 52-3, 61
Spencer, Sara Ellen 53, 114
Spratt, Joseph 37, 164
Spring Ridge 14, 22, 23, 25
Staines, Rev. Robert 16, 18
Stamp, Edward 61
Steamship services 69, 77-80
Streetcars 47-9, 98, 146, 150, 152, 161
Streetlights 32, 38, 67

Tate, D'Arcy 93
Tatlow, R.G. 89, 90
Taylor, Thomas 93
Taylor, W.J. 90
Teague, John 61
Telephones 38, 67
Templeman, William 46, 87, 160
Terms of Union (confederation) 28, 84-5, 156
Terry's 50, 51
Texada Scandal 44
Thunderbird Park 19
Tickle, Billy 64, 69
"Tillicum" canoe 19, 157
Tingley, Stephen 125
Tod, John 20, 30, 136, 145
Todd, J.H. 149
Tolmie, S.F. 94, 96-7, 165
Tolmie, W.F. 23, 25, 84, 122, 165
Tourists 68-9, 71, 75, 77, 78, 79, 136
Trapp, T.J. 39
"Triangle run" 77-8
Trounce, Thomas 61, 151
Trutch, Joseph 26, 84, 128
Tulk, A.E. 94, 95
Tupper, Charles 88, 140
Tupper, Charles Hibbert 29, 90, 93, 94, 95, 140
Turner, J.H. 35, 46, 87, 88, 89, 91, 148, 149
Twigg, H.D. 95
"Tynemouth" 120
Tyrwhitt-Drake, M.W. 148

Union Club 34, 42-3
Unions (organized labour) 37, 93, 94, 118, 168, 169
United Farmers of B.C. 21, 93
U.S.A. 10, 15, 21, 22, 26, 57, 77, 79, 80, 85, 95
University of B.C. 77, 96
Uplands 137, 138
Uplands Farm 30, 136
Uplands Golf Club 137

Vancouver, Capt. George 10
Vancouver, City of 11, 12, 21, 49, 56, 71, 75,
    77, 86, 92, 93, 95, 96, 97, 162
Vancouver Improvement Company 105, 161
Vancouver Island Coach Lines 98, 167
Victoria:
Bungalow Construction Company 130
College 77
Cougars 146
Gas Works 38
Golf Club 137
Machinery Depot 79, 148, 164
Phoenix Brewing Company 153
Public Market 39, 62
Rice & Flour Mills Company 79
School of Music 119
Sealing Company 37, 148
Standard 42, 44, 49
Terminal & Sidney Railway 39, 46, 163, 167
Theatre 35
Times 29, 44-6, 90
Transfer Company 39, 43
Volunteer Rifles 122
West 151, 164
Von Alvensleben, Alvo 38
Voss, Capt. John 19, 77

Waddington, Alfred 21, 32
Wade, F.C. 43, 91, 94
Walkem, George 10, 26, 44, 57, 81, *84-5*,
    132, 156, 162
Walkem, George Alexander 93
Wallace, Hubert & Clarence 143
War: Crimean 20, 155
First World 12, 42, 53, 57, 74, 92, 94, 144,
    146, 155, 164
Second World 12, 49, 57, 97, 98, 99, 155
Ward, Robert 113
Warren, George 79
Weiler Brothers 33, 34, 112
Westby, W.J. 167
Whelan, Lawrence 66
White Horse Hotel 10
White Lunch 39
Williams, Parker 90, 168
Willows Farm 145
Willows Hotel 144, 146
Wilson, Biggerstaff 60, 62
Wilson, H.G. 60
Wilson, Lieut. Charles 17, 20

Wilson, Victoria Jane 39, 72-3
Wilson, W & J 60, 61
Wilson, William Ridgeway 153
Wilson-Brown, G.H. 72, 116
Winch, Ernest & Harold 97, 163
Windsor Hotel 34
Windsor Park 136, 142
Winter, George 131
Wismer, Gordon 98, 100
Wolfenden, Richard 151
Women's Suffrage 91, 92
Wood, Frederick 121
"Woodhall" 141
Wood-block paving 32
Work, John 15, 20, 21, *30*
Work Point Barracks 155, 160
Wright, Andrew 143

Yarrows 78, 143, 155
Yates, James 20, 153
Yates, J. Stuart 88, 153
Yorkshire Guarantee Corporation 47, 67
Young, H.E. 83